This pathbreaking book offers a new perspective on a central group of music theory treatises that have long formed the background to the study of Renaissance music. Taking theorists' music examples as a point of departure, it explores fundamental questions about how music was read, and by whom, situating the reading in specific cultural contexts. Numerous broader issues are addressed in the process: the relationship of theory and praxis; access to, and use of, printed musical sources; stated and unstated agendas of theorists; orality and literacy as it was represented via music print culture; the evaluation of anonymous repertories; and the analysis of repertories delineated by boundaries other than the usual ones of composer and genre. In particular this study illuminates the ways in which Renaissance theorists' choices have shaped later interpretation of earlier practice, and reflexively the ways in which modern theory has been mapped on to that practice.

Cristle Collins Judd is Associate Professor of Music Theory at the University of Pennsylvania and editor of *Tonal Structures in Early Music* (1998).

CAMBRIDGE STUDIES IN MUSIC THEORY AND ANALYSIS

GENERAL EDITOR: IAN BENT

Published titles

READING RENAISSANCE MUSIC THEORY

Hearing with the Eyes

CRISTLE COLLINS JUDD

PUBLISHED BY THE PRESS SYNDICATE OF THE UNIVERSITY OF CAMBRIDGE
The Pitt Building, Trumpington Street, Cambridge, United Kingdom

CAMBRIDGE UNIVERSITY PRESS
The Edinburgh Building, Cambridge CB2 2RU, UK   www.cup.cam.ac.uk
40 West 20th Street, New York, NY 10011-4211, USA   www.cup.org
10 Stamford Road, Oakleigh, Melbourne 3166, Australia
Ruiz de Alarcón 13, 28014 Madrid, Spain

First published 2000

Printed in the United Kingdom at the University Press, Cambridge

Typeface Monotype Bembo 11/13 pt.   System QuarkXPress™ [SE]

A catalogue record for this book is available from the British Library

ISBN 0 521 77144 7 hardback

For Katie, Hannah, and Sarah
In memoriam Philippa and Jamie

CONTENTS

ILLUSTRATIONS

Figures

Music examples

Tables

FOREWORD BY IAN BENT

Theory and analysis are in one sense reciprocals: if analysis opens up a musical structure or style to inspection, inventorying its components, identifying its connective forces, providing a description adequate to some live experience, then theory generalizes from such data, predicting what the analyst will find in other cases within a given structural or stylistic orbit, devising systems by which other works – as yet unwritten – might be generated. Conversely, if theory intuits how musical systems operate, then analysis furnishes feedback to such imaginative intuitions, rendering them more insightful. In this sense, they are like two hemispheres that fit together to form a globe (or cerebrum!), functioning deductively as investigation and abstraction, inductively as hypothesis and verification, and in practice forming a chain of alternating activities.

Professionally, on the other hand, "theory" now denotes a whole subdiscipline of the general field of musicology. Analysis often appears to be a subordinate category within the larger activity of theory. After all, there is theory that does not require analysis. Theorists may engage in building systems or formulating strategies for use by composers; and these almost by definition have no use for analysis. Others may conduct experimental research into the sound-materials of music or the cognitive processes of the human mind, to which analysis may be wholly inappropriate. And on the other hand, historians habitually use analysis as a tool for understanding the classes of compositions – repertoires, "outputs," "periods," works, versions, sketches, and so forth – that they study. Professionally, then, our ideal image of twin hemispheres is replaced by an intersection: an area that exists in common between two subdisciplines. Seen from this viewpoint, analysis reciprocates in two directions: with certain kinds of theoretical inquiry, and with certain kinds of historical enquiry. In the former case, analysis has tended to be used in rather orthodox modes, in the latter a more eclectic fashion; but that does not mean that analysis in the service of theory is necessarily more exact, more "scientific," than analysis in the service of history.

The above epistemological excursion is by no means irrelevant to the present series. Cambridge Studies in Music Theory and Analysis is intended to present the work of theorists and of analysts. It has been designed to include "pure" theory – that is, theoretical formulation with a minimum of analytical exemplification; "pure" analysis – that is, practical analysis with a minimum of theoretical underpinning; and writings that fall at points along the spectrum between the two extremes. In these capacities, it aims to illuminate music, as work and as process.

However, theory and analysis are not the exclusive preserves of the present day. As subjects in their own right, they are diachronic. The former is coeval with the very study of music itself, and extends far beyond the confines of Western culture; the latter, defined broadly, has several centuries of past practice. Moreover, they have been dynamic, not static fields throughout their histories. Consequently, studying earlier music through the eyes of its own contemporary theory helps us to escape (when we need to, not that we should make a dogma out of it) from the preconceptions of our own age. Studying earlier analyses does this too, and in a particularly sharply focused way; at the same time it gives us the opportunity to re-evaluate past analytical methods for present purposes, such as is happening currently, for example, with the long-despised methods of hermeneutic analysis of the late nineteenth century. The series thus includes editions and translations of major works of past theory, and also studies in the history of theory.

The present volume is the first to address music theory before the Baroque period. Cristle Collins Judd takes as the focus of her study four principal music theorists in the period 1516 to 1588: Pietro Aron, Sebald Heyden, Heinrich Glarean, and Gioseffo Zarlino – two Italians, one German, one Swiss – men with certain theoretical-practical interests in common and at the same time fascinating differences of education, training, social position, environment, religious outlook, profession, personal aspirations, and even choice of language, which stamp their treatises with distinctive characters. Preceding the first of their treatises by a mere fifteen years was an event of enormous historical importance: the first publication of printed polyphonic music, by Petrucci in 1501. This event ushered in music's "print culture," and in so doing transformed the way in which theorists were to write about music.

Professor Judd reveals to us the far-reaching inplications of this process. Not only could music examples now be printed in treatises, but those examples came to form a symbiotic relationship with the steadily increasing printed repertory. It is possible for us now to see into the mind of the theorist and gauge his motives for selecting the material that he did – motives that are at times as ideological and strategic (often prompted by hidden agendas), as they are practical. Let me not spoil the narrative; for Professor Judd tells it almost like a detective story. It is a compelling tale of intellectual history, of private book collecting, of rhetoric, of image creation, and of manoeuvrings for position and power. It takes us at different times into the typographic details of printed partbooks and the intracacies of modal theory, into the writing of commonplace books, into the tensions between catholic and reformed religious practices, and into the world of human relations.

Reading Renaissance Music Theory offers a radically new manner of looking at the music theory of the past – a vital way that will be of interest to historians of the Renaissance, of Humanism, and of the Reformation, of cultural historians, scholars of orality and literacy, of those engaged in the history of printing, the book and textual studies, as well as to historians of music and music theory. "Hearing with the Eyes," its subtitle, hints at the multifarious role of music examples, which interrupt the verbal discourse and at the same time enrich it, which must be interpreted by the eye and reconstructed by the inner ear, which stand as tokens for repertories while also shaping those same repertories, and which also raise broader issues about the nature of reading itself that go far beyond the specifically musical.

PREFACE

Like all good adventures, the writing of this book has taken me down paths that I hardly knew existed when I began. The journey commenced with a paper I was invited to give at a celebration in honor of Harold Powers' sixty-fifth birthday. That paper – which at the time, I viewed as an explication of Pietro Aron's modal theory – ultimately led me to considerations of orality, visuality, literacy, and textuality in relation to music theory. These are areas with a vast, fascinating, and often contentious literature, relatively little of which had been brought to bear on questions of printed music and notions of musical literacy. As I read about reading, I was drawn into the world of the history of the book and considerations of the materiality of the text. What emerged for me from those perspectives was the sense of a unique point of contact between music and writing about music in the examples and citations of music theory treatises.

Music examples have commonly occupied a minor role in histories of music theory and an even lesser place in broader humanistic studies; indeed, they normally merit mention only to the extent that they appear to clarify (or contradict) passages of text. Examples appear too obvious to merit scrutiny: they are out in the open; they are normally signed neatly with an "e.g." or precise captions; they may be carefully framed; they are set apart visually; they may even be indexed. On the face of it, the purpose of such examples is obvious: they ensure the authenticity of the discourse that surrounds them; they verify its truth content.

Reading out from music examples to the repertories they implicitly represent suggests entirely new perspectives on the connections among a group of treatises, theorists, and music sources whose interpretation has long formed the backbone of musical scholarship of the Renaissance. Appropriated musical texts act as crucial markers of the intellectual and social milieus inhabited by music theorists, their treatises, and the practice they (re)present. The intersection of music and printing evidenced through music examples offers an unexplored vantage point from which to address the emergence of a "musical print culture." This culture had dramatic ramifications not only for the writing of music theory, but also for the wider significance of the resulting discourse. Renaissance theorists' choices shaped the reception of sixteenth-century musical practice, while reflexively influencing the ways in which modern theory has been mapped onto that practice.

This study weaves together strands of religion, politics, and printing as they impinge on, and are exemplified by, music-theoretic discourse. In the process, numerous broader issues are considered: the nature of the relationship of theory and praxis; contemporaneous access to, and use of, practical sources; stated and unstated agendas of theorists; orality and literacy as represented via music print culture; the evaluation of anonymous repertories; and the analysis of repertories delineated by boundaries other than the usual ones of composer and genre.

Studies of early printed music have generally focused on the relationship between publication and performance, concluding that music prints stand apart from the considerations of other printed materials, while studies of music theory treatises have accorded relatively little attention to the examples contained within them, treating such examples as internal supplements and repositories of repertory. Another view is possible when the music examples of theory treatises – and, by extension, early printed musical texts themselves – are not assumed to be associated purely, or even primarily, with aural performance. This entails a consideration of the materiality of printed musical texts not only from the perspective of printing history but in a broader exploration of the kinds of multiple readings that historians of the book have proposed for other printed sources. That is, I want to highlight an understanding of printed music books and music theory treatises as part of a broader culture of the book. The ramifications of such an approach move this book beyond the narrow field of its specific focus: while locally this study bridges the fields of music history and music theory, it also draws more broadly on the fields of Renaissance and Reformation studies, studies of the craft of printing and history of the book, and cultural history.

Four case studies form the core of this book: each examines the interplay of individual theorists and treatises with both local and widely disseminated repertories. These are followed by a more wide-ranging essay that traces the reception of a single work, the motet *Magnus es tu Domine*, through a number of anthologies and theoretical sources, from 1504 until the present. Pietro Aron's *De institutione harmonica* (1516) and Gioseffo Zarlino's *Le istitutioni harmoniche* (1558, R1573) frame the theoretical texts chosen for consideration here. The "harmonic institution(s)" of their titles may be used not only to invoke the specific theoretical fundamentals of these texts, but also to highlight the intertextuality of a number of institutions as mediated by (and as mediators of) music-theoretic discourse. The chronological boundaries of the study reflect the advent of printed polyphonic music (Petrucci's *Odhecaton* (1501)) and the emergence of a music print culture in the sixteenth century. The theorists examined here are often cited for their innovations – for example, Aron's discussion of mode in polyphony (1525), Sebald Heyden's single-tactus theory (1537), Heinrich Glarean's exposition of a twelve-mode system (1547) and Zarlino's synthesis of *musica practica* and *musica theorica* in a single treatise (1558). These theorists and treatises also represent divergent geographical, theological, educational, social, and intellectual positions while they are bounded by an apparently common relationship to chant tradition on the one hand, and the circumstances of printed musical transmission on the other.

During the writing of this book, I have received invaluable assistance from many individuals. First and foremost, I owe a debt to my colleagues in the Music Department at the University of Pennsylvania; they have provided an environment that has been wonderfully conducive to the writing of this book and assured that I had the time and means to complete it. Lawrence Bernstein, Jeffrey Kallberg, and Eugene Narmour all listened and generously responded to my queries with critical acumen as the arguments presented here were gradually developed. I owe special thanks to Gary Tomlinson and Christopher Hasty. Their prompt and careful readings of early drafts helped me avoid many pitfalls; their willingness to listen over and over again as I struggled to find the shape of this book was a constant source of encouragement and inspiration. I have been fortunate to have graduate students at Penn share in the formation of this material during the course of several seminars. Their questions and observations have greatly focused my arguments; work by Christopher Amos, Olivia Bloechl, and Carol Whang was especially helpful. Marjorie Hassen, librarian of the Otto Albrecht Music Library and God's gift to music faculty, has never failed to answer my requests, while Brad Young procured microfilms of music and treatises from far and wide. Beyond Penn, Jessie Ann Owens offered incisive and practical advice from the time I first began work on this topic and read versions of the manuscript in several stages. Bonnie Blackburn generously shared her extraordinary expertise on so many of the subjects touched on here and provided a most helpful reading of the entire manuscript, complemented by the assistance of the indefatigable Leofranc Holford-Strevens. Harold Powers's timely and thoughtful reading of the penultimate draft greatly improved the structure of the final version. Ian Bent guided me through the publication process, offering suggestions that improved both the argument and its presentation.

One of the great joys of working on a book that touched so many disciplinary areas has been the long and fruitful conversations with so many colleagues inside and outside musicology. Over and over I have benefited from the willingness of colleagues with greater specialized knowledge to listen to my ideas and share the fruits of their research. The participants in the "History of the Material Text" seminar at Penn provided a forum for presenting this work to a non-musicological audience and the queries and interest from many in that group shaped this work in subtle ways. Joseph Farrell of Classical Studies, Ann Matter of Religious Studies, and Ann Moyer of History have answered numerous questions, helped trace obscure sources, and aided with translations.

Each of the case studies of this book allowed me to engage the work of different communities within the world of musicology and music theory. Margaret Bent, Harold Powers, and David Fallows offered helpful comments on my original work on Pietro Aron. Royston Gustavson, Susan Jackson, Bartlett Butler, and Volker Schreier answered questions about sixteenth-century Nuremberg. A perceptive comment by Kate van Orden led me to consider the nature of commonplace books and their role in relation to musical thought in connection with Glarean's manuscripts. Linda Austern pointed me to several references about commonplace books and Renaissance exemplarity. Jane Bernstein, Jonathan Glixon, Robert Kendrick, Mary Lewis, Giulio Ongaro, and Katelijne Schiltz were uncommonly generous in helping me gain some understanding of the complicated world of mid-century Venetian printing, ecclesiastical history, and cultural context. Benito Rivera freely shared his archival work on Zarlino and materials from his forthcoming book on Zarlino and Willaert's music. Frans Wiering shared his unparalleled knowledge of sixteenth-century modal cycles and his intimate acquaintance with Zarlino's treatises. On Josquin, Richard Sherr endured an endless series of e-mails about *Magnus es tu Domine* and related matters; Patrick Macey responded thoughtfully to an early version of this material; Herbert Kellman and Stacey Jacoy arranged to make materials from the Renaissance Archives at the University of Illinois available to me; Peter Urquhart assisted in the search for obscure recordings; and Marc Perlman helped me broaden my thinking beyond my own disciplinary blinders.

A Fellowship for University Teachers from the National Endowment for the Humanities, a Faculty Research Fellowship from the School of Arts and Sciences at the University of Pennsylvania, and a Summer Research Fellowship and travel funds from the Research Foundation of the University of Pennsylvania facilitated my research. Publication subventions from the Society for Music Theory and the Research Foundation at Penn defrayed the expenses of plates and examples.

An earlier version of part of Chapter 3 originally appeared as "Reading Aron reading Petrucci: The Music Examples of the *Trattato della natura et cognitione di tutti gli tuoni* (1525)," *Early Music History* 14 (1995), 121–52. A preliminary version of parts of Chapters 5 and 6 was published in "Musical Commonplace Books, Writing Theory, and 'Silent Listening': The Polyphonic Examples of the *Dodecachordon*," *The Musical Quarterly* 82 (1998), 482–516.

Numerous libraries supplied microfilms and answered queries, including the British Library, the Library of Congress, the Sibley Library at the Eastman School of Music, the Biblioteca Casanatense, the Stadtbibliothek Nürnberg, the Civico Museo Bibliografico Musicale Bologna, the Bayerische Staatsbibliothek, the Österreichische Nationalbibliothek Musiksammlung, the Gesellschaft der Musikfreunde, and the Musikwissenschaftliche Institut Vienna. I am especially grateful to Irene Friedl and Wolfgang Müller for their assistance when I was working with the Glarean Nachlaß at the Munich Universitätsbibliothek, and to Cornel Dora for his assistance in the Stiftsbibliothek St. Gallen.

My family has endured the writing of this book with near-saintly patience. Katie has grown into a young lady as this text has materialized, Hannah was born as it was conceived, and Sarah arrived in the midst of it. To these, our three graces, I dedicate this book. As always, my husband, Robert Judd, made the completion of this project possible in ways so numerous that I hardly recognize them all myself – with quiet good humor, a healthy dose of skepticism, gentle generosity, and acts of unspoken kindness throughout.

PART I

BEGINNINGS

PROLOGUE: *EXEMPLI GRATIA* . . .

PRINT CULTURE, CYBER CULTURE, AND "READING" MUSIC

In conferences, lectures, and day-to-day conversations about music, we routinely employ sounding music examples as an integral part of our discourse *about* music. Such sounds may include anything from the humming of a phrase or line, to a partial rendition at the keyboard, to live or recorded performances of entire works. Traditionally, when such oral/aural events are transformed for the medium of print, sounding words and sounding music are replaced by written text and notated examples. In the late 1990s the advent of hypermedia – CD-ROMs and the promulgation of electronic journals – holds the promise, if not yet the actuality, of transforming the way we present our published discourse about music. Readily apparent – perhaps facile – parallels between the so-called "print revolution" and the "cyber revolution" abound. Yet the similarities provide a particularly appropriate point of departure for this book. Thus I begin a book broadly concerning the nature of exemplarity in theoretical writing with my own (textual) example in the form of an anecdote that highlights the broader resonance of the study undertaken here.

I have been engaged over the last few years with a pedagogical initiative that attempts to take advantage of the possibilities of hypermedia for undergraduate instruction in music theory. During the same time, I worked on this book – a book that assumes a traditional printed form in its pursuit of the ways in which sixteenth-century music theorizing shaped and was shaped by possibilities intimately linked to the emergence of a music print culture. The two projects have far more in common than I initially realized. While beginning the study of the examples in Pietro Aron's *Trattato della natura et cognitione di tutti gli tuoni* (1525), I was also undertaking an experimental design of materials for an undergraduate theory course that supplemented the printed examples of a standard theory textbook with a point and click web interface of matching audio excerpts for the hundreds of short excerpts. The motivation for the web experiment grew out of the difficulties of addressing the needs of students with an extraordinarily wide range of abilities in day-to-day music classes. What most characterized these students' ability to engage their textbook were the different levels of their "music-reading" abilities. At one end of the spectrum were "musically literate" students, those capable of imagining or recollecting the sounds represented by the frequent examples in their theory text-book. More common were students who had greater difficulty when confronted by examples, but who realized the notation (albeit imperfectly) through a combination of singing and working the examples out at the piano, even though many of the examples were pianistically quite challenging and beyond most of these students' skills. And then there were the students who openly rejoiced with the appearance of each music example; their response to the difficult, even forbidding, notation was simply . . . to skip it. The web project was an attempt to mediate the notation, to provide at least a minimal means of "hearing" the music and in the best case scenario to help students develop the skills to conceptualize such examples without the crutch of audio files. Ultimately it led toward a format which attempted to focus on the skills related to hearing sounds in real time which were contrasted with the very different visual and atemporal possibilities offered by notational representations in which students could "see" relationships that they often were not capable of perceiving aurally.

As I explained the purpose of this endeavor to a well-meaning reporter from an alumni periodical, she exclaimed with real excitement, "Oh, this is just what I need! I just finished reading Charles Rosen's *The Romantic Generation* and I loved it, but I don't read music." My first reaction was to wonder how anyone could read such a book without even the possibility of comprehending its copious examples. Indeed of all the music books to read without being able to read music, Rosen's struck me on first thought as the least likely candidate. Figure 1.1, an opening from *The Romantic Generation*, was chosen more or less at random. Not every page has this much music, but many do. How, I wondered, could anyone who didn't read music read a book like Rosen's? As it turns out, *The Romantic Generation*, is extraordinarily idiosyncratic in its manipulation of music examples. The book includes a compact disc of Rosen performing, but it is not specifically keyed to the examples of the book. Rather it creates for the listener/reader the musical world of the Romantic generation, or more to the point, it allows the reader/listener to partake of Charles Rosen's communion with the Romantic generation. The same is true of the notated examples. Although they are often couched in service of a technical point, and even included within sentences, the prose survives remarkably well without them. Rosen has made a point of including first editions wherever possible, and if that was not possible, the example is reproduced from a near-contemporary edition. That these have not been reset is no mere economizing on the publisher's part: Rosen is deliberately using the visual image as a material connection to the Romantic generation. We are intended to *see* (and by implication hear) *their* music. Ironically, the originals of some of these examples have deteriorated so severely that actually reading them as they appear in the text with any assurance of accuracy is difficult if not impossible. But I was left to wonder in what sense this reporter and I had read the same book, in what sense we formed part of a community of readers. We had read the same words, but only one of us had "read" the music.

During this same period of pedagogical experimentation with sound files on web pages for theory courses, I came back to work on Pietro Aron's *Trattato*, a treatise on modes in polyphonic music from 1525. Aron's treatise was one that I felt I knew rather well. Like many before me, I think I expected Aron to act in some sense as a kind of tour guide to a repertory and way of thinking about it as I began rereading him with facsimiles of various Petrucci music prints in hand. Instead, I began to have some sense of his interaction with the world of printed music books. The implications of that interaction forced me to stand back and begin to think about the significance of music-theoretical treatises as material objects, as books which partake of a whole host of conventions and contexts that we overlook when we focus solely on the immaterial content of their abstract theorizing.

When musical sources from the first half of the sixteenth century have entered the realm of discussions of the "history of the book" and "print culture," they have been primarily music books, not hybrid volumes like theory treatises that integrate words and music. The argument has normally been advanced that musical sources stand apart from the usual considerations of other printed materials. By and large, scholars of other disciplines have by a sort of tacit agreement avoided musical sources, while musicologists entering the interdisciplinary fray have tended to reinforce the "otherness" of musical sources, linking them closely to an intended performing market. But music and writing *about* music confront and confound all sorts of assumptions in the orality–literacy debates that have been a central feature of studies of the history of the book and the history of reading. At the same time, theory treatises, the central texts of this book, demonstrate how fragile an argument separating musical sources from other sorts can be.

HEARING WITH THE EYES: THE NATURE OF MUSICAL EXEMPLARITY

The oxymoron "aural image" highlights the special nature of musical exemplarity and notational representation. The notated music example is doubly distant from the aural phenomenon that it ultimately represents: the notation stands for sound, but, excised and framed as an example, points both back to a presumed whole that it represents (synecdoche) and also forward from the new discourse of which it becomes part. In Gelley's words, "the function of example is precisely to divert us from the two limiting terms – the whole *from which* and the whole *toward which* – and disclose an *in between*, an opening for picturing, for illustrative realization."[1] In moving from an analogical mode to an iconic, the example itself becomes exemplar, inducing an imitative realization on the part of the audience.

---

[1] Alexander Gelley, "Introduction," *Unruly Examples: On the Rhetoric of Exemplarity* (Stanford: Stanford University Press, 1995), 3.

Still another version (I^b), even closer to the Beethoven song, continues the D minor:

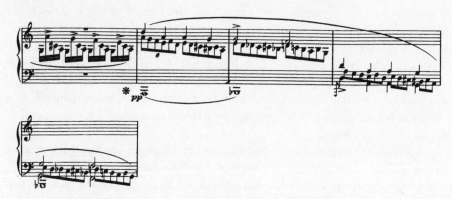

This leads to a second playing of the lyrical versions I^a and I^b now in the subdominant major, F, the relative major of D minor:

As a secondary tonality of an exposition, the subdominant is very rare and absolutely unclassical. It is, however, established directly out of the harmony of the opening bass, and it leads directly to the chord of its own supertonic (G minor) and back to D minor in a series of broken phrases. We return to C major and the opening theme by a simple sequence of rising subdominants: D minor, G minor, C minor.

1.1 Rosen, *The Romantic Generation*, 106–07

As I have observed, the chord of the tonic major in root position is evaded by Schumann until the end of the piece. After a short stretto in faster tempo, the opening theme reappears on a tonic pedal, but still unresolved, with the dissonant harmony of D minor insistently present; and it is rounded off with a half cadence and a fermata, which serve to prolong the tension of the "exposition":

1.1 *(cont.)*

Rhetorical exemplarity has a richly complicated history that extends to modern and postmodern philosophy.[2] Words reconstitute "things" in their own mold by encompassing them as examples. Examples are necessarily dependent texts that occur in the context of another text – hierarchically superior – which systematizes them. They must be recognizable, whether the recognition relies on tradition and memory, or reference to a commonly accepted textual world. The example brings that which is outside within the text. Simultaneously, it is marked by discontinuity, on which it depends for its recognition.[3]

Non-discursive examples display an inborn resistance to the frame of the text, perhaps none more so than music. Music disrupts the discourse, halts its progression, interrupts the rhythm of words. There are times when notation serves a purely iconic function – we are meant to *see* notation, but not hear it. At other times, the notation serves as a generalized reminder of music as sounding phenomenon, and at still other times, the notation is meant to be "read" and "heard," although the reading and hearing may take many forms. By means of the visual representation, the reader takes control of the sounds represented. They may be imagined or actualized in or out of real time, completely or partially. The meaning of the example may be apprehended through a synoptic reading or by means of a glance. Notation allows the writer to speak of music as "sound" within the confines of the printed page, offering a specific point of reference which serves as the only potential guarantee of the possibility of shared understanding of abstractions of sounding moments in the context of music both as it sounds and as it is written about.

Music examples pose a particularly interesting challenge precisely because of their ability to function simultaneously as visual image and aural trace. Some examples from Thomas Morley's *A Plaine and Easie Introduction to Practicall Musicke* (1597), a treatise that stands at the very end of the century with which I am most directly concerned, highlight these possibilities.

By the time Morley wrote, music printing and music print culture were no novelties; his treatise reflects certain traditions of music-theoretic discourse that

---

[2] A concise summary is supplied in Gelley, *Unruly Examples*. In particular he contrasts the following passages from Kant and Derrida:

> How to take an *Exempel* and how to cite a *Beispiel* for clarification of an expression involve quite separate concepts. The *Exempel* is a special case of a *practical* rule, insofar as it conceives the practicality or impracticality of an action. Whereas a *Beispiel* is only the notion of the particular (concretum) standing within the concept of the general (abstractum), and merely the theoretical presentation of a concept. (Immanuel Kant, *Metaphysik der Sitten*, ed. W. Weischedel (Frankfurt: Suhrkamp, 1977), cited in Buck "Kants Lehre vom Exempel," 150–51, cited in Gelley, p. 8.)

> What is at stake is exemplarity and its whole *enigma* – in other words, as the word enigma indicates, exemplarity and the *récit* which works through the logic of the example . . . The trait that marks membership inevitably divides, the boundary of the set comes to form, by invagination, an internal pocket larger than the whole; and the outcome of this division and of this abounding remains as singular as it is limitless. (Jacques Derrida, "The Law of Genre," *Glyph:Textual Studies* 7 (1988), 206, cited in Gelley, p. 10.)

[3] This discussion has been shaped by John D. Lyons, *Exemplum:The Rhetoric of Example in Early Modern France and Italy* (Princeton: Princeton University Press, 1989) and Gelley, *Unruly Examples*.

became well established in the course of the sixteenth century – traditions that we as modern readers take for granted. The first series of examples from Morley (Fig. 1.2) comes early in the dialogue.[4] This example is useful for understanding how a theorist manipulates notation and the printed page in an attempt at creating verisimilitude. So the master says: "Here is one: sing it." We are intended to *see*, but not yet *hear* the example that follows on from the master's words. The master is presenting the notation to the student, Philomathes, who is to realize it. Morley then attaches solmization syllables to the excerpt when it is repeated, so we know that Philomathes has sung it. Not only do we know that he has sung it, but the dialogue tells us that he has sung it well! By extension, the conventions of dialogue suggest that *we*, the readers, know to sing it because we recognize Morley as the director who simultaneously stands outside the dialogue, but who is embodied within as the "master." Similarly, we are outside the dialogue, but participate vicariously through the voice of the students. Through aural and active reference – to sing, peruse, see, hear – Morley's language frames his examples, even as the treatise remains a visual object manipulated by its reader. Its careful spatial organization supports the illusion of simultaneity between the dialogue and its visual representation.

Polyphonic examples are more problematic, particularly in the context of a dialogue, especially those moments when Morley puts the polyphony in the mouth of an individual, as he is wont to do. Frequently, format becomes a clue for understanding how the example is to be read. We know from the layout and placement at the end of the treatise that the examples are to be performed by a group, not imagined by an individual (Fig. 1.3). Other examples in score or pseudo-score pose no challenge to the modern reader; there is no doubt that by the end of the sixteenth century, score was a format associated with music for study.[5] What then of the examples notated in parts? Figure 1.4 reproduces one three-part example from the copy of Morley's treatise held by the Library of Congress. This copy contains annotations in an early seventeenth-century hand. In this instance, the letters provide points of reference for guiding the eye in relating the parts. The relative infrequency of such annotations in surviving sources suggests that earlier in the century such a reading together of disparate parts was a skill assumed on the part of least some readers and writers of treatises. Morley's treatise highlights in striking ways the two foci of this study: the material means by which music (notation) is transmitted and the ways in which such notation is read.

---

[4] It is worth noting that monophony poses far fewer problems than polyphony in terms of reading music examples. The question of how the individual realizes such notation is not a particularly interesting one, given the range of possibilities. (See the discussion of silent reading and silent listening pp. 11–16.)

[5] For a concise overview of the formats associated with music theory treatises, see Jessie Ann Owens, *Composers at Work: The Craft of Musical Composition 1450–1600* (New York: Oxford University Press, 1997), 34–63. For more general descriptions of formats, see Donald Krummel and Stanley Sadie, eds., *Music Printing and Publishing* (New York: Norton, 1990), especially the glossary by Stanley Boorman, 489–551.

6 The first part.

Ma. How then muſt you ſing it when there is no ſigne?

Phi. I crie you mercie, it muſt be ſharpe: but I had forgotten the rule you gaue mee, and therefore I pray you ſet mee another example, to ſee if I haue forgotten any more?

Ma. Here is one: ſing it.

Phi.

Vt re mi fa ſol la fa ſol la mi fa.

Ma. This is well ſong:
Now ſing this other.

Phi.

vt re mi fa ſol la mi fa ſol la

Ma. This is right: but could you ſing it no other wiſe?

Phi. No otherwiſe in tune, though I might alter the names of the notes.

Ma. Of which, and how?

Phi. Of the three firſt, thus and ſo foorth of their eyghtes.

&c.

The three firſt notes may be altered in name though not in tune.

fa ſol la

Ma. You do well. Now for the laſt tryall of your ſinging in continuall deduction ſing this perfectly, and I will ſaie you vnderſtand plainſong well enough.

Phi. I know not how to beginne.

Ma. Why?

Phi. Becauſe, beneath *Gam vt* there is nothing: and the firſt note ſtandeth beneath *Gam vt.*

1.2 Morley, *A Plaine and Easie Introduction*, 6, music examples within the dialogue

EXCURSUS: SILENT READING, SILENT LISTENING

Multi-faceted notions of what is signaled by the phrase "reading music" exist both within and without the musicological community. There does appear to be some level of consensus among musicologists and historians of the book who work in early print culture that musical notation implies realization in performance. As Stanley Boorman most succinctly phrased it:

> [The arrangement of printed volumes of polyphony in partbook format] means that the titles were useless to anyone except a complete set of performers. The act of silently studying the music from such books was, if not impossible, very tedious . . . This makes implicit what is implied by format, that the sort of use-for-reference that characterizes, say, legal printing, is an impossibility for almost all printed music. Thus until the appearance of these volumes in score, one cannot say that there was a *reading* public for musical printing but only a *using* public.[6]

Boorman was addressing a non-musicological audience and he may have deliberately simplified his claim. He ties the ability to "read" (as opposed to perform) music to the format in which it was transmitted. For his audience (a conference on print culture), Boorman's focus on format would have had resonances with the ongoing debate in print culture circles about "silent reading" and the relationship of the phenomena to visual cues such as word demarcation that were regulated both in changing habits of manuscript production as well as through the medium of printed books.[7] More than that, it stood entirely to reason that Boorman would be the scholar addressing this audience about printed music. His extensive studies of the output of Ottaviano Petrucci were among the first to embrace the importance of print history and analytical bibliography in the study of musical sources.[8]

Boorman's statement about the silent study of such sources may seem self-evident in relation to modern music-reading habits. While the primary use for books like Petrucci's undoubtedly *was* performance or as a means to a performance (when partbooks served as the sources for material copied into manuscript choirbooks), the later appearance of score format and its association with music for study need not necessarily be taken as evidence of the impossibility of studying the music of such books silently (what Boorman seems to mean by "reading"). The format

---

[6] Stanley Boorman, "Early Music Printing: Working for a Specialized Market," in *Print and Culture in the Renaissance: Essays on the Advent of Printing in Europe*, ed. Gerald P. Tyson and Sylvia S. Wagonheim (Newark DE: University of Delaware Press, 1986), 222.

[7] Paul Saenger, "Silent Reading: Its Impact on Late Medieval Script and Society," *Viator* 13 (1982), 367–414.

[8] Of Boorman's extensive writings on Petrucci, see especially, "Petrucci at Fossombrone: A Study of Early Music Printing, with Special Reference to the Motetti de la Corona (1514–19)," Ph.D. dissertation, King's College, University of London (1976); "The 'First' Edition of the *Odhecaton A*," *Journal of the American Musicological Society* 30 (1977), 183–207; "Limitations and Extensions of Filiation Technique," in *Music in Medieval and Early Modern Europe: Patronage, Sources and Texts*, ed. Iain Fenlon (Cambridge: Cambridge University Press, 1981), 319–46; "Petrucci's Type-setters and the Process of Stemmatics," in *Formen und Probleme der Überlieferung mehrstimmiger Musik im Zeitalter Josquins Desprez*, ed. Ludwig Finscher (Munich: Kraus International Publications, 1981), 245–80; "The Uses of Filiation in Early Music," *Text: Transactions of the Society for Textual Scholarship* 1 (1984), 167–84, and his contributions, including the glossary, in *Music Printing and Publishing*, ed. Krummel and Sadie.

1.3 Morley, *A Plaine and Easie Introduction*, 194–95, partbook format

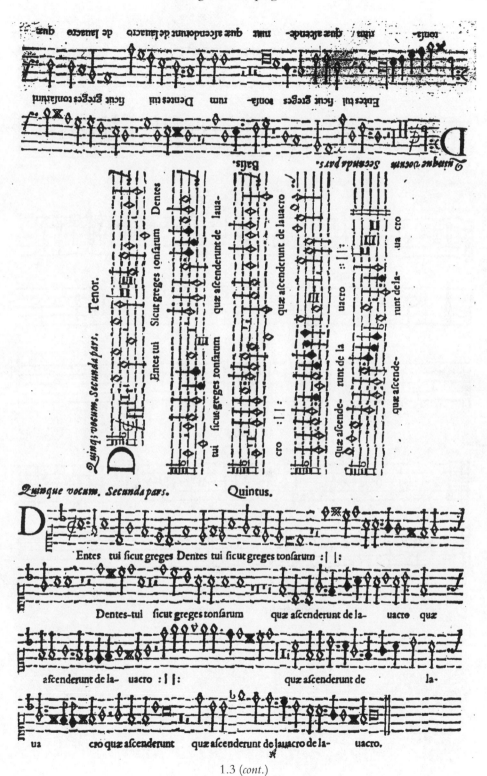

1.3 (*cont.*)

1.4 Morley, *A Plaine and Easie Introduction*, 30, three-part example with seventeenth-century annotations

may not have been as formidable for reading and study to musicians who were accustomed to it as it is for the modern musician long in the habit of relying on score notation.[9] Boorman's emphasis on silent study and its association with format has resonances with a central article on medieval reading habits by Paul Saenger from a few years before.[10] Saenger's thesis ties the advent of silent reading to thirteenth- and fourteenth-century developments, specifically the spatial separation of word units. The change from partbook to score might be taken as an obvious visual cue that serves (like word demarcation) to provide a visual patterning to the page that encourages synoptic reading. Yet ironically, musical notation, in *any* format, seems to have been frankly forbidding to Saenger, who, when claiming that silent reading was uncommon in classical antiquity, invoked a parallel with musical notation:

A written text was essentially a transcription which, like modern musical notation, became an intelligible message only when it was performed orally to others or to oneself.[11]

For Boorman, the hurdle lay in the notational format and its difficulty in apprehension; the score, Boorman seems (commonsensically) to suggest, can be silently apprehended as a representation of a musical entity, while parts cannot. For Saenger, it is not the format but the very nature of the musical notation that is prohibitive. In the more extensive statement of his thesis on the relationship of word demarcation and the development of silent reading in *Space between Words*, Saenger explicitly connected the development and use of musical notation (of monophonic chant) with the word demarcation process. Although he never directly addresses the phenomenon of reading music, it is clear that Saenger *always* assumes an audible performance of these musical sources. Yet because all of Saenger's sources are monophonic, the question of how they are conceptualized by an individual (whether silently or out loud) is not particularly interesting from the present point of view. The issue is greatly complicated when polyphony enters the realm, not only because of the potential demands of the notation highlighted by Boorman, but also because aural realization is impossible by an individual: either an instrument or other singers are necessary for performance. This forces the issue of how an *individual* "reads" polyphony.

In contrast to Saenger (and in a very different context), Rose Rosengard Subotnik sees a central problem in the way musicologists "read" music, pretending that scores are books:

⁹ The most extensive recent argument for reading in parts appears in Owens, *Composers at Work*, 48–56 and *passim*. For an earlier discussion, see Robert Judd, "The Use of Notational Formats at the Keyboard: A Study of Printed Sources of Keyboard Music in Spain and Italy c. 1500–1700," D.Phil. thesis, University of Oxford (1989). Both are concerned with different kinds of evidence than that presented here but contribute to a larger picture that partbooks could be (and were) read by some segment of the musically literate population. In the decades since Boorman's article appeared, there have been a number of significant studies that offer a more nuanced interpretation of the successive/simultaneous dichotomy and the fixation on the score. The most recent is Owens, *Composers at Work*.

¹⁰ Saenger, "Silent Reading," and developed more extensively in *Space Between Words: The Origins of Silent Reading* (Stanford: Stanford University Press, 1997).   ¹¹ Saenger, "Silent Reading."

Our perceptions and analytical concerns as musicologists [are] almost completely dependent on scores, as if the latter were books. One is tempted to argue that structural listening makes more use of the eyes than of the ears. Certainly, to an important extent structural listening can take place in the mind through intelligent score-reading, without the physical presence of an external sound-source. But whereas the absence of concrete sound constitutes a debatable loss in the case of literature, it represents nothing less than a catastrophic sacrifice for music.[12]

But what is it that we mean when we talk about "reading" music? The act of reading in which I am interested is so basic that Boorman and Subotnik appear to take it for granted: the sense in which one apprehends or realizes notated music from a page, a skill that might be termed "silent listening" or "silent hearing."[13] More specifically, though, I am interested in the process as it occurs when reading a verbal text that incorporates notation – pages like those I highlighted from Charles Rosen's *The Romantic Generation* – with its inevitable disjunction in two symbolic systems. Thus this book implicitly addresses the general question of what it is to "read" music while simultaneously considering explicitly the specific nature of musical exemplarity.

The examples drawn from Morley highlight some of the issues of format and function in relation to notated music within sixteenth-century texts, but these examples are "newly composed" and thus implicitly internal to the text in which they are contained. Even as the means of presentation changes, the music of Morley's treatise still issues from his pen. More interesting – for the ways they point outside the text – are examples appropriated from other sources and it is those on which this book concentrates. By contrast to the apparent ease with which Morley was able to control and manipulate his examples, theory treatises from the late fifteenth century through the first half of the sixteenth century show their authors constantly renegotiating the relationship with print, while refining the means of notational presentation.

---

[12] Rose Rosengard Subotnik, "Toward a Deconstruction of Structural Listening: A Critique of Schoenberg, Adorno, and Stravinsky," in *Deconstructive Variations* (Minneapolis: University of Minnesota Press, 1996), 148–76, esp. 161. For an earlier version of this essay, see *Explorations in Music, the Arts, and Ideas*, ed. Eugene Narmour and Ruth Solie (Stuyvesant NY: Pendragon Press, 1988), 104.

[13] I invoke these ungainly terms only for the purposes of maintaining a distinction between reading music and reading other sorts of texts.

2

MUSIC THEORY INCUNABULA
PRINTED BOOKS, PRINTED MUSIC

The advent of printing had multiple ramifications for the nature of musical exemplarity. Although in some sense music theory books were no different from other works in the ways they bridged manuscript and print culture in the late fifteenth century when the first treatises were printed, the use of music notation within a treatise blurs the orality/visuality dichotomy sometimes associated with the arrival of print culture. Technical limitations of musical notation clearly posed an obstacle to certain sorts of publications, shaping both the look and genre of book as printed. Thus an understanding of the first printed theory books provides the necessary background for exploring the conventions of exemplarity in sixteenth-century treatises. Although only a handful of treatises appeared in the last years of the fifteenth century, between 1500 and 1600 some 326 separate works on the theory of music were issued in a total of 611 editions by 225 printers in 75 cities throughout Europe.[1]

THE TREATISES OF FRANCHINO GAFFURIO AND THE MANUSCRIPT TRADITION

Among the most important early printed treatises in terms of their influence on the sixteenth century were the writings of Franchino Gaffurio. His three most significant treatises, *Theorica musicae* (1492), *Practica musicae* (1496), and *De harmonia musicorum instrumentorum opus* (1518) – often described as a theoretical trilogy – provided a complete study in theoretical and practical music. Gaffurio's treatises provide the backdrop for the present study, even as they stand apart from it in one important detail: when Gaffurio's treatises were published there was no "music print culture," that is, there was no printed polyphonic repertory. Gaffurio's examples are in fact among the first instances of printed polyphonic music. Despite his obvious participation in an incipient print culture, Gaffurio was clearly writing from within a culture of manuscripts. Six theoretical works are still extant in manuscript form with dates ranging from 1474 to 1487 and at least two others were known to have existed.[2]

---

[1] These statistics are based on Åke Davidsson, *Bibliographie der Musiktheoretischen Drucke des 16. Jahrhunderts* (Baden-Baden: Verlag Heitz, 1962).

[2] Five manuscripts are discussed in Clement Miller, "Early Gaffuriana: New Answers to Old Questions," *Musical Quarterly* 56 (1970), 367–88. Bonnie J. Blackburn, Edward E. Lowinsky, and Clement A. Miller, eds., *A Correspondence of Renaissance Musicians* (Oxford: Clarendon Press, 1991), 166–74, describe a sixth manuscript treatise.

Gaffurio consistently reworked manuscript treatises for modified printed versions with new dedicatees, thus treating them as new works of equal stature. What most distinguishes Gaffurio's treatises from the case studies that follow in this book is the nature and production of his music examples, which are tied directly to manuscript culture. A brief survey of early printed theory books follows, in which Gaffurio's figure most prominently.

Gaffurio's *Theoricum opus musicae disciplinae* (Naples, 1480),[3] an early version of his *Theorica musicae*, was the first printed book broadly devoted to the study of music.[4] Like many music incunabula, almost all of which were liturgical books like missals and breviaries, the *Theoricum opus* included no actual printed music, but left space for its insertion by hand.[5] Illuminated initials would also have been added by hand. As a work firmly in the realm of *musica speculativa* – that part of theory concerned with establishing the nature and essence of music on a strictly philosophical and scientific basis – there was little call for notation in Gaffurio's treatise.[6] In essence, it followed Boethius's *De institutione musica* which would not itself be printed until 1492. Gaffurio's move to Naples in 1478 may have supplied the impetus toward publication. Following his patron, Prospero Adorno, into exile, Gaffurio entered into the cultural context of the court of Ferdinand I of Aragon. Unlike many other patrons of the period who were interested almost exclusively in manuscripts as unique, personal, and precious objects, Ferdinand was a strong champion of printing and favored its development. Talented typographers were readily available in Naples and the *Theoricum opus* posed no particular technical challenge.[7]

Other theory treatises followed shortly after. Ramis de Pareja's *Musica Utriusque cantus practica* (Bologna, 1482),[8] like the *Theoricum opus*, was published in upright quarto format.[9] It, too, contains almost no music, but the printed solution was

---

[3] Facsimile with introduction by Cesarino Ruini, Musurgiana 15 (Lucca: Libreria Musicale Italiana, 1996); Facsimile, Monuments of Music and Music Literature in Facsimile, II, 100 (New York: Broude Brothers, 1967).

[4] The later version of the book published in 1492 is much better known and usually treated as the definitive version of the treatise. On the background to the 1480 edition, see Ruini, "Introduction."

[5] Mary Kay Duggen, *Italian Music Incunabula: Printers and Type* (Berkeley: University of California Press, 1992), 42–75. Duggen categorizes music incunabula according to four types on the basis of their treatment of music notation: space for music; printed staves; music printed from woodcuts; and music printed from type.

[6] The treatise is in five books of eight chapters each. The first deals with the praise, classification, and invention of music; the second with terminology and the physical characteristics of sound. Book III is on arithmetic proportions and the intervals while Book IV concerns Greek doctrine of intervals. The final book concerns Greek tetrachords and *tonoi* along with Gregorian modal theory. On Gaffurio's misinterpretation of the relationship of Greek, Boethian, and ecclesiastical theory, see Claude Palisca, *Humanism in Italian Renaissance Musical Thought* (New Haven: Yale University Press, 1985), 293–98. For a general introduction to Gaffurio's speculative theory, see Walter Kurt Kreiszig, introduction to his translation of *Theorica musice* as *The Theory of Music* (New Haven: Yale University Press, 1993).   [7] Ruini, "Introduction," 41.

[8] Facsimile ed. G. Vecchi, Bibliotheca Musica Bononiensis, II, 3 (Bologna: Forni, 1969); translation by Clement A Miller, Musicological Studies and Documents 44 (Neuhausen-Stuttgart: Hänssler-Verlag, 1993).

[9] Descriptions of book format throughout refer specifically to the production of the book and are not used in a more casual sense to designate size, which was dependent on the size of paper used in the production of the book. For a concise description of paper sizes and formats, see Jane Bernstein, *Music Printing in Renaissance Venice: The Scotto Press (1539–1572)* (New York: Oxford University Press, 1998), 62–68.

slightly more sophisticated than blank space for the insertion of notes. Like many missals, Ramis's treatise was supplied with printed staves on which notes are to be added.[10] In this case, the addition was a single poorly printed three-line staff, which, as Duggan observed, was insufficient for the notation described by the text. Gaffurio's solution in the copy of the treatise lent to him by Spataro was to add two staves in the margin[11] (compare Figs. 2.1a and 2.1b). *Musica practica* was obviously intended as an inexpensive textbook. In contrast to *Theoricum opus*, the print quality is poor, the layout and typeface are inelegant, and there are numerous errors. All this suggests careless and hasty printing. Indeed, Bottrigari called the treatise (of which he owned two copies) the worst example of printing he had ever seen.[12]

A second treatise, Nicolo Burzio's *Musices opusculum*,[13] appeared in Bologna in 1487. It adopted what was to be the favored solution for including musical notation in books about music: woodcuts. Woodcut music illustrations made possible the printing of music theory books in the absence of expensive mensural types or complex fonts for plainchant neumes. Woodcuts offered an affordable solution to the problem of music examples and craftsmen to make them were in ready supply.[14] The results, as seen in Burzio's treatise (Fig. 2.2), were not always elegant, however. Most music incunabula that include woodcuts of music are in fact theory treatises: in addition to Burzio's *Musices opusculum*, Gaffurio's *Practica musicae* and Bonaventura de Brescia's *Regula musicae planae*[15] use woodcuts for music examples. The reprinting of the latter suggests the efficacy of woodcuts in the printing process as a means of including music in books from the late fifteenth century.[16]

In contrast to all earlier printed theory treatises, including the two versions of his *Theorica*, Franchino Gaffurio's *Practica musicae* (Milan, 1496; Brescia, 1497) was an extraordinarily beautiful folio volume that set new standards for the printing of music theory treatises. Numerous examples of Roman and Ambrosian plainchant on a four-line staff and of mensural music on a five-line staff are printed throughout

---

[10] Ramis's laborious notation in letter names (which follows from his not entirely consistent rejection of Guidonian syllables) posed a real obstacle to understanding without the aid of staff notation.

[11] Duggan, *Italian Music Incunabula*, 51–53; Albano Sorbelli, "Le due edizioni della *Musica Practica* di Bartolomé Ramis de Pareja," *Gutenberg-Jahrbuch* 5 (1930), 106. The two copies of the treatise in the Bologna Civico Museo Bibliografico Musicale were once in the possession of the theorist Ercole Bottrigari. One of these had previously belonged to the theorist Giovanni Spataro. Spataro, a pupil of Ramis, lent the treatise to Gaffurio and it came back filled with Gaffurio's criticisms in marginalia. The episode is detailed in Miller's commentary and also in Blackburn *et al.*, eds., *Correspondence*.   [12] Miller (commentary to translation), 12.

[13] Facsimile ed. Domenico Massera, Bibliotheca Musica Bononiensis, II, 4 (Bologna: Forni, 1969). Translation, Clement A. Miller, Musicological Studies and Documents 67 (Neuhausen-Stuttgart: American Institute of Musicology, 1983).   [14] Duggan, *Italian Music Incunabula*, 64.

[15] Bonaventura da Brescia, *Breviloquium musicale* (Brescia: Angelo Britannico, 1497); *Regula musicae planae* (Brescia: Angelo Britannico, 1497; R Milan: Giovanni de Legnano, 1500). Facsimile, Milan: Bollettino Bibliografico Musicale, 1934.

[16] The treatise by Bonaventura da Brescia contains woodcuts on twenty-eight pages. These are primarily chant examples in roman notation of fairly crude effect. Like the anonymous cantorinus, *Compendium musices*, also an unimposing quarto volume published with woodcut chant examples, such manuals proved extremely popular as elementary manuals for priests who needed to learn the rudiments necessary for singing chant. They were reprinted throughout the sixteenth century with typeset music substituted for the earlier woodcuts.

Tractat⸿ ſcd̕s

elleuabitur grauiora ſeu acutiora loca tenebũt. Signabimus igi
tur nunc duplicez diapaſon vnaz a littera e. in c. acuta z aliaz ab
eadez in c. ſupacutaz vt incboãtes p̃ diuerſa loca ꝯnotẽt uoces

Sallitur per uo uoces iſtas: tas is ces uo uo per tur li ſal
Sallitur per uo uoces iſtas tas iſ ces uo per tur li ſal
C. D. E. F. G. G. A. ♭. C. C. H. A. G. g. F. E D. C. c. d. e. f. g.
g. a. ♮ c. c. ♭. a. g. g. f. e. d. c. Si autez lector non ita facile per
notulas poteſt diſcurrere cũ uocis elleuatione ſeu depreſſione
ad monochordũ recurrat z a tertia uoce incipiens uſꝗ ad eius
octauaz conſcendat z ad tertiaz uocez ſcandar vt dictũ fuit ca
pitulo Multi uolentes. totũ igitur ꝙ dictuz fuit debere fieri
cuz iſtrũmto: in b̊ ſine eo facere ſciet notulis pectis.

Sicte muſice declaratio   Cap. ſm
Et autem de bijs ſignis atꝗ notulis pleioꝛ
habeatur cognitio: aliqua circa b̊
ſubtilius inueſtigabimus.   Solent. n. alia ſigna
in cantibus poni per que diſtãtia intercapedinũ co
gnoſcitur iequalis: quoꝛ alteꝛ ſic. b rotũdo ſcribitur: alterũ. ue
ro ſic ♮ quadrũ figuratur. Primũ ſignũ b molle dicitur ſiue: b
rotunduz ſecunduz ucro ♮ quadratũ ſiue ♮ duꝛ ♮ ꝗdratũ z b
rotundũ appellantur a figure qnalitate ſed b molle aut ♮ duꝛ
dicitur ex eo ꝙ canentes per litteras gregoꝛiſ quãdo ab a in b
faciunt ſemitoniũ illud b dicũt molle qꝛ cũ in arſyz z theſiz ſal
tus ſit per ſemitoniũ magis molleſcit uox illa qua quãdo p to
nũ ſicut a b molle a b quadꝛ duꝛe ſic etia quãdo per ſemiditonũ
magis molle quã per ditonũ. ſicut g. b. molle. g. b quadꝛe dure
Similiter diatheſſaron magis molle -ꝗ tritonus. ſicut f. b. mo
lle. f. b. quadꝛe duriſſime. Ex his paret erꝛoꝛ quoꝛũdã cantoruz
qui dicunt b molle aut b quadꝛatum. duobus eniz modis erꝛant
pꝛimo quia ipſi cantant peꝛ ſyllabã guidonis z non per litteꝛas
gꝛegoꝛii. neqꝛ igitur b molle neqꝛ b quadꝛe duꝛe pꝛonuntiant.
ſed fa aut mi ſecũdo non faciunt rectaz relationez paz quando
dicunt b quadꝛatũ debent coꝛꝛeſpondenter diceꝛe b ꝛotunduz

2.1a Ramis, *Musica practica*, showing printed staff (Civico Museo Bibliografico Musicale. Reproduced by permission.)

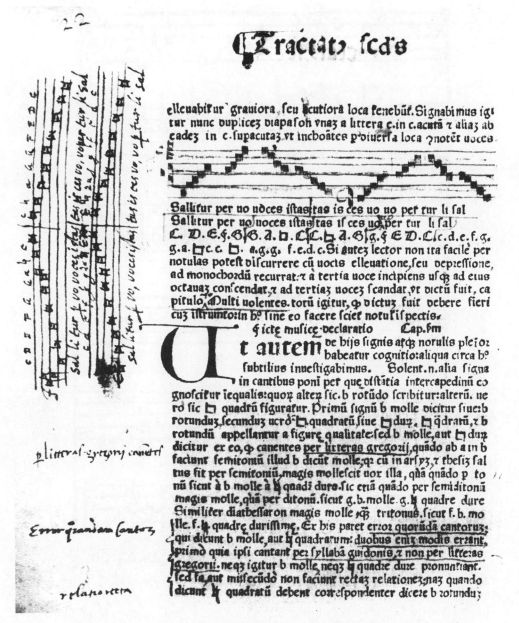

2.1b Ramis, *Musica practica*, with Gaffurio's annotations (Civico Museo Bibliografico Musicale. Reproduced by permission.)

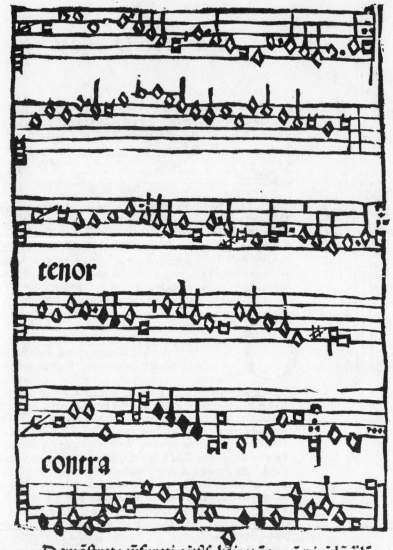

2.2 Burzio, *Musices opusculum*, woodcut example of polyphony

the book. It is arguable that no single book on music had as great an influence on musical thought of the sixteenth century as the *Practica musicae*. Leading theorists of diverse national origins cited, paraphrased, or appropriated Gaffurio (and his examples) throughout the course of the century.[17] The *Practica* complements the *musica speculativa* of the *Theorica* and *De harmonia* in its focus on sounding music and concern with proportions. Books I and III are concerned with intervals and

---

[17] Like all of Gaffurio's treatises, the *Practica musicae* is essentially scholastic in method, filled with quotations of ancient authorities, mostly as known to Gaffurio through contemporary Latin translations.

counterpoint, while Book II is on notation and Book IV concentrates on mensural proportions. The relationships of the alternate books are visually signaled in the 1496 edition by the elegant borders that mark the beginnings of each book[18] (see Fig. 2.3).

A sense of how integral the notation is to the subject matter of the *Practica* and the ways in which the woodcuts of the treatise mimic a manuscript is readily apparent in the liberal illustration of Book I (on the elements of music and plainchant). Shorter examples are placed directly in the text. Most often they are placed flush right in the text block, but on pages particularly filled with examples, they are inserted within text, even mid-syllable, in the most economic use of the available space (see Fig. 2.4). Gaffurio does not caption his examples, rather they follow directly from description as demonstration, even as one has to sometimes read past them in order to make sense of the words they interrupt because of the practicalities of placement. "Authorities" and sources are highlighted marginally, as in the contrast of the Gregorian and Ambrosian versions of the *Nos qui vivimus* chant shown in Figure 2.5. While the chant examples might seem to point outside the treatise, they are part of a long history in which chant provided the primary means of musical instantiation carrying with it the authority of the Church and tradition. Chant and mode, for example, were inseparable concepts for the fifteenth-century musician. What is special about Gaffurio's treatment, stemming from his location in Milan, is his acknowledgment of both local and Roman chant tradition.[19]

Miller highlights the composers of polyphony cited in the *Practica*, noting particularly the changes in citations from the earlier manuscript version of Book IV of the treatise, the *Tractatus praticabilium proportionum* (c. 1482).[20] While some eighteen composers are named in the *Practica*, the citations are neither frequent, nor scattered throughout the treatise: most occur in two lists in Book III, the book on counterpoint. First, in a discussion of discords in counterpoint, Gaffurio mentions Dunstable, Binchois, Dufay, and Brassart. Later in a chapter on the use of similar perfect consonances, Gaffurio provides an example of writing in parallel tenths and remarks that Tinctoris, Guielmus Guarneris, Josquin, Weerbecke, Agricola, Compère, Obrecht, Brumel, and Isaac have used a similar passage (see Fig. 2.6). The contrast of generations is striking in the two lists. In each case, however, the composer is associated in the most general way with a practice. Two composers are mentioned in other places as well – Tinctoris and Bonadies; Tinctoris was Gaffurio's close associate, Bonadies his teacher. Indeed, Tinctoris is the most cited of all composers (this apart from references to his theoretical

---

[18] The craftsmanship of the borders and frontispiece has been long admired in studies of incunabula. For a discussion and references, see James Haar, "The Frontispiece of Gafori's *Practica musicae* (1496)," *Renaissance Quarterly* 27 (1974), 7–22. Neither the frontispiece nor the borders were reused in the 1497, 1508 or 1512 editions although the music examples and diagrams appear to have been printed from the same blocks as the earlier edition. (On the blocks, see H. Edmund Pool, "Definition, Early Stages and Woodblock Printing," in *Music Printing and Publishing*, ed. D. W. Krummel and Stanley Sadie (New York: Norton, 1990), 10.)

[19] For a detailed discussion of Gaffurio's chant examples, see Clement Miller, "Gaffurius's *Practica Musicae*: Origin and Contents," *Musica disciplina* 22 (1968), 105–28.   [20] Miller, "Early Gaffuriana," 375.

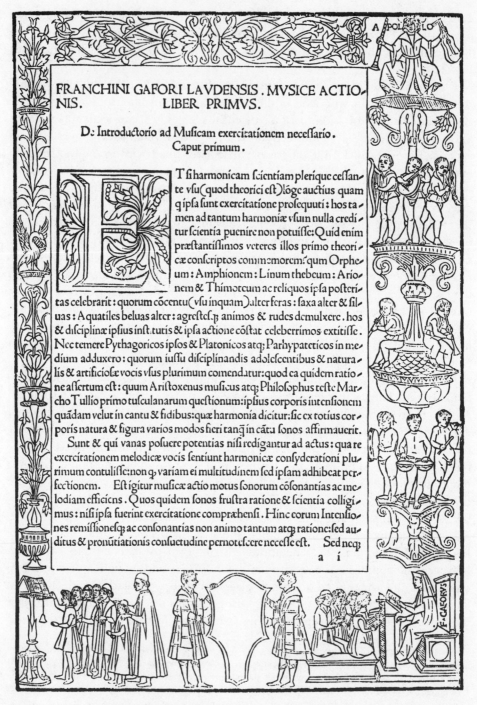

2.3a Gaffurio, *Practica musicae*, title page borders, Books I and III

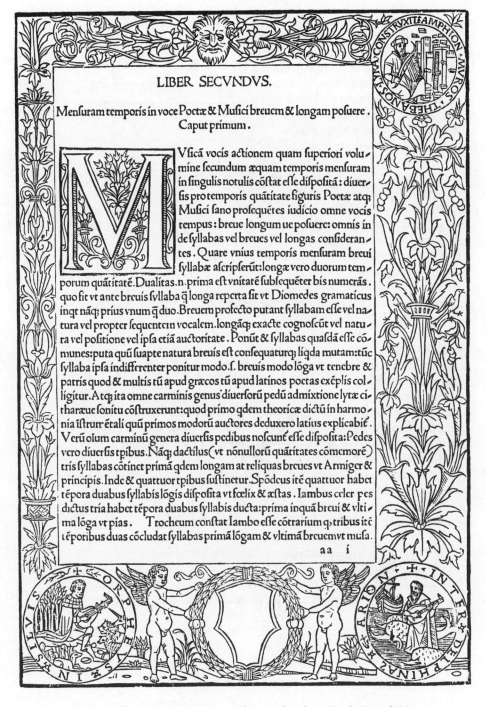

2.3b Gaffurio, *Practica musicae*, title page borders, Books II and IV

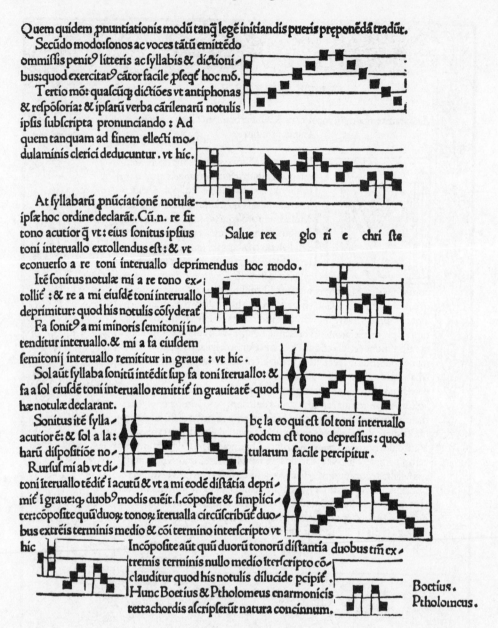

Quem quidem pnuntiationis modū tanǧ legē initiandis pueris preponēdā tradūt.

Secūdo modo:sonos ac voces tātū emittēdo ommiſſis penit⁹ litteris ac ſyllabis & dictioni bus:quod exercitat⁹ cātor facile pſeqǧ hoc mó.

Tertio mó: quaſcūǧ dictióes vt antiphonas & reſpóſoria: & ipſarū verba cārilenarū notulis ipſis ſubſcripta pronunciando : Ad quem tanquam ad ſinem ellecti mo dulaminis clerici deducuntur . vt hic.

At ſyllabarū pnūciationē notulæ ipſæ hoc ordine declarāt.Cū.n. re ſit tono acutior ǧ vt: eius ſonitus ipſius toni interuallo extollendus eſt: & vt econuerſo a re toni interuallo deprimendus hoc modo .

Itē ſonitus notulæ mi a re tono ex tollit : & re a mi eiuſdē toni interuallo deprimitur: quod his notulis cóſyderaſ

Fa ſonit⁹ a mi minoris ſemitonij in tenditur interuallo. & mi a ſa eiuſdem ſemitonij interuallo remititur in graue : vt hic .

Sol aūt ſyllaba ſonitū intēdit ſup fa toni iteruallo: & fa a ſol eiuſdē toni interuallo remittit in grauitatē quod hæ notulæ declarant.

Sonitus itē ſylla acutior ē: & ſol a la: harū diſpoſitióe no

Rurſuſ mi ab vt di toni iteruallo tēdiſ i acutū & vt a mi eodē diſtātia depri mit i graue:cǧ duob⁹ modis euēit. ſ.cópoſite & ſimplici ter:cópoſite qūu duoǧ tonoǧ iterualla circūſcribūt duo bus extrēis terminis medio & cói termino interſcripto vt hic

Salue rex   glo ri e chri ſte

bǫ la eo qui eſt ſol toni interuallo eodem eſt tono depreſſus: quod tularum facile percipitur .

Incópoſite aūt qūu duorū tonorū diſtantia duobus tm ex tremis terminis nullo medio iterſcripto có cluditur quod his notulis dilucide pcipiſ . Hunc Boetius & Ptholomeus enarmonicis tettachordis aſcripſerūt natura concinnum.

Boetius.
Ptholomeus.

2.4 Gaffurio, *Practica musicae*, woodcut examples

Gregoriani .   phonario cóperíes pnotatas.   Extat & altera feptimi toni pfalmodía quã Gregoriani obferuant fup antiphona Nos q viuimus benedicimus dominũ in cófinali terminata cũ acqfite deducta fit & fola voce in acutũ diminuta:vt prefenti formula pcipié

añt Nos q ví uí mus   be ne dí cí mus   do mí num. p̃s In e xí tu

yf ra el de e gíp to   do   mus íacob de po pu lo barba ro .

Hæc.n.pfalmodía in princípío p fimílé retinet q̃rto tono modulatíoné in medío
fexto qa antíphona cómifcet' eí propriam diatefíaton fpeciem.f. tertíã cóprehendés
Ambrofiani In fine tertío Verũ Ambrofiani:& fi antiphonã ipfam ifídé notulis & clauibus pro-
fequuntur:alteram tamen huius pfalmodíæ modulationem celebrant:náq; incipiũt
in confinali ipfius antiphonæ chorda.f.in Gfolrcut grauí vbí fua diapétes figura ter-
mínatur in acutum:ficutí & in cæterís obferuant autenticís:hoc modo .

añt. Nos q ví uí mus   be ne dí cí mus do mí num p̃s In e xí tu

yf ra el ex e gíp to   dom⁹Iacob de popu lo barba ro.

2.5 Gaffurio, *Practica musicae*, comparison of Gregorian and Ambrosian
settings of *Nos qui vivimus*

pronouncements).[21] In Book IV (on proportions in mensural music), Gaffurio does make observations related to specific compositions: Busnois's *Missa L'homme armé*, Ockeghem's chanson *L'autre d'antans*, Dufay's *Missa de Sancto Anthonii*, and Dunstable's *Veni sancte spiritus*. Strikingly, three of the four works were already cited by Tinctoris in his *Proportionale*;[22] Gaffurio includes specific examples from these works. In the one instance in which Gaffurio introduces a new citation, Dunstable's *Veni sancte spiritus*, he prints the tenor. From all appearances, the other polyphonic examples are newly composed; if excerpted from other works, they have yet to be identified. Thus even though Gaffurio's treatise is a printed text, it operates within traditions of a musical culture that remains one of manuscript transmission and circulation. Although he could refer to specific composers and generally to aspects of their practice with a sense that his readers participated in the same tradition, he could with little certainty assume any knowledge of specific compositions. As *maestro di cappella* of Milan Cathedral, he composed motets and masses that were collected together with the work of other composers in the manuscripts known as the Gaffurio Codices. The scholastic tradition in which he writes does not suggest excerpting from "real" music. Rather, he provides illustrations as an extension of his textual discourse.

While the printing of the *Practica musicae* had an undeniable and extraordinary impact on sixteenth-century theorizing – there are more than seventy-five extant copies of just the first two editions – the ways in which the means of production affected its composition are less obvious. If anything, the use of woodcuts allowed Gaffurio to circumvent the primary obstacle to printing a theory treatise – the production of music examples – with no obvious concession to the technical limitations of the medium. Indeed, the book has long been admired for its artistry. Thus even though Gaffurio's treatises, especially the *Practica*, stand at the head of sixteenth-century writing about music, setting an artistic standard of production which would not be met again for many years, as books their genesis is very much in the world of manuscript culture.

Even so, the number of examples in the *Practica* is staggering. In addition to the chant examples of Book I, there are some 155 polyphonic examples, most of which (111) occur in Book IV of the treatise, on proportions in mensural music. As will be discussed in subsequent chapters, these examples became a printed musical repertory of sorts for later theorists. *Practica musicae* draws together in a single volume books that often existed independently as manuscripts.[23] The comparable treatises in Tinctoris's output were *Liber de natura et proprietate tonorum* (1476) on the modes, *Liber de arte contrapuncti* (1477) which discusses principles of consonance and disso-

---

[21] From one of Gaffurio's citations, Bonnie J. Blackburn was able to identify a previously unknown work of Tinctoris. See "A Lost Guide to Tinctoris's Teachings Recovered," *Early Music History* 1 (1981) 29.

[22] By and large, Tinctoris uses other composers to illustrate what *not* to do. See Margaret Bent, "Harmony and Discords," in *Music Theory and Analysis 1450–1650*, ed. Anne-Emmanuelle Ceulemans and Bonnie J. Blackburn (Louvain-la-Neuve, forthcoming).

[23] As can be seen by the manuscript precursors of three of the four books of the *Practica*.

In hoc exemplo: omnes primæ notulæ in octauam pofitæ quádecenter difpofitæ
fant quia funt immobiles(interpofita etiam femibreui paufa).   Verum quinta
cantus minima minímæ paufam immediate fequens q̃ in octaua fit cum tenore nó
admittitur propter remiffam octauam immediate præcedenté.   Sunt & qui(interpofita etiam paufa femibreui)duas confimiles concordantias perfectas immediate afcendentes aut defcendentes non admittunt:quáquam his complures dif-
fentiunt cum paufa femibreuis integram temporis menfuram obfcruet.   Con-
decenter item duæ aut plures femibreuium paufæ duas confimiles concordátias
perfectas confequenter afcendentes aut defcendentes mediabunt : fiue in tenore
fiue in cantu feu etiam in contratenore aut in Baritonáte deductæ fint.   Quid
infuper credendum cenfemus ijs qui organizantibus obftant ne plures q̃ tres fe-
mibreues in cantu vnifonas pronuntient? quod propterea affeuerant: ne cantus
uideatur in tenorem conuerfus ac tenor in cantum . hoc noftra quidem fenten-
tia ridiculum eft . Solent enim perfæpe cantilenarum compofitores tenorem atq̃
contratenorem diminutioribus pernotare figuris ac cantú tardioribus: quod re-
centiores frequentant vt hic notiffimo conftat experimento.

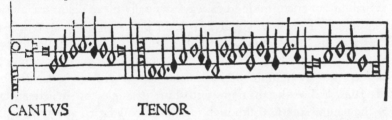

CANTVS   TENOR

Eft & celeberrimus quidam in contrapuncto proceffus notularum videlicet Ba-   Tinctoris
ritonantis ad cantus notulas inftitutus confimilibus notulis per decimam inui-   Gulielmus
cem procedentibus: tenore ad fingulos concorditer commeante . quem Tincto-   guarnerij
ris: Gulielmus guarnerij: Iufquin defprct: Gafpar: Alexander agricola : Loyfet: Iufquin
Obrech: Brumcl: Ifaac ac reliqui Iucundiffimi compofitores in fuis cátilenis fæ-   Gafpar
pius obferuarunt . quod & præfentis cócentus cófyderatione percipitur.   Agricola
                                                          ee ij   Loyfet
                    Verte folium.   Obrech
                                                                                  Brumel
                                                                                  Ifaac

2.6 Gaffurio, *Practica musicae*, composers listed in the margin

nance and rules for counterpoint, and *Proportionale musices* (*c.* 1473–74) which deals
with aspects of mensural notation.[24]

This highlights the areas of theoretical discourse in which notated music examples most frequently occur: mode, mensural theory, and counterpoint.[25] A treatise
like Gaffurio's *Practica musicae* thus reflects long-standing conventions of when and

---

[24] For an overview of Tinctoris's treatises, dating, and content, see *J. Tinctoris: Opera theoretica*, ed. Albert Seay,
Corpus scriptorum de musica 22 ([Rome]: American Institute of Musicology, 1975).

[25] The present study is not primarily about specific pronouncements on mode, mensural theory, and counterpoint, and the discussion that follows of examples that appear in these parts of theory treatises for the most part
requires minimal knowledge of the intricacies of these theories.

where music examples occur, even as his discussion of proportions stands at the brink of changing musical priorities.

PRINTED MUSIC

During the 1470s and 1480s, a number of music books were also printed. Most were produced from metal type in a process that required two impressions: music notation was added to the lines and spaces of a previously printed staff. Even in the early decades, printing of music became a specialized trade practiced by a handful of craftsmen based in a few cities.[26] The music produced in the last three decades of the fifteenth century consisted mostly of liturgical books like missals and graduals that used plainchant notation – primarily Roman, but also Ambrosian and Gothic. Most were in a large folio format appropriate for use on the altar.[27] In Venice, by the end of the century, smaller types were produced for quarto and octavo formats that extended the marketing of service books by both lower cost and convenience of size. Yet the availability of such music fonts was essentially meaningless for music theory treatises; the size of the fonts coupled with the limitation to chant typeface was of no use for a treatise like Gaffurio's with its requirements for mensural notation. Similarly, the fonts were both too costly and too large for such unassuming practical books as the anonymous *Compendium musices* and the *Regulae* of Bonaventura da Brescia. For the diagrams and short examples of such treatises, woodcuts were the natural solution, although such woodcuts varied enormously in quality. Woodcuts continued to be used throughout the sixteenth century. Perhaps the most spectacular example is Andrea Antico's *Liber quindecim missarum* (RISM 1516[1]), a folio choirbook that was a remarkable achievement, even for a professional woodcutter of music like Antico.

While the techniques of printing plainchant were highly developed by 1500, there was no corresponding evolution in the printing of mensural music at the same time. This may be seen to be in equal parts a reflection of market and technological demands. Although isolated instances of some mensural type may be documented,[28] the twenty-year privilege to print and sell music books in Venice obtained by Ottaviano Petrucci of Fossombrone in 1498 marks the beginning of what was to become music print culture.

In many ways, the present book begins with the publication by Petrucci of books of polyphony. Petrucci's *Harmonice musices Odhecaton A* published in May 1501 was

---

[26] Duggan, *Italian Music Incunabula*, 68.

[27] Duggan, *Italian Music Incunabula*, cites 121 missals printed from movable type in Italy alone; those from Rome and Milan all used large plainchant fonts.

[28] The first font of mensural type appears to have been used in an essentially non-musical book: Francesco Niger's *Grammatica* (Venice: Theodor Franck of Würzburg for Johann Lucilius Santritter, 1480). The book contains six pages of mensural notation in music printed from type. As opposed to earlier books like Ramis's treatise in which staves were printed and notation was added by hand, here notes and clefs were provided with the staves to be added. For a facsimile, see Duggan, *Italian Music Incunabula*, figure 36, p. 100.

the first book of polyphony printed by double impression with movable type. The achievement had a profound effect on both the dissemination of polyphonic music and the writing of music theory. Although the books were expensive, they nevertheless placed music notation in the hands of a new class of music readers in conveniently sized, easily manipulated volumes. Petrucci's first publications were in oblong choirbook format, as shown by Figure 2.7, from the *Odhecaton*. In 1504, with the publication of his third book of motets, *Motetti C*, Petrucci switched to the oblong partbook format that remained the characteristic format of most of the ensemble music published in the century (see Fig. 2.8).

COMMUNITIES OF READERS

While the picture of who actually owned such music books and how they used them remains unclear, one community of readers stands out: writers on music like Pietro Aron and Heinrich Glarean. In different ways, both of their treatises are unimaginable without the access to music afforded by the Petrucci sources. There was no necessary reason for sixteenth-century theorists to work from printed editions rather than manuscripts, but the picture that emerges from their practice of citations makes it clear that they did so. The different circles in which theorists like Aron, Heyden, Glarean, and Zarlino moved, as well as rapid changes in the burgeoning music print culture and the growth of a musically literate public in the first half of the sixteenth century, means that the specific nature of the relationships between theoretical writing, ways of reading, and printed sources takes a different shape in each of their treatises. While the use of music examples in a theory treatise may appear obvious or trivial to a modern reader – an inevitable concomitant of the emergence of a music print culture – and thus hardly the likely point of departure for historico-theoretical study, it is that very familiarity that has caused scholars to overlook how dramatically different were the relationships of different theorists (and by association their readers) to musical sources. Indeed, the invocation of printed musical sources by theorists betokened an irreversible change in the interplay of music theory, practice, printed repertories, and communities of readers. Re-examining that interplay has major ramifications not only for the interpretation of sixteenth-century musical and printed culture, but also for our understanding of our own relationship to that culture and the ways in which it has shaped us as scholars and musicians.

Writing about music conveys, encompasses, and conceptualizes music itself through the mediation of musical notation. Because the examples are embedded in a discursive domain, they partake of the constraints of that format as well as those of the original (musical) format. These intersections offer points of departure for exploring fundamental questions – how was music read? by whom? and to what purpose? – in specific cultural contexts.

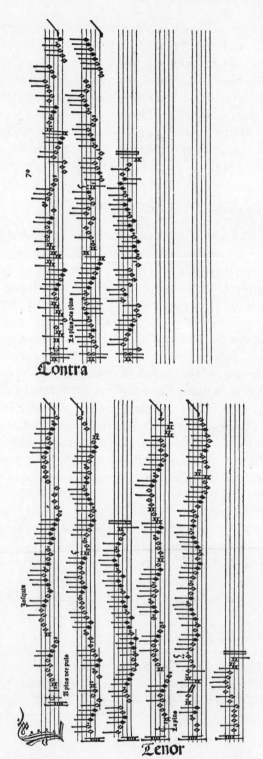

2.7 Petrucci, *Odhecaton*, Josquin, *La plus des plus*

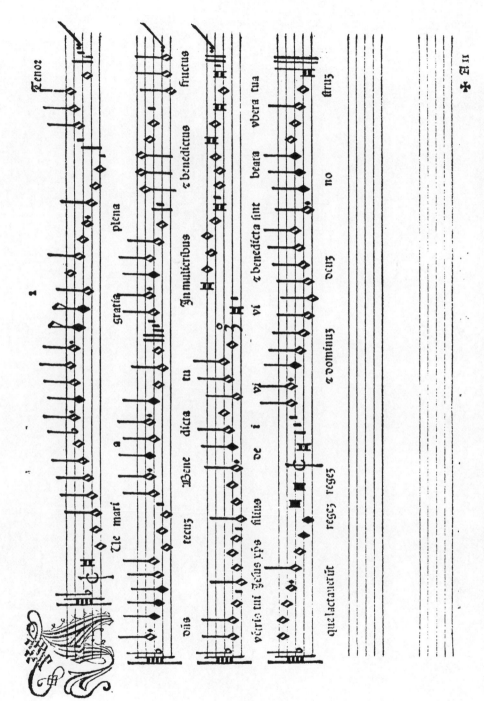

2.8 Petrucci, *Motetti C*, Josquin, *Ave Maria*, tenor (British Library, K.1.d.4. Reproduced by permission.)

PART II

1520–1540: PIETRO ARON AND SEBALD HEYDEN

3

PIETRO ARON AND PETRUCCI'S PRINTS

> And note that all the songs and composers mentioned here, one by one, are found in a book called One Hundred Songs Printed in Order. I have taken this trouble so that you may more easily reach the goal of understanding.
>
> Pietro Aron, *Toscanello*, III: 19

Pietro Aron's *Trattato della natura et cognitione di tutti gli tuoni* (1525)[1] has often been singled out in histories of music for explicitly linking traditional eight-mode theory with polyphonic music. Although a number of earlier treatises suggested the relevance of modal theory for composers of polyphony, Aron established the connection in a novel way: by citing actual compositions and asserting the modal categories to which they belonged. As has long been observed, most of the compositions Aron cited appeared in collections issued from the press of Ottaviano Petrucci in the first quarter of the sixteenth century. The symbiotic relationship of Aron's treatise with a printed musical repertory – the first such connection in the history of music theory – suggests the *Trattato* as the logical point of departure for an examination of the intersections of music theory, musical practice, and print culture. Thus this chapter reads Aron as a reader of Petrucci, so to speak, in a fundamentally contextual or "external" view of his citations.[2] My concern is not primarily with the intricacies of Aron's theorizing and his pronouncements on modality.[3]

---

[1] *Trattato della natura et cognitione di tutti gli tuoni di canto figurato non da altrui piu scritti* (Venice: Bernardino de Vitali, 4 August 1525). Facsimile, ed. Willem Elders, Musica Revindicata (Utrecht: Joachimsthal, 1966); Chapters 1–7 translated in Oliver Strunk, *Source Readings in Music History* (New York: Norton, 1950), 205–18; revised in Gary Tomlinson, ed., *Strunk's Source Readings in Music History*, vol. 3: *The Renaissance* (New York: Norton, 1998), 137–50; A supplement to the *Trattato* was published separately without title page or indication of the author (Venice: Bernardino de Vitali, 1531).

[2] For an overview of "internal" versus "external" reading and the significance of appropriation of texts, see Roger Chartier, "Texts, Printing, Readings," in *The New Cultural History*, ed. Lynn Hunt (Berkeley: University of California Press, 1989), 156–58 and *passim*.

[3] The significance of Aron's connection of mode and polyphony has been the subject of a wide variety of historical and theoretical interpretation: in particular, Leeman Perkins ("Mode and Structure in the Masses of Josquin," *Journal of the American Musicological Society* 26 (1973), 189–239) based a study of the masses of Josquin on principles derived from the *Trattato*, while Peter Bergquist ("Mode and Polyphony around 1500," *Music Forum* 1 (1967), 99–161) argued that Aron's classifications were essentially irrelevant for polyphony, despite the

Rather I am interested here in the means by which a musical repertory, as defined by its appearance in printed form, not only conditioned, but effectively shaped Aron's use of citations. By extension, the process affected his practice of music theory in affording the very possibility of such an approach. Examining Aron's citations in the larger context of the specific printed repertory from which he drew them and considering the implications of his reading and appropriation of that repertory offers new insight into the meaning of his citations. Viewing the *Trattato* from this vantage point raises issues of how we are to read and understand the music associated with theorists' writings and the larger repertory from which it is drawn, while confronting fundamental assumptions of how music prints were used in the first quarter of the sixteenth century. A complex picture of the significance of print culture for different communities of musical readers emerges.[4] This approach also highlights issues of orality, literacy, and visuality in relation to music prints, perhaps by their very nature the most difficult exemplars of all to understand in the context of print culture.

From the distance of our twentieth-century perspective it can be difficult to appreciate just how extraordinary the gesture of citing a musical composition by title and composer within a theory treatise was. Such a gesture was deeply dependent on the availability of printed music. The idea of referring to specific compositions could hardly be considered common in the first part of the sixteenth century. While Tinctoris named several specific compositions and supplied the relevant musical passages in his *Proportionale*, his criticism of his contemporaries (for his citations were primarily a means by which to point out errors) seems not to have been well received and he cited fewer compositions in subsequent treatises.[5] Gaffurio, who followed Tinctoris in his use of citations and examples drawn from real music in manuscript versions of his *Practica musicae*, was much more circumspect in the printed version of the treatise.[6]

From the so-called Spataro correspondence, one gains a sense of the ways in

footnote 3 (*cont.*)

claims of his treatise. More recently – in an article provocatively entitled "Is Mode Real? Pietro Aron, the Octenary System, and Polyphony" (*Basler Jahrbuch für historische Musikpraxis* 16 (1992), 9–52) – Harold Powers proposed a literal interpretation of the *Trattato*, based on a close reading that deduced Aron's methods of modal categorization from the internal logic of the treatise. Powers offered an explanation of the means by which Aron mapped a synthesis of modal theory (based on the Italian tradition stemming from Marchetto of Padua) onto an early sixteenth-century repertory. Specifically, Powers showed that Aron's concern extended only to the tenor parts of the compositions he adduced in support of the relevance of modal theory for a polyphonic repertory. In the process of demonstrating the internal consistency of Aron's endeavor, Powers raised a larger philosophical question about the nature of modality in early sixteenth-century thought as represented by Aron and its relationship to musical practice.

[4] On interpretative communities, see especially Roger Chartier, *The Order of Books: Readers, Authors, and Libraries in Europe between the Fourteenth and Eighteenth Centuries*, translated by Lydia Cochrane (Stanford: Stanford University Press, 1994), 1–23.

[5] Bonnie J. Blackburn, "Did Ockeghem Listen to Tinctorris?" *Johannes Ockeghem: Actes du xie colloque international d'études humanistes*, ed. Philippe Vendrix (Tours: Klincksieck, 1998), 597–640.

[6] One cannot be sure that all of his unattributed examples are of his own invention or whether some have been taken from existing compositions. See the discussion of Gaffurio's examples and citations in chapter 2, p. 23.

which a small group of writers discussed works of a shared repertory, often sending their own compositions back and forth to each other for criticism and mentioning others by title only, which suggests recognition on the part of the recipient of the letter.[7] The majority of the compositions come from citations of Aron's and Spataro's own works (twelve and twenty-seven respectively); the next most frequently cited composers are Josquin (six masses and one motet, all available in Petrucci prints) and Willaert (six motets, hymns, and Magnificats of which two are unknown). Some of the works cited in the correspondence also appear in the Spataro choirbooks.[8] To move such a discussion from the shared repertory of this smaller circle and essentially a manuscript culture to the larger audience of a printed treatise demanded a different strategy.

AN OVERVIEW OF ARON'S PUBLICATIONS

An author wishing to publish a music treatise in the early sixteenth century inherited a tradition of exemplarity from manuscript treatises and incunabula, and with it an awareness of the relatively uncommon phenomenon of naming specific composers and compositions. Along with this came an understanding of the technical and financial obstacles facing such an undertaking. This background is necessary to an interpretation of the particularities of the *Trattato*. Equally helpful is an understanding of Aron's social status and the place of this treatise in his output. Relatively little is known about Aron's life apart from the information supplied in the prefaces and dedications of his five treatises and a handful of letters that are included in the Spataro correspondence.[9]

Aron's published treatises, in order of appearance were:

(1) *Libri tres de institutione harmonica editi a Petro Aaron Florentino interprete Jo. Antonio Flam. Foro Cornelite* (Bologna: Benedictus Hectoris, 1516);

(2) *Thoscanello de la Musica* (Venice: Bernardino and Matheo de Vitali, 23 July 1523); revised with a supplement as *Toscanello in Musica di Messer Piero Aron Fiorentino . . . nuovamente stampato con l'aggiunta da lui fatta et con diligentia corretto* (Venice: Bernardino and Matheo de Vitali, 5 July 1529; Reprint Venice: Marchio Sessa, 19 March 1539; Reprint Venice: Domenico Nicolino, 1562);

(3) *Trattato della natura et cognitione di tutti gli tuoni di canto figurato non da altrui piu*

---

[7] The Spataro correspondence was published by Bonnie J. Blackburn, Edward E. Lowinsky, and Clement A. Miller, eds., *A Correspondence of Renaissance Musicians* (Oxford: Clarendon Press, 1991). Table 4, xxxviii–xliv, catalogues 114 compositions mentioned in the letters. Of these, more than half (some sixty-five) are today unknown. Although the correspondence includes extensive discussion on the publication of Spataro's music treatise, no explicit reference to printed music appears in the letters it reproduces.

[8] Compare Blackburn *et al.*, eds., *Correspondence*, Table 4 with the inventory in Frank Tirro, *Giovanni Spataro's Choirbooks*, Renaissance Musical Sources in the Archive of San Petronio in Bologna, vol. 1, Renaissance Manuscript Studies 4 (Neuhausen-Stuttgart, American Institute of Musicology, 1986), 157–63.

[9] The most detailed study of Aron's life and works remains Peter Bergquist, "The Theoretical Writings of Pietro Aaron," Ph.D. dissertation, Columbia University (1964). Blackburn *et al.*, eds., *Correspondence*, provides a few additional details on Aron's life (74–100 and *passim*). The outline presented here relies on Bergquist and Blackburn *et al.* For details of facsimiles and translations of Aron's treatises, see the Bibliography.

scritti (Venice: Bernardino de Vitali, 4 August 1525); a supplement to the *Trattato* was published separately without title page or indication of the author (Venice: Bernardino de Vitali, 1531);

(4) *Lucidario in Musica, di alcune oppenioni antiche, et moderne con le loro oppositioni, et resolutioni, con molti altri secreti appresso, et questioni da altrui anchora non dichiarati* (Venice: Girolamo Scotto, 1545);

(5) *Compendiolo di molti dubii, segreti et sentenze intorno al canto fermo, et figurato . . .* (Milan: Jo. Antonio da Castelliono, [*c.* 1550]).

Aron was probably born about 1480, but nothing is known of his background or education other than that he always identified himself as a Florentine and that he was a priest by 1516. The inconsistent spelling of his name (both Aaron and Aron) coupled with its extremely uncommon occurrence in sixteenth-century Italy led Bonnie J. Blackburn to suggest that he may have been a converted Jew.[10] His early writings, and the many unconventional formulations they contain, suggest that he lacked the traditional education of a musician; he himself made reference to the tenuous circumstances of his birth in the preface to the *Toscanello* (1523). Neither did his career path follow the usual order from choirboy, to singer, to holy orders or university, and finally to *maestro di cappella* – the route of theorists like Gaffurio and Zarlino. Nor was he a 'teorico' like his (sometime) friend Giovanni Del Lago – a career ecclesiastic whose interest was not in sounding phenomenon but in the abstractions of the mensural system, problems of notation, arcane canons, the Greek genera, and Pythagorean tuning. Aron's treatises – marked by their single-minded approach to *musica practica* – appear to have been intended for students of music, prospective composers, singers, and a growing audience of amateur music makers. Three books, *De institutione harmonica*, *Toscanello*, and the *Compendiolo*, are primarily elementary textbooks, while the *Trattato* and *Lucidario* engage more specialized, but still essentially practical, topics. The *Toscanello* was without doubt the most popular of his books: it survives in at least four editions between 1523 and 1562 and was cited by Zarlino and other later theorists. By writing in Italian for all but the first of his treatises, Aron seems to have aimed at the audience that Gaffurio rather disdainfully acknowledged in allowing an Italian translation of his *Practica musicae* to be released (*Angelicum ac divinum opus musicae* (Milan, 1508)): those lacking the necessary learning to read the original in Latin.

Aron published his first treatise, the *Libri tres de institutione harmonica* (1516), while a priest in Imola. The unimposing title page, reproduced in Figure 3.1, is the only ornamental aspect of the entire treatise. The humanist Giovanni Antonio Flaminio is highlighted on the title page as translator, a role necessitated by Aron's confessed inability to write in Latin himself. Flaminio's role extended beyond mere translation, however, and he supplied a preface to all three books of the treatise as well as insertions in the text, particularly with reference to Greek terms. Unfortunately, the combination of Flaminio's lack of musical knowledge and

---

[10] For a full account of this persuasive hypothesis, see Blackburn *et al.*, eds., *Correspondence*, 89–92.

Aron's own deficiencies resulted in a deeply flawed book that was the subject of a stinging critique by Gaffurio.[11]

The printer of *De institutione harmonica*, Benedetto Faelli, had never printed music and this treatise consists entirely of text.[12] Had Aron requested music examples, it seems likely that Faelli's response would have been that he was unable (or unwilling) to oblige.[13] Aron appears to have lacked any financial means for subsidizing the publication and the treatise is a modest production. *De institutione harmonica* consists of three books focused on practical music with minimal attention to speculative theory. Book I covers plainsong, solmization, intervals, and modes in thirty-five chapters; Book II is concerned primarily with mensural notation; Book III focuses on counterpoint. Not surprisingly, the lack of music examples – even the simple representations of note values commonly found in such treatises – results in extraordinary verbal circumlocutions. This is particularly true of the section on counterpoint, where a series of chapters is necessitated by Aron's description of basic cadence patterns in two voices. First he outlines the pattern of the superius, using solmization syllables; the intervallic relationship of the tenor with these patterns follows. The beginning of this passage is reproduced in Figure 3.2 and represented notationally in Example 3.1.

Despite the many apparent musical and linguistic shortcomings of this first treatise, it is clear that Aron was well regarded in Imola. He was employed from at least 1520 as a singer and teacher at the cathedral. In that year, he was specifically employed by the city to teach the art of music free of charge to poor clerics and other persons serving the musical chapel.[14] *De institutione harmonica* may have served as a textbook in this context, not unlike Ramis's relatively cheaply produced

[11] Flaminio and Gaffurio's manuscript correspondence is reprinted in the introduction to the facsimile of *Libri tres de institutione harmonica*. The correspondence between Aron and Gaffurio apparently does not survive. For the most recent discussion of this incident, see Blackburn *et al.*, eds., *Correspondence*. The polemic generated among a group of late fifteenth- and early sixteenth-century theorists that included Gaffurio, Ramis, Aron, Del Lago, and Spataro is an extraordinary chapter in the history of music theory. In almost every instance, Spataro seems to have been the central figure, if not the instigator. See also, Bonnie J. Blackburn, "On Compositional Process in the Fifteenth Century," *Journal of the American Musicological Society* 40 (1987), 210–84.

[12] In addition to Aron's treatise, Faelli's editions of music theory books included Burzio's *Musices opusculum* (1487) and Spataro's polemic *Errori de Franchino Gafurio* (1521). Faelli underwrote the expenses of publishing the Burzio volume (which contained one woodcut example), set by Ugo de Rugeriis (shown in Fig. 2.2). See Blackburn *et al.*, eds., *Correspondence*, 991. Spataro's *Errori* is similarly unadorned.

[13] The concern with music examples as an obstacle to publication is highlighted in Spataro's communications with Aron when Spataro is seeking Aron's assistance in publishing a treatise. Spataro mentions several times that he will send a manuscript for publication as soon as he has cut the examples. "Cut" is ambiguous because it could mean to delete or to have the examples cut by an engraver. Since Spataro does speak of an "intagliatore" in one letter (no. 55, para. 7), it seems that he was thinking, even as late as 1533, of woodcuts. This may be related to his observation in his letter to Del Lago of January 1529 (no. 17) that the treatise on proportions would be difficult to print because it had some figures that he had never seen in print (half-blackened notes and other figures), and that it would be very expensive and require folio format. See Blackburn *et al.*, eds., *Correspondence*. I am grateful to Bonnie J. Blackburn for her guidance on what Spataro might mean in these communications.

[14] New documents on Aron's employment in Imola are reproduced in Blackburn *et al.*, eds., *Correspondence*, 79–80 and 96–100. The employment by the city, which offered significant financial benefits beyond those he was receiving from his employment at the cathedral, seems to have been motivated by a desire to keep Aron in Imola when he received an offer of employment elsewhere.

LIBRI TRES DE INSTITVTIONE
HARMONICA EDITI A PETRO
AARON FLORENTINO IN,
TERPRETE IO.ANTO.
NIO FLAM.FORO
CORNELITE.

3.1 Aron, *Libri tres de institutione harmonica*, title page

TERTIVS 49

anteq̃ ad finem cantus ipſe peruenlat/fierl ſolent/quanq̃ mul/
tæ ſunt quidem cãtilenæ/quarum ſinem uarium admodum eſſe
cernimus/quia(uti componenti libuit) uel per Redditum/uel
per Coronatam terminari uidemus. Verum/ut ſciat unuſquiſq̃
quonam modo intelligendæ ſint cadentiæ iuxta ſeculi huius cõ
ſuetudinem/locos omneis ad faciendum illas neceſſarios/quęq̃
ſuſpenſe ſint/& q̃ nõ. Item quomodo in cãtilenis diſponẽdę ſint
quia ſunt admodum neceſſariæ/ſuo quidẽ ordine declarabimus.

❡ CADENTIARVM GENERA DVO. CAP. xxxvi.

c   Adentiarum quidem/quod in primis ſciendum eſt/du/
plex eſt compoſitio. Hinc fit:ut illarum genera ſint duo:
Nam aliæ quidem ſunt ſimplices/duplicatæ uero aliæ.
Et ſimplices quidem ſunt/cum prima nota ſemel tantum pro/
nunciatur/ut/cum dicitur FA MI FA. SOL FA SOL. Du/
plicatæ uero/cum prima illa nota repetitur/& dicimus FA FA
MI FA. SOL SOL FA SOL. Idem eſt de cæteris intelli/
gendũ. Tales igiſ duplicate uocanſ. Vt autem ĩ tali cadẽtiarum
differentia ſcire poſſis/quid tibi agendum ſit/illud memoria te/
nere debebis/q̃ quando in Cantu FA FA MI FA dicetur in
C ſol fa ut oportebit tenorem i octaua ſubeſſe/uel in ſexta/quæ
quidem octaua in C fa ut erit. Igiſ/ſi prima illa tenoris nota prio
ri fa/quod eſt in cantu reſpondens octauam fecerit/ſecundum
fa ſeptimam faciat. Tertia uero ideſt MI/quæ non ipſo ordine:
ſed re ultima eſt in ſexta reſpondeat. Hoc ubi feceris cum termi
natione ipſa/ſiue cadentia/hoc eſt cum ultimo fa deuenies in
octauam/& gratiſſimus fiet concentus. Quod ſi tenor cum an/
tedicto primo fa ſextam fecerit/ſecundum illud FA ſeptimam
reddat. Tertia uero nota MI fiat ſexta/& ultimum FA ſimiliter
in octauam deſinat. Et ſic ubicunq̃ fuerint duplicatæ cadentiæ
per octauam terminari/uel ſextam poterunt. Illud ſciendum eſt
in prima cadentiæ nota tenorem cum cãtu facere quintam poſ/
ſe. Sed reliquarum cadentiæ ipſius notarum/quem dedimus/or
do ſeruandus eſt.

❡ DE CADENTIIS SIMPLICIBVS. CAP. xxxvii.

3.2 Aron, *De institutione harmonica*, fol. 49ʳ, discussion of two-part cadences

Ex. 3.1 Transcription of cadences (*De insitutione harmonica*, fol. 49ʳ⁻ᵛ)

Musica practica. Giovanni Spataro's role as Aron's mentor also seems well established by this time; the publication of the treatise in Bologna might be connected to his association with Spataro.

Aron probably left Imola in 1522; by 1523 at the latest, he was in Venice. There he obtained a position as the tutor to the (illegitimate) sons of Sebastiano Michiel, the Grand Prior of the Knights of St. John of Jerusalem. Michiel was the dedicatee of Aron's *Toscanello*, a treatise printed shortly after his arrival in Venice. The title is a reference to Aron's native Tuscany, a further indication of his pride in his Florentine origins. The treatise was probably completed while he was still in Imola. The frequently reproduced frontispiece (Fig. 3.3), showing Aron as a teacher, may have been commissioned there. The contrasts of the *Toscanello* with *De institutione harmonica* are many. Although both were quarto volumes, *Toscanello* was printed on paper twice the size of *De institutione harmonica*, with elaborate initials, intricate diagrams, and a noteworthy number of music examples. Most frequently observed by modern scholars as an innovation was Aron's decision to write in Italian. Writing in Italian was obviously a pragmatic move on Aron's part, given his self-confessed inability to write in Latin, but the appearance of such a treatise in the vernacular points both to a new audience for such treatises and a breaking down of the prejudice against non-Latin texts that Aron described in the preface of *De institutione harmonica*. Only many years later, in his *Lucidario* (1545), would Aron justify writing in Italian by appeals to the tradition of Dante, Boccaccio, and Petrarch.[15] Such elevated currents of humanist thought seem hardly likely to have been the motivating factor in the choice of Italian for the *Toscanello*. The treatise hardly touches on such lofty theoretical concerns as the Greek genera, much less speculative theory. Instead, its first book is a manual of notation, after a brief opening discussion of the praises, origin, and definition of music. Book II is concerned with the practicalities of polyphonic composition: the principles of counterpoint, the construction of chords, proportions, and tuning.

---

[15] On Pietro Bembo's initiatives for writing in Italian, see chapter 7 and the discussion of Zarlino's *Le istitutioni harmoniche*.

3.3 Aron, *Toscanello*, frontispiece

The contrast of both format and style with *De institutione harmonica* is vividly illustrated by a comparison of the discussion of cadences in the two treatises. Figure 3.4 (transcribed as Ex. 3.2) is the part in the treatise comparable to the page reproduced from *De institutione harmonica* in Figure 3.2 above. Aron still relies on solmization syllables for his description, but now illustrates the discussion with an example demonstrating possible cadences, easily extending the two-voice discussion of *De institutione harmonica* to a four-voice framework.

More unusual is the schematic way that Aron chooses to represent the perfect consonances in the *Toscanello* (Fig. 3.5). The same representational impulse lies behind the table of counterpoint that is among the most often cited features of this treatise (Fig. 3.6). Here Aron has represented in the most concise manner the possible relationships of individual voices in a four-part texture.[16] Such a representation would have been impossible in *De institutione harmonica*, or in simple musical notation, requiring as it does an abstraction of intervallic relationships, albeit a practical rather than speculative abstraction.

Stylistically, visually, and in its subject matter, the *Trattato* that followed two years later is very much a companion to the *Toscanello*. It includes the same woodcut frontispiece of Aron teaching (shown in Fig. 3.3). Issued from the same publisher, the border of its title page suggests a more elevated context for the treatise (Fig. 3.7). The title itself proclaims Aron now a canon of Rimini (a benefice presumably bestowed by Michiel) and "maestro di casa" of Michiel's household.[17] While the subject matter of the *Trattato*, like *Toscanello*, stems from *De institutione harmonica*, the treatment is more radical. Music examples, however, are few and far between in the *Trattato*. On the evidence of the precedent of the *Toscanello*, Bernardino was capable of printing quite elegant examples and diagrams. Aron's patronage at this point was secure and the treatise was issued relatively shortly after the *Toscanello*. It is not mere economizing by either printer or patron that results in lack of examples in the *Trattato*. Rather, the availability of printed music taken along with Aron's stated intention of demonstrating how the modes are to be recognized in "figured song" (i.e. polyphony) leads him to a new rhetorical and theoretical strategy: the inclusion of citations by composer and title for almost every modal final listed. Yet, while citing polyphonic compositions by title and composer was unusual, presenting modal theory by means of instantiation was not. The *Trattato* does not reflect various humanist initiatives at recovering ancient Greek modal theory that motivated so much sixteenth-century speculation on modality. Indeed, there was an evident reluctance on

---

[16] On such "chord tables" generally, see Jessie Ann Owens, *Composers at Work: The Craft of Musical Composition 1450–1600* (New York: Oxford University Press, 1997), 24–25; Helen Bush, "The Recognition of Chordal Formation by Early Music Theorists," *Musical Quarterly* 32 (1946), 227–43; and Benito Rivera, "Harmonic Theory in Musical Treatises of the Late Fifteenth and Early Sixteenth Centuries," *Music Theory Spectrum* 1 (1979), 80–95.

[17] How Aron came by the canonicate in Rimini is unclear, since it is not very close to Venice and Michiel is not known to have had connections there, but it is difficult to imagine anyone else who could have secured it for Aron.

LIBRO

alla natura di eſſo primo, et ſecódo tuono. del che eſſendo dette cadenze in
B fa ♮ mi, E la mi, et C ſol fa, il canto nó ſarebbe grato, mà fuora di ogni
ſua intonatione, come ſi uede in alcune cópoſitioni con poco fondamento
fatte. Coſi il terzo, et quarto tuono p eſſer cópoſto di mi mi, et mi la ſecóda
ſpecie del dià pénte, et dià teſſáron, le ſue cadenze ſaranno in E la mi, A la
mi re, et G ſol re ut, mà raro. Il qnto, et ſeſto tuono ſará formato di Fa fa, et
Vt fa terza ſpecie del dià pénte, et dià teſſáron: le ſue cadenze ſaráno in F
fa ut, A la mi re, C ſol fa, et qualche uolta i G ſol re ut. Il ſettimo, et ottauo
tuono p eſſer formato di ut ſol quarta ſpecie del dià pénte, et re ſol prima
del dià teſſáron, le ſue cadenze ſono G ſol re ut, A la mi re, et C ſol fa. Per la
qual coſa eſſaminando li ſopradetti modi faccio giudicio, che in breue té=
po arriuerai alla intelligenza della retta compoſitione. Et queſto a te ſia a
ſofficiëza detto p meſſe, motetti, canzone, frottole, barzellette, madrigali,
ſtrambotti, capitoli, et ſonetti. Et tutte le dette cadéze ſi dichiarcráno nella
figura ſeguente.

E quali cadenze ſecondo la intentione del cópoſitore ſi fanno di quá=
tità maggiore, et ſempre mai ſi oppone la ſettima diſſonáza nanzi la
ſeſta precedente lottaua, pur che nó ſiano ſemplicemente compoſté,
ma ſimili alle ſeguenti, et ſuperiori, come qui.

3.4 Aron, *Toscanello*, discussion of cadences in four parts

Ex. 3.2 Transcription of cadences (*Toscanello* II: 18)

Aron's part to break with traditional theory in any way if present practice could be made to seem to conform to it – even if the conformity was illusory.[18] What Aron had effectively accomplished was the substitution of the authority of a contemporary printed polyphonic repertory for that of the Church as represented by chant, a potentially heretical gesture when thus described. Looked at another way, Aron's gesture placed all composed music under the ecclesiastical authority of modal theory.

Aron's move from Imola to Venice and his changed employment circumstances may have played a role in his invocation of printed music. As a cathedral singer and teacher of music in Imola he had access to the choirbooks and music manuscripts of that institution. There is no indication that he moved in similar institutional circles in Venice and it is unclear what the musical establishment of Michiel's order was like and what involvement Aron might have had beyond his duties as tutor to Michiel's sons. Books like Petrucci's music prints may well have been more easily accessible to Aron after his arrival in Venice and in an environment like Michiel's household.

ARON'S CITATIONS IN THE *TRATTATO*

One can construct a remarkably complete picture of how Aron went about choosing his examples, observing what he "left out" as well as what he cited. He refers to

---

[18] This sense of illusory conformity lies behind Power's rhetorical questioning of the "reality" of mode. Powers, "Is Mode Real?"

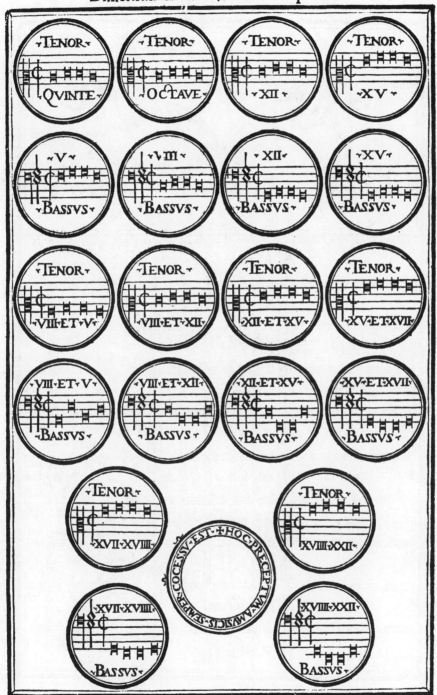

3.5 Aron, *Toscanello*, illustration of perfect consonances

Tauola del contrapunto.

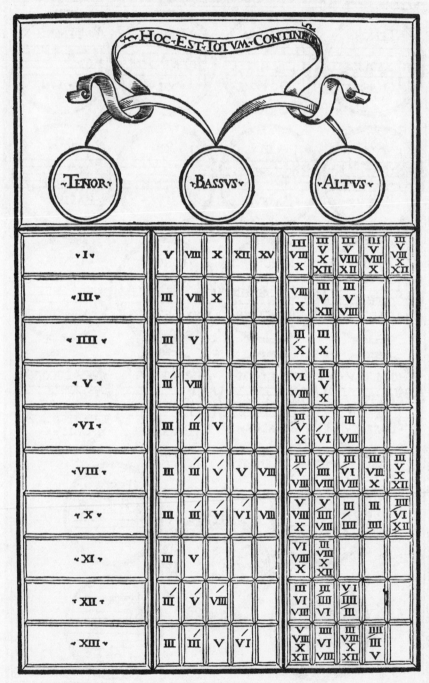

3.6 Aron, *Toscanello*, table of counterpoint

TRATTATO DELLA NATVRA ET COGNITIONE DI TVTTI GLI TVONI DI CANTO FIGVRATO NON DA ALTRVI PIV SCRITTI COMPOSTI PER MESSER PIERO AARON MVSICO FIORENTINO CANONICO IN RIMINI MAESTRO DI CASA DEL REVE.do ET MAGNIFICO CAVALIERE HIEROSOLIMITANO MESSER SEBASTIANO MICHELE PRIORE DI VINETIA.

3.7 Aron, *Trattato*, title page

polyphonic compositions not only in the *Trattato*, but also in the 1529 *Aggiunta* to the reprint of *Toscanello*, suggesting that he found the process worth continuing. The opening chapters of the *Trattato* cite examples of polyphony ascribed to modal categories;[19] the *Aggiunta* cites examples in that other notoriously "difficult" area of sixteenth-century music theory: musica ficta.[20] It appears that it is only at these moments (discussion of mode and accidentals), when the gulf between the theory Aron articulates and polyphonic practice is greatest, that he refers to specific polyphonic compositions.

Reconstructing Aron's collection of printed sources is a relatively straightforward task. In the *Toscanello* supplement he refers specifically to Petrucci's *Odhecaton* and his reasons for including examples (see the passage quoted as epigraph for this chapter). Equally certain is his use of the first three of Petrucci's *Motetti de la Corona* anthologies. Not only does he refer to the prints in chapter 3 of the *Trattato*,[21] but in the *Aggiunta* he points to citations by placement on a page (that is, by voice, staff, and text: e.g., "In the motet, *Ave nobilissima*, in the second contrabass at the end of the second line over the words, 'ab omnibus malis et fraudibus. . .'").[22] Another Petrucci print, *Motetti C*, is named in the *Trattato*,[23] and his other undeniable source is Petrucci's second anthology in the *Odhecaton* series, *Canti B*.[24] Probably, but not as certainly, Petrucci's first and second volumes of masses by Josquin should be included in the list.[25] Together, as Table 3.1 illustrates, these sources account for almost all the works Aron cites by name in chapters 4 to 7 of

---

[19] There are no citations in the later chapters discussing cadences, hexachords, or the solmization of tones outside the gamut. The two subsequent treatises, the *Lucidario* and the *Compendiolo*, do not use citations and have relatively few examples. These were written after Aron had left Venice to join the Order of the Crutched Friars in Bergamo. The subject matter and style of the treatises, as well as the relatively antiquated repertory Aron cited in his treatises from the 1520s, along with his distance from the Venetian musical establishment, all appear to have played a role in the lack of citations in these books. Aron's citations in the *Aggiunta* to the *Toscanello* must have seemed decidedly outdated in the later reprintings of the treatise.

[20] At the same time that I presented my first preliminary work on Aron's citations in the *Trattato*, Margaret Bent was working on a close reading of the *Aggiunta* examples ("Accidentals, Counterpoint, and Notation in Aaron's *Aggiunta* to the *Toscanello*," *Journal of Musicology* 12 (1994), 306–44. Bent's study is analogous in many ways to Powers's reading of the *Trattato* examples ("Is Mode Real?")). I have incorporated Bent's numbering of the *Aggiunta* citations in my discussion of the *Toscanello* that follows. She notes the difficulty that Aron encounters in describing accidentals and comments on his convoluted language.

[21] "For example, 'Cela sans plus' by Josquin, 'Peccata mea Domine' by Jean Mouton (in the *Motetti de la Corona*), 'Le serviteur,' 'Hélas m'amour,' 'La dicuplaisant,' &c."

[22] *Toscanello*, trans. Bergquist, III: 17. For a catalog of these indications, see Bent, "Accidentals, Counterpoint, and Notation," 327–34.

[23] Had Aron not explicitly cited *Motetti C* one might question his access to this source, since he cites only three motets from this collection, far fewer than from any of the other prints he uses in the *Trattato* and *Aggiunta*.

[24] Although Aron never explicitly names *Canti B*, the order of his selections as well as composer indications suggests this as one of his primary sources.

[25] Three masses which appear in the second volume of the masses are cited, but there is no way of positing this as Aron's source with absolute certainty; several works from the first volume of Josquin's masses printed by Petrucci are cited more specifically in the *Aggiunta*, which offers circumstantial evidence that Aron likely had access to both volumes.

Table 3.1 *Aron's citations (*Trattato*, chapters 4–7) and their sources*

Chapter 4

Modes 1 and 2 *D sol re*

Motetti de la Corona II, 7	Jacotin, *Rogamus te virgo Maria* (mode 1)
Motetti de la Corona II, 8	A. Caen, *Judica me Deus* (mode 1)
Motetti de la Corona II, 16	Mouton, *Congregati sunt* (mode 1)
Motetti de la Corona I, 11	Mouton, *Beata Dei genitrix* (mode 2)
[*Motetti a 5,* 1]	Regis, *Clangat plebs flores* (mode 1)

Mode 1 *D la sol re* **with flat signature**

Motetti de la Corona II, 3	A. Caen, *Nomine qui Domini*
Canti B, 43	*Pour quoy fut fuie cette emprise*

Mode 1 *G sol re ut* **with flat signature**

[*Missarum Liber II,* 1]	Josquin, *Missa Ave maris stella*
[*Missarum Liber II,* 6]	Josquin, *Missa D'ung aultre amer*
Motetti de la Corona I, 8	Févin, *Nobilis progenie*
Motetti de la Corona I, 21	Févin, *Vulnerasti cor meum*

Mode 2 *G sol re ut* **with flat signature**

Canti B, 2	Compère, *Virgo celesti*
?	Hayne, *D'ung aultre amer*
[*Odhecaton,* 20]	Hayne, *De tous biens playne*
Canti B, 7	Pierre de la Rue, *Ce n'est pas*
Canti B, 24	Orto, *D'ung aultre amer*

Modes 1 and 2 *A la mi re*

Odhecaton, 64	Josquin, *La plus des plus* (mode 1)
Odhecaton, 51	Compère, *Se mieulx* (mode 2)

Mode 1 *D la sol re* **with a flat signature**

(see Spataro correspondence)	Busnois, *Pourtant si mon*
(see Crawford)[a]	Constanzo Festa, *Gaude virgo*
Canti B, 1	Josquin, *L'homme armé*
Odhecaton, 30	Japart, *Hélas qu'il est à mon gré*

Mode 1 *D la sol re* **(no signature)**

Canti B, 28	Pierre de la Rue, *Fors seulement*
Canti B, 50	Brumel, *Je déspite tous*
Motetti de la Corona I, 1	Mouton, *Gaude Barbara*

Mode 2 *D la sol re*

[*Missarum Liber II,* 2]	Josquin, *Missa Hercules dux Ferrariae*

Chapter 5

Mode 3 *E la mi*

Motetti de la Corona II, 6	Jacotin, *Michael archangele*
Odhecaton, 63	Ockeghem, *Malheur me bat*
Motetti de la Corona II, 2	Jacotin, *Interveniat pro rege nostro*

Mode 3 *G sol re ut*

Odhecaton, 4	*Nunca fué pena mayor*

Mode 3 *A la mi re*

Motetti de la Corona III, 7	Josquin, *Miserere mei Deus*

Table 3.1 (*cont.*)

[*Motetti de la Corona I*, 4?]	Eustachio [?], *Laetatus sum*
Motetti de la Corona II, 11	*Benedic anima mea Dominum*
Mode 4 *A la mi re*	
Motetti C, 34	*O Maria Rogamus te*

Chapter 6

Mode 5 *F fa ut*	
Motetti de la Corona III, 6	Josquin, *Stabat mater dolorosa*
Motetti de la Corona III, 10	Josquin, *Alma redemptoris*
Odhecaton, 13	Caron, *Hélas que pourra devenir*
[*Antico*]	Mouton, *Quaeramus cum pastoribus*
Motetti de la Corona II, 12	Mouton, *Illuminare illuminare Jerusalem*
[*Missae 1*]	Pierre de la Rue, Sanctus and Agnus, *Missa de beata virgine*
Mode 6 *F fa ut*	
Odhecaton, 5	Stokem, *Brunette*
Odhecaton, 41	Compère, *Vostre bergeronette*
Odhecaton, 42	Busnois, *Je ne demande*
Odhecaton, 48	Agricola, *Allez regretz*
Odhecaton, 93	Hayne, *A l'audience*
Motetti de la Corona I, 13	Févin, *Sancta Trinitas unus Deus*
Motetti de la Corona I, 20	Févin, *Tempus meum est ut revertar ad eum*
Motetti de la Corona I, 22	Mouton, *Celeste beneficium*
Motetti de la Corona I, 23	Févin, *Egregie Christi*
Modes 5 and 6 *B fa mi* **with flat signature**	
Canti B, 48	Hayne, *La regretée* (mode 5)
[*Antico*]	Josquin, *O admirabile commercium* (mode 6)
Mode 5 *C sol fa ut*	
Canti B, 40	Obrecht, *Si sumpsero*

Chapter 7

Mode 8 *C fa ut*	
Canti B, 12	Orto, *Mon mari m'a diffamée*
Canti B, 27	*E la la la*
Mode 7 *G sol re ut*	
?	Mouton, *Missa Ut sol*
[*Missae 1*]	Pierre de la Rue, Gloria from *Missa de Beata Virgine*
(see Spataro correspondence)	Zanetto [Giovanni del Lago], *Multi sunt vocati*
Motetti de la Corona I, 18	Hylaere, *Ascendens Christus in altum*
Mode 8 *G sol re ut*	
Odhecaton, 56	Agricola, *Si dedero*
Odhecaton, 72	*C'est possible qui l'homme peut*
Odhecaton, 78	Josquin, *O venus bant*
Odhecaton, 89	*Disant adieu madame*
Canti B, 11	*Je suis amie*
Canti B, 18	*Myn morghem ghaf*

Table 3.1 (*cont.*)

Canti B, 21	Ninot, *Hélas hélas*
Canti B, 29	Compère, *E d'en revenez vous*
Motetti C, 7	*Beata dei genitrix*
Mode 7 C *sol fa ut*	
Odhecaton, 59	Compère, *Mes pensées*
Odhecaton, 66	*Madame hélas*
Canti B, 19	Josquin, *Comment peult*
Motetti C, 40	*Mittit ad virginem*
Odhecaton, 2	*Je cuide si ce temps*
Mode 8 C *sol fa ut*	
Odhecaton, 29	*Ne l'oserai je dire*

Note:

[a] David Crawford speculates that the *Gaude virgo* found in Casale Monferrato, Archivio Capitolare, MS D(F) is the composition to which Aron refers. D. Crawford, *Sixteenth-Century Choirbooks in the Archivio Capitolare at Casale Monferrato* (Rome: American Institute of Musicology, 1975), 70.

the *Trattato*.[26] The bulk of the citations comes from seven Petrucci prints first published between 1501 and 1519: *Odhecaton A*, *Canti B*, *Motetti C*, Josquin's *Missarum liber II* and *Motetti de la Corona I*, *II* and *III*. A fuller tabulation included in the Appendix to this chapter gives an overview of these Petrucci prints, noting information about their content and indicating those works Aron cited in the *Trattato* and in the *Aggiunta* to the *Toscanello*. Interestingly, although the same primary sources are used for both, the overlap of citations between the two is minimal.

From the background of the conventional and conservative explanation of modal theory in *De institutione harmonica*, Aron's avowed purpose in the *Trattato* is nothing short of remarkable. With no little pride, Aron proposes to confront a problem that his theoretical colleagues had avoided:

And knowing it to be exacting and strange, I judge that it was abandoned by the celebrated musicians already referred to not through ignorance but merely because it proved otherwise troublesome and exacting at the time. For it is clear that no writers of our age have explained how the many different modes are to be recognized, although to their greater credit they have treated of matters which cannot be readily understood. I, therefore, not moved by ambition of any kind, but as a humble man, have undertaken this task, hoping that in humanity and kindliness my readers will excuse whatever errors I may make. I show briefly what I know to be necessary, for I see that many are deceived about the true

[26] Strunk, *Source Readings*, 205–06, listed sources for most of Aron's citations, but made no distinction between those sources which Aron undeniably used, and those which may or may not have been available to him. Tomlinson's modifications to Strunk's list (pp. 137–39) reflects my preliminary research for this chapter. Table 3.1 encloses uncertain sources in square brackets, along with additional references to manuscript sources or lost works. Strunk's list is alphabetical, obscuring many of the relationships observed below and, with the exception of the *Odhecaton*, does not indicate the placement of examples within source prints. Bergquist, "Theoretical Writings," also followed Strunk's list. Citations for five works for which Strunk cited no source are given here, along with minor corrections to his list, now incorporated in Tomlinson's revision.

understanding, and regarding this I hope in some measure to satisfy them.[27] (trans. Strunk/Tomlinson, *Source Readings,* 139–40)

What actually sets Aron's treatise apart is not that he is going to show how the modes are recognized, but that he is going to do so with specific citations of polyphonic examples. Aron's priorities for adducing the mode of the examples he cites reflect a hierarchical interrelationship that proceeds from the mode of the tenor or a pre-existing plainsong to a consideration of final, species of the perfect fifth and/or fourth, and psalm-tone *differentiae*.[28] The tenor defines the mode unless a plainsong melody appears in another part which then takes modal priority;[29] the mode of a polyphonic composition is that of the pre-existent melody on which it is based. Otherwise, the final absolutely determines the mode in works with the regular finals D and E. The same is true of the regular finals F and G, although if contradicted by the species of the consonances the possibility of irregular endings on the *confinalis* or *differentiae* must be considered. The species govern irregular endings on A, B(♭), or C. The species and *differentiae* are used together to determine the mode of compositions that do not end on regular finals and that contain contradictory or incomplete species.

The first seven chapters of the *Trattato* set out these "rules," and here Aron cites the polyphony for which this treatise is often noted. While refining his procedures for identifying the modes, Aron expresses his misgivings at the prospect:

[H]aving reached this point, I am left somewhat in doubt. Yet I intend rather to go on reasoning with you, seeking a rule by means of which you may arrive at a clear understanding of each of the tones in question.[30]

These misgivings may be in part formulaic – Aron was in the habit of excusing himself, begging the reader's indulgence, and noting his own shortcomings – but

[27] "Et aspettando essa fastidiosa et strana non fo giuditio che dagli celeberrimi sopra detti musichi per ignoranza da loro abbandonato sia, ma sol per altro incommodo et opportuno fastidio lasciato hanno, et chiaro si vede che da nessuno al nostro secolo scritto si truova, Onde per maggiore laude trattato hanno di quello che facilmente intender non si puo, della qual cosa si cognosce varii et varii modi, Io adunque mosso non per ambitione alcuna, ma come infimo ho preso tal fatica sperando che da tutti per sue humanita et gentilezze se alcuno error sara scusato sia, mostrando brevemente quello che necessario cognosco. Conciosia cosa che assai della vera intelligenza ingannarsi veggo, della qual cosa spero in qualche particella satisfarti" (*Trattato*, chapter 1, sig. aʳ).

[28] The invocation of the *differentiae* as "irregular" finals is the most unusual proposal of Aron's treatise. Although he refers to the psalm-tone *differentiae*, his wide-ranging discussion applies these psalm-tone pseudo-finals (as Powers has called them) to both sacred (non-psalm) and secular genres. Although a precedent for such procedures might by adduced from Burzio's *Musices opusculum* (1487), the use of the term *differentiae* there refers specifically to antiphons and possibly, by analogy, to other chants. Aron's extension to non-chant-based and secular works represents a departure from traditional modal theory in its blurring of psalmodic conventions and modal tenets.

[29] Carl Dahlhaus, trans. Robert Gjerdigen, *Studies in the Origins of Harmonic Tonality* (Princeton: Princeton University Press, 1990), 201–02, asserts that, for Aron, the tenor can no longer govern the mode when there is no cantus firmus, voices are composed simultaneously, or the tenor ambitus is matched in the superius. This does not accord with the examples actually cited in the *Trattato*, which clearly have been classified on the basis of the tenor. See also Bernhard Meier's discussion of the theoretical basis of the "tenor principle" (Bernhard Meier, trans. Ellen Beebe, *The Modes of Classical Vocal Polyphony* (New York: Broude Brothers, 1988), 70–74).

[30] Strunk/Tomlinson, *Source Readings*, 142–43.

they also project Aron's determination to find the "rules" and the observance of those rules by which any piece of polyphony could be modally categorized.

An examination of the works Aron cites reveals a classification system consistent with the procedures outlined above. While some refinement is necessary as he proceeds, Aron is able to illustrate each modal classification with citations of composed polyphony. In spite of these frequent references to polyphony, however, Aron hardly goes further than his predecessors in his technical references to polyphony in the context of modal theory. In his discussion of many of Aron's difficult-to-understand assignments, Powers has shown the reasoning by which Aron came to his assignments and stressed the fact that he was concerned with the tenor voice alone.[31] This may in part be a reflection of the nature of polyphonic notation as a collection of individual lines. A musical piece is presented as a collection of discrete lines, sharing at best a common space (in choirbook notation) but not in any way conjoined. Each line may be readily read individually. The question of which voice to "look to" for the mode itself is predicated on an understanding of how to "look at" the notational representation of a composition.

It might appear that Aron has chosen his citations as "best representations" of the categories that he described; indeed they have long been examined from this perspective. Yet approaching these compositions from the context of the sources from which they were taken rather than modern editions of individual works, suggests that ordering, expediency, misreading, and visual orientation were just as often the criteria for Aron's choices. His way of reading music is not just dependent on, but shaped by, the conventions of a group of printed materials texts.

The choice of Aron's citations, taken in conjunction with the order in which they appear, reveals his working method and reflects an unprecedented relationship between a theorist and sources of printed polyphonic music. Aron accepts Petrucci's authority as arbiter of repertory in a way that simultaneously bolsters his own credibility by instantiating his writing with references to printed sources, available in multiple copies with fixed notation. Chapter 4 of the *Trattato* begins the citation process systematically: the first citations – *Motetti de la Corona II*, numbers 7, 8, and 16 – are the only motets from that print that fit this modal category and they are cited in the order in which they appear in the motet print (see Table 3.1.). Aron supplies examples for every possible termination and signature in this chapter. This is the only chapter that refers to Josquin's masses, although examples from that print could have been adduced to demonstrate other modes. More examples are given in chapter 4 than in any other section of the treatise, and Aron draws from the widest variety of sources here.[32] The

---

[31] Powers, "Is Mode Real?" Aron's use of the tenor reflects its traditional basis as *fundamentum concordationis* in polyphonic combinations of two or more voices.

[32] Three of the works cited in this chapter are unknown in any printed source. One, Busnois's *Pourtant si mon*, is mentioned in the Spataro correspondence (Blackburn *et al.*, eds., *Correspondence*, 350 and 832), and may have been known to Aron through those circles. Similarly *Multi sunt vocati* (cited in chapter 7) was mentioned by Aron in a letter to Giovanni Del Lago (Blackburn *et al.*, eds., *Correspondence*, 707) and was frequently cited in the correspondence. The tenor of Del Lago's composition is given in letter 86, reproduced in facsimile in Blackburn *et al.*, eds., *Correspondence*, 848–49.

citations of chapter 5 are slightly more circumscribed and less systematic. Aron cites no compositions for one termination he describes (an A final with flat signature) although he could have cited the tenors of two of the Josquin motets at the opening of *Motetti de la Corona III*, his presumed source for *Miserere mei Deus*.[33] Especially revealing is Aron's description of the villancico *Nunca fué* as terminating irregularly on G. As Bergquist noted, Aron misinterpreted the form of the piece, which in fact ends regularly on the modal final E.[34] This misreading is symptomatic of Aron's visual orientation, glancing through the *Odhecaton* and taking the last note of the tenor parts as the end of the piece, notwithstanding notational and performative conventions that indicate otherwise.[35]

Reading Aron through his citations suggests that his process of gathering changed as he continued to work on the *Trattato*. Expediency takes over in chapters 6 and 7, where one can imagine Aron thumbing through a small group of prints at hand searching for examples, completing the appropriation of the repertory for his pedagogical purposes. As Table 3.1 shows, the first five citations in the list of Mode 6 works all come from the *Odhecaton* and follow the order of the print; the next four are taken in order from *Motetti de la Corona I*, comprising all the motets from that print in this modal category.[36] Similarly, in chapter 7, the listing of Mode 8 works with finals on G moves in order from the *Odhecaton*, to *Canti B*, and finally to *Motetti C*. Aron follows the same sources in the same chronological order for Mode 7 ending on C: *Odhecaton*, *Canti B*, *Motetti C*. Most telling, perhaps, is the final Mode 7 (or first Mode 8) chanson *Je cuide si ce temps*. As Powers pointed out, the grammatical construction of Aron's description is ambiguous: he could be describing *Je cuide si ce temps* as either Mode 7 or Mode 8.[37]

Onde gli presenti canti cioe Mes pensies di Compere, Madame Helas, Cenent peult di Josquino, et Mittit ad virginem no altrimenti che del settimo son chiamati, et Je vide sece tamps, &t Loserai dire del tuono ottavo et non settimo come la sua forma et continuo processo ti dimostrano &c. (*Trattato*, chapter 7, sig. d^r)

Powers argued that Aron must be including it in his Mode 7 list on the basis of the "modal" features of the tenor: it has a *differentia* appropriate to either Mode 7 or Mode 8, with a regular Mode 7 ambitus:

---

[33] The two motets are *Huc me sydereo* and *Ave nobilissima* which share the same Mode 4 tenor with A final and flat signature. However, Aron need not have consulted *Motetti de la Corona III* in the writing of this chapter. The tenor of *Miserere mei Deus*, with its ascending and descending "miserere" ostinato, is precisely the sort of tenor that Aron might have recalled, rather than looked at, for his modal classification.

[34] Bergquist, "Theoretical Writings," 286.

[35] Rather than suggesting a kind of musical incompetence, Aron's "misreading" may simply be indicative of the way in which the repertory of the *Odhecaton*, already retrospective at the time of its initial publication in 1501, was understood twenty-five years later. In the *Aggiunta* Aron distinguishes between the "moderns," represented by examples drawn from the *Motetti de la Corona* repertory and the "ancients" represented by examples taken from the *Odhecaton* (*Toscanello*, trans. Bergquist, III: 19).

[36] Unlike chapter 4, and to a slightly lesser degree chapter 5, Aron is no longer concerned to instantiate every possible termination; see, most notably, his treatment of endings on *A la mi re*.

[37] Powers, "Is Mode Real?" 39.

Thus "Mes pensées" by Compère, "Madame hélas" and "Comment peut" by Josquin, and "Mittit ad virginem" can be assigned only to the seventh tone; and also "Je cuide si ce temps"; and "Ne l'oserai je dire" will be of the eighth tone and not of the seventh, as its form and extended downward *processo* will show you. (trans. Strunk/Tomlinson, *Source Readings*)[38]

Recognizing the placement of the chanson within the *Odhecaton* suggests that an addendum is likely; one may conjecture that Aron had turned back to the start of the *Odhecaton* to begin his listing anew for Mode 8 only to discover his omission of a Mode 7 chanson.

Aron makes no explicit distinction of genre in his citations among motet, mass, and chanson, and he appears to make no effort to represent each genre in each classification. This is particularly true for masses. After the citations from Josquin's second book of masses in chapter 4, Aron appears to have made no further reference to other mass prints or manuscripts. He cites Pierre de la Rue's *Beata virgine* mass twice,[39] but any *Beata virgine* masses would have fallen into these modal categories because of the plainchants on which they were customarily based. Similarly the (now unknown) Mouton *Missa Ut sol* might well have received its Mode 7 classification from the solmization basis implied in its title. It is notable that two of these mass citations, as well as the reference to Del Lago's *Multi sunt vocati*, none of which is part of the core Petrucci repertory, occur among the citations for Mode 7 on *G sol re ut*. Here Aron relies, at most, on a single Petrucci exemplar. Indeed, even that work, Hylaere's *Ascendens Christus in altum*, may have been "remembered" or been taken from some other (manuscript) source, since Aron makes no other citations from the *Motetti de la Corona* anthologies in this chapter. This suggests the possibility that he was no longer referring to those partbooks (although he certainly had access to them four years later when he prepared the *Aggiunta* to the *Toscanello*). The relatively few citations for Mode 7 on G also point to a dearth of settings that would qualify for that mode in the repertory he had to hand.[40]

Twenty-six works are cited in chapter 4 (Modes 1 and 2); eight in chapter 5 (Modes 3 and 4); eighteen in chapter 6 (Modes 5 and 6); and twenty-one in chapter 7 (Modes 7 and 8). Aron's citations are more evenly distributed across the modal spectrum than the actual repertory from which he drew them: approximately half of the works in the Petrucci prints from which he worked would fall into his Modes

---

[38] Strunk translated it as Mode 8: "Thus 'Mes pensées' by Compère, 'Madame hélas' and 'Comment peut' by Josquin, and 'Mittit ad virginem' can be assigned only to the seventh tone. But 'Je cuide si ce temps' and 'Ne l'oserai je dire' will be of the eighth tone and not of the seventh, as their form and extended downward procedure will show you" (Strunk, *Source Readings*, 218). Tomlinson amended the translation to follow Powers's interpretation.

[39] The Sanctus and Agnus Dei are cited as examples of Mode 5 on *F fa ut*; the Gloria is cited for Mode 7 on *G sol re ut*.

[40] This dearth of examples is highlighted in a hypothetical modal categorization of Josquin's motets following Aron's criteria; see Cristle Collins Judd, "Modal Types and *Ut, Re, Mi* Tonalities: Tonal Coherence in Sacred Vocal Polyphony from about 1500," *Journal of the American Musicological Society* 45 (1992), 431–36.

1 and 2 category, with G finals in *cantus mollis* by far the most common, as the tables in the Appendix demonstrate. Indeed this "abundance" of examples may well be responsible for what appears to be a more thorough approach in chapter 4. His citations generally minimize any tonal distinctions among the motet and chanson repertories. Only three of 147 chansons in *Odhecaton* and *Canti B* finish on E in the tenor, while the proportion of such endings in the motet collections (thirteen of 109) is higher:[41] Aron cites one chanson and two motets with terminations on E. Motets that would be described as Modes 5 and 6 are more frequent than chansons, but Aron cites them in near equal numbers (nine motets, eight chansons, and one mass). And while Modes 7 and 8 categories are more frequent among chansons than motets, the repertory at hand represents nothing like the lop-sided proportion of Aron's selection (fifteen from the chanson collections to three from motet prints), which reflects more the particular sources he used for this chapter (*Odhecaton, Canti B,* and *Motetti C*) than the larger array of sources he had to hand.[42] In other words, Aron is making no attempt to "represent" the repertory; instead he is appropriating the contents of a group of prints for his own purposes and the presumed convenience they offer his reader.

SPECIFIC EXAMPLES: WORKS ENDING ON *A LA MI RE*

Sixteenth-century theoretical discussions of mode subsequent to Aron's *Trattato*, as well as those from recent times, suggest that Aron's assignments of works ending on *A* and *C* are among his most problematic. A modern conception which posits "modality" as a system akin to "tonality" would argue that most of the compositions Aron cites do not function as "A" or "C" tonalities.[43] The role of "regular" as opposed to "irregular" terminations in eight-mode theory mediated by Aron's invocation of the psalm-tone *differentiae* as an explanation for endings on A and C was vitiated by the theorizing of Glarean and others. Powers illustrated the internal theoretical consistency and logic which led Aron to his categorizations, showing why and how Aron's essentially scholastic approach relied on a medieval and monophonic conception of modality.[44] An external reading of the interplay of Aron's citations and Petrucci's prints sheds further light on these "problematic" assignments. This reading suggests not only the way in which the Petrucci repertory influenced the realization of Aron's theorizing, but also offers a tantalizing glimpse

---

[41] Two other motets in which the tenor extends cadences on E followed by a termination on B might also be added to this group: Jacotin's *Interveniat pro rege nostro* and Carpentras's *Cantate Domino.* I have maintained the generic distinctions suggested by the prints in the discussion which follows; thus, the seven works with Latin incipits in *Odhecaton* and *Canti B* have been counted among the "chansons" as a reflection of the print titles.

[42] It is striking that Aron refers only to the earliest of his Petrucci prints in this chapter; he may well have viewed the three anthologies which first appeared between the years 1501 and 1504 as a related series since his citations also reflect the order of publication. The different formats of the books would make this seem unlikely, however. *Odhecaton* and *Canti B* were in oblong choirbook; *Motetti C* was a set of four partbooks.

[43] See for example Bergquist's discussion of *Se mieulx* in "Theoretical Writings."

[44] Powers, "Is Mode Real?" hastened to point out that the assignments are more revealing of Aron's theorizing than representative of the music he discussed.

into generic and tonal associations suggested by these citations. The two subsets of his classifications which cite instances of terminations on *A la mi re* will serve as demonstrations. The first set is the pair of chansons cited in chapter 4 for Modes 1 and 2:

Alcuni altri tenori finiranno in A la mi re. bisogna considerare et examinare se el processo suo e conveniente et rationale a tal terminatione, perche essendo fini irregularmente terminata al primo et secondo tuono et non procedendo colla sua forma propria potrebbe facilmente non essere di quel tuono, dato che sia fine irregulare et termine del suo seculorum overo differenza, questo e, che el terzo et quarto tuono ha simil luogo quanto alla differenza come seguitando intenderai. Si che per questa ragione trovandosi adunque la sua conveniente forma, saran chiamati del primo tuono come La plus de plus di Iosquino, el quale per el discorso degli diapenti e sua ascensione e primo tuono, Et del secondo Si mieulx di Loiset compere come manifestamente si comprende (Aron, chapter 4).

Some other tenors terminate at *A la mi re*. It is necessary to consider and examine whether their *processo* is appropriate and reasonable for that ending, because if [a tenor] ends irregularly terminated for Modes 1 and 2 and does not proceed with its proper form, it could easily not belong to the former [Mode 1], even though *A la mi re* is [both] irregular final and a termination for its psalm-tone. That is because Modes 3 and 4 have the same place for the psalm-tone difference, as you will understand later on. If then in this way of reasoning you find its form appropriate, it will be called Mode 1, like *La plus des plus* of Josquin, which from the course of its species of the fifth and its ascent is Mode 1. And *Se mieulx* of Loyset Compère is Mode 2, as is manifestly to be understood (Powers, "Is Mode Real?" 32).

Aron here first raises the possibility of "irregular endings" and allows that a tenor ending on *A la mi re* may signal Modes 1, 2, 3, or 4 depending on its "processo."[45] He then cites two examples: Josquin's *La plus des plus*, which he assigns straightforwardly to Mode 1 on account of its species of the fifth and its "ascent"; and Compère's *Se mieulx*, which he assigns to Mode 2 "come manifestamente si comprende." A facsimile of the tenor of *Se mieulx* from the *Odhecaton* is given in Figure 3.8. (A facsimile of *La plus des plus* appears as Fig. 2.7). As Powers pointed out, by any of the criteria Aron outlined for his modal assignments – psalm-tone *differentia*, species, and *processo* – the assignment of this tenor to Mode 2 is incomprehensible, in stark contrast to the ease with which Aron's assignments of *La plus des plus* is comprehended.[46] In a complicated argument, Powers suggested that *A la mi re* must be understood as an instance of *confinality*, noting that Aron never explicitly invoked confinality as the basis of modal governance of a tenor by an irregular termination; I suggested elsewhere that Aron set himself the task of categorizing the tenor and that a process of elimination of his possibilities for tenors ending on A left Mode 2 by default, as it were.[47] Neither explanation sits very easily with Aron's assertion that his classification of *Se mieulx* to Mode 2 is "manifestly to be under-

[45] See Powers, "Is Mode Real?" 30–31, on Aron's use of the term *processo* to correspond to the more familiar term *ambitus.*   [46] Powers, "Is Mode Real?" 32–34.

[47] Powers, "Is Mode Real?" 34; Cristle Collins Judd, "Aspects of Tonal Coherence in the Motets of Josquin," Ph.D. dissertation, King's College London (1993; UMI 9501876), 42–44.

stood." In light of my observations about how Aron "read" the Petrucci prints, I can suggest another, contextual explanation of the citation. *Se mieulx* is the first example (no. 51) in the *Odhecaton* without a flat in the signature that ends on A in the tenor (see Appendix, Table A1 for the signatures and finals of all the compositions in the *Odhecaton*). Its inclusion among Aron's citations may simply represent the comprehensiveness characteristic of chapter 4 that falls by the way in succeeding chapters as Aron begins to cite possible termination points without adducing examples. *La plus des plus* (no. 64) is the next work in the *Odhecaton* with an ending on A. There are only three other possibilities in that print for Aron to consider: Agricola's *Crion nouel* (no. 75), Stokem's *Ha! traitre amours* (no. 86), and the anonymous *Puisque de vous* (no. 91); *Canti B* offers only the two settings of *J'ay pris amours* (no. 3 and no. 30). Aron would certainly have assigned all of these chansons – *Se mieulx* is the sole exception – to Mode 1, primarily because of prominent descending fifths proper to Mode 1 that conclude the tenor, exactly as in *La plus des plus*. Beyond Aron's sample group of prints, there does exist a complex of chansons which share certain tonal and textual features with *Se mieulx*,[48] but there was nothing comparable in the repertory in front of him in the *Odhecaton* and *Canti B*. The chansons which end on A, and indeed the motets ending on A, would all be described by Aron on the basis of their species and *processo* in relatively straightforward terms as ending on a psalm-tone *differentiae*;[49] *Se mieulx* does obviously stand apart in that context. Although Aron's "come manifestamente si comprende" may still strike us as an enigma, his assignment is less incomprehensible when one looks through these prints as he apparently did, noting the importance he attached to the *Odhecaton*, the placement of *Se mieulx* in that print, and the placement of this citation in the most "comprehensive" chapter of the *Trattato*.

Aron's comments on the Mode 3 and 4 works ending on A follow in the next chapter:

Alcuni altri anchora in A la mi re del terzo troverai, negli quali essendo in essi el processo conforme saranno giudicati di esso terzo tuono come Miserere mei deus di Iosquino. Letatus sum di Eustacio et Benedic anima mea dominum dove la prima parte finisce nel suo confinale, la seconda nel finale, et la terza nella differenza, et molti altri cosi si troveranno. Ma se saranno con el segno del B molle. Dico che questi maggiormente si chiameranno del terzo tuono dato che nel principio o mezzo non siano proceduti con el debito et conveniente modo, perche chiaramente si vede la regolar sua compositione di mi mi et mi la, la qual si genera da detto A la mi re, ad E la mi acuto, congiunto el superiore Diatessaron quale e mi la, benche di questi pochi se ritruovino per la incommodita dello ascenso suo, excettuando se non fussino a voce simili overo mutate, gli quali saranno giudicati del terzo o quarto tuono quanto alle spetie et discensioni, et non per cagione della differenza ne processo, per tanto si conclude che tal canti piu tosto saranno chiamati del quarto tuono per

---

[48] E.g. Compère's *Se pis ne vient*. I am grateful to Mary Kathleen Morgan for bringing this relationship to my attention.

[49] On Aron's use of *differentiae* as "pseudo finals," see Powers, "Is Mode Real?" 35, and Judd, "Aspects of Tonal Coherence," 46.

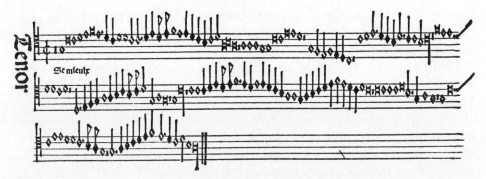

3.8 Compère, *Se mieulx*, tenor (*Odhecaton*, fol. 56ᵛ)

la discendente continuatione, come O maria rogamus te nel libro de motetti c et molti altri con questo modo facilmente potrai intendere (Aron, chapter 5).

You will also find certain other compositions ending on *A la mi re*; when these observe the appropriate *processo* they will be assigned to the third mode. For example, *Miserere mei Deus* by Josquin, *Laetatus sum* by Eustachio, and *Benedic anima mea Dominum* in which the first part ends on the confinal, the second on the final, and the third on the difference, etc. But when they have a flat signature, they are in my opinion to be assigned to the third mode the more readily, even though at the beginning and in their course they fail to proceed in the due and appropriate way, for it is evident that the regular structure of the mode – namely, *mi-mi* and *mi-la*, arising from the interval *A la mi re* to high *E la mi*, to which is added the upper diatessaron *mi-la* – will prevail. But because of the inconvenience of their upward range, few such pieces will be found, unless written for equal voices or *voce mutate*. Compositions of this sort are to be assigned to the third or fourth mode in view of their species and downward range, not because of their difference or *processo*. Thus it may be inferred that, in view of their extended downward range, they will in preference be assigned to the fourth mode. For example, *O Maria rogamus te* in the *Motetti C* and many others which you will readily recognize on the same principle (after Strunk/Tomlinson, *Source Readings*, 147).

There are three points to highlight in summary: (1) Aron argues that compositions that end on *A la mi re* and observe the appropriate *processo* belong to the third mode and cites three examples (Josquin's *Miserere*, Eustachio's [?] *Laetatus sum*[50] and *Benedic anima mea Dominum*); (2) he discusses the addition of a flat signature which transforms the species of fifth and fourth to those proper to Mode 3, that is, from *re-*

---

[50] Strunk, *Source Readings*, 205, misidentifies this work, citing *Motetti de la Corona II*. There is no known *Laetatus sum* attributed to Eustachio; the only setting of *Laetatus sum* in the Petrucci prints consulted by Aron is attributed to Andreas de Silva, and fits the tonal profile of the motets he discusses here. The attribution to Eustachio [de Monteregalis] belongs properly with the third motet cited in this list *Benedic anima mea Dominum*. For the purposes of the following discussion I will refer to the setting of *Laetatus sum* by Andreas de Silva, while acknowledging that Aron may have been referring to another setting of this text. Letters from 1531 (see Blackburn *et al.*, eds., *Correspondence*, 440–55) do make brief reference to a *Laetatus sum* by Aron. The description makes it unlikely that this was the work referred to in the *Trattato*.

la and *re-sol* to *mi-mi* and *mi-la*; and (3) he discusses assignments to Mode 4 based on extended downward range, for which he cites *O Maria rogamus te*, specifically mentioning that it appears in *Motetti C*.

The three instances of Mode 3 terminating on A are all psalm motets – *Miserere mei Deus* (Psalm 50 with refrain), *Benedic anima mea Dominum* (Psalm 102), and *Laetatus sum* (Psalm 121): each sets a complete psalm text and all invoke a psalm tone to some degree. These motets share the same cleffing and ranges and each concludes on E in the penultimate *pars* and A in the final *pars*. Aron describes this explicitly for *Benedic anima mea Dominum*: the first part ends with the tenor on the confinal (B); in the second it ends on the octave of the final (E); and the third on the psalm-tone *differentia* (in the context of this citation, presumably A). The conclusion of each *pars* of the motet is given in Examples 3.3a–c. The endings of the *prima* and *secunda partes* do indeed follow Aron's description, but the conclusion of the tenor of the *tertia pars* on C-sharp is unexpected in the context in which this citation is made. Aron seems to be invoking what he describes elsewhere as an extended final cadence where one part (tenor or cantus) sustains the final.[51] The two such cadences given earlier in chapter 5 are reproduced in Example 3.4; Aron might accept by analogy such an extension of a termination on *A la mi re*, as indicated on Example 3.3c, even though *A la mi re* can attain the status only of psalm-tone pseudo-final.[52] Such an explanation on Aron's part is visually suggested by the last system of the tenor with its cadence to A on the final word of text, followed by an obvious extension to a notated C-sharp, shown in facsimile in Figure 3.9. Equally, though, his description of the ending of the *tertia pars* on its difference could refer to the C-sharp with which the tenor ends, for *C* is a difference of tone 3 and the presence of a sharp is immaterial to Aron in this context (again highlighting both the visual and abstract distance of Aron's theory from the aural realization of the music he cites).[53]

For Mode 4, Aron cites one example under the heading of terminations on *A la mi re*: *Rogamus te/O Maria* from *Motetti C*.[54] In terms of the *tonality* of the motets, the distinction he makes appears to be an arbitrary one: *Rogamus te* has the same cleffing

---

[51] "And if sometimes, as has become the custom, the composer prolongs his work, amusing himself with additional progressions, you will, in my opinion, need to consider whether the final, as altered by the composer, is suited to and in keeping or out of keeping with his composition, for if reason guide him in what is suited to the tone he will at least see to it that some one part (namely, the tenor or cantus) sustains the final, while the others proceed as required by the tone, regular or irregular, with pleasing and appropriate progressions like those shown below, or in some more varied manner according to his pleasure and disposition" (Strunk, *Source Readings*, 212).

[52] However, the same logic would have suggested that *Miserere mei Deus* concluded with an extended cadence on E; see Judd, "Aspects of Tonal Coherence," 61–64.

[53] On the meaning of such sharp signs, see Margaret Bent, "Diatonic ficta," *Early Music History* 4 (1984), 1–48 and *eadem*, "Accidentals, Counterpoint, and Notation." Aron's visual orientation is also evident in early citations of the *Aggiunta* where he seems to be collecting examples in much the same way as he concludes the *Trattato*, although as Bent suggests in some of the later *Aggiunta* examples he does apparently mentally reconstruct the entire musical texture.

[54] The work is also known as an untexted instrumental ensemble fantasy attributed to Isaac with the title "La mi la sol," the solmization pattern of its tenor.

Ex. 3.3a *Benedic anima mea Dominum*, end of *prima pars*

Ex. 3.3b *Benedic anima mea Dominum*, end of *secunda pars*

Ex. 3.3c *Benedic anima mea Dominum*, end of *tertia pars*

Domino.

Domino.

Domino.   ↑ (extended cadence)

Domino.

Ex. 3.4 Aron's examples of an extended final cadence to E

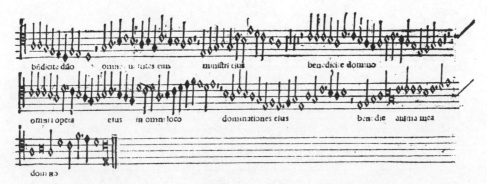

3.9 Conclusion of tenor, *Benedic anima mea Dominum* (*Motetti de la Corona II*, 11) (British Library K.1.d.14; reproduced by permission.)

as the other motets; its *prima pars* concludes on E in the tenor; its *secuna pars* on A. Although he has just discussed terminations on *A la mi re* with a flat signature, *Rogamus te*, like the other works ending on A, has no flat signature (see Fig. 3.10).[55] But unlike the case of *La plus des plus* and *Se mieulx* discussed above, there is a real modal distinction of authentic and plagal. The tenor of *Rogamus te* is based on an ostinato which emphasizes the species of fourth proper to Mode 4. The limited tenor range and its "downward" emphasis are surely responsible for Aron's categorization.

The intellectual interplay of Aron's medieval and monophonic modal theory and his modern and visual reliance on printed sources of polyphony raises a host of questions about how he accommodated the two, and in what sense, if any, his accommodation relates to practical realities. His categorizations of *La plus des plus* and *Se mieulx* on the one hand, and *Miserere mei Deus*, *Benedic anima mea Dominum*, and *Laetatus sum* on the other, do reflect a "real" tonal distinction – one embodied in hexachordal manipulation which is the shared basis of Aron's theory and the compositions he examined.[56] The tonal distinction is recognized in Aron's modal terms precisely because *A la mi re* is *not* vested with the authority of a final.[57]

The generic association of these tonalities – with endings on A – that Aron perhaps unwittingly suggests holds true not only for the prints he surveyed, but more widely: endings on A in *re* tonalities occur primarily in chansons; endings on

[55] Powers seems to have read Aron too literally here, implying that he cites *Rogamus te/O Maria* as an example with a flat signature: "When there is a flat signature, however, a la mi re cannot be a psalm-tone pseudo-final; in principle, chant theory does not provide for 'transformed' psalm-tones. In a piece with a b-flat in the signature where the species mi/fa/sol//re/mi – (a/b-flat/c//d/e) – and mi/fa/sol/la – (e/f/g/aa or E/F/G/a) – are associated with a termination at a la mi, an assignment to Mode 3 or Mode 4 would be appropriate 'because its regular composition is clearly seen'; since the processo [of a tenor] is not likely to extend up through the higher species of the fourth, however, it is the degree of extension in the lower part of the compass only that will determine the choice between authentic or plagal for such a tenor. According to Aron, it should usually be Mode 4, and his citation is an anonymous *O Maria rogamus te* from Petrucci's *Motetti C*" ("Is Mode Real?" 35).

[56] For further discussion of this point, see Judd, "Reading Aron Reading Petrucci," 140–42.

[57] With Glarean's recognition of A as the final of the Aeolian modal pair, these pieces are all subsumed by that modal category and indeed, Glarean does cite Josquin's *Miserere* as an example of the Hypoaeolian mode.

3.10 *O Maria*, tenor (*Motetti C*, 34) (British Library, K.1.d.4. Reproduced by permission.)

A in *mi* tonalities occur in motets, especially psalm motets. Indeed the tonal framework of *Benedic anima mea Dominum* could almost serve as a prototype for a group of motets which follow this scheme.[58] But such generic distinctions, if observed by Aron, were hardly pertinent to the purpose to which he turned his citations.

AFTER THE *TRATTATO*: CITATIONS IN THE *AGGIUNTA* TO THE *TOSCANELLO*

The reception of the *Trattato* can best be described as mixed: Spataro berated the treatise as "without order and truth" and apparently supplied an extensive critique,[59] while Iluminato Aiguino spoke reverently of Aron as his honored teacher in his two published treatises on the modes which followed Aron's model.[60] It is difficult to gauge both the reaction to the *Trattato* and the specifics contained within Spataro's now lost critique. However, in the new edition of the *Toscanello* four years later, Aron adds a supplement that deals primarily with the notation of accidentals in response to Spataro's critique of the original edition of *Toscanello*. He continues

---

[58] Psalm motets are prominent in the most "modern" of Aron's repertory, the *Motetti de la Corona* anthologies (each volume concludes with a psalm motet in addition to several scattered through the volume) and the generic and tonal distinctions represented by Aron's citations may also reflect the chronological distance of the chanson prints he cites. On text types in the *Motetti de la Corona* anthologies, see D. Gehrenbeck, "*Motetti de la Corona*: A Study of Ottaviano Petrucci's Four Last-known Motet Prints," S.M.D. dissertation, Union Theological Seminary (1970; UMI 7112440), 234–56.

[59] "Al venerabile Petro non voglio scrive[re] de tale cosa, perché lui è al tuto sdegnato con me, et que[sto] nasce perché io asai cercai retrarlo da la impresa de quello suo tractato de tonis ultimamente da lui impresso, el quale è reuscito proprio come io li scripsi, cioè senza ordine et verità, contra el quale ho scripto apresso a cento foglii, li quali scripti sono apresso di me" (Blackburn *et al.*, eds., *Correspondence*, 374). ("I don't want to write to Aaron; he is sore at me because I tried to dissuade him from publishing his treatise on the modes. I wrote him 100 folios about it; just as I predicted, it came out without order and truth" (Summary from Blackburn *et al.*, eds., *Correspondence*, 375–76)).

[60] Aiguino's treatises were *La illuminata de tutti I tuoni di canto fermo, con alcuni bellissimi secreti, non d'altrui più scritti* (Venice: Antonio Gardano, 1562) and *Il tesoro illuminato di tutti i tuoni di canto figurato, con alcuni bellissimi secreti, non da altri più scritti* (Venice: Giovanni Varisco, 1581). On Aiguino's theory, see Peter Schubert, "The Fourteen-Mode System of Illuminato Aiguino," *Journal of Music Theory* 35 (1991), 175–210.

the process of citation used in the *Trattato*, relying on the same sources, but citing relatively few of the same pieces (see the Tables of the Appendix). Table 3.2 outlines the citations of the *Aggiunta* in the three categories in which Aron invokes them: the avoidance of tritones; exceptions to the rules on tritones; and the responsibility of composers to notate accidentals to show their intentions.[61] Even more so than in the *Trattato*, Aron is looking through these partbooks, as one can see from the ordered citations and the clusters of citations from individual prints. Although Bent argues that Aron moves from citations relying on individual parts to the full texture, he may have simply used the procedure of working through a piece two voices at a time as described in the Spataro correspondence. He does seem to have selected his examples slightly differently however. Unlike the citations of the *Trattato*, there is a clear emphasis in the *Aggiunta* on two composers: Mouton and Josquin. Further, when he moves away from these composers (in the middle of the citations on notational practice) he seems to move either to works he knows well or to works contained in manuscripts, suggesting a shift from visual collection to aural recollection. Finally, he specifically sets up a distinction of ancient and modern that is defined by printed collections: seven works from the *Odhecaton* are cited as examples by ancient composers. A mere four years earlier, Aron had made no such distinction.[62]

Aron's reading of Petrucci's anthologies for the *Trattato* and the *Aggiunta* to the *Toscanello* may be characterized as personal, silent, and visual, in marked contrast at times to the aural reality represented by the notation. For his purposes, the notation as it existed in print became an authoritative, visual text that need not necessarily be the object of performance. Aron's reading for the *Trattato* relied on several volumes as sources, rather than close study of relatively few pieces; this suggests distance from the more personalized and circumscribed music manuscript culture that characterized his interactions with Spataro and Del Lago. The volumes he used for citations in the treatise were easily manipulated and need not have functioned as reminders of a repertory Aron "knew" or had even necessarily "read" before. Aron's working method in relation to his sources in the *Trattato* seems quite transparent, and suggests a shift from the methodical, even systematic approach of chapter 4 to the sorts of cursory "glances" reflected in chapter 7. These latter citations reflect minimal revision, juggling, or reordering in the preparation of his text as a whole. This style of reading – glancing and collecting – also initiates the citations of the *Aggiunta*, but then again changes to suit his particular purposes as Aron progresses. Yet in his position as theorist and author, he suggests the availability of a community of readers who shared, or at least accepted, his appropriation of the Petrucci prints as both pedagogical material and source of authority.

---

[61] See Bent, "Accidentals, Counterpoint, and Notation," for a detailed discussion of Aron's citations in the *Aggiunta*.

[62] Bent concludes her examination of Aron's citations by suggesting a "progressive" view of notation. It is also a view of notation that is implicitly tied to the regularizing function of printed music books.

Table 3.2 *Aron's citations* (Aggiunta *to the* Toscanello) *and their sources*

Tritone avoidance

Motetti de la Corona I, 5	Mouton, *Nos qui vivimus*
Motetti de la Corona I, 11	[Mouton, *Beata dei genetrix*]
Motetti de la Corona I, 19	Mouton, *Benedicta est celorum regina*
Motetti de la Corona II, 16	Mouton, *Congregate sunt*
Motetti de la Corona I, 5	Mouton, *Nos qui vivimus*
Motetti de la Corona I, 2	Josquin, *Memor esto*
Liber primus missarum Josquin, 3	Josquin *Missa Gaudeamus*
Liber primus missarum Josquin, 1	Josquin, *Missa L'homme armé super voces musicales*
Liber primus missarum Josquin, 2	Josquin, *Missa La sol fa re mi*
Motetti de la Corona I, 10	Févin, *Benedictus dominus deus meus*
Motetti de la Corona II, 21	L'heritier, *Dum complerentur*
Motetti de la Corona I, 3	Carpentras, *Bonitatem fecisti*

Exceptions to the tritone rule

Liber primus missarum Josquin, 1	Josquin, *Missa Clama necesses* [*Missa L'homme armé super voces musicales*]
Liber primus missarum Josquin, 2	Josquin, *Missa La sol fa re mi*

Composer's intentions

Motetti de la Corona I, 2	Josquin, *Memor esto*
Motetti de la Corona III, 2	Josquin, *Praeter rerum*
Motetti de la Corona III, 3	Josquin, *Ave nobilissima*
Motetti de la Corona III, 4	Josquin, *Virgo salutiferi*
Liber primus missarum Josquin, 1	Josquin, *Missa L'homme armé super voces musicales*
Motetti de la Corona I, 1	Mouton, *Gaude Barbara*
Motetti de la Corona I, 5	Mouton, *Nos qui vivimus*
Motetti de la Corona I, 10	Févin, *Benedictus dominus deus meus*
Motetti de la Corona II, 4	Richafort, *Miseremini mei*
?	Festa, *Fors seulement*
Motetti de la Corona I, 12	Longueval, *Benedicat nos imperialis maiestis*
?	Verdelot, *Ave virgo gratiosa*
?	La Rue, *Il es bien*
?	L'heritier, *Miserere mei deus*
?	Festa, *Ecce deus savator meus*
Odhecaton, 1	Orto, *Ave Maria*
Odhecaton, 12	Agricola, *Cest mal charche*
Odhecaton, 15	La Rue, *Pour quoy nun*
Odhecaton, 30	Japart, *Helas!*
Odhecaton, 37	Compère, *Nous sommes*
Odhecaton, 40	Isaac, *He logerons nous*
Odhecaton, 69	Obrecht, *Tandernaken*

Petrucci undoubtedly did originally intend his volumes for groups of performers, but Aron's appropriation of the repertory in the *Trattato* is exactly the kind of "use-for-reference" of early music prints that Stanley Boorman discounts.[63] Aron's continuation of that appropriation four years later in his supplement to the *Toscanello* suggests that what may seem a novel way of reading for 1525 was in fact shared, at least to some extent, by some portion of his readers. Even with Aron's precedent, however, references to printed polyphonic music hardly became commonplace in Italian theoretical writing. The initial expense of Aron's Venetian treatises is documented by Spataro's inability to sell the six copies of the *Toscanello* that he had Aron send him. By comparison, he noted that Gaffurio's *Practica musicae* which was twice the size and contained many music examples cost less, while the Italian version of Gaffurio's treatise was even cheaper.[64]

When Spataro enlisted Aron's assistance in getting his own treatise published (which he dedicated to Aron) he commented that he had considerably reduced the examples. In another letter, he remarks on Aron's on-going negotiations with the printer on format, woodcuts, and paper.[65] Spataro's *Tractato di musica* appeared in 1531, two years after the *Aggiunta* from the same publisher.[66] Spataro only occasionally cites composers, notably Dufay and Josquin and even less frequently cites specific works (Dufay's *Missa di Sancto Antonio*, Josquin's *Missa Malheur me bat*). In a determined gesture, the "specialness" of the relatively few music examples is signaled by frames on the woodcuts which visually set the music apart (see Fig. 3.11). Not until Zarlino's *Le istitutioni harmoniche* of 1558 would a theorist take up the citation of printed polyphony with anything like the enthusiasm of Aron's enterprise, and again it would be primarily in the area of modal theory.

The interpretation I have proposed for Aron's music citations in the *Trattato* and *Aggiunta*, along with the view of Aron as a reader of Petrucci's anthologies it suggests, raises numerous general questions about theoretical citations from printed music sources which are explored further in subsequent chapters. Implicit among them is the question of Aron's status as theorist. His invocation of printed sources now appears, of course, as both eminently practical and closely tied to the nature of his material in the *Trattato* and the *Aggiunta*. Indeed, the reliance of a theorist on printed sources seems inevitable given the undeniable impact of music printing. Publishing so many examples in the *Trattato* would have been highly unlikely, if not impossible. Citations from Petrucci's prints provided at least the appearance of commonality when Aron could count neither on readers' access to manuscript sources nor on their memory of individual tenor parts. But Aron's very reliance on printed sources might also be construed as reflecting a kind of musico-theoretical inferiority that combined a resort to the visual in lieu of aural memory with an assertion of his own qualification through association with Petrucci's prints and the composers contained in them.

---

[63] See chapter 1, 11–16.   [64] Blackburn *et al.*, eds., *Correspondence*, Letter 9.   [65] *Ibid.*, 434, 465.
[66] Giovanni Spataro, *Tractato di musica* (Venice: Bernadino de Vitali, 1531); facsimile ed. Giuseppe Vecchi, Bibliotheca Musica Bononiensis, II, 14 (Bologna: Forni, 1970).

CApITOLO

Declaratione de le figure:nel superposito exemplo assegnate.   Capitolo. XXI.

LA intentione di Fráchino e stata:che in questo segno ☉ prima in lo preaducto suo concento locato:due minime/ ouer el suo ualore per una integra mensura siano pronuntiate in cantando: & etiã ha considerato:che le semibreue posite da poi la prima sesqualtera siano perfecte:perche ha inteso:che tale semibreue siano gubernate dal segno/ut hic ☉ in principio di tal concento locato:ma dice/che ciascuna de le semibreue predicte sesqualterate/sara diminuta de la sua parte terza:& questo dice accadere:pche si a ciascuna de le predicte semibreue secódo el segno circulare punctato nó sesqualterato: haueua uirtu & ualore di tre minime: data dapoi la sesqualtera: tale sua uirtu & ualore ternario:sara riducto in binario: Adóche qua bisogna ad uertire:che se ciascuna de le predicte tre minime cótenute da ciascuna de le predicte semibreue sesqualterate:perde la sua parte terza (come ha dicto Fráchino)el sequitera:che la semibreue pfecta sesqualterata solaméte restera diminuta/ rispecto la subtractione de la parte terza di ciascuna sua terza parte.s.de la terza parte di ciascuna di quelle tre minime di essa semibreue contenute:& nó/che(in quanto al numero) essa semibreue sia riducta di ternario in binario numero de le sue sequenti minore propin/que.s.in due minime:impoche(come disopra e stato dimostrato)tale semibreue sesqualterate/nó prderãno:el numero ternario de le sue propin/que minime:perche resterãno in uirtu/& ualore di tre minime diminute:

3.11 Spataro, *Tractato*, sig. ci^v

The traditional view holds Aron up as an "innovator" and "progressive":

> One can easily see that Aron, in such varied ways as his use of the vernacular, his desire for a consistent indication of accidentals, his disapproval of conflicting signatures, and his emphasis on a practical terminology, proves himself a Renaissance man in touch with the progressive music thinking of his day.[67]

Another perspective suggests taking his relationship to printed sources as a revealing starting point, thus recognizing a rather different second and third "first" in the *Trattato*: publishing a theory treatise in Italian rather than Latin, of course; but then, explicitly connecting mode with a particular polyphonic repertory; and finally, defining that repertory through printed sources. Such departures from the norm stand in striking contrast to the purely medieval basis for Aron's actual modal theory and were perhaps only even conceivable because of his position as an "outsider," lacking access to both the materials and training, musical and otherwise, available to his theoretical peers. One cannot gainsay the significance of those "firsts" for subsequent theoretical discourse, however. Whether he intended to do so or not, Pietro Aron's conscious reliance on printed sources betokened an irreversibly changed relationship between theorists and a community of readers defined by a shared, printed musical image.

APPENDIX

Sources of Aron's citations

Table A3.1 *Harmonice musices Odhecaton*[68]

No.	Attribution	Text	Clefs	Tenor signature	Final[69]	Aron[70] 1525	1529
1	**Orto**	*Ave Maria*	**c2-c4-f3-f5**	♭	**F**		30
2		*Je cuide se ce temps*	g2-c3-c3-f4		C	VII	
3	[Stokem]	*Hor oires une chanzon*	c1-c2-c3-c3-c4	♭	G		
4		**Nunca fué pena mayor**	**c1-c4-c3-c4**		**G**	**III**	
5	**Stokem**	**Brunette**	**c1-c4-c4-c3-f4**	♭	**F**	**VI**	
6		*J'ay pris amours/De tous biens*	c1-c3-c4-f4	♭♭	G		
7	Japart	*Nenciozza mia*	c2-c4-f4-f4	♭	F		
8		*Je ne fay plus*	g2-c2-c3-c4	♭	G		
9	Hayne	*Amours amours*	c2-c3-c4-f4	♭	G		
10	Josquin	*Bergerette savoyenne*	g2-c3-c3-f3		C		
11		*Et qui le dira*	c1-c3-c4-f4	♭	G		

[67] Gustav Reese, *Music in the Renaissance* (London: J. M. Dent, 1954), 183.

[68] RISM 1501: table based on facsimile ed. (New York, 1973) of RISM 1504². Modern ed. by H. Hewitt (Cambridge, MA. 1942). I am grateful to David Fallows for supplying attributions for nos. 3, 31, 71, and 80.

[69] Concluding pitch class of tenor is given. In multi-part works, the final of each section is given, separated by ‖. The termination of the bassus is given in square brackets when it differs from the tenor.

[70] Works in bold type are cited by Aron. Citations from the *Trattato* are indicated in the column headed "1525." Aron's modal classification is indicated with roman numerals; dashes indicate citation without modal classification. Citations from the *Aggiunta* to the *Toscanello* appear in the column headed "1529"; numbering follows Bent, "Accidentals, Counterpoint, and Notation," 327–34.

Table A3.1 (*cont.*)

No.	Attribution	Text	Clefs	Tenor signature	Final	Aron 1525	Aron 1529
12	**Agricola**	*C'est mal cherche*	**c1–c3–c4–f4**	♭	**G**		31
13	**Caron**	*Hélas que pourra devenir*	**c1–c3–c3–c4**	♭	**F**	**V**	
14	Josquin	*Adieu mes amours*	c1–c3–c4–f3	♭	G		
15	**LaRue**	*Pourquoy non*	**c2–c3–c3–f4**	♭♭	**F**		32
16	Stokem	*Pourquoy je ne puis dire/Vray dieu*	c2–c4–c4–f4	♭	F		
17		*Mon mignault/Gracieuse*	c2–c3–c4–f4	♭	G		
18		*Dit le burguygnon*	c1–c3–c4–f4	♭	G		
19	Stokem	*Hélas ce n'est pas*	c1–c4–c4–f4	♭	G		
20	**[Hayne]**	*De tous biens playne*	**c2–c3–c4–f4**	♭	**G**	**II**	
21	Japart	*J'ay pris amours*	c1–c3–c3–f4	♭♭	G		
22[71]	Compère	*Ung franc archier*	c1–c3–c4–f4	♭	G		
23	Japart	*Amours amours*	c1–c4–c4–f4	♭	F		
24	[Japart]	*Cela sans plus non souffi pas*	c2–f3–f3–f4	♭♭	C		
25		*Rompeltier*	c1–c3–c4–f4	♭	G		
26	Compère	*Alons fere nos barbes*	c1–c3–c4–f4	♭	G		
27	[Japart]	*Tmeiskin*	c1–c3–c4–f4	♭	G		
28	Japart	*Se congie pris*	c1–c3–c4–f4	♭	G		
29		*L'oseraie dire*	**g2–c3–c3–f3**	♭	**C**	**VIII**	
30	**Japart**	*Hélas qu'il est à mon gré*	**g2–c1–c2–c4**		**D**	**I**	33
31	[Japart]	*Amours fait molt/Il est de bonne*	c2–c4–c3–f4	♭	G		
32	[Ninot]	*Nostre chamberière*	c1–c3–c4–f3	♭	F		
33	[Busnois]	*Acordes moy*	c2–f3–c4–f4	♭	G		
34	Japart	*Tam bien mi son pensada*	c1–c3–c4–f4	♭	G		
35		*Le serviteur*	**c2–c3–c4–f4**	♭♭	**C**	**[-]**	
36	[Mouton]	*Jamais jamais*	g2–c3–c3–f4	♭	G		
37	**Compère**	*Nous sommes*	**g2–c3–c3–f3**		**C**		34
38	Agricola	*Je n'ay dueil*	c2–c4–c4–f4		D		
39	Busnois	*J'ay pris amours tout au rebours*	c2–c4–c4–f4	♭	A[D]		
40	**[Isaac]**	*Helogierons nous*	**c2–c3–c4–f4**	♭	**G**		35
41	**Compère**	*Vostre bargeronette*	**c1–c3–c4–f3**	♭	**F**	**VI**	
42	**Busnois**	*Je ne demande*	**c2–c4–f4–f4**	♭	**F**	**VI**	
43	Tadinghen	*Pensif mari*	c1–c3–f4	♭	G		
44	Isaac	*La morra*	c1–c3–f4	♭	G		
45	Compère	*Ne doibt*	c1–c4–f4	♭	G		
46	Compère	*Male bouche/Circumdederunt*	c2–c4–f3		D		
47	Agricola	*L'homme banni*	c2–c4–f4	♭	G		
48	**Agricola**	*Allez regretz*	**c2–c2–c4**	♭	**F**	**VI**	
49		*La stangetta*	c1–c4–f4	♭	G		
50	Isaac	*Hélas*	c1–c3–c4	♭	F		
51	**Compère**	*Se mieulx*	**c1–c4–f3**		**A**	**II**	
52	Tinctoris	*Hélas*	c1–c3–f4		D		
53	Compère	*Venez regretz*	c1–c4–f3	♭	F		
54	Ockeghem	*Ma bouche rit*	c1–c4–f4		E		
55	Agricola	*Royne des fleurs*	c2–c4–f4		D		

[71] Hewitt exchanges Compère *Ung franc archier* (no. 22) and Japart *Se congie pris* (no. 28) without comment.

Table A3.1 (*cont.*)

No.	Attribution	Text	Clefs	Tenor signature	Final	Aron 1525	1529
56	**Agrigola**	*Si dedero*	**c2–c4–f4**		**G**	**VIII**	
57	Hayne	*Allez regretz*	c2–c4–f4	♭	F		
58	Compère	*Guerises moy*	c1–c4–f4	♭	G		
59	**Compère**	***Mes pensées***	**c1–c3–c4**		**C**	**VII**	
60	Vincenet	*Fortune par ta crualte*	c1–c3–f3	♭♭	C		
61	**Josquin**	***Cela sans plus***	**c1–c4–f3**	♭	**G**	**[–]**	
62	Brumel	*Mater patris*	c3–c3–c4	♭	G		
63	**Ockeghem**	***Malheur me bat***	**c1–c4–c4**		**E**	**III**	
64	**Josquin**	***La plus des plus***	**c1–c4–f3**		**A**	**I**	
65	Agricola	*Allez mon cueur*	c1–c4–f4		E		
66		***Madame hélas***	**c1–c3–f3**		**C**	**VII**	
67	Compère	*Le corps / Corpusque meum*	c2–c4–f3		D		
68	Compère	*Tant ha bon oeul*	c2–c4–f4		D		
69	**Obrecht**	***T'andernacken***	**c2–c4–f4**	♭	**A**		**36**
70		*Si à tort on m'a blasmé*	c1–c3–f3		G		
71	[Hayne]	*Les grans regretz*	c1–c3–f3	♭	G		
72		***Est il possible***	**c1–c3–f3**		**G**	**VIII**	
73	Bourdon [in index]	*De tous biens*	c2–c4–f4	♭	G		
74		*Fortuna d'un gran tempo*	c2–c4–f3	♭	F		
75	Agricola	*Crions nouel*	c1–c4–f3		A		
76	Isaac	*Benedictus*	c2–c3–f4	♭	G		
77	Compère	*Le renvoy*	c2–c4–f4	♭	G		
78	**Josquin**	***O venus bant***	**c1–c4–f4**		**G**	**VIII**	
79		*Ma seule dame*	c1–c4–f4	♭	F		
80	Ghiselin	*L'Alfonsina*	c2–c3–f4	♭	G		
81	Agricola	*L'heure est venue / Circumdederunt*	c2–c4–f4		D		
82	Agricola	*J'ay beau huer*	c1–c4–f3	♭	G		
83	[Hayne]	*Mon souvenir*	c1–c3–f3	♭	G		
84	Compère	*Royne du ciel / Regina celi*	c2–c4–f3		G		
85		*Marguerite*	g2–c1–c4	♭	D		
86	Stokem	*Ha! traitre amours*	c1–c4–c4		A		
87	Compère	*Mais que ce fust*	c1–c4–f3	♭	G		
88	Orto	*Venus tu m'a pris*	c1–c3–f3	♭♭	C		
89	**Compère**	***Disant adieu à madame***	**c1–c4–f4**		**G**	**VIII**	
90		*Gentil prince*	c1–c4–f4	♭	G		
91		*Puisque de vous*	c1–c4–f4		A		
92	Obrecht	*Tsat een meskin*	c1–c3–c4–f3		G		
93	**Hayne**	***A l'audience***	**c3–c4–f4–f4**	♭	**F**	**VI**	
94	Bruhier	*La turatu*	c1–c3–c4–f4	♭	G		
95	Josquin	*De tous biens playne*	c2–c4–f3–[f3]	♭	G		
96	Obrecht	*Meskin es hu*	c1–c3–c3–f4	♭	D[G]		

Table A3.2 *Canti B*[72]

No.	Attribution	Text	Clefs	Signature	Final	1525[73]
1	**Josquin**	*L'homme armé*	**c1–c3–c3–f3**	♭	**D**	**I**
2	**Compère**	*Virgo celesti*	**c1–c3–c4–c4–f4**	♭	**G**	**II**
3	Obrecht	*J'ay pris amours*	c1–c2–c4–f4		A	
4	[Bruhier]	*Vray Dieu*	c1–c3–c4–f4		D	
5	Compère	*Lourdault*	c1–c3–c4–f4	♭	G	
6	[Raulin]	*Je suis trop jeunette*	g2–c3–c3–f4	♭	G	
7	**LaRue**	*Ce n'est pas jeu*	**c2–c4–c4–f4**	♭	**G**	**II**
8	Busnois	*L'autrier que passa*	c2–c3–f3–f4	♭	G	
9		*Réveillez-vous*	c1–c4–c4–f4		D	
10		*En chambre polie*	g2–c3–c4–f3	♭	F	
11	**[Compère]**	*Je suiz amie du fourrier*	**c1–c3–c4–f4**		**G**	**VIII**
12	**Orto**	*Mon mary m'a diffamée*	**c2–c3–f3–f4**	♭	**C**	**VIII**
13	Obrecht	*Cela sans plus*	c1–c3–c4–f3		G[C]	
14		*Bon temps*	c2–c4–c4–f4	♭	D	
15		*A qui dir élle sa pencee*	c1–c3–c4–f4	♭	G	
16	Lannoy [in index]	*Cela sans plus*	g2–c3–c3–f3		G	
17		*Mon père m'a mariée*	c1–c3–c4–f4	♭	G	
18		*Mijn morken gaf*	**c1–c3–c4–f4**		**G**	**VIII**
19	**Josquin**	*Comment peult avoir*	**g2–c3–c3–f4**	♭	**C**	**VII**
20		*Comment peult*	c2–c4–c4–f4		G	
21	**Ninot**	*Hélas, hélas, hélas*	**c1–c3–c4–f4**		**G**	**VIII**
22	LaRue	*Tous les regretz*	c2–c4–f3–f5		D	
23	Vaqueras	*Veci la danse barbari*	c1–c4–c4–f4		G	
24	**Orto**	*D'ung aultre amer*	**c1–c4–c4–f4**	♭	**G**	**II**
25	Brumel	*Noé, noé, noé*	c1–c3–c4–f4	♭	G	
26		*Una moza falle yo*	c1–c3–c3–f4	♭	G	
27	**[Ninot]**	*Et la la la*	**c1–c3–c4–f3**		**C**	**VIII**
28	**LaRue**	*Fors seulement*	**c1–c1–c1–c4**		**D**	**I**
29	**Compère**	*Et dun revenis*	**c1–c3–c4–f3**		**G**	**VIII**
30	Japart	*J'ay pris amours*	c1–c2–c4–c4		A	
31	Japart	*Je cuide/De tous biens*	c1–c3–c4–f4	♭	G	
32	De Vigne	*Franc coeur/Fortuna*	c1–c2–c4–c4–f4		G	
33	Lourdoys (Braconnier)	*Amours me trocte*	c1–c3–c4–f4	♭	F	
34	Josquin	*Baisez moy*	c1–c2–c3–c4	♭	G	
35	Obrecht	*Vanil ment [=Wat willen]*	c1–c3–c3–f4	♭	G	
36	Bulkyn	*Or sus, or sus*	c1–[c3]–c3–f3		G	
37		*Baisez moy*	[c1]–c3–[c2]–c4–[c4]–f4		G	
38		*Avant avant*	c2–[c4]–c4–f4		D	
39	Brumel	*Ave Ancilla Trinitatis*	c3–f4–f4	♭	G	
40	**Obrecht**	*Si sumpsero*	**g2–c3–f3**	♭	**C**	**V**
41		*Mon père m'a donné mari*	c1–c3–c4–f4	♭	G	
42	Ghiselin	*De tous biens*	c2–c3–f3	♭	G	
43		*Pour quoy*	**c2–c4–f4**	♭	**D**	**I**
44	[Isaac]	*Adieu fillette*	c1–c4–f4	♭	G	
45	Compère	*Chanter ne puis*	c2–c4–f4	♭	G	
46	Agricola	*Je vous emprie [=Si vous voullez]*	c1–c3–f4		C	
47	Compère	*A qui dirage*	c1–c4–f4	♭	G	
48	**Hayne**	*La regretée*	**c1–c3–f3**	♭	**B♭**	**V**
49	Brumel	*En amours*	c2–c4–f4	♭	G	
50	**Brumel**	*Je despite tous*	**g2–c2–c4**		**D**	**I**
51	Compère	*Le grant désir*	c2–c4–f4		D	

---

[72] RISM 1502²; table based on facsimile ed. (New York, 1975). Modern ed. by H. Hewitt (Chicago, 1967).
[73] Works from *Canti B* are cited only in the *Trattato*, not in the *Aggiunta* to *Toscanello*.

Table A3.3 *Motetti C*[74]

No.	Attribution	Text	Clefs	Signature	Final	1525[75]
1	Josquin	*Ave Maria [...benedicta tu]*	g2-c3-c3-f3	♭	G	
2	Brumel	*Ave celorum Domina*	c1-c3-c3-c4	♭	G	
3	Josquin	*Liber generationis*	c1-c3-c4-f4		G[E]‖A‖E	
4	Josquin	*Factum est autem*	c1-c4-c4-f4		G[E]‖E[A]‖G	
5	Nico. Craen	*Tota pulchra es*	c2-c3-c4-f5		E‖E	
6		*Davidica stirpe*	g2-c3-c3-f3	♭	C[F]‖F	
7		***Beata Dei genitrix***	**c1-c4-c4-f4**		**G‖G**	**VIII**
8	Josquin	*Missus est*	c2-c4-c4-f4	♭	B♭[G]	
9		*Ergo sancti martires*	c2-c4-f3-f4	♭	D	
10		*Concede nobis Domine*	c1-c4-c4-f4	♭	G‖G	
11	[Obrecht]	*Requiem eternam*	c1-c3-c4-f4		E‖E	
12	[Ninot]	*Psallite noe*	c1-c3-c4-f4	♭	F	
13	[Ninot]	*Si oblitus fuero*	c1-c3-c4-f4	♭	G‖G	
14		*Civitatem istam*	c1-c3-c4-f4		G[C]‖A	
15	[Ockeghem]	*Ut hermita*	c1-c3-c3-f4		E‖E	
16	[Josquin]	*O bone et dulcis/Pater noster*	c1-c3-c4-f4		D	
17		*Missus est*	c1-c2-c3-c4		E[A]‖D	
18	[Isaac]	*Alma redemptoris*	c1/c2-c3-c3-f3	♭	A‖F	
19		*Miles mire probitatis*	c2-c4-c4-f4	♭	F‖F	
20		*Ave regina/O decus innocentie*	c1-c2-c4-f4	♭	F‖F	
21		*Virgo precellens*	c1-c3-c4-f4	♭	G‖G‖G‖G‖G	
22		*O sacrum convivium/Qui pacem*	c1-c4-c4-f4	♭	F	
23		*O admirable*	c1-c4-c4-f4	♭	F	
24	[Mouton]	*Sancti Dei omnes*	c1-c4/c3-c4-f4	♭	F‖F	
25		*Confitemini*	c1-c3-c4-f4	♭	G[C]‖G	
26		*Respice me in felicem*	c1-c4-c4-f4	♭	G	
27		*Trinitas deitas*	c1-c4-c4-f4	♭	A[D]‖G	
28	[Compère]	*Profitentes unitatem*	c1-c2-c3-f3		E[A]‖A[D]	
29		*Filie regum [In honore tuo]*	c1-c4-c4-f4		A‖E[A]	
30		*Miserere mei*	c1-c3-c3-f4	♭	G	
31		*Si bona suscepimus*	c1-c3-c4-f4		B[E]‖A	
32	[Josquin?]	*Magnus es tu*	c1-c4-c4-f3		E[A]‖E	
33	[Josquin?]	*Planxit autem*	c1-c3-c4-f4	♭	F‖F‖F‖F	
34	**[Isaac]**	***Rogamus te/O Maria***	**c1-c3-c4-f4**		**E‖A**	**IV**
35		*Inviolata*	g2-c3-c3-f3		C‖E‖E‖E‖C‖ C‖E‖E‖C‖ G[C]‖C‖C	
36		*Gloria laus*	c1-c4-c4-f4		D‖A[D]‖A[D]‖A	
37		*Gaudeamus*	c1-c3-c4-f4	♭	G‖G‖G‖G‖G	
38		*Huc omnes pariter*	c1-c4-c4-f4	♭	C[F]‖F	
39		*O dulcissima*	c1-c3-c3-f4	♭	G‖G	
40	**[Josquin]**	***Mittit ad virginem***	**g2-c3-c3-f3**		**C‖C**	**VII**
41		*Salvatoris mater pia*	c1-c3-c3-c4	♭	G‖G‖G	
42		*In lectulo*	c4-c4-f4	♭	D[G]	

[74] RISM 1504[1]; table based on film of D–Mbs. Partial modern ed. in R. Sherr, *The Petrucci Motet Anthologies* (New York, 1991).

[75] Works from *Motetti C* are cited only in the *Trattato*, not in the *Aggiunta* to *Toscanello*.

Table A3.4 *Missae Josquin*[76]

No.	Attribution	Text	Clefs	Signature	Final	1529[77]
1	**Josquin**	*L'Homme armé super voces musicales*	**c2–c4–c4–f4**		**D‖D‖D‖D‖D**	**8, 13, 19**
2	**Josquin**	*La sol fa re mi*	**c1–c4–c4–f4**		**E‖E‖E‖E‖A**	**9, 14**
3	**Josquin**	*Gaudeamus*	**g2–c3–c3–f3**		**A‖A‖A‖A‖A**	**7**
4	Josquin	*Fortuna desperata*	c1–c3–c3–f3	♭	F‖F‖F‖F‖F	
5	Josquin	*L'homme armé sexti toni*	c1–f3–c4–f5	♭	F‖F‖F‖F‖F	

Table A3.5 *Missarum Josquin liber secundus*[78]

No.	Attribution	Text	Clefs	Signature	Final	1525[79]
1	**Josquin**	*Ave maris stella*	**g2–c3–c3–f3**	♭	**G‖G‖G‖G‖G**	**I**
2	**Josquin**	*Hercules dux ferrariae*	**c2–c4–c4–f4**		**D‖D‖D‖D‖D**	**II**
3	Josquin	*Malheur me bat*	c2–c4–c4–f4		E‖E‖E‖E‖E	
4	Josquin	*L'ami baudichon*	c1–c3–c3–f3		C‖C‖C‖C‖C	
5	Josquin	*Una musque de buscaya*	c1–c3–c4–f4	♭	B♭‖B♭‖G‖B♭‖B♭	
6	**Josquin**	*D'ung aultre amer*	**c1–c4–c4–c4**	♭	**G‖G‖G‖G‖G**	**I**

[76] RISM J666 (1502); table based on facsimile ed. (Rome, 1973).

[77] Works from the first volume of Josquin masses are cited only in the *Aggiunta* to *Toscanello*, not in the *Trattato*.

[78] RISM J670 (1505); table based on facsimile ed. (Rome, 1973).

[79] Works from the second volume of Josquin masses are cited only in the *Trattato*, not in the *Aggiunta* to *Toscanello*.

Table A3.6 *Motetti de la corona libro primo*[80]

No.	Attribution	Text	Clefs	Signature	Final	1525	1529
1.1	**Mouton**	*Gaude Barbara beata*	g2-c2-c3-c4		**A‖D**	I	?
1.2	**Josquin**	*Memor esto verbi tui*	c1-c4-c2-f3		**B[E]‖E[A]**		6, 15, 20
1.3	**Carpentras**	*Bonitatem fecisti*	c1-c3-c4-f4		**A[D]‖C[A]**		12
1.4	De Silva	*Laetatus sum*	c1-c3-c4-f4		E[A]‖A[A]	[III]	
1.5	**Mouton**	*Nos qui vivimus: In exitu Israel*	c1-c4-c4-f4		**G‖G‖G**		1, 5, 21
1.6	Thérache	*Clare sanctorum*	c1-c3-c4-f4		G		
1.7	Mouton	*Laudate Deum*	c1-c3-c4-f4		G‖G		
1.8	**Févin**	*Nobilis progenie*	g2-c3-c3-f3	♭	**G**	I	
1.9	Mouton	*Ecce Maria genuit*	g2-c2-c3-c4	♭	B♭		
1.10	**Févin**	*Benedictus Dominus Deus*	g2-c3-c4-f4	♭	**G‖G**		10, 22
1.11	**Mouton**	*Beata Dei, genitrix Maria*	c1-c1-c4-f3		**D**	I/II	2
1.12	**Longueval**	*Benedicat nos*	c1-c3-c4-f4	♭	**G‖G**		25
1.13	**Févin**	*Sancta Trinitas*	c1-c3-c4-f4	♭	**F**	VI	
1.14	Divitis	*O desolatorum consolator*	c1-c3-c4-f4	♭	G‖G		
1.15	Févin	*Gaude francorum regia corona*	c1-c3-c4-f4	♭	G		
1.16	Mouton	*Christum regem regum*	c3-c3-c4-f4	♭	G		
1.17		*Contremuerunt omnia membra*	c3-c4-c4-f4		E		
1.18	**Hylaire**	*Ascendens Christus*	g2-g2-c3-c4		**G**	VII	
1.19	**Mouton**	*Benedicta es*	c2-c4-c4-f4		**G**		3
1.20	**Févin**	*Tempus meum est*	c1-c3-c4-f4	♭	**F‖F**	VI	
1.21		*Vulnerasti cor meum*	g2-c2-c3-f4	♭	**A[D]‖G**	I	
1.22	**Mouton**	*Celeste beneficium*	c2-c3-c4-f4	♭	**F‖F**	VI	
1.23	**Févin**	*Egregie Christi confessor*	c1-c3-c4-f4	♭	**F‖F**	VI	
1.24	[Févin]	*Dilectus Deo*	c1-c4-c4-f4		C		
1.25	Josquin	*Christum ducem*	c2-c3-c4-f4		E		
1.26	Brumel	*Laudate Dominum*	c1-c3-c4-f4		D[G]‖G		

[80] RISM 1514[1]; table based on film of I-Bc. Partial modern eds. in D. Gehrenbeck, "*Motetti de la Corona*: A Study of Ottaviano Petrucci's Four Last-Known Motet Prints," S.M.D. dissertation, Union Theological Seminary (1970; UMI 7112440), and R. Sherr, *Selections from Motetti de la Corona* (New York, 1992).

Table A3.7 *Motetti de la Corona libro secondo*[81]

No.	Attribution	Text	Clefs	Signature	Final	1525	1529
2.1	Thérache	*Verbum bonum et suave*	c1–c4–c4–f4		G		
2.2	**Jacotin**	*Interveniat pro rege nostro*	c3–c4–c4–f4		B[E]	III	
2.3	**Caen**	*Nomine qui Domini*	c1–c3–c4–f4	♭	D	I	
2.4	**Richafort [Mouton]**	*Miseremini mei*	c1–c4–c3–f4		A‖E[A]		23
2.5	Lupus	*Postquam consummati sunt*	c1–c3–c4–f4		A		
2.6	**Jacotin**	*Michael Archangele*	c1–c3–c4–f4		A‖E	III	
2.7	**Jacotin**	*Rogamus te, Virgo Maria*	c1–c3–c4–f4		A‖D	I/II	
2.8	**Caen**	*Judica me, Deus*	c2–c2–c4–f4		E[A]‖D	I/II	
2.9	Caen	*Sanctificavit Dominus*	c1–c3–c4–f4		G‖G		
2.10	Maistre Jan	*O benignissime Domine Jesu*	c1–c3–c4–f4		A		
2.11	**Eustachius**	*Benedic anima mea*	c1–c3–c4–f4		B[E]‖E‖C♯‖[A]	III	
2.12	**Mouton**	*Illuminare Hierusalem*	g2–c2–c3–f3	♭	F‖F	V	
2.13	Mouton	*O Christe Redemptor*	g2–c2–c3–f3	♭	G‖G		
2.14	Mouton	*Corde et animo*	c1–c3–c4–f4	♭	F		
2.15	Mouton	*Amicus Dei, Nicolaus*	g2–c2–c3–c4		G‖G		
2.16	**Mouton**	*Congregati sunt gentes*	c1–c3–c4–f4		D‖D	I/II	4
2.17	**Mouton**	*Peccata mea, Domine (a5 ex 4)*	c3–c3–f4–f4	♭♭	G	[-]	-
2.18	Mouton	*Factum est silentium*	g2–c2–c3–c4		G‖G		
2.19	Mouton	*Homo quidam*	c1–c3–c4–f4	♭	F		
2.20	Mouton	*Maria Virgo*	c1–c3–c4–f4	♭	G‖G		
2.21	**Lhéritier**	*Dum complerentur*	c1–c3–c4–f4	♭	G‖G		11
2.22	Mouton	*Non nobis Domine*	c1–c3–c4–f4	♭	F‖F		
2.23	Mouton	*Noe noe psallite*	g2–c2–c3–c4	♭	G		
2.24	La Fage	*Elisabeth Zacharie*	c1–c3–c4–f4		B[G]‖G		
2.25	Eustachius	*Omnes gentes plaudite*	c1–c3–c4–f4		E[A]‖D		

[81] RISM 1519[1]; table based on film of GB-Lbm. Partial modern eds. in Gehrenbeck, "*Motetti de la Corona*", and Sherr, *Selections*.

Table A3.8 *Motetti de la Corona libro tertio*[82]

No.	Attribution	Text	Clefs	Signature	Final	1525	1529
3.1	Josquin	*Huc me sydereo*	c1–f4–c3–c4–f4–f4	♭	A‖A[D]		
3.2	**Josquin**	***Praeter rerum seriem***	**c1–c3–c3–c4–f4–f4**	♭	**G‖G**		**16**
3.3	**Josquin**	***Ave nobilissima creatura***	**c1–c4–c4–c4–f4–f4**	♭	**A‖A[D]**		**17**
3.4	**Josquin**	***Virgo salutiferi***	**c1–c4–c4–c4–f4**	♭	**B♭‖C‖G**		**18**
3.5	Le Brung	*Recumbentibus undecim discipulis*	c1–c4–c4–f4–f4	♭	C‖C‖G		
3.6	**Josquin**	***Stabat mater dolorosa***	**g2–c3–c3–c4–f4**	♭	**G[C]‖F**	**V**	
3.7	**Josquin**	***Miserere mei Deus***	**c1–c3–c4–c4–f4**		**E‖E‖A**	**III**	
3.8	Mouton	*Quis dabit oculis nostris*	c1–c3–c4–f4		A‖G[E]‖E		
3.9	Pesenti	*Tulerunt Dominum*	c2–c4–c4–f4		E[A]‖G[E]		
3.10	**Josquin**	***Alma redemptoris mater***	**c4–c3–c3–f3**	♭	**A‖F**	**V**	
3.11	Josquin	*Domine ne in furore*	c4–c4–c4–f4		A‖G[E]		
3.12	Mouton	*Quam pulchra es*	c4–c4–c4–f4	♭	C[F]‖C[F]		
3.13		*Ecce nunc benedicite*	c2–c3–c4–f4		E		
3.14	Compère	*O bone Jesu*	c1–c3–c3–f3		G		
3.15	[Mouton]	*Felix namque es*	g2–c3–c3–c4	♭	G‖G		
3.16	Carpentras	*Cantate Domino*	c1–c3–c4–f3		B[E]‖B[E]		

[82] RISM 1519²; table based on film of GB-Lbm. Partial modern eds. in Gehrenbeck, "*Motetti de la Corona*", and Sherr, *Selections*.

MUSIC ANTHOLOGIES, THEORY
TREATISES, AND THE REFORMATION

NUREMBERG IN THE 1530S AND 1540S

> But, as for that which pertains to teaching examples . . . here they will
> find only the choicest, and those acquired from the best musicians by
> means of unusual effort.
>
> Sebald Heyden, Musicae, 1537

The imperial city of Nuremberg was one of the most important centers on the trade route from Venice to the north and the nexus of printing and publishing for the German-speaking world in the sixteenth century.[1] Between 1490 and 1550, more than sixty booksellers and printers were active in the city, which was also home to a strong music-theory tradition. The distinctive northern humanistic leanings of the city's theorists were shaped by associations with the Latin schools of the city – particularly those of St. Sebald, St. Lorenz, the Spitalskirche of the Holy Ghost, and St. Egidius.[2] Among theory treatises published in Nuremberg were:[3]

Johannes Cochlaeus, *De musica* (1511) and *Tetrachordum musices* (1512);
Sebald Heyden, *Musicae stoicheiosis* (1532), *Musicae* (1537), and *De arte canendi* (1540);

---

[1] The best English-language overview of Renaissance Nuremberg is Gerald Strauss, *Nuremberg in the Sixteenth Century: City Politics and Life Between Middle Ages and Modern Times*, rev. ed. (Bloomington: Indiana University Press, 1976). The most important study of musical life in sixteenth-century Nuremberg is Bartlett Butler, "Liturgical Music in Sixteenth-Century Nürnberg: A Socio-musical Study," Ph.D. dissertation, University of Illinois (1970), 2 vols. (UMI 71–14,690). Several recent studies have begun to address Nuremberg's music publishing firms in the period of concern here: Mariko Teramoto and Armin Brinzing, *Katalog der Musikdrucke des Johannes Petreius in Nürnberg*, Catalogus Musicus 14 (Kassel: Bärenreiter, 1993); Mariko Teramoto, *Die Psalmmotettendrucke des Johannes Petrejus in Nürnberg*, Frankfurter Beiträge zur Musikwissenschaft 10 (Tutzing: Schneider, 1983); Susan Jackson, "Berg and Neuber: Music Printers in Sixteenth-Century Nuremberg," Ph.D. dissertation, The City University of New York (1998), 2 vols. (UMI 9820545); and Royston Gustavson, "Hans Ott, Hieronymus Formschneider, and the *Novum et insigne opus musicum* (Nuremberg 1537–38)," Ph.D. dissertation, University of Melbourne (1998).

[2] The general background to musical life in sixteenth-century Nuremberg provided here relies heavily on the magisterial study of Butler, "Liturgical Music in Sixteenth-Century Nürnberg."

[3] Publication dates given here indicate the first publication in Nuremberg. Cochlaeus's *De musica* was first published in Cologne in 1507; Listenius's treatise was first published in Wittenberg in 1533. See the Bibliography for full details of publishers and reprintings. This selective list of treatises was compiled from Paul Cohen, *Die Nürnberger Musikdrucker im sechzehnten Jahrhundert* (Erlangen: Höfer & Limmert, 1927); Åke Davidsson, *Bibliographie der Musiktheoretischen Drucke des 16. Jahrhunderts* (Baden-Baden: Heitz, 1962); Teramoto and Brinzing, *Katalog der Musikdrucke*; and Teramoto, *Die Psalmmotettendrucke*.

Johann Spangenberg, *Quaestiones musicae in usum scholoae Northusianae* (1536);

Nicolaus Listenius, *Musica* (1539);

Heinrich Faber, *Ad musicam practicam introductio* (1550) and *Compendiolum musicae* (1555);

Adrian Petit Coclico, *Compendiolum musices* and *Musica reservata* (1552);

Ambros Wilphlingseder, *Musica Teutsch* (1561) and *Erotemata musicae practicae* (1563);

Several of these treatises were also published in Wittenberg and point either directly or indirectly to the reformist sympathies of their authors. Any book published in Nuremberg had to be approved by the City Council and Nuremberg became a center for the production of Lutheran and other Reformation theological literature, even as it precariously maintained its position as an imperial city with professed loyalty to the Catholic Emperor. Nuremberg was one of the first cities to embrace the Reformation and it was exceptional in that both patricians and the populace sided with Luther. Bonds between Nuremberg and Wittenberg were established as early as 1517. Many Lutheran clergy, trained in Wittenberg, were put into place in the city's churches and schools. In 1530, Nuremberg signed the Augsburg Confession, but the City Council carefully attempted to avoid a break with Charles V, adopting a "policy of appearances." This policy conceded nothing theological but sought to minimize the external differences in the celebration of the liturgy and the mass in Nuremberg retained most of the external features of the Roman mass, with a complete ordinary and in the proper of the mass only the loss of the offertory. German was used for the didactic portions of the liturgy and a separate sermon service was established between *Frühmeße* and the celebration of *Tagamt*. Chorales were part of the sermon service; chant was retained for the mass. Of the offices, vespers and a psalm office before *Tagamt* remained. Rather than the appointment of specific psalms, the Psalter was sung (in Latin) in numerical order throughout the year.[4]

The publication in Nuremberg of the treatises by Heyden, Spangenberg, and Listenius, along with the appearance of several large music anthologies, took place in the decade following the adoption of the Nuremberg *Kirchenordnung* in 1533. This intersection offers extraordinarily fertile ground for an exploration of the convergence of early Lutheran tastes, the music which will have served those tastes, and musical and theoretical representation of Reformation, Catholic, and Imperial ideologies. The importance of music in the liturgy, its traditional status in the quadrivium, and its expanding role in society guaranteed its position in cultural life even though the city of Nuremberg was neither a cathedral, court, nor university city. The patricians were directly or indirectly responsible for musical developments, as for almost all other aspects of the closely regulated life of the conservative city. The

---

[4] A detailed discussion of the implications of the "policy of appearances" for the Nuremberg liturgy and the political expediency which necessitated it is contained in Butler, "Liturgical Music in Sixteenth-Century Nürnberg," 78–154.

close association of music and education in the Latin schools fostered the notion that Latin and musical excellence were essential components of the patrician style.[5]

The relatively large group of treatises published between 1532 and 1540 was accompanied by a similar boom in music publishing. The first books of polyphonic music printed from movable type published in Nuremberg appeared in 1534,[6] following the publication from woodblocks of Hans Gerle's lute tablature.[7] Two printers were responsible for almost all of the music issues in the ensuing decade: Formschneider and Petreius. An unprecedented number of large anthologies of motets issued from their presses between 1537 and 1542 and both firms published anthologies of masses in 1539.[8] All told, Formschneider and Petreius printed more than 300 motets just between 1537 and 1539.

MUSIC IN THE LATIN SCHOOLS: THE NUREMBERG TRADITION

Many of the authors of treatises listed above were directly affiliated with schools in Nuremberg; their treatises were textbooks intended for use in the Latin schools. The theologians and musicians who worked and taught at these schools during the sixteenth century included Cochlaeus, Heyden, Wilphlingseder, Leonhard Lechner, Veit Deitrich, and Andreas Osiander.[9] The rector (also called the school master) of the Latin school was expected to be not only a scholar but also a competent musician: he was responsible for the school choir that was charged with providing both chant and polyphony daily in the church. A contemporary illustration from a Latin grammar book published in Nuremberg provides an indication of the form that musical education may have taken. The woodcut from the frontispiece of Paulus Naivis's *Latinum idioma*, shown in Figure 4.1, illustrates a schoolroom with music notation on a board in the background.[10]

---

[5] Butler, "Liturgical Music in Sixteenth-Century Nürnberg," 47–52.

[6] Hans Ott, ed., *Hundert und ainundzewintzig newe Lieder von berümbtenn dieser Kunst gesetzt* (Nuremberg: Formschneider, 1534) [RISM 1534[17]; Gustavson F20].

[7] Hans Gerle, *Musica teusch auf die Instrument der grossen und kleinen Geygen auch Lautten* (Nuremberg: Formschneider, 1532) and *idem, Tabulatur auff die Lautten* (Nuremberg: Formschneider, 1533) ed. Hélène Charnassé, *Hans Gerle: Tablature pour les Luths (Nuremberg: Formschneider, 1533),* Publications de la Société Française de Musicologie 5, 1 (Paris: Chez Heugel, 1975–78) [Howard Mayer Brown, *Instrumental Music Printed before 1600: A Bibliography* (Cambridge MA: Harvard University Press, 1965), 1533/1; Gustavson F21].

[8] It is interesting to observe an order of publishing similar to that of Petrucci's, spanning a comparable time period: first, collections of secular songs (*Odhecaton* (1501)), followed closely by motets (*Motetti A* (1502)), followed by masses. (In Petrucci's case, the first mass publications were individual composer prints (1503) followed by his *Fragmenta missarum* (1505) and *Missarum diversorum auctorum liber primus* (1509).)

[9] Coclico lived and taught in Nuremberg, although not at any of the Latin schools. On Coclico's close association with Berg and Neuber, see Jackson, "Berg and Neuber."

[10] Paulus Niavis, *Latinum idioma pro parvulis editum* (Nuremberg: Friedrich Creussner, 1494). This appears to have been a popular textbook in German Latin schools, first published in Nuremberg in about 1482 and reprinted throughout the German-speaking areas of Europe. This frontispiece is frequently cited and reproduced. Most recently, see Jessie Ann Owens, *Composers at Work* (New York: Oxford University Press, 1997), 83, and Heinz Zirnbauer, *Musik in der alten Reichsstadt Nürnberg*, Beiträge zur Geschichte und Kultur der Stadt Nürnberg Herausgegeben im Auftrag des Stadtrats Nürnberg von der Stadtbibliothek 9 (Nuremberg: GAA-Verlag, n.d.), 19.

4.1 Paulus Niavis, *Latinum idioma*, frontispiece (Stadtbibliothek Nürenberg. Reproduced by permission.)

COCHLAEUS AND THE PRE-REFORMATION TRADITION

Johannes Cochlaeus was appointed the school master of St. Lorenz in 1510; he was highly sought after for the position by members of the City Council who desired his combination of humanistic learning and musical credentials.[11] His music treatise, *Tetrachordum musices* (1511), was written for use at the school. The didactic work, in question and answer form, went through at least seven editions. The treatise is a slender, upright quarto of thirty folios. As its name implies, it is organized as a tetrachord with four parts comprising: the elements of music; Gregorian chant; the eight tones; and mensural music. These are listed at the bottom of the title page, reproduced in Figure 4.2.[12]

The treatise was closely tied to the pedagogy of the Latin school, concluding with four-part hymns that were demonstrations of the various poetic meters which were apparently sung daily at the beginning and end of lessons.[13] The Iambic illustration, *Veni creator spiritus*, is reproduced in Figure 4.3. The simple homorhythmic style along with indications of line breaks would make it easy enough to read these parts together, although text is underlaid only for the upper voice, the part sung by the school boys. The ordering of voices on the page reflects the contrapuntal discussion of the treatise, implying compositional priorities: cantus, tenor, bassus, and finally altus. The pedagogical orientation of the treatise suggests the examples were provided for "recitation" as part of the textbook, much on the model of Latin grammars. Indeed, Cochlaeus refers in this section of the treatise to his *Quadrivium grammatices*, also published Nuremberg in 1511. As a textbook, the *Tetrachordum musices* provided the means for the boys to gain the required abilities to fulfill their obligations to provide plainsong and polyphony for the church.[14] Most of the examples are didactic teaching material consisting of monophony in Gothic chant

---

[11] Part of the communication between the Council member Kress and Cochlaeus is reproduced in Klaus Wolfgang Niemöller, *Untersuchungen zu Musikpflege und Musikunterricht an den deutschen Lateinschulen vom ausgehenden Mittelalter bis um 1600*, Kölner Beiträge zur Musikforschung 54 (Regensburg: Gustav Bosse, 1969), 330–31. The cantor (until 1509) and school master of St. Sebald (the other most prominent Latin school in Nuremberg) from 1510 to 1516 had been a student of Cochlaeus's in Cologne, extending Cochlaeus's influence across the schools of the city.

[12] The *Tetrachordum musices* was based in part on Cochleus's earlier *Musica*, published in 1507 in Cologne. The *Musica*, in turn, relied heavily on the *Opus Aureum* of Wollick and Schanppecher. The background to *Tetrachordum musices* is discussed in Clement Miller, introduction to the translation of *Tetrachordum musices*, Musicological Studies and Documents 23 (n.p.: American Institute of Musicology, 1970). See also Karl G. Fellerer, "Die Köllner Musiktheoretische Schule des 16. Jahrhunderts," in *Renaissance-muziek 1400–1600 donum natalicium Rene Bernard Lenaerts*, ed. Jozef Robijns, Musicologica Lovaniensia 1 (Leuven: Katholieke Universiteit Seminarie voor Muziekwetenschap, 1969), 121–30. On Wollick and Schanppecher, see Klaus Niemöller, *Nicolaus Wollick und sein Musiktraktat*, Beiträge zur rheinischen Musikgeschichte 13 (Cologne: Arno Volk Verlag, 1956) and *idem, Die Musica figurativa des Melchior Schanppecher*, Beiträge zur rheinischen Musikgeschichte 50 (Cologne: Arno Volk Verlag, 1961).   [13] Niemöller, *Untersuchungen*, 339.

[14] *Ibid.*, 339–44, documents the kinds of polyphony that might have been sung in the first part of the century in pre-Reformation Nuremberg. There is relatively little information available, and Cochlaeus's treatise does not offer any pointers to specific repertories. It is not clear how much music was supplied by the school masters and cantors of the various churches, but few if any compositions by most of them are known to survive.

Tetrachozdum Muſi

ces Joannis Coclei Mozici. Artiũ Ma=
giſtri:Nurnberge nuper cõtextum:p iuuentu=
tis Laurentiane eruditione imprimis:dein ad ce=
terorũ in muſicis Tyrũculorũ ſalubriorem
planiorẽq̃ eruditionem/nunc prima
ſui Aeditiõe Typis calcographo
rum exaratum.deo Au=
ſpice,in lucem
prodit.

Bilibaldi Pirckheimer Ad Io.Coclitẽ Epigrãma.

Ingenium Codes tribuit tibi docta Minerua
Deliciaſq̃ Venus/pulcher Apollo lyram
At numeros faciles varia & diſcrimina vocum
Mercurius pariter Theſpiadumq̃ chorus
Quid mirum ſuperas ſi cunctos arte canendi
Cum faueant ceptis/numina tanta tuis

Chelidonius Muſophilus ad lectorem.

Delius antiſtes Muſarum carmen olimpo
Concentu vario dulciſonoq̃ canit
Quin pelago ludunt modulamina blanda canore
Sirenes.aer audit aueſq̃ ſuas
Necnon & lætas numeris vocalibus odas
Orpheus Eliſio perſonat.atq̃ Linus
Codes pieridum ſocius.iuuat arte Camenas
Pegaſeumq̃ melos percinit atq̃ docet

Huius Tetrachordi Quattuor tractatus.

Primus	De Muſices elementis	
Secundus	De Muſica Gregoriana	Quorũ quilibet decẽ ca=
Tertius	De Octo tonis Meli	pita complectitur
Quartus	De Muſica menſurali	

4.2 Cochlaeus, *Tetrachordum musices*, title page

notation (*Hofnagel*), as in his examples of the modes (Fig. 4.4). The brief section on counterpoint includes examples on ten-line staves.[15] It concludes with four-part harmonizations in Gothic chant notation of the psalm tones (Fig. 4.5). The psalm tone appears variously in either the discantus or tenor voice.

Cochlaeus left Nuremberg in 1515. He earned a doctorate in theology in 1517

---

[15] For an overview of the use of ten-line staves in theory treatises and the kinds of examples for which they are normally used, see Owens, *Composers at Work*, 38–45. Benito Rivera, "Harmonic Theory in Musical Treatises of the Late Fifteenth and Early Sixteenth Centuries," *Music Theory Spectrum* 1 (1979), 80–95, discusses Cochlaeus's examples of cadences which are presented on a ten-line staff.

Tǔc veniǎt rifus/tǔc paup cornua fumit   Tǔc dolor & curæ/rugaʠ frǒtʃ abǐʦ
Confcia mẽs recti famæ mẽdacia ridet   Sed nos in viciū credula turba fum
Sⅽ₃ vt fuluū fpectaſ in ignibus aurū   Tẽpore fic duro eſt infpiciẽda fides
Donec eris fœlix/multos numerabis amicos Tpa fi fuerint nubila/folus eris/
¶ Carmina vero/quæ nos fub hoc melo quottidie in noua noſtra fchola cani⸗
mus/his tanⱪ abortiua fubiunguntur.
Mane tuū petim᾽ numẽ/o fpūs alme   Senfibus anfis nubila craffa fuges
Pectora nfa facro᾽pfunde liquore Helicǒis Vt fontes nfos docta Thalia colat
Mentibus o nfis illabere/redde furorem   Diuinū/vates quo caluere facri

Melos Jambicum.

Veni creator fpūs.Mẽtes tuorū vifita/imple fupna gſa.Quæ tu creaſti pectora

Tenor

Baſſus

Altus

Cǒditor alme fiderū/Eterna lux credẽtiū/Chriſte redẽptor oīm/Exaudi p̄.fup.
Veni redẽptor gẽtiū/Oſide partū virgis/Mireſ oſne fcℏm/Taſ decet part᾽ deū
A fol᾽ort᾽ cardie:Adufⱪ₃ terræ limitẽ:Chriſtū canam᾽ principẽ:Natū ma.vir.
Hoſtis herodes impie:xp̄m venire qd times:nǒ arripit mortalia:q reg.dat.ce.
¶ Hæc metra Iambica fūt dimetra:ⱪ in facris hymnis frequẽtiora funt. At fiſe
genus nec apud Horaciū:nec apud Boeciū repire potui. Vnū Iambicū habet
Horatii Epodon trimetrū Plura habet Boecius fed trimetra quoⱪ.

                                                      F iiij

4.3 Cochlaeus, *Veni creator spiritus*, *Tetrachordum musices*, sig. Fiiiʳ

in Ferrara and was ordained to the priesthood in Rome.[16] He published no music
books after the *Tetrachordum musices*, devoting himself to theological writing that
was virulent in its opposition to Lutheranism and Calvinism.[17] His music theoretical legacy was carried out in very different ways by two of his pupils: Sebald

[16] The outlines of Cochlaeus's career are given in Clement A. Miller, "Cochlaeus [Dobneck, Wendelstein],
Johannes," *New Grove Dictionary of Music and Musicians*, ed. S. Sadie (London: Macmillan, 1980), IV: 4, 512.

[17] A worklist of Cochlaeus's publications is provided in Martin Spahn, *Johannes Cochlaeus: ein Lebensbild aus der Zeit
der Kirchenspaltung* (Berlin: F. L. Dames, 1898).

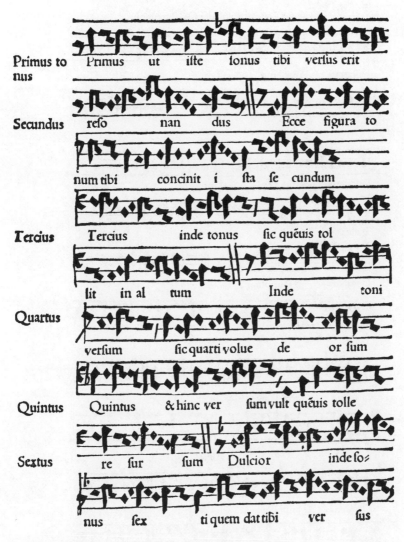

4.4 Cochlaeus, *Tetrachordum musices*, sig. Dii^v, examples of the modes

Heyden and Heinrich Glarean. The first was a staunch reformer with Calvinist sympathies; the latter was a Catholic humanist with ties to Erasmus. The two men shared a background molded by the pedagogy of the German Latin school and university study, but that background played out in very different ways because of the theological agendas that ultimately shaped their music-theoretic writing.

4.5 Cochlaeus, *Tetrachordum musices*, sig. Fii[r], harmonizations of the psalm tones

REFORMATION IDEOLOGY AND THE WRITINGS OF
SEBALD HEYDEN

If reprints may be taken as any indication, Cochlaeus's *Tetrachordum musices* remained the standard textbook of the Nuremberg schools into the 1530s.[18] In 1532, the first of three treatises by Sebald Heyden, his *Musicae* Στοιχείωσις [*stoicheio-*

---

[18] The treatise was printed in 1511 by Weissenburger, in 1512 and 1514 by Stuchs, in 1514, 1516, 1517, 1520, and 1526 by Peypus. (These dates are cited after Cohen, *Die Nürnberger Musikdrucker* and Davidsson, *Bibliographie*.) The treatise was never published outside Nuremberg.

sis] was published by Peypus, the same printer of all of the later reprints of Cochlaeus's *Tetrachordum musices*. The content of Sebald Heyden's music treatises is often discussed without an understanding of the role of music in the Latin schools, in the liturgy, and in Nuremberg more generally in the 1530s. Such an approach obscures the fundamental meaning of Heyden's use of polyphonic examples in the second and third versions of his music treatise. Similarly the convenience of a facsimile and translation of the 1540 edition has had the unfortunate effect of deflecting attention away from the earlier versions as *De arte canendi* is viewed as the definitive work.[19] The continuities of both pedagogy and content, as well as his debt to Cochlaeus, are often remarked, while the distinctiveness of his single-tactus mensural theory is highlighted.[20] The different relationship of Heyden, in comparison to his predecessors, with both chant and polyphony and by extension with his music examples is less obvious, especially when the final version of his treatise is read primarily as a self-contained theoretical exposition.

Heyden entered the school at St. Lorenz in 1505 and was a pupil there when Cochlaeus arrived. He matriculated at the University of Ingolstadt in 1513, and returned to Nuremberg in 1519. His first appointment was at the school of the Spitalkirche, followed by an appointment as rector of the St. Sebald school in 1525. The first Lutheran masses in Nuremberg had been celebrated at St. Sebald and St. Lorenz in 1524; the City Council issued a prohibition against the saying of Roman mass on 16 March 1525.[21] Heyden was clearly in sympathy with the reformer faction in Nuremberg relatively shortly after his return to the city following his university studies. In 1523, he supplied the Reichstag with a new text for the Marian antiphon "Salve regina," changing it to a Christological text: "Salve regina, mater misericordiae" became "Jesu Christe, rex misericordiae".[22] His first publications in 1524 and 1525 were theological tracts, but in the 1530s he began publishing a series of textbooks. The first was the *Formulae puerilium colloquiorum*, published in 1530 and reprinted through the eighteenth century. This elementary textbook was a simple Latin–German wordbook, also published under the title *Nomenclatura*.[23] His "Elements of Music," *Musicae stoicheiosis*, followed the *Formulae* and the *Leges scholasticae* in 1532.[24] All three editions of Heyden's music treatise are dedicated to Hieronymus Baumgartner, a Nuremberg patrician and member of the City Council, but the prefatory letters are completely rewritten in each edition. These prefaces provide a fascinating means for understanding Heyden's changing relationship to music examples and printed music.

---

[19] Sebald Heyden, *De arte canendi* (Nuremberg: Petreius, 1540), facsimile, Monuments of Music and Music Literature in Facsimile, II, 149 (New York: Broude Brothers, 1969), translation and transcription by Clement Miller, Musicological Studies and Documents 26 (n.p.: American Institute of Musicology, 1972).

[20] This theory is discussed further below.   [21] Butler, "Liturgical Music in Sixteenth-Century Nürnberg," 78.

[22] The full text appears in Alfred Kosel, *Sebald Heyden (1499–1561): Ein Beitrag zur Geschichte der Nürnberger Schulmusik in der Reformationszeit* (Würzburg: Konrad Triltsch, 1940), 8.

[23] Peter O. Müller, "Sebald Heydens Nomenclatura," *Sprachwissenschaft* 18 (1993), 59–88. These books are frequently found bound with other texts of Latin schools, such as Johannes Murmellius's *Loci communes*. Such is the case with two of the five copies in the university library in Munich (shelfmarks 8°Philol 1486 and 8°Philol 705).

[24] A bibliography of Heyden's writings appears in Kosel, *Sebald Heyden*, 57–59.

To understand the preface to the first edition of 1532, it is important to take account of the political and theological situation in Nuremberg. Polyphony appears to have been more or less removed from the reform liturgy in Nuremberg churches from as early as 1525, even though it continued to play an important role in the liturgies of other Lutheran centers such as Augsburg and Wittenberg.[25] Three factions – the patricians, the clergy, and educators – had a strong stake in the issue of liturgy and music that was being fiercely debated in 1532 in the final stages of the preparation of Nuremberg's *Kirchenordnung*. At the time, it would appear that Latin chant was the predominant music of the liturgy and that the boys of the Latin schools fulfilled daily choir duties. Sacred polyphony – in Latin or German – appears to have been practiced for recreational, educational, and devotional purposes, but was not normally included in the liturgy.[26] In this climate, Heyden's textbook, and particularly its dedication, was an extraordinarily strong attempt to force the hand of Baumgartner in the crafting of the *Kirchenordnung*.[27] Five of the forty-four pages of the treatise are devoted to the prefatory letter to Baumgartner, followed by three pages of epitaphs for Hieronimus Ebner, a recently deceased Nuremberg patrician. The treatise itself covers topics similar to those of Cochlaeus's *Tetrachordum musices*, although in a more superficial way. There is a marked difference, however. Even though relatively few music examples appear (and the four of polyphony are all demonstrations of proportions), none of the monophonic examples is in chant notation. Even the simple monophonic representations of the modes (shown in Fig. 4.6) are presented in mensural notation. The preface supplies the reason for this departure from tradition: Heyden is using this treatise as an attack on the current practice of music in the liturgy.[28] He is not, as one might imagine to be the case with a musician–educator, trying to reinstate polyphony. Far from it. Rather, he is arguing against schoolboys being forced to sing chant in church, claiming that they are overtaxed by this burden. He further suggests that the use of a foreign language in worship was detrimental because the boys could not understand what they were singing. As he framed it, the primary objective of Heyden's book was to enable the serious student to benefit from music-making in the Ciceronian sense that held up the study and practice of music as refreshment for the mind. He shared the Platonic humanists' fears of the dangers of music and preferred to limit its use to those who had already demonstrated ample self-discipline in their studies. True worship as intended by the church

---

[25] For a detailed discussion of the musical changes in the liturgy in the period 1524–1535, see Butler, "Liturgical Music in Sixteenth-Century Nürnberg," 395–409.

[26] Butler, "Liturgical Music in Sixteenth-Century Nürnberg," 425.

[27] Butler, "Liturgical Music in Sixteenth-Century Nürnberg," advances this argument and provides a detailed summary of the preface to Heyden's *Musicae*, 417–26.

[28] Miller points out that Heyden claims that anyone who understands the elements of mensural music will also understand plainsong as his justification for omitting chant notation ("Sebald Heyden's *De arte canendi*: Background and Contents," *Musica disciplina* 24 (1970), 82).

Per hæc Interualla diligenter obferuata, faáíle tum erit, de
cuiuslibet cantus Tono iudicare, hoc modo.

OMNis cantus in re finiens, qui fuæ melodiæ tractũ per
re & la, Diapente potißimum effingit, Primi Toni eft. Sin
per fa & re Hemiditonum, Secundi eft.

Exenplum primi.

Exemplum Secundi.

CANTilenæ quæ in mi deficrint, fi mi & fa Diapente
cũ Hemitonio fæpius fonuerint, Tertij Toni funt. Verũ fi mi
et la Dia teffaron fubinde repetiuerint, Quarti.

Exemplum Tertij Toni.

Exemplum Quarti Toni.

Cantio terminata in fa, quæ fuperne Diapente fa crebrius

4.6 Heyden, *Musicae stoicheiosis* (1532), examples of the modes (Bayersiche
Staatsbibliothek Mus.th. 1560°. Reproduced by permission.)

fathers, in Heyden's view, did not require protracted singing of chant, but did
require increased spiritual concentration.[29]

The text of the *Musicae stoicheiosis* became the substance of Heyden's later
editions of the treatise, although its form was altered so radically as to be hardly

[29] fols. A2[r]–A2[v]: Ita et Musicam nulla alia caussa magis admittamus, quam ut inde animis ex severioribus studiis
defessis, pristinum vigorem restauremus. Ut ita non viciosis voluptatibus augendis, sed virtutibus amplectendis:
non emasculandis iuvenum animis, sed ad honestatem ac fortitudinem accendendis, ipsa deserviat. Atq[ue] utinam
saltem non ineptius de Musica olim statuissent templariarum Ceremoniarum autores. Sic enim ea, quae ingenuis
pueris cotidie in templis iamdiu decantanda fuerunt, non tam labor, quam defessoru[m] ex recenti studio
animoru[m] recreatio habita fuissent. Quod equidem et priscos illos primaevae Ecclesie Proceres, ita voluisse con-
tenderim, ut nulla alia ratione eiusmodi Musicas Ceremonias instituerent, quam ut plebs pueriq[ue] Christiani
habere[n]t, quibus se ab audito verbo, caeterisq[ue] id genus seriis exercitiis, oblectarent reficerentq[ue]. Est enim
et spiritui suus ludus sua[que] remissio, sicubi nimium intensus defatigetur. Alioqui quod ad rem divinam serio
adtinebat, certe non intensiore voce, sed collectiore animo faciendum erat.　　　*(continued on next page)*

recognizable.[30] As Miller observed, through the change from narrative to question-and-answer format and the insertion of music examples, the edition grew from twenty-six folios in 1532, to 115 pages in 1537, and 163 in 1540.[31]

THE EXAMPLES OF HEYDEN'S *MUSICAE* (1537) AND THE NUREMBERG MUSIC ANTHOLOGIES

Heyden's *Musicae, id est artis canendi* (1537) began with a newly written preface. The polemic on plainchant was largely removed (although overt treatment of plainsong was still noticeably absent from the treatise). In its place was a discussion and justification of the many polyphonic examples that had now been added to the treatise. From the perspective of the present study, this preface constitutes one of the very few occasions when a theorist provides information not only on how he intends his examples to function, but where he has obtained them. No doubt this section of the preface appears because such inclusion of examples was still not customary in a treatise. The precedent for Heyden's inclusion of some forty-four notated examples comes in no small part from Gaffurio's *Practica musicae*, because the enlarged version of Heyden's treatise focuses almost entirely on questions of tactus and proportion,[32]

footnote 29 (*cont.*)

[And so let us admit Music for no other reason rather than to restore thereby the native vigor to souls exhausted by more taxing studies, so that it might serve not to increase vicious pleasures, but to embrace virtues; not to emasculate the spirits of youths, but to incite them to honor and courage. And would that at least the authors of the templar ceremonies had not in former times made incompetent regulations concerning Music. For then those things that well-born boys have had to sing daily in churches for a long time now, would have been regarded not so much a burden as a recreation for spirits exhausted from recent study. Which is what I at least should contend that those ancient leaders of the primeval Church wanted, so that they instituted musical ceremonies of this kind for no other reason than that the people, including Christian boys, would have a means of delighting and refreshing themselves from listening to the Gospel and other serious exercises of that kind. For the spirit has its own proper sport and relaxation, whenever it becomes excessively taxed and fatigued. Otherwise, where matters of divinity were seriously concerned, certainly one had to do not with additional taxing of the voice, but with a more collected spirit.]

fols. A3ᵛ–A4ʳ: Tum etiam quod hanc artem solos eos decere contendo, qui alioqui gravibus negociis occupati aut ingenuis studiis addicti, sicubi ita sudando lassitudinem contrahant, ut habeant, quo sese successivo tempore oblectando reficiant. Nam de illiteratis ac ociose inertibus cum Platone pronuncio, eos per varios canendi modos, multomagis corrumpi ac emasculari quam refici.

[Then too, as for my contention that this art becomes only those who, being otherwise occupied by serious business or devoted to noble pursuits, so that whenever they incur weariness by so exerting themselves, they might have a means of refreshment by delighting themselves in the time that follows, I hold with Plato's opinion about the unlettered and those who live in sluggish ease, that they are much more corrupted and emasculated by the various modes of singing than restored.]

[30] Although the *Musicae stoicheiosis* is frequently treated as a separate treatise, as Miller ("Sebald Heyden's *De arte canendi*," 79) observes, Heyden clearly indicates that the 1540 version is the third edition.

[31] Miller, "Sebald Heyden's *De arte canendi*," 79.

[32] Briefly, Heyden viewed tactus and mensuration signs as inseparable. He argued for a simplification of traditional theories of proportions. In sum, he argued that a single, uniform tactus was applicable to all mensuration signs; mensuration signs, in turn, had a constant, unchanging meaning in relation to tactus. Clement Miller summarizes the relationships for all tactus-mensuration relationships in "Sebald Heyden's *De arte canendi*," 85. To no small degree, Heyden's mensural theory has to be seen as an attempt to understand, recover, and interpret compositional and notational procedures that were already antiquated by the time Petrucci printed his repertory in

even though in scope and content, the *Practica* is a very different sort of book. Unlike Aron, Heyden could not count on his readers being able to go to his examples outside the treatise; mere citation would not suffice. Indeed, as he makes clear in a section of the preface discussed below, he has only had the good fortune to study these examples himself through the generosity of Ulrich Starck, a Nuremberg patrician and book collector. And Heyden's notational alterations (in service of his theory of the relationship of mensural signs and tactus) mean that his readers cannot look to just any version of these works, but must observe the specific notational features as Heyden transmits them. When he begins the discussion of examples, he first explains why he has included them:

But, as for that which pertains to teaching examples [praeceptionum exempla], just as boys will find virtually none in the "Elements" [Στοιχειωσις],[33] so here they will find [only] the choicest, and those acquired from the best musicians by means of unusual effort. But since I knew it was scarcely possible that proper altos, tenors, and basses (as they are popularly called) could be found just anywhere for each of the four different vocal parts, due to this scarcity of singers I adopted the plan of writing down only such examples as could be sung correctly among actual groups of boys of about the same age. Among them are [examples] of the kind that we popularly call *fugae*, in which, within a single row of notes, two or three other voices follow their course at fixed intervals [spatiis].[34]

Although Heyden's use of *fugae* for many of his examples is regularly remarked upon, the more obvious point of this section of the preface – that these two- and three-part excerpts are particularly appropriate for singing by the boys who are the intended readers (omitted in the rewritten preface to the edition of 1540) – has been overlooked.[35] Heyden's interest in and inclusion of such examples is a marked departure from other such textbooks, going much further in their pedagogical usefulness than the polyphonic examples of hymns to demonstrate meters that concluded Cochlaeus's *Tetrachordum musices*. These are not arcane mensural examples intended primarily for study; they are specifically chosen to allow boys to sing polyphony in the absence of other voice parts. There was not a tradition of students in Latin schools buying music books, which from all the evidence were very expensive. Rather they copied out and memorized materials provided by their teacher.[36] Generally the teacher supplied these materials by writing them out on a large board in the front of the room[37] (see the illustration in Fig. 4.1). Heyden's treatise

---

the early part of the century. They remained a theoretical preoccupation because of Gaffurio's extensive discussion and exemplification of proportions.   [33] Heyden's treatise of 1532.

[34] The preface of *Musicae, id est artis canendi* is reproduced in Teramoto, *Die Psalmmotettendrucke*, 53–57. My commentary is based on the copy of the treatise in the Bayerische Staatsbibliothek (4° Mus Th 664). I am grateful to Joseph Farrell for his assistance with this translation.

[35] For example, Miller observes: "He sought out the most complex and complicated works to use as examples, works that were intricate in both mensuration and polyphonic texture. For example, from a total of 54 polyphonic compositions in *De Arte Canendi*, 16 are *fugae* for two or three voice parts" ("Sebald Heyden's *De arte canendi*," 84).   [36] This "notebook" culture is discussed further in chapter 5.

[37] Friedrich Sannemann, *Die Musik als Unterrichtsgegenstand in den Evangelischen Lateinschulen des 16. Jahrhunderts*, Musikwissenschaftlichen Studien 4 (Berlin: E. Ebering, 1904), 61–62.

combines the two functions by incorporating examples directly into the textbook. Using so many *fugae* also had the pragmatic effect of saving space: Heyden is able to print extensive polyphonic excerpts that fill only the space of monophonic examples. He need print only a single line from which one or more additional voices are derived (see Fig. 4.7, a duo by Josquin). Had Heyden not used so many *fugae* as examples, the book would have had to be at least half as long again to contain the same amount of polyphony.

The publication of a treatise incorporating so many music examples was also tied to the development in Nuremberg of single-impression printing of music with movable type earlier in the same decade. Formschneider and Petreius between them published an enormous and unprecedented amount of music. Both began their careers as printers in the mid-1520s.[38] In 1536, Petreius published Spangenberg's *Quaestiones musicae in usum scholae Northusiae*, a work dedicated to and published by Georg Rhau of Wittenberg in the same year.[39] Petreius first used a music font, modeled after one designed by Formschneider in 1534, for the publication of Heyden's treatise the year after Spangenberg's. Although Petreius had previously published works like Spangenberg's using woodcuts, it is highly unlikely that he would have been willing to attempt the number of examples of Heyden's treatise and the use of white mensural notation without the ability to typeset the music. By publishing Heyden's treatise, in the form it took in 1537, Petreius may have been attempting to position himself in relation to the market for printed music as he prepared to follow Formschneider's lead. Formschneider's printing of music for the most part was under the editorial direction of Johannes Ott who held the privilege for the music books he printed; his press was not a full-time operation.[40] Petreius,

[38] An overview of Nuremberg printers is available in Teramoto, *Die Psalmmotettendrucke*, 84–85. Petreius's first prints were primarily theological titles, including two by Heyden. (*Adversus hypocritas calumnatiorum* (1524) and *Usum Christum mediatorum esse* (a second edition of *Adversus hypocritas*)). Formschneider, famed as a woodcutter (in Albrecht Dürer's shop), typecutter, and die sinker, began his career as a printer in 1527. In 1532 and 1533, Formschneider printed two lutebooks for Hans Gerle: *Musica Teutsch* and the *Tabulatur auff die Lautten*. In both, woodcuts are used for all the examples. (Heyden's pronouncements against the lute and the distraction that playing it poses for his students suggests by counterexample that a market existed for Gerle's books among patrician families.) It is not surprising the Gerle would choose Formschneider to publish these books, given his reputation as a cutter. In 1534 Formschneider designed, cut, and produced a single-impression music font for the publication of Senfl's *Varia carminum genera* (Gustavson F27), among one of the first uses of such single-impression fonts. See Donald W. Krummel, "Early German Partbook Typefaces," *Gutenburg Jahrbuch* 60 (1985), 81. In the same year, Formschneider printed his first music book commissioned by Johannes Ott, *121 Newe Lieder*. Ott's imperial privilege to publish music was probably the impetus for Formschneider to create a music font. Petreius also began his music printing with a lute book in 1536, *Ein Neugeordnet künstlich Lautenbuch*.

[39] Spangenberg's oft-reprinted didactic treatise is a Latin school text on plainsong. The small octavo volume consists of a series of basic questions and answers. Its publication in Nuremberg during what was still a tumultuous period in terms of the liturgy might represent a response at some level to Heyden's polemic on the requirements for boys to sing chant and his deliberate avoidance of any reference to plainsong in the first edition of his treatise. It also suggests the possibility of its use at other Latin schools in the city while reflecting the many connections of Nuremberg publications to Wittenberg. The few examples in the treatise (mostly of psalmody) are in Gothic chant notation.

[40] Ott was a bookseller and publisher who moved to Nuremberg in 1531. He appears to have been a man of some learning with access to a number of manuscript sources, including the Lochamer Liederbuch and Isaac's *Choralis constantinus*. For the most recent study of Ott, see Gustavson, "Hans Ott."

Quis cantus eſt Primi Toni?

Omnis cantus Primi toni eſt, qui in re finiens, tractum
ſuæ melodiæ per re la Diapente potiſſimum effingit.

Monodia Primi Toni.

Tonus.   Pſalmus.   Magnificat.

Exemplum.

Fuga duum Ioſquini, in Subdiateſſaron, poſt duo těpora.

P 2   Quis

4.7 Heyden, *Musicae* (1537), p. 107, example of the first mode (Bayerische
Staatsbibliothek, 4° Mus.th. 664. Reproduced by permission.)

on the other hand, was a publisher, printer, and bookseller who was adding music to his already substantial list of theoretical and pedagogical titles.

Beyond the pedagogical premises and the technological implications of Heyden's examples, his choices reflect a particular aesthetic sensibility that may be tied closely to Nuremberg and Reformation ideology. Heyden's examples represent a group of composers who were to be featured in the motet and mass prints that Form-schneider and Petreius would issue in the next few years:

> But the boys should realize that I have received these *fugae* on loan not from any old source, but from the best and most approved musicians: Josquin, Obrecht, Pierre de la Rue, Heinrich Isaac, and the like. So that they may hold these books of ours in the greater esteem for this reason as well, provided they know that the examples thus written down here are to be regarded not just as the best, but even so to speak as miracles of the musical art.

The names Josquin and Isaac in particular would be repeatedly highlighted in sub-sequent prefaces of motets and masses; Senfl would be added to their number.[41] Table 4.1 lists Heyden's examples from the 1537 treatise in a compressed form ordered by composer.[42] While Heyden identifies the composer in the majority of his examples, he is far less consistent in identifying the work from which the example is drawn. Most of the examples (thirty-four of forty-five) are excerpted from masses. Heyden's concentration on two- and three-part examples and *fugae* may have pointed him to masses and the reduced texture commonly found in certain parts of polyphonic settings of the ordinary, most notably the Benedictus, Pleni sunt, and Agnus Dei. But the reliance on excerpts from polyphonic masses points to a conundrum of sorts. If, as all the evidence suggests, polyphony was not used liturgically in Nuremberg in this period, why would Heyden include excerpts from polyphonic masses in his treatise? While there may have been a move to restore polyphony from some factions within the city, Heyden seems rather

---

[41] Until the recent work of Teramoto, Gustavson, and Jackson cited above, almost all of the work on these Formschneider and Petreius prints (and the later Berg and Neuber anthologies) had taken as a point of departure the many attributions to Josquin, particularly of psalm motets. For an overview, see Howard Meyer Brown, "Hans Ott, Heinrich Finck and Stoltzer: Early Sixteenth-Century German Motets in Formschneider's Anthologies of 1537 and 1538," in *Von Isaac bis Bach: Studien zur älteren deutschen Musikgeschichte*, ed. Frank Heidlberger (Kassel: Bärenreiter, 1991), 73–84. On the making of the "German" Josquin, see especially Patrick Macey, "Josquin as Classic: *Qui habitat, Memor esto*, and Two Imitations Unmasked," *Journal of the Royal Musical Association* 118 (1993), 1–43; Stephanie Schlagel, "Josquin des Prez and his Motets: A Case Study in Sixteenth-Century Reception History," Ph.D. dissertation, University of North Carolina-Chapel Hill (1996; UMI 9715763); Jessie Ann Owens, "How Josquin Became Josquin," in *Music in Renaissance Cities and Courts: Studies in Honor of Lewis Lockwood*, ed. Jessie Ann Owens and Anthony M. Cummings (Warren MI: Harmonie Park Press, 1997).

[42] A detailed list of Heyden's examples, comparing the 1537 and 1540 editions, supplied with Heyden's captions appears in the Appendix to this chapter. This list was greatly facilitated by the inventories in Mariko Teramoto and Armin Brinzing, *Katalog der Musikdrucke*, and the commentaries on the examples of the 1540 edition by Clement Miller, trans. *De arte canendi*, Musicological Studies and Documents 26 ([Rome]: American Institute of Musicology, 1972) and *idem*, "Sebald Heyden's *De arte canendi*," 79. The numbering of examples in Table 4.1 and the Appendix follows Teramoto and Brinzing.

Table 4.1 *Composers and works represented in Heyden, Musicae (1537)*

Composer	Work	1537	Composer named	Title given	Concordance in Petrucci print
Agricola	*Missa Malheur me bat*	13, 40	✓	—	*Misse Alexandri Agricola, 1504*
	Missa Le serviteur	44	✓	—	*Misse Alexandri Agricola, 1504*
Sixt Dietrich	*Omnis caro foenum*	42	—	✓	
Ghiselin	*Missa Gratieuse*	31–33; 36–37	✓	—	*Misse Ghiselin, 1503*
	Missa Narayge	20	✓	✓	*Misse Ghiselin, 1504*
Isaac	*De radice Jesse*	28	✓	✓	*Misse 1505*
Josquin	*Missa Quant j'ay au cueur*	12, 14	✓	—	*Motetti B 1503*
	Ave verum corpus	18, 43	✓	—	*Missarum Josquin Liber Tertius 1514*
	Missa ad fugam	25	✓	—	*Liber Primus Missae Josquin 1502*
	Missa Gaudeamus	16	✓	—	*Missarum Josquin Liber Secundus 1505*
	Missa Hercules Dux Ferrariae	8, 41	✓	✓	*Liber Primus Missae Josquin 1502*
	Missa L'homme armé sexti toni	1	✓	—	*Liber Primus Missae Josquin 1502*
	Missa L'homme armé super voces musicales	23, 24, 26	✓	✓	*Missarum Josquin Liber Secundus 1505*
	Missa Malheur me bat	19	✓	—	*Missarum Josquin Liber Tertius 1514*
	Missa Mater patris	3, 4, 5	✓	—	*Missarum Josquin Liber Tertius 1514*
	Missa sine nomine	38	✓	—	
Listenius	*Exemplum pariter Prolationis*	15	✓	—	*Motetti B 1503*
[Moulu]	*Sic unda impellitur unda*	6	✓	—	*Misse Obrecht 1503*
Obrecht	*Missa Je ne demande*	21, 29, 30	✓	✓	*Misse Obrecht 1503*
	Missa Salve diva parens	9	✓	✓	*Canti C 1503*
Ockeghem	*Prennez sur moi*	10	✓	—	*Motetti B 1503*
Orto	*Domine non secundum*	17	—	—	*Misse de Orto 1505*
	Missa L'homme armé	34	✓	✓	*Misse de Orto 1505*
	Missa La belle	35	✓	✓	*Misse de Orto 1505*
	Missa J'ay pris amour	7	✓	✓	
Rhau	*Exercitii sex vocum*	2	✓	✓	
la Rue	*Missa L'homme armé*	27	✓	✓	*Misse 1503*
Senfl	*O salutatris hostia*	39	✓	✓	
	Fortuna	11	✓	✓	
Weerbecke	*Missa Octavi toni*	45	✓	✓	*Misse Gaspar 1507*

unlikely to have been part of such an effort.[43] Heyden's gesture, taken in conjunction with other evidence, suggests that the music had become totally divorced from the liturgy that engendered it. While there is ample evidence of the "recreational" and devotional use of sacred vocal polyphony in Italy, the liturgical associations of the music remained in effect because of its continued use in services. For German Protestants in a conservative center like Nuremberg, however, the liturgical connections had been severed – hence the enjoyment of such pieces, especially those with Latin texts and theological implications, as aesthetic and educational objects. Heyden further objectifies the examples in his *Musicae* by reproducing them shorn of any text. Although it is not difficult to supply text for a Benedictus or Pleni sunt, Heyden's emphasis on solmization in the treatise suggests that these examples would have been sung by the boys as untexted solmization exercises.[44]

The printing of examples within the treatise further suggests that Heyden assumed that his readers (namely, his pupils) were unlikely to have access to the work from which his excerpts were drawn. His not entirely consistent approach to naming compositions and pointing in any specific way to the place quoted would make it difficult for his reader to identify the work cited.[45] Heyden does seem to provide the names of composers when he was aware of them, in part, no doubt, for the authority they convey. He also names the two theorists from whom he borrows examples: Rhau and Listenius. The question remains why Heyden would choose this particular repertory to cite and what might have happened between 1532 and 1537, beyond the technical ability to print music, so dramatically to have changed the two editions of his treatise.

The next section of the preface offers a tantalizing clue:

In so acquiring these examples, I have certainly been placed under no small obligation by Ulrich Starck, a gentleman both distinguished in the first place by his birth and reputation, and one who is also a very great lover of music, and on this account worthy of being remembered in these books. For he, perfect gentleman that he is [*humanissimus*], had lent me for some time towards this project the finest books of songs that he has. And on this account the boys, too, will owe him well-earned thanks, for as long as they perceive that they are the more easily instructed because of the clarity of [these] examples.

Book collectors are sometimes acknowledged in other slightly later music prints for providing sources, but this is the only instance of which I am aware in which a theorist specifically credits an individual with supplying access to music.[46] Even

---

[43] Butler suggests that the arrival of Veit Dietrich in Nuremberg may have been the first step in the restoration of polyphony and that the publication of Ott's anthologies in 1537–38, as well as his dedication of his book of masses to the council in 1539, may have played a part. Heyden's Calvinist sympathies led him toward a much more restricted view of the role of music in the liturgy than was typical of attitudes of those connected more closely to Luther and trends in Augsburg and Wittenberg.

[44] The early examples in the book include not only clefs, but identify the place of the syllables on each line of the staff. On Heyden's view of solmization and hexachord theory, see Miller, "Sebald Heyden's *De arte canendi*."

[45] The process is very different for the modern reader with easy access to various indices and collected editions.

[46] Heyden's reference to Starck was mentioned in Sandberger, *Bemerkungen zur Biographie Hans Leo Haßlers und seiner Brüder sowie zur Musikgeschichte der Städte Nürnberg und Augsburg im 16. und zu Anfang des 17. Jahrhunderts,*

though many of the examples are retained in the revised version of the treatise issued in 1540, there Heyden drops the mention of his debt to Starck, perhaps because so much more polyphonic music has become readily available in local publications between 1537 and 1540, for between them, Formschneider and Petreius had printed an enormous number of motets and two large collections of masses. It may also signal Heyden's desire to move beyond a primarily local audience of schoolboys.

Ulrich Starck (1484–1549) was a Nuremberg patrician whose family was engaged in trade.[47] Ulrich was wealthy enough to have commissioned a Christus-corpus for the east end of St. Sebald.[48] Like many of the patriciate, his travels and business contacts were convenient for acquiring music from many parts of Europe. To date, my efforts to recover any of Starck's books have been unsuccessful,[49] but from Heyden's examples it is possible to posit that they comprised some or all of the Petrucci prints listed as concordances in Table 4.1: *Missae Agricola*, *Ghiselin*, *Josquin* (I, II, and III), *Obrecht*, *de Orto*, *la Rue*, *Weerbecke*, and possibly *Motetti B*. With the exception of the third book of Josquin masses, all of these were published between 1502 and 1507 and it is not uncommon to find mass prints like these by individual composers grouped in binders' copies. If Starck owned many or most of these editions, they were probably bound as two, or at most three, sets of distinct partbooks. The duos and trios are generally indicated in the parts of the Petrucci prints, as are the resolutions of canons. It would have been easy enough for Heyden to search such publications for his examples. Although he appears to have worked with a repertory similar to Aron's, it is difficult to assert with complete confidence that Heyden was working from Petrucci exemplars. The nature of his tactus theory leads him to significant changes in mensuration signs.[50] The similarity of the canons and resolutions does suggest a source at least closely related to Petrucci.[51] It is possible that Starck's books

Denkmäler der Tonkunst in Bayern, Jg. V/I (Leipzig: Breitkopf and Härtel, 1904), 14, but as far as I am aware, there has been no speculation about what books Heyden may have borrowed from Starck.

[47] Dürer did a black chalk sketch of him in 1527 that is in the British Museum; the attribution is based on a medal reproduced in *Die deutschen Schaumünzen des XVI. Jahrhunderts*, ed. Georg Habich (Munich: F. Bruckman, 1929–34), vol. I.2, pl./nr. 967.   [48] Private communication from Bartlett Butler.

[49] Starck married Katherina Imhoff in 1513. The Imhoff were very wealthy and their family archive still exists, so it is possible that evidence of Starck's books may yet be recovered. I am grateful to Susan Jackson for this information and for her assistance in my attempts to discover Starck's books. Recently Eugene Schreurs has shown that the scribe Petrus Alamire was an Imhoff from Nuremberg, a tantalizing connection for possible sources of music. (Eugeen Schreurs, "Petrus Alamire: Music Calligrapher, Musician, Composer, Spy," in *The Treasury of Petrus Alamine: Music and Art in Flemish Court Manuscripts 1500–1535*, ed. Herbert Kellman (Amsterdam: Ludion Ghent, 1999), 15–27.)

[50] It seems likely that many (if not all) of the differences in mensuration signs between the Petrucci sources and Heyden's examples were changes introduced by Heyden to demonstrate his single tactus theory. See especially the comparison in Miller, "Sebald Heyden's *De arte canendi*," 87, of Heyden's version with Petrucci's of an excerpt from an Isaac mass.

[51] Gustavson, "Hans Ott," has shown that almost all of Ott's sources for the *Novum et insigne opus musicum* must have been manuscripts. This suggests a German manuscript tradition, no longer extant, for many Josquin works. Petreius's mass print of 1539 (*Liber quindecim missarum*), on the other hand, took the first five masses from a Petrucci edition.

used by Heyden may have been notebooks derived from Petrucci's prints rather than the prints themselves.[52]

Heyden's examples also point to a number of more general trends reflected in the music published in Nuremberg between 1537 and 1542. First, his emphasis on the works of Josquin and Isaac is reflected in the prefaces and organization of the large motet prints produced by Formschneider and Petreius. Along with Senfl (whom Heyden mentions in his preface of 1540), these are the musicians regularly singled out for commendation by Ott in his prefaces. Both Ott and Petreius tend to order works in their motet collections beginning with Josquin, followed by Isaac and/or Senfl, and then filled out with lesser-known German composers.[53]

Heyden's emphasis on the use of music for study and recreation also recurs in the dedications of prints by Ott and Petreius. Petreius addresses the preface of his *Modulationes aliquot quatuor vocum selectissimae* (1538) to "Studioso Musicae Lectori." His mass print of 1539, *Liber quindecim missarum*, was addressed to "Syncero Musicae Amatori."[54] Ott's mass print of 1539, *Liber tredecim missarum*, was dedicated to the Nuremberg City Council. In explaining his decision to publish the volume of masses he says: "I judged that it is most convenient, after two volumes of Motets (as they call them), to publish Masses, lest the studious had lacked something in our works."[55] Ott also singles out the works of his *Secundus tomus novi operis musici* for their ingenuity:

As regards the *cantiones* which we now publish, we hope that we will satisfy even learned musicians. We did not choose them for their ready availability but after careful listening and consideration, chose those which stood out for their *suavitas* and *ingenium*. (Singers will readily understand this when they come to grips with them.) One cannot form a correct opinion about a song heard only once.[56]

The majority of the extant copies of the two volumes of the *Novum et insigne opus musicum* were originally the property of Latin schools, further suggesting the connection of these prints with the curriculum for which Heyden's treatise was written.

A practice reminiscent of Heyden's use of duos was also evident in Protestant

---

[52] See the discussion of the "Tschudi Liederbuch" in chapter 6 for an illustration of such a notebook by a humanist compiler, completed probably around 1540.

[53] Indices of the Ott and Petreius prints are available in Harry B. Lincoln, *The Latin Motet: Indexes to Printed Collections, 1500–1600*, Musicological Studies 59 (Ottawa: The Institute of Mediaeval Music, 1993). These should be used with caution. An index for the two Ott prints known collectively as *Novum et insigne opus musicum* is available in Gustavson, "Hans Ott." Brown, "Hans Ott," also lists the contents of these prints. The Petreius prints are indexed in Teramoto and Brinzing, *Katalog der Musikdrucke*.

[54] The prefaces of the *Modulationes aliquot quatuor vocum selectissimae* and the *Liber quindecim missarum* are reproduced in Teramoto, *Die Psalmmotettendrucke*, 68.

[55] The preface is reproduced and translated in Gustavson, "Hans Ott," 579.

[56] The preface is reproduced and translated *ibid.*, 573.

cities like Nuremberg in the publication of *bicinia* and *tricinia*, sometimes as textless compositions.[57] In fact, Heyden's examples could be viewed as one of the first such collections. The preface to Ott's *Trium vocum carmina a diversis musicis composita* (1538) is strikingly similar in its avowed purpose to Heyden's description of gathering of examples in his 1537 treatise:

We present to you a great number of choice songs of three voices, composed by the most proven professors of music, young and old. We collected these pieces with singular zeal, not simply in order that, of their kind, the most delightful monuments of the highest minds might not perish, but that also we might incite the studies of the young to an art which is the most delightful of all and one to be diligently embraced. There are notable commendations of the old Greek poets – of Theognis, of Homer, and of others – by which they honor Music as a perpetual companion of honesty and erudition; also, there are clear judgements of the Philosophers which remain that testify that, for the good of the State, the young should diligently learn music. If this Art should possess nothing beyond delight and amusement, surely this would not be insufficient as a great commendation, especially since this life is not able to be made joyful (on account of cares and business concerns) except when it is tempered by some learned delight. We therefore esteem that this, our study, goes forth proven in all its goodness; thus we show care for the State and for Youth, and we vindicate the most pleasant labors of notable musicians from disaster. Since these songs did not have words of one single language, we judged it more helpful, with the words omitted, to signify the songs by numbers. It was seen that this matter would be held to be a blemish, if the songs, in German, French, sometimes in Italian, or in Latin, were to be mixed together. Thus the makers of the music are seen to have regarded the songs of three voices more as a learned mixture of sounds than of words. The learned Musician may enjoy himself in this delight, even though there are no words placed under the notes. Nor were we very troubled concerning the names of the Authors, since each of them has their own notable music, from which learned Musicians may be able to recognize them easily.[58]

The composers represented in the one hundred songs of this print are the same ones featured in Heyden's examples: Josquin, Isaac, Obrecht, Ghiselin, Ockeghem, Pierre de la Rue, Sixt Dietrich, and Agricola, rounded out with works by composers like Senfl, Brumel, Hayne van Ghizeghem, Richafort, and Compère, some of whom were to appear in the final version of Heyden's treatise.[59] The emergence of these collections of duos and trios – as pieces for study, recreation, and education –

---

[57] The best discussion of the general trends behind the appearance of these publications is John E. Lindberg, "Origins and Development of the Sixteenth-Century Tricinium," Ph.D. dissertation, University of Cincinnati (1988; UMI 9019795).

[58] The preface is reproduced and translated in Gustavson, "Hans Ott," 601. For a slightly different translation, see Lindberg, "Origins and Development of the Sixteenth-Century Tricinium," 20.

[59] An index of the print is provided in Lindberg, "Origins and Development of the Sixteenth Century Tricinium," 245–48. Lindberg questions the motivations for Ott's omission of texts, suggesting that he may have viewed the book as a "solfege anthology." He dismisses this possibility, saying that no other such anthologies were published at the time (22). However, the Heyden examples may have functioned as just such an anthology. Lindberg also notes the many concordances with Petrucci's *Odhecaton* and Egenolff's *Liederbuch*, both untexted anthologies. However, as he points out, the *Odhecaton* is unlikely to have been Ott's source (23).

reinforces the understanding that Heyden's treatise suggests of the place of music within Nuremberg society.[60]

CHANGES BETWEEN HEYDEN'S *MUSICAE* (1537) AND HIS *DE ARTE CANENDI* (1540)

The basic outline of Heyden's treatise remains the same between the 1537 edition of the treatise and the 1540 revision: two books, the first of which treats the elements of music, the second tactus and mensuration. Since the completion of the second edition, Heyden had had the opportunity to study Tinctoris's *Proportionale*, lent to him by Georg Forster, a humanist who was, among other things, the editor of *Frische teutsche Liedlein*,[61] a collection of 382 German songs. Heyden made note of the composers that Tinctoris cites: Dunstable, Dufay, Binchois, Ockeghem, Busnois, and Caron. His mention of Josquin and Isaac is no longer present in the preface. Instead, he highlights Johannes Ghiselin's *Missa Gratieusa* and Obrecht's *Missa Je ne demande*, works that are accorded special attention in the treatise.

The publication of a number of compositions in the years intervening between the latter two versions of his treatise placed Heyden in an interesting position with respect to his examples. Music that was apparently relatively little known (and available to him through the collection of Ulrich Starck) was now more widely available as a result of Ott's and Petreius's mass prints of 1539. Each contained three works from which Heyden had excerpted examples in his treatise.[62] It was perhaps the availability of these masses that led him to a disclaimer in the preface of the new version that could equally have applied to his 1537 treatise:

It is indeed evident that in some examples which are not mine but which were acquired from others to demonstrate the rules, I have changed the form of the notes, or in some other examples I have placed the note forms with different signs, applying a form other than that used by the composer himself. In this I have no doubt that any fair judge will believe it was done for a proper and just reason, because, despite the changes in notes and signs, the nature of a song is entirely complete and unchanged in what pertains to contrapuntal composition and the intent of the composer, and it always remains unaltered. Moreover, this can be defended with just reason, partly because the somewhat older musical structure is more pleasing to my spirit, and partly to give chirping young boys (I like to speak so) a specimen, as it were, of the manifold variety of mensural music, in which it is very easy to transcribe

---

[60] Georg Rhau's publication of tricinia (*Tricinium tum veterum tum recentiorum in arte music symphonistarum* (Wittenberg: Georg Rhau, 1542)) explicitly states that the collection is printed for children to sing and for use by schools and churches. The preface and translation along with an extended discussion of this print appear in Lindberg, "Origins and Development of the Sixteenth-Century Tricinium," 29–37, and *passim*. Lindberg, citing Wofram Steude, "Untersuchungen zu Herkunft, Verbreitung und spezifische Inhalt mitteldeutscher Musikhandschriften des 16. Jahrhunderts," Ph.D. dissertation, University of Rostock (1972), 72, notes that Rhau frequently used manuscript pieces from the library of Friederic der Weise as source material.

[61] 2 volumes, Petreius, 1539–40 = RISM 1539[27] and 1540[21].

[62] Of works cited by Heyden, RISM 1539[1] contained (following the Petrucci publications) Josquin's *Missa Fortuna desperata*, *Missa Gaudeamus*, and *Missa L'homme armé super voces musicales*. RISM 1539[2] also contained Josquin's *Missa Fortuna desperata* and *Missa L'homme armé super voces musicales*, as well as Brumel's *Missa Bon temps*.

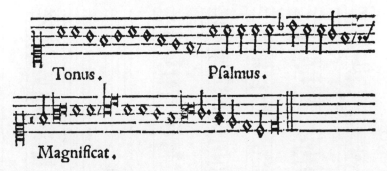

4.8 Heyden, *De arte canendi* (1540), p. 137, monophonic example of the first mode
(Bayerische Staatsbibliothek 4° Mus.th. 665. Reproduced by permission.)

any song, even if changed ten times from one form to another. This is done with such
equity that no composer can complain it has been the cause of any harm to him. Yet we
have done this scarcely once or twice, and only in demonstration of simple rules which are
totally uncontroversial, for we were aware that original and perfect examples must be used
in controversies and confutations.

I was glad to mention these points here of my own accord and in anticipation, as it were,
so that some dilettante does not attack through malice and calumny such an example he may
discover accidentally, and claim that falsehoods were substituted for truth.[63]

As can be seen by the comparative table of the examples of the two treatises in
the Appendix to this chapter, the process in 1540 was primarily an additive one,
often supplying extra examples from works for which excerpts had been included
in 1537. Thirteen works are omitted. Two of these were by other theorists (Rhau
and Listenius) and were replaced by examples drawn from "real" compositions. The
most significant change comes at the end of the treatise where the original examples numbered 38–44 have been replaced by a new series of examples in a demonstration of the modes. The monophonic examples have been separated out into a
chapter of their own and are more spaciously set (compare Fig. 4.8 with Fig. 4.7, p.
97). The polyphonic examples are no longer *fugae* and duos. All of these have been
replaced with three- and four-part compositions presented in choirbook format
(compare Fig. 4.9, pp. 106–7, with Fig. 4.7, p. 97). Only the final four-part
example, the Agnus Dei III from Weerbecke's *Missa Octavi toni*, has been retained.

Heyden supplies only minimal explanation of modal theory, relying instead on
his examples in lieu of textual description for a subject that he obviously feels must
be incorporated in the treatise, but which is of little interest to him. Even as he
almost completely replaces the original examples, his text is virtually unchanged
between the two editions.

[63] Miller, trans. *De arte canendi*, 22–23.

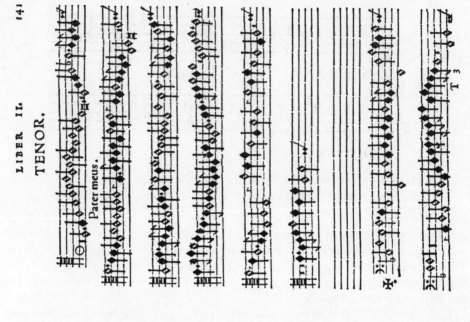

MVSICAE
Exemplum Primi Toni.

DISCANTVS.

Pater Meus agricola est.   Alexander Agric.

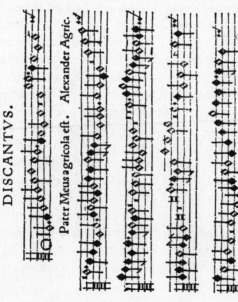

BASSVS.

Pater meus

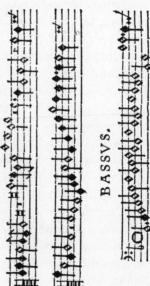

LIBER II.
TENOR.

Pater meus.

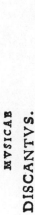

TENOR.

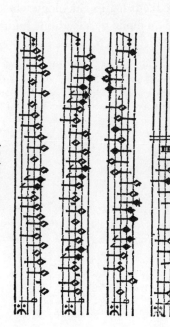

Exemplum

MVSICAE

DISCANTVS.

142

BASSVS.

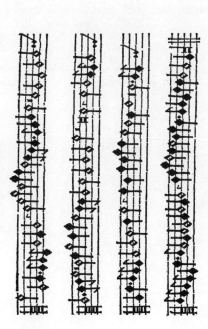

4.9 Heyden, *De arte canendi* (1540), pp. 140–43, Polyphonic example of the first mode (Agricola, *Pater meus*) (Bayerische Staatsbibliothek, 4° Mus.th. 665. Reproduced by permission.)

Here I will purposely refrain from describing the modes at length. For why is it necessary to pursue religiously the ranges of authentic and plagal modes, as they are called, and the *differentiae* added to them, when we perceive that they are hardly taken into account in figural music? So let it be sufficient here to have shown as simply as possible how the modes of all more commonly known *cantilenae* should be recognized, and how psalms and the *Magnificat* should be intoned, as it is called. Anyone who wishes more details should seek it from other sources.[64]

HEYDEN'S EXAMPLES AS EXEMPLARS

Beyond the local theological and pedagogical impact that Heyden's treatise may have had, the repertory represented by his examples functioned for a number of later theorists as a musical source in its own right. Heyden was rarely credited; his examples were reproduced under the authority of the composer to whom he attributed them. His examples were frequently used in contexts quite divorced from his theoretical stance and for purposes at odds with those for which he gathered the examples. Thus the music of his treatise reappeared in a nested series of appropriations by Glarean, Faber, Zanger, Finck, and Wilphlingseder.[65] The most interesting of these borrowings is by Heinrich Glarean. In his own gathering of examples, Glarean connected the examples of Heyden's treatise with one of the anthologies with which it shared repertory, issued in Nuremberg shortly after the treatise, Petreius's *Liber quindecim missarum* of 1539. These same examples would now be divorced from the tactus theory for which they stood in Heyden's treatise, and the Reformation ideology which framed their inclusion, and put to service in a treatise on mode by a Catholic humanist.

---

[64] Miller, trans., *De arte canendi*, as amended by Frans Wiering, "The Language of the Modes: Studies in the History of Polyphonic Modality," Ph.D. dissertation, University of Amsterdam (1995), 176. Wiering provides a detailed discussion of Heyden's two sets of examples for the eight modes, 176–83.

[65] Concordances with these treatises are listed in Teramoto and Brinzing, *Katalog der Musikdrucke*.

APPENDIX: A4.1 *Heyden's examples in the Musicae (1537) and De arte canendi (1540)*

1537	Caption	Composer	Work	1540	Caption	Composer, Work
1	Fuga in subdiapente	[Josquin]	[Benedictus, *Missa L'homme armé sexti toni*]	1	(as 1537)	
2	Exemplum exercitti sex vocum ex Rhauo	Rhau	example from treatise	omitted		
				2	Exercitium vocum Musicalium. N.P.	[Nicolaus Piltz]
3	Exemplum bmolle acuti Systematis. Fuga. author Josquin	Josquin	[Pleni sunt coeli, *Missa Mater patris*]	3	(as 1537)	
				4	Fuga trium vocum, quarum duae in unisono, tertia in Subdiapente.	—
4	Exemplum hdurum acuti Systematis. Fuga Josquini	Josquin	[Benedictus, *Missa Mater patris*]	5	(as 1537)	
5	Exemplum bmolle medii Systematis. Fuga duorum ex eodem. Josquini	Josquin	[Agnus Dei II, *Missa Mater patris*]	omitted		
(new items in 1540)				6	Fuga duorum, ex eadem clave, post perfectum tempus.	—
				7	Fuga duorum in unisono	—
				8	Fuga trium in unison	—
6	Exemplum hdurum medii Systematis. Fuga trium ex eodem.	[Moulu?]	[*Sic unda impellitur unda*]	9	(as 1537)	
7	Exemplum bmolle partis infimae Systematis. Ex Iay prys amours De Orto. Fuga duorum ex eadem clave.	de Orto	[Agnus Dei II] *Missa J'ay pris amour*	11	(as 1537)	
8	Exemplum h durum partis infimae Systematis, sive Bassi. Fuga duorum in Epidiapente, ex Hercule Iosquini.	Josquin	[Pleni sunt coeli] *Missa Hercules Dux Ferrariae*	12	(as 1537)	
9	Exemplum tertium infimi Systematis, vulgatior Bassi formula. Fuga duorum	Obrecht	[Qui cum patre, *Missa Salve diva parens*]	10	(as 1537)	
10	Exemplum cantus ficti, sive bmollis	Ockeghem	[*Prennez sur moi*]	13	(as 1537)	

APPENDIX: A4.1 (*cont.*)

1537	Caption	Composer	Work	1540	Caption	Composer, Work
11	iste fuerit, hduri. Okengem. Fuga trium vocum, in Epidiatessaron, post perfectum tempus. Sequitur exemplum Notularum utriusque speciei. *Fortuna*. Ludovici Senfii, ad voces Musicales. (new items in 1540)	Senfl	*Fortuna*	14	(as 1537)	
				15	Exemplum Brumelii, in quo quinta Longa a prima in ordine Brevi imperficitur.	Brumel, Christe, *Missa Victimae paschali* [tenor only]
				16	Exemplum Iosquini ex L'homme Arme sext Toni	Josquin, Kyrie II, *Missa L'homme armé sexti toni* [tenor only]
12	Exemplum Prolationis Maioris integrae, diminutae & Proportionatae. (new items in 1540)	[Isaac]	[Kyrie II, *Missa Quant j'ay au cueur*]	17	(as 1537)	
				18	Sequitur aliud exemplum Prolationis perfectae, ex Missa Prolationum Iohannis Ogekhem	Ockeghem, Kyrie I, *Missa Prolationum*
				19	Ex Missa Bon temps Brumelii.	Brumel, Agnus Dei II, *Missa Bon temps* [bassus only]
				20	Sequitur aliud exemplum Henrici Isaac Ex Paschali illius	Isaac, Sanctus, *Missa Paschale* [missing altus]
13	Exemplum	[Agricola]	[Kyrie, *Missa Malheur me bat*]	22	(as 1537)	
14	Aliud exemplum Temporis perfecti, integri, Diminuti, et Proportionati. (new items in 1540)	[Isaac]	[Kyrie II, *Missa Quant j'ay au cueur*]	21	(as 1537)	
15	Exemplum pariter Prolationis, Temporis, ac Modi Minoris ex Libello Listenii	Listenius		23	Exemplum. Kyrie ex Malheur me bat. A. Agricola	Agricola, Kyrie I, *Missa Malheur me bat*
				omitted		

16	Exemplum Proportionis Duplae	[Josquin]	[Benedictus, Missa Gaudeamus]	26	(as 1537)	
17	Exemplum Proportionis Triplae	[de Orto]	["cito anticipent," from Domine non secundum]	27	(as 1537)	
18	Quadrupla Proportio quam habet Notionem.	[Josquin]	[secunda pars, Ave verum corpus]	28	(as 1537)	
19	Exemplum. Fuga duorum Josqin	Josquin	[Agnus II, Missa Malheur me bat]	29	(as 1537)	
20	Exemplum Ioannis Ghiselin.	Ghiselin	[Cum sancto spiritu, Missa Narayge]	30	(as 1537)	
				31	Quem in sacrae mensa coenae	—
				32	Exemplum	—
21	Exemplum in Ie ne demande Oberti. Qui tollis	Obrecht	Qui tollis, Missa Je ne demande [tenor only]	33	(as 1537)	
22	Exemplum primi Modi per C2. Duo in unum Iosquini	Josquin	[In nomine, Missa L'homme armé super voces musicales]	34	(as 1537)	
23	Exemplum Secundi Modi, per O C. Duo in unum Josquini.	Josquin	[Qui venit, Missa L'homme armé super voces musicales]	35	(as 1537)	
24	Exemplum Tertii Modi, per. Duo in unum Iosquini.	Josquin	[Benedictus, Missa L'homme armé super voces musicales]	36	(as 1537)	
25	Sequitur exemplum variarum Diminutionum.	[Josquin]	[Benedictus, Missa ad fugam]	37	(as 1537)	
(new items in 1540)				38	Exemplum Henrici Isaac, ex Prosa de Maria Magdalena	Isaac, Qualis sit, from Coeli terrae maris
				39	Exemplum Oberti in Ie ne demande	Obrecht, [Qui tollis,]Missa Je ne demande [superius and tenor only]
				40	Primum argumentum N.P.	[Nicolaus Piltz]
26	Primum Argumentum unica ac eiusdem perpetui Tactus ex Lommearme	Josquin	[Agnus Dei II,] Missa L'homme armé super	41	(as 1537)	

APPENDIX: A4.1 (cont.)

1537	Caption	Composer	Work	1540	Caption	Composer, Work
	Iosquini. Fuga trium vocum ex unica, quarum prima Proportionatum valorem: Altera Diminutum: Tertia Integrum canit.		*voces musicales*			
27	Alterum Argumentum Petri de la Rue est, ex Lomme arme ipsius. Fuga quatuor vocum ex unica	Pierre de la Rue	[Agnus II,] *Missa L'homme armé*	42	(as 1537)	
28	Tertium Argumentum Henrichi Isaac est, ex Prosa historiae de Conceptione Mariae, in quo Tripla Proportio promiscue nunc Diminuto, nunc integro Notularum valori opponitur	Isaac	*De radice Jesse*	43	(as 1537)	
29	Exemplum. Ie ne demande Oberti	Obrecht	[Kyrie I] *Missa Je ne demande* [tenor only]	omitted		
30	Exemplum. Sanctus. Ie ne demande Oberti.	Obrecht	[Et in spiritum [Credo]] *Missa Je ne demande* [tenor only]	omitted		
(new items in 1540)				44	Exemplum ex Naraige Ghiselini	Ghiselin, [Kyrie I,] *Missa Narayge* [tenor and bassus only]
				45	Exemplo sint prioris exempli Diminutae voces, quibus si dimidium figurarum auferas, ita habebunt	"
				46	Exemplum	—
				47	Exemplum ex Missa Fortuna Iosquin	Josquin, [end of Credo,] *Missa Fortuna desperata* [superius and tenor only]
				48	Exemplum Primum Kyrie ex Lhomme arme Iosquini	Josquin, Kyrie I, *Missa L'homme armé super voces musicales* [tenor and bassus only]

No.	Exemplum	(as 1537)	Work
49	Exemplum Christe eleyson ex Lhomme arme Iosquini.		Josquin, Christe, *Missa L'homme armé super voces musicales* [tenor and bassus only]
50	Exemplum ex Missa Prolationum Iohannis Ockegem.	(as 1537)	Ockeghem, [Osanna,] *Missa Prolationum*
51	Exemplum ex Naraige Iohannis Ghiselin	(as 1537)	Ghiselin, [Sanctus,] *Missa Narayge* [tenor and bassus only]
52	Exemplum ex Ghiselino	(as 1537)	Ghiselin, [Sanctus, *Missa La belle se siet* superius and tenor only]

No.	Exemplum	Composer	Work	Concordance	(as 1537)
31	Exemplum Ghiselini	Ghiselin	[Qui tollis, *Missa Gratieuse* [tenor only]]	54	(as 1537)
32	Exemplum Sexti Canonis Et resurrexit. Ioannis Ghiselin.	Ghiselin	[Et iterum, *Missa Gratieuse* [tenor only]]	55	(as 1537)
33	Ghiselin. Canon Primo per 1/3. Secundo per 1/2. Tertio ut iacet.	Ghiselin	[Gloria, *Missa Gratieuse* [tenor only]]	53	(as 1537)
34	Ex Lomme arme de Orto.	de Orto	[Agnus Dei I] *Missa L'homme armé* [bassus only]	omitted	
35	Alterum Exemplum. Agnus ultimum ex La belle de Orto.	de Orto	Agnus Dei III, *Missa La belle* [superius only]	56	(as 1537)
36	Ghiselin. Patrem	Ghiselin	Credo, [*Missa Gratieuse* [tenor only]	25	(as 1537)
37	Sanctus Ghiselin	Ghiselin	Sanctus, [*Missa Gratieuse* [tenor only]	24	(as 1537)
38	Exemplum/Fuga duum Iosquini, in Subdiatessaron, post duo tempora.	Josquin	[Pleni sunt coeli, *Missa sine nomine*]	omitted	
39	Exemplum. Duo, Petri de la Rue. O salutaris hostia	Pierre de la Rue	[Pleni sunt,] *Missa O salutaris hostia*	omitted	
40	Exemplum. Duo Alexand. Agric.	Agricola	[Crucifixus, *Missa Malleur me bat*]	omitted	
41	Exemplum Iosquini. Fuga trium, hic in Epidiapent[e] ille in Subdiatessa[ron]	Josquin	[Agnus Dei II, *Missa Hercules Dux Ferrariae*]	omitted	

APPENDIX: A4.1 (*cont.*)

1537	Caption	Composer	Work	1540	Caption	Composer, Work
42	Exemplum.	[Sixt Dietrich]	Omnis caro foenum	omitted		
43	Exemplum. Iosquin, Duo.	Josquin	[Ave verum corpus [beginning of prima pars]]	omitted		
44	Exemplum. Fuga duorum Temporum in Diatessaron Alexan. Agricolae (new items in 1540)	Agricola	[Christe, Missa Le serviteur]	omitted		
				57	Exemplum Primi Toni. Pater meus agricola est. Alexander Agric.	Agricola, *Pater meus*
				58	Exemplum Secundi Toni. Ave mater omnium. Gaspar	Weerbecke, *Ave mater omnium*
				59	Sequitur exemplum Tertii Toni	—
				60	Exemplum Quarti Toni. Agnus. Malheur me bat. Alex. Agric.	Agricola. Agnus Dei I, *Missa Malheur me bat*
				61	Exemplum Quinti Toni Iohannis Ockegen. Et in terra.	Ockeghem, Gloria *Missa Prolationum*
				62	Exemplum Sexti Toni. Fuga ad minimam Iosquini in Lhomme arme Sexti Toni. Agnus	Josquin, Agnus Dei III, *Missa L'homme armé sexti toni*
				63	Sequitur exemplum Septimi Toni Iosquini, ex Lhomme arme. Osanna Iosquini ex Lhomme arme.	Josquin, Osanna, *Missa L'homme armé super voces musicales*
45	Exemplum. Gaspar. Octavi	Weerbecke	[Agnus Dei III,] *Missa Octavi toni*	64	(as in 1537)	

PART III

THE POLYPHONY OF HEINRICH GLAREAN'S *DODECACHORDON* (1547)

EXEMPLA, COMMONPLACE BOOKS, AND WRITING THEORY

> This was to be the end of the book, certainly of monstrous size if one considers the examples, but of no great size at all if one looks at the text.
>
> Heinrich Glarean, *Dodecachordon*, 1547

For the twentieth-century reader, Heinrich Glarean's *Dodecachordon* stands as a monument of Renaissance music theory. The work is impressive even as a physical object, proclaiming its importance through its luxurious folio format and elegant printing and spacious layout of more than 470 pages, including more than two hundred extensive music examples and diagrams.[1] In keeping with its format, the work's title page (reproduced in Fig. 5.1) signals the *Dodecachordon*'s unique position in musical writing from the first half of the sixteenth century. This is a book that announces its place alongside the rapidly proliferating texts of classical antiquity: commentaries on Ovid, editions of Aristotle, Glarean's own edition of Boethius, and so on. The importance of the *Dodecachordon*'s format as a marker of the intellectual arena to which it aspires is vividly illustrated by a comparison with Glarean's first printed book on music, the *Isagoge in musicen*,[2] an upright quarto with a traditional frontispiece and woodcut border by Hans Holbein the younger (shown in Fig. 5.2).[3] The *Isagoge* was among Glarean's earliest publications and was a simple didactic treatise of ten chapters intended as a schoolbook introduction to music.[4] His *Helvetiae descriptio* (Basle, 1515) preceded the *Isagoge*; works on grammar, geography, arithmetic, and history followed, as did commentaries and editions of the writings of Boethius, Erasmus, Ovid, Horace, and Julius Caesar, among others. In the course of this publication career, Glarean's changing stature is reflected not only

---

[1] By elegant printing I refer here only to physical features. The volume was plagued with inaccuracies, as witnessed by the five pages of *errata* and Glarean's hand-corrections of numerous additional errors (both textual and musical) in several surviving copies of the *Dodecachordon*.

[2] *Isagoge in musicen e quibusque bonis authoribus lat. et graec. ad studiosorum utilitatem multo labore elaborata* (Basle: J. Froben, 1516). Translated with introduction by Frances Berry Turrell as "The *Isagoge in Musicen* of Henry Glarean," *Journal of Music Theory* 3 (1959), 97–139.

[3] On the reuse of this woodcut in subsequent publications from Froben's firm (including Erasmus' *Epistola ad Dorpium*) and Holbein's relationship with Basle humanists, see Turrell, "*Isagoge*," 106–08.

[4] Thus in tradition it belongs with the writings of Nuremberg and Cologne theorists like Wollick and Cochlaeus, Glarean's teacher. It was intended for use in the humanist curriculum of the German Latin schools, as were Heyden's treatises of a few years later. The *Isagoge* is frequently preserved in contemporary bindings with other school books, usually Latin grammars and arithmetic books.

GLAREANI

ΔΩΔΕΚΑΧΟΡΔΟΝ

Plagij	Authentæ
A Hypodorius	D Dorius
Hypermixolydius Ptolemæi	
B Hypophrygius	E Phrygius
Hyperæolius Mar. Cap.	
C Hypolydius	F Lydius
	Hyperphrygius Mar. Cap.
D Hypomixolyd.	G Mixolydius
Hyperiaſtius uel Hyperionicus Mar. Cap.	Hyperlydius Mart. Cap.
E Hypoæolius	A Aeolius
Hyperdorius Mart. Capell.	
G Hypoionicus	C Ionicus Porphyrio
Hypoiaſtius Mart. Cap.	Iaſtius Apuleius & Mar. Cap.
*F Hyperphrygius	*B Hyperæolius
Hyperlydius Politia. ſed eſt error	

B A S I L E Æ.

5.1 Glarean, *Dodecachordon*, title page

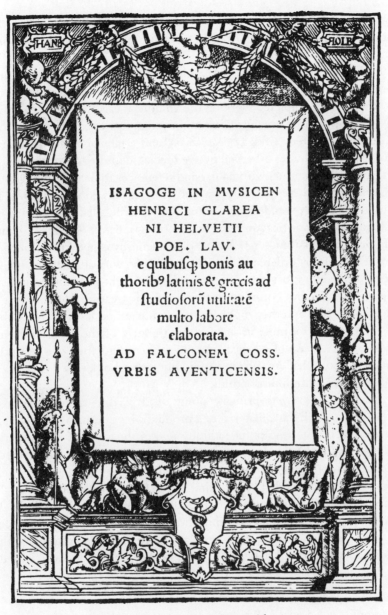

ISAGOGE IN MVSICEN
HENRICI GLAREA
NI HELVETII
POE. LAV.
e quibuſcʒ bonis au
thorib⁹ latinis & grǣcis ad
ſtudioſorũ utilitaté
multo labore
elaborata.
AD FALCONEM COSS.
VRBIS AVENTICENSIS.

5.2 Glarean, *Isagoge in musicen*, title page

in the breadth of subjects on which he lectured and published, but also in the shift from books that are essentially primers to overtly learned commentaries and editions.

The *Dodecachordon* appeared in 1547, thirty-one years after the *Isagoge*, and near the conclusion of Glarean's published output.[5] Various indications, however, suggest that he had completed work on the volume as early as 1539.[6] In contrast to the *Isagoge*, the title page presents Glarean's name in its humanist version, followed by the unadorned Greek title, *Dodecachordon*, and a tabular representation of the signal focus of the volume: the seven octave species identified by final and arranged in plagal and authentic pairs with names and references to names from classical and Hellenistic sources where necessary to "authenticate" his constructions.[7] The title page is followed by an extended preface and a series of detailed tables giving first the three classes of authorities on which the text is based – Greek, Latin, and "Symphonetæ" (i.e., composers). A table of contents by chapter titles follows, then an index of polyphony ordered alphabetically by title, with attribution and number of voices indicated for most examples, and a detailed eight-page topical index. Such tables and indices are not common features of music treatises from the first half of the sixteenth century and they highlight the significant position of quoted authority and appropriated example in shaping the rhetoric of the *Dodecachordon*. In its size, rhetorical style, use of *exempla*, and physical configuration it is not primarily other musical books that are called to mind but rather books like Erasmus's *Adagia* and Glarean's own edition of Boethius.

This chapter takes as its primary point of departure an assessment of the *Dodecachordon* as a *book* – as a material text produced by a humanist writer in northern Europe. Such a starting point radically revises the view of a treatise that has been studied by subsequent generations primarily as a self-contained theoretical examination of mode and a repository of repertory.

Determining the intended readership of the *Dodecachordon* and untangling its influence in the sixteenth century from its later reception is no easy task.[8] Unlike the *Isagoge* it was not intended as a Latin-school primer, nor was it aimed at an audience of professional musicians, nor does it appear to have been directed at the burgeoning market of musical amateurs. Instead, its style and production point directly

---

[5] For a descriptive catalog of Glarean's works, see Otto Fridolin Fritzsche, *Glarean, sein Leben und seine Schriften* (Frauenfeld: Verlag J. Huber, 1890).

[6] The chronology of the writing of the *Dodecachordon* is discussed further below. Briefly, Glarean appears actively to have been working on the *Dodecachordon* in the 1520s and 1530s. He indicated in a letter to Damian a Goes in 1539 that he had completed work on the treatise in that year with the exception of a few examples that he was commissioning. (Cited in Clement Miller, "The *Dodecachordon*: Its Origins and Influence on Renaissance Musical Thought," *Musica disciplina* 15 (1961), 161.) In the treatise itself he explains that the publication was delayed by the difficulty in having the music examples printed.

[7] See Harold Powers, "Mode," III.4, *New Grove Dictionary of Music and Musicians*, ed. S. Sadie (London: Macmillan, 1980), XII: 12, 408–09. The gesture was particularly important because it shows Glarean finding classical warrant for the pseudo-classical names of chant theory (e.g. from the ninth-century *Alia musica*).

[8] One of the ways in which its influence quickly extended beyond that community was witnessed by Zarlino's appropriation of Glarean's modal labels in 1549, discussed below in chapter 7.

to a rather narrowly defined community of university-trained northern humanist readers. A consideration of the *Dodecachordon* from the intellectual perspective of the Swiss-German humanist community of the 1520s and 1530s points to specific methods of reading that guided the production of this treatise and reveals the manner in which the religious upheaval of those decades is reflected in the contents of the work.[9] Among the many extant copies of the *Dodecachordon*, several presentation copies survive, suggesting at least one potential group of users of the book. They represent a group of humanist readers, often with training in philosophy and theology.[10]

That Glarean's *Dodecachordon* is the production of a humanist writer on music must surely qualify as one of the most oft-repeated statements of modern musicology.[11] The most explicit study of Glarean's examples in this century, Schering's article of 1911, set the tone for most subsequent work on the treatise.[12] Describing the treatise as a "classical anthology of polyphonic works from the period of about 1480–1540," Schering focused almost exclusively on the polyphonic examples of the treatise with only a fleeting mention of one chant item at the conclusion of the article. He surveys the "anthology" contents by "type" (contrapuntal pedagogical examples, textless compositions, polyphonic compositions with fragmentary texts, and polyphonic compositions with complete texts), highlighting the composers and compositions represented in the treatise. Miller's introduction to his English translation of the treatise some fifty years later is not dissimilar in his treatment of the music examples, although he does briefly highlight the chant examples before launching into his own typology of the polyphonic examples based on genre: pedagogical, motets, mass sections, and contrafacta and secular compositions.[13] Thus the *Dodecachordon* became the window through which subsequent generations learned

---

[9] See Sarah Fuller, "Defending the *Dodecachordon*: Ideological Currents in Glarean's Modal Theory," *Journal of the American Musicological Society* 49 (1996), 191–224 for a discussion of the dedication of the volume and its theological implications.

[10] For example, *MunU 2°Art. 127* is dedicated to Wolfgang Hunger, a professor and then Reichsgericht in Ingolstadt (d. 1555). The copy passed to his son Albrecht Hunger who served as vice-chancellor of the University of Ingolstadt for twenty-six years after holding posts as Professor of Philosophy and Theology. Albrecht Hunger's will left his library to the university. *Mbs 2° L.impt.c.n.mss 73 (olim 2° Mus.th.214)* is dedicated to Johann Albrecht Widmanstetter. Widmanstetter was a Nuremberg humanist who published a partial translation of the Koran in 1543. (See Riezler, "Widmanstetter, Johann Albrecht," *Allgemeine Deutsche Biographie* (Leipzig: Verlag Duncker and Humblot, 1897), XLII: 360.) *SGall Mag.-Nr. NN rechts II 6–4.Vitrine* was dedicated to Deithelm Blarer, the abbot of St. Gall who was in the process of restoring the abbey library. The dedicatory letter highlights Glarean's references to the monastery in the treatise and expresses the hope that his book will find a place in the fine monastery that was home to Notker and the important writer on music Hermannus Contractus. He also presented a copy of his last publication, the *Epitome* of Marcus Junianus Justinus (Basle: Heinrich Petri, 1562), to the abbot. These presentation copies are discussed further in n. 33.

[11] See Fuller, "Defending the *Dodecachordon*," 217n for a listing of the most prominent studies of Glarean's humanism.

[12] Arnold Schering, "Die Notenbeispiele in Glarean's Dodekachordon (1547)," *Sammelbände der Internationalen Musikgesellschaft* 13 (1912), 569–96. One welcome exception is Fuller's recent examination of the plainsong examples in "Defending the *Dodecachordon*." See also Harold Powers, "Mode," III.4ii, *New Grove*, XII: 409.

[13] Clement Miller, introduction to the English translation of the *Dodecachordon*, Musicological Studies and Documents 6 ([Rome]: American Institute of Musicology, 1965), 26–34.

an earlier repertory, as though the examples of the treatise simply comprised another music print, an anthology of the best of its day.[14] In this sense, Glarean's examples served primarily as a repository of repertory, even though Glarean as an editor has been frequently faulted. Equally, the examples have also been seen in the sense that they most obviously function in the text: as illustrations of the mensural and modal precepts Glarean describes.[15]

The three books of the *Dodecachordon* are clearly delineated in subject matter and by type of example. The first book follows in the tradition of the *Isagoge*, providing basic definitions and expanding on the materials found there. Book II, which concerns the modes in monophony, outlines the criteria and authorities on whose works Glarean's theory is based. The central theoretical statement of the treatise occurs in chapter 7 of Book II and concerns the octave species and the identification and naming of twelve modes. These are succinctly summarized in two adjacent figures. The first, reproduced here as Figure 5.3, illustrates the six authentic modes and the "harmonic" division of the octave. (The misplaced f-clef in this figure is not noted in the Errata, although it is corrected by hand in many copies of the treatise.) Immediately beneath them are the paired plagal modes created by "arithmetic" division of the octave. The second figure (Fig. 5.4) orders the pairs of modes based on the seven octave species, thus listing fourteen modes; two of are then discarded. The source of this octave species model is most obviously seen in Glarean's annotations to Gaffurio's *Practica musica* (See Fig. 5.5). On Gaffurio's harmonic and arithmetic division of the octave, Glarean has inserted the name of the mode in his twelve-mode system. The marginalia form the basis of his comments entered in the tabular representation of the division of the octave species presented in the *Dodecachordon* (compare Fig. 5.5 with Fig. 5.6). The subsequent chapters of Book II are taken up with the copious illustration of these modes with plainchant exemplars.[16]

Book III contains the necessary instruction for consideration of polyphony: an opening section on notation and mensuration followed by examples of the twelve

---

[14] Chapter 9 explores this relationship of anthologies and theoretical writing through the reception history of the motet *Magnus es tu Domine*.

[15] For a detailed survey of some of the polyphonic examples as they relate to Glarean's descriptions of the modes, see Frans Wiering, "The Language of the Modes: Studies in the History of Polyphonic Modality," Ph.D. dissertation, University of Amsterdam (1995), 186–95. Wiering's thorough analysis is an excellent examination of the overt relationship of the examples and the text they accompany.

[16] In her recent article, Sarah Fuller eloquently outlined the ideological themes advanced in the second book of the *Dodecachordon* and the way in which the chant examples are used to demonstrate the validity of the theoretical system. As she points out, the number of chant examples in the *Dodecachordon* is without parallel in the contemporary theoretical literature. She cites the newly composed untexted examples in Tinctoris's *Liber de natura et proprietate tonorum* and the formulaic antiphons of Gaffurio's *Practica musicae* as points of contrast. She sees Glarean's choice of chants as narrating a theological agenda and providing the Christian pillar supporting Glarean's claim for a twelve-fold modal system ("Defending the *Dodecachordon*"). There is also the medieval twelve-mode tradition that Glarean cited; for the continuation of chant terminology in twelve-mode doctrine, a music-theoretical support from chant theory further situates Glarean as Catholic humanist. See Powers, "Mode," III.4iii, *New Grove*, XII: 409. The basis of Glarean's Catholic humanist agenda is even more strongly articulated when the examples of Book II and Book III are considered from the sixteenth-century perspective on *exempla*.

5.3 Glarean, *Dodecachordon*, 82, diagram of the authentic and plagal modes

5.4 Glarean, *Dodecachordon*, 83, diagram of the authentic and plagal modes

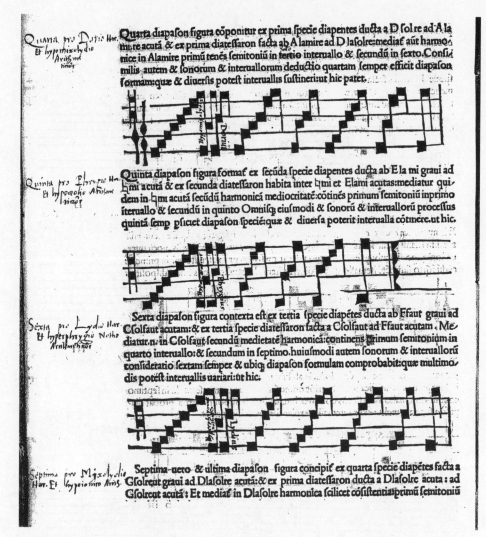

5.5 Glarean's annotations of the octave species in his copy of Gaffurio's *Practica musicae* (Munich University Library, 2° Inc.Lat. 1209. Reproduced by permission.)

modes in polyphony and concluding with a pæan to the skills of composers, Josquin des Prez foremost among them. It is not my purpose here to elucidate the technical details of Glarean's modal theory – at any rate, that has been done admirably elsewhere[17] – but rather to understand the manner in which his argument about the modes is articulated and its relationship to music print culture as represented by his polyphonic examples in Book III. Thus, I, too, will focus on the

[17] Among numerous detailed studies of Glarean's modal theory, see Bernhard Meier, "Heinrich Loriti Glareanus als Musiktheoretiker," in *Aufsätze zur Freiburger Wissenschafts- und Universitätsgeschichte* (Freiburg im Breisgau: Verlag Eberhard Albert Universitätsbuchhandlung, 1960), Harold Powers, "Mode," §III, 4 (ii) "Glarean's 12 modes," *New Grove*, XII: 407–11, and Wiering, "The Language of the Modes," 183–95.

		Hypodorius
Prima diapason species ex A, in a.	Ani- Har- chmcmon.	
Secundus.		
Hic est Aeolius modus apud Aristoxenum. Nonus.	Ari- Har- mon.	
Secunda diapason species ex B, in b.		Hypophryg.Hypolidius
Quartus	Ari- Har- chmcmon.	
Hæc diuisio in diatonico non habet locum, propter tritonum ac semidiapente. Hyperæolius.		
Tertia diapason species ex C, in c.		Dorius
Sextus. Vetus.	Ari- Har- chmcmon.	
Hic nostra ætate quinti nomen habet, apud Aristoxenum Iastius, apud alios Ionicus. Vndecimus.	Ari- Har- mon.	
Quarta diapason species ex D, in d.		
Hic Hyperiastius ab Aristoxeno nominatur. Hypomixolydius. Octauus.	Ari- Har- chmcmon.	
Primus.		Phrygius
Quinta diapason species ex E, in e.		
Hic est hypoæolius modus apud Aristoxenum. Decimus.	Ari- Har- chmcmon.	
Tertius.		Lydius
Sexta diapason species ex F, in f.		
Et hæc diuisio diatonico inepta est propter Semidiapente ac tritonu. Hyperphrygius.	Ari- Har- chmcmon.	
Quintus. Verus		Mixolydius
Septima diapason species ex G, in g.		
Hic nostra tempestate sexti nomen habet apud Aristoxenum Hypoiastius. Duodecimus.	Ari- Har- chmcmon.	
Septimus.	Ari- Har- mon.	
Ptolemæi octauus, cum secundo natura Idem.		Hypermixo.

Dis diapason Itema maxima

5.6 Glarean, *Dodecachordon*, 71, table of the octave species

polyphony contained within the treatise, but I do so with the explicit goal of understanding that music within the rhetorical framework of the treatise as a whole. To view the examples as an "anthology" is to divorce them from their surroundings; equally to read them as simple illustrations of textual precepts – as Miller does when he asserts that "Glarean's chief concern in presenting polyphonic musical examples was to demonstrate his modal system" – also misses an important aspect of the treatise.

THE IDEOLOGY OF HUMANIST PRODUCTION:
GATHERING AND FRAMING

The exemplum in Renaissance discourse

The use of illustrative materials identified as "examples" within both written and oral discourse dates to the rhetorical treatises of classical antiquity. The most direct precedents for the sixteenth century were the use of *exempla* in medieval sermons. In this sense, the *exemplum* was a literary genre of illustrative narrative with demonstrative function placed within a larger narrative scheme.[18] While simultaneously continuing in this tradition, *exempla* take on a greater role in the rhetorical strategies advocated by sixteenth-century humanists. Pragmatically described, the humanist educational initiative sought to replace existing scholastic and professional training with a curriculum based on rhetorical study of classical authors that was designed to teach its students to speak fluent, classical Latin. Humanist thought depended on example, viewing the twin discursive practices of gathering and framing materials as a central mode of transaction with classical antiquity.[19]

Erasmus's *De duplici copia verborum ac rerum*, first published in 1512 and in numerous subsequent editions,[20] is among the most explicit source describing (and prescribing) the use of examples. Book II of his *De copia* provides "an enormous supply of examples exhibiting the greatest possible diversity [vis quam maxima masimeque varia]."[21] The *Copia* itself stands as a model of the ways in which one integrates such examples in a structured (and moral) reading of texts. Indeed one witnesses in the writings of Erasmus a deliberate conflation of the "methodological" with the "morally sound."[22] For Erasmus "no discipline is so remote from rhetoric" (the specific disciplines cited are mathematics and natural science) as not to be useful in enriching the collection of examples.[23] Rather, the copious deployment of examples becomes the stuff of rhetoric itself.[24] In part, this may be seen as the response to a burgeoning print culture in which the raw materials – primarily texts of classical

---

[18] See Fritz Kemmler, *"Exempla" in Context: A Historical and Critical Study of Robert Mannyng of Brunne's "Handlyng Synne"* (Tübingen: Gunter Narr Verlag, 1984), for an overview of illustrative narratives, especially chapter 2, "Aspects of 'Exempla'," and chapter 5, "Towards a Theory of Illustrative Narratives ('Exempla')."

[19] Mary Thomas Crane, *Framing Authority: Sayings, Self, and Society in Sixteenth-Century England* (Princeton: Princeton University Press, 1993).

[20] Erasmus, *De duplici copia verborum ac rerum commentarii duo*, translated and annotated by Betty I. Knott as *Copia: Foundations of the Abundant Style*, Collected Works of Erasmus, Literary and Educational Writings 2 (Toronto: University of Toronto Press, 1978). Selected excerpts are reproduced below.

[21] *De copia*, 607. Cited here after the translation in Ann Moss, *Printed Commonplace-Books and the Structuring of Renaissance Thought* (Oxford: Oxford University Press, 1996), 109.

[22] See especially the discussion in Anthony Grafton and Lisa Jardine, *From Humanism to the Humanities: Education and the Liberal Arts in Fifteenth- and Sixteenth-Century Europe* (Cambridge, MA: Harvard University Press, 1986), 122–57. The importance of understanding the morality implicit in the proper procedure of disciplined reading as promoted by Erasmus will become clear in my discussion of Glarean's letter below (pp. 141–49).

[23] *De copia*, 638.

[24] On "copia," see Terrence Cave, *The Cornucopian Text: Problems of Writing in the French Renaissance* (Oxford: Clarendon Press, 1979).

antiquity now added to the material world and scriptural word as sources – proliferated at such a rate as to threaten to overwhelm readers if not structured in a framework that revealed pattern and hierarchy.

I will use an extended passage of excerpts from *De copia* to illustrate the Erasmian concept of example and its centrality to rhetorical enterprise, not only through the literal reproduction of the words of Erasmus's text but by following his model. By appropriating his words, excised from their original context and reframed to my purposes here, I appeal outside my text to another while simultaneously reconstructing and regulating the text to which I appeal:

A most effective means of making what we are saying convincing and of generating copia at the same time is to be found in illustrative examples, for which the Greek word is παρα-δειγματα [*paradeigmata*]. The content of examples can be something like, unlike, or in contrast to what we are illustrating, or something greater, smaller, or equivalent . . . We include under "examples" stories, fables, proverbs, opinions, parallels or comparisons, similitudes, analogies, and anything else of the same sort. Most of these are introduced not only to make our case look convincing, but also to dress it up and brighten, expand, and enrich it. Anyone therefore who chooses to furnish himself with a mass of material from the possibilities here listed can make what he has to say as copious as he likes, without thereby producing a meaningless accumulation of words; furthermore the variety of the material will prevent boredom.

Erasmus connects exemplarity with its classical Aristotelian antecedent in *paradeigma*, freeing it from the narrower medieval associations with sermon and narration. The *exemplum* is to Erasmus a representation of the world that is limited neither by verbal form nor intended effect nor type of source, but the collected material reaches exemplary significance when set into context:

In the development of copia, then, illustrations play a leading role, whether the speech is the sort that debates what action should be taken, or urges to a particular course of action, or is intended to console someone in grief, or is laudatory or vituperative; in short, whether one is trying to convince one's audience, move them, or give them pleasure.

It is not enough to provide oneself with an enormous and very varied supply of illustrations, and to have them ready for use at a moment's notice; one must also be able to handle them with variety. Variety can be provided by the very nature of the illustrative examples themselves. . .

One should therefore apply as many different illustrations as possible at each point, derived not only from the whole range of Greek and Latin literature, but also from the history of other nations.

Exempla allowed the writer to take beliefs about reality and reframe them into something that suited the direction of a new text. The example simultaneously gestured outside a text, toward something commonly recognized by writer and reader that had been systematically excised from its original context, while regulating that reality within the discourse that now framed it. Thus the example becomes a subordinate text, occurring within a superordinate text, leaving to the reader or listener the activity of actualizing or expanding it and allowing the experienced reader to recognize large networks of textual kinship and significance, to relate to sources of authoritative knowledge.[25] While this understanding of *exempla* revolves around a means of production, that production was enabled by a method of reading which relied on classified collection via the central pedagogical tool of the humanist reader: the notebook.

The humanist's notebook[26]

Not inadvisedly, but at the suggestion of his teacher, the diligent student should carefully correct his textbooks, pick out phrases and pithy remarks by inserting indicators, put a mark against the most memorable passages, or better still, excerpt them, and write what he has extracted in a little book designed for the purpose . . . For in the course of our reading we often meet many things worth remembering which we forget if we do not make extracts of them. If we wanted to find them again, we would be obliged to go through almost the whole book over again, but, if we had collected them as little excerpts, they would be to hand whenever we wanted them. Remarks which relate to the same subject–matter should be noted down and collected together in one particular place in the notebook.[27]

Two themes emerge from this passage: a description of a method of reading in which important passages are physically highlighted in their original source – or better yet, copied into a book specially designed for the purpose – and a recommendation to organize the extracts by topic. Ordering not only assists in the recollection of the marked passages but also allows access, making them immediately available, ready for use. Collections of excerpts also have a fundamental place in the teaching procedures Erasmus recommends in *De copia*. Commonplace heads (the *loci*) provide an organized system for storing and retrieving materials. Such a system insures

both that what you read will stay fixed more firmly in your mind and that you will learn to make use of the riches you have acquired by reading . . . Finally, whenever occasion demands, you will have ready to hand a supply of material for spoken or written composition, because you will have as it were a well organized set of pigeonholes, from which you may extract what you want.[28]

These ideas of reading, collecting, and indexing as a help in producing new works were the central tenets of northern humanist pedagogy in the first half of the

---

[25] John D. Lyons, *Exemplum: The Rhetoric of Example in Early Modern France and Italy* (Princeton: Princeton University Press, 1989) provides an extended discussion of the ways in which *exempla* are intimately bound to a representation of the world and serve to represent a common ground of belief that forms a recognizable shared reality between writers and readers. The practice of *exempla* allows the writer to connect a general statement with specific and convincing instances.

[26] The summary discussion of commonplace books which follows is deeply indebted to Moss, *Printed Commonplace-Books*.

[27] Johannes Murmellius, *Opusculum de discipulorum officiis: quod enchiridion scholasticorum inscribitur* (Cologne, 1505), 84. Cited and translated in Moss, *Printed Commonplace-Books*, 88.

[28] *De copia*, 638. Cited here after the translation in Moss, *Printed Commonplace-Books*, 111. Thus, the notebook provides not only a collection of usable material, but an accessible collection because the commonplace heads provide the means of retrieval.

sixteenth century. The commonplace book represented a specialized segment of a broader "notebook" culture which pervaded all aspects of writing and production. Prescriptions for commonplace books consist of pedagogic instructions for putting together systematized notebooks into which quotation from mainly printed texts were to be transcribed by hand under pre-established headings (the *loci* of the *loci communes* by which such collections were normally identified). The commonplace book bore the responsibility for shaping the mind of every schoolboy – defining his mental horizons, framing his linguistic abilities through its formative and programmatic compilation of *exempla*. The role of the teacher in this process was as guide and filter, determining what was morally edifying and pragmatically useful for inclusion in the notebook.

The commonplace book played a central role in shaping the intellectual universe of a compiler, yet it represents structures so fundamental that he had no reason to make it visible. Attempting to reveal the traces of commonplace books offers an understanding not only of a compiler's method of production in relation to the notebook, but perhaps more significantly, how that notebook mediated the literary world he inhabited and the cultural matrix in which he was implicated for the production of a future work. The concept of notebook as mediation in the collection of examples for the *Dodecachordon* provides the focus for this chapter. By highlighting the relationship of a group of manuscripts and the way they were compiled, I will demonstrate the ways in which Glarean's framing of examples broadly reflects the precepts of Erasmus's *De copia*.[29]

Yet a disclaimer at this point is not only necessary, but inevitable. Erasmus is writing about writing (words) and there are a number of ways in which his prescriptions for gathering and framing may and may not apply to musical notation or to other iconic or symbolic representations. The notebook Erasmus describes is a model for production in kind. Certainly, such musical notebooks exist. A tradition of keeping notebooks of musical phrases for use in subsequent compositions has been documented by Jessie Ann Owens. For example, Owens cites the instructions of Johannes Frosch to his pupils to collect phrases from the compositions of good composers for incorporation and adaptation in subsequent compositions by the student.[30] Not surprisingly, these instructions come from a northern humanist pedagogue writing in a deliberately learned Latin style, following very much in the path of the Murmellius quotation cited above. Such notebooks are best distinguished from the commonplace tradition, however, because in the purely pragmatic bent of their collecting they lack not only the moral framework that

---

[29] I do not intend to suggest thereby a direct relationship with *De copia*, although given his relationship with Erasmus, it is hard to imagine that Glarean was unfamiliar with it. Rather I am taking *De copia* as a well-known representative of a pervasive humanist pedagogy, a pedagogy particularly reflected in the teaching and writing of northern humanists. Fuller, "Defending the *Dodecachordon*," highlights numerous references to Erasmus in the treatise.

[30] Frosch, *Rerum musicarum opusculum* (Strasbourg: Petrus Schoeffer and Mathias Apiarium, 1535), sig. E, cited in Jessie Ann Owens, *Composers at Work: The Craft of Musical Composition 1450–1600* (New York: Oxford University Press, 1997), 190–91. See also Owens's discussion of notebooks, pp. 122–24 and her Table 6.1.

characterizes the commonplace book but also its most characteristic feature: ordered collection.[31]

My interest here is in a different sort of notebook in which the ordered and collected musical materials are being "read" for incorporation in the rhetorical context of a theoretical treatise. To understand the *Dodecachordon* as the material production of a humanist writer in northern Europe requires revising the view of its music examples to take account of the broader conventions of *exempla* within which they operate. That means taking seriously Erasmus's injunction that examples are the stuff of rhetoric itself and considering the ways in which Glarean's gathering and framing of examples operates within a rhetorical world epitomized by *copia*.

GLAREAN'S *DODECACHORDON* AS A HUMANIST TEXT

Glarean's books

Glarean provides an exceptional opportunity for exploring these perspectives because a significant portion of his personal library has long been known to survive in the collection of the university library of the Ludwig Maximilian University in Munich.[32] Most significant for the present study are four types of books that survive in the collection: (1) the writings of other theorists, including a manuscript collection of several medieval treatises, and Glarean's annotated copies of Boethius's *De musica* and Gaffurio's *De harmonia musicorum instrumentorum* and *Practica musicae*; (2) printed music collections, manuscript anthologies of motets and masses in the hands of his students, and musical works copied into other books; (3) books by Erasmus, biblical commentaries, and many editions of Greek works of antiquity and the church fathers; and (4) corrected presentation copies of the *Dodecachordon*.[33]

---

[31] Thus I would make a greater distinction between miscellanies and commonplace books than Owens does when she says: "Composers also used bound manuscripts of different sizes. Some of them were small notebooks that functioned like commonplace books: a kind of workbook for jotting down ideas and working out compositions as well as for copying music" (*Composers at Work*, 122).

[32] Among the musical items in his library are printed partbooks, annotated theory treatises, and music manuscripts. The typescript catalogues and card catalog of the Rare Book Room of Munich University Library contain extensive annotations by successive librarians as well as a number of scholars who have studied the provenance and binding of the Glarean books in recent years. The Glarean Nachlaß came to the Munich collection by way of his student Knöringen, who purchased Glarean's library shortly before his death. Knöringen became the librarian at Ingolstadt and willed his collection of 6062 volumes to the university. The Ingolstadt collection passed to Landshut in 1800 and to Munich in 1826. For a history of the library, see Ladislaus Buzás, *Geschichte der Universitätsbibliothek München* (Wiesbaden: Otto Harrassowitz, 1972). I am grateful to Irene Friedl and Dr. Wolfgang Müller for guiding me through the many unpublished sources on the collection held in the Rare Book Room and for their generous assistance during my two visits to Munich. Music manuscripts from this collection with Glarean's annotations are described in Clytus Gottwald, *Die Musikhandschriften der Universitätsbibliothek München* (Wiesbaden: Otto Harrassowitz, 1968). A partial description of the library holdings associated with Glarean appears in Iain Fenlon, "Heinrich Glarean's Books," in *Music in the German Renaissance*, ed. John Kmetz (Cambridge: Cambridge University Press, 1994), 74–102.

[33] Each of these copies contains a dedicatory letter to the recipient in Glarean's hand and corrections are penned throughout the text. The ones consulted for this study are found in the Sibley Library of the Eastman School of Music, the Library of Congress, the University Library and the Bavarian State Library, Munich, and the Abbey

The traces of Glarean's working method offered through these books provide tantalizing hints of how he read other theorists by means of his annotations; how he collected and organized musical compositions and the implicit direction for such
collecting witnessed in the surviving notebooks of his students; how he ordered
motets and masses within printed collections through his additions of modal headings; and, more generally, how he interacted with printed books in the production
of his own books. Particularly relevant to the discussion at hand are: his copies of
Boethius, *Opera philosophica minora et theologica* (Venice, 1497–99) and of Gaffurio's
Practica musicae (Brescia, 1497) and *De harmonia musicorum instrumentorum opus*
(Milan, 1518); loose bifolios of music manuscripts bound in with Gaffurio's *De harmonia*; two bound sets of printed music partbooks; and a set of manuscript partbooks.

The *exempla* of the *Dodecachordon*

The notated music examples of the *Dodecachordon* reflect the extraordinary nature
of the treatise as represented by its subject matter and presentation. Glarean deemed
the examples central to the text and insisted on including them despite the long
publication delay and difficulties he experienced on their account.[34] He himself
draws attention to their inordinate composite length at the end of the volume when
he remarks, "This was to be the end of the book, certainly of monstrous size if one
considers the examples, but of no great size at all if one looks at the text" (271).
Some eighty monophonic examples and 115 polyphonic examples are printed in
the treatise and additional works are cited. The polyphonic examples fall into
clearly defined groups that represent three distinctive modes of gathering and
framing: the first, illustrating mensuration, is drawn almost entirely from other theorists' treatises and provides an interesting view into theoretical intertextuality. The
next (and largest) group of examples comprises the demonstration of the twelve
modes in polyphony. The final group of examples cites works of individual composers in support of their merits, sometimes with, sometimes without modal
ascription. Tables 5.1a–c list these groups of Glarean's examples, in order of appearance with titles and attributions as they appear either in the index or in the body of
the *Dodecachordon*.

Library of St. Gall. The photocard reproduction of the Sibley copy begins with the title page, thus omitting the
dedicatory poem. The fact that Glarean presented copies to humanists whose libraries were often valued and
willed to other collections accounts for the large number of surviving presentation copies. (See note 10 above.)
These copies also contain annotations by later users that offer clues to the subsequent reading of the text, discussed further in chapter 9.

[34] Glarean described these difficulties in a letter to Damian a Goes in 1539, cited in Clement Miller, "The
Dodecachordon," 161. The subsequent (abridged) edition of the *Dodecachordon* as *Musicae epitome ex Glareani
Dodecachordon* (Basle: Hieronymus Curio, 1559) concludes with the mensural examples of Book III and includes
none of the discussion or examples of modes in polyphony that follow, resulting in a book of only 150 rather
than 470 pages.

Table 5.1A *Glarean's polyphonic mensural examples* (Dodecachordon, *III: 4–12*)

No.[a]	Composer[b]	Title	Source[c]
1	Gaffurio	punctum divisionis	Gaffurio II: 10
2	"	punctum perfectionis ac additionis	Gaffurio II: 12
3	"	diminution	Gaffurio II: 15
4	"	imperfection of notes	Gaffurio II: 2
5	"	imperfection via *partes propinquae*	Gaffurio II: 3
6	"	coloration in perfect mensuration	Gaffurio II: 9
7	[Glarean]	coloration in perfect mensuration	—
8	Gaffurio	alteration with punctis divisionis	Gaffurio II: 13
9	— [Glarean?]	syncopation	[ascribed to Josquin in *SGall 463*]
10	Heyden [Isaac]	prolatio triplex [Kyrie II from *Missa Quant i'ay au cueur*]	Heyden 12, 14
11	Ghiselin	[*cum sancto* from Gloria of *Missa Narayge*]	Heyden 20
11a	[Josquin]	[Benedictus from *Missa ad Fugam*]	Heyden 25
	[Hexachords]		
12	Rhau	Si Deus pro nobis	Heyden 2
13	Josquin	Voces in Lydian: Benedictus from *Missa L'homme arme VI toni*	[Heyden]
14	"	Voces in Aeolian: Benedictus from *Missa Gaudeamus*	[Heyden 16; *MunU 448*]
15	"	Deduction of voces in a canon: Agnus Dei from *Missa Hercules Dux Ferrariae*	[Heyden 41]
16	Senfl	Voces in Ionian and ligatures: *Fortuna ad voces musicales*	Heyden 11
	[Proportions]		
17	Gaffurio	proportio dupla	Gaffurio IV: 46
18	"	"	Gaffurio IV: 47
19	Cochlaeus	proportio tripla	Cochlaeus IV: 5
20	Gaffurio	"	Gaffurio IV: 51
21	Cochlaeus	proportio quadrupla	Cochlaeus IV: 6
22	" [renotated Glarean]	"	[renotated Glarean]
23	Gaffurio	"	Gaffurio IV: 53
24	"	"	Gaffurio IV: 69
25	Cochlaeus	sesquialtera	Cochlaeus IV: 7
26	Gaffurio	"	Gaffurio IV: 72
27	Obrecht	[Qui tollis from *Missa For seulement*]	*MunU 239*
28	"	[Sanctus from *Missa For seulement*]	*MunU 239*
29	Gaffurio	proportio sesquialtera	Gaffurio IV: 44

Notes:

[a] Numbering follows Miller's edition. Only examples actually printed in the treatise (as opposed to citations) are included in this table.

[b] Attributions follow Glarean (index and text); conflicting attributions, titles not identified by Glarean, and original text of contrafacta are provided in brackets.

[c] Sources: Gaffurio, *Practica musicae* (1497, examples are indicated by book and then numbered consecutively); Cochlaeus, *Tetrachordum musices* (1511, examples are indicated by book and numbered consecutively); Heyden, *Musicae* (1537, numbering follow Teramoto); *MunU 239* is the manuscript appended to Glarean's copy of Gaffurio's *De harmonia*; *MunU 448* is Glarean's copy of *Liber quindecim missarum* (RISM 1539[1]).

Table 5.1b *Glarean's polyphonic examples for the twelve modes*
(Dodecachordon, *III: 13–25*)

Mode	No[a]	Composer[b]	Title
Hypodorian	30	Josquin	Pleni sunt [*Missa Hercules Dux Ferrariae*]
	31	Pierre de la Rue	Pleni sunt [*Missa O salutaris*]
	32	Bertrand Vaqueras	*Domine non secundum (I, II)*
	33	Josquin	*Domine non secundum*
	34	Josquin	*Adjuva nos* [*Part IV, Domine non secundum*]
	35	[anon.]	*Deus meus*
	36	Antonius a Vinea	*Ego dormio (I)*
Aeolian	37	Obrecht	*Monad in Aeolian mode*
	38	Josquin	*Monad in Aeolian mode* [Agnus Dei II from *Missa Mater Patris*]
	39	Josquin	Pleni sunt from *Missa Sine nomine*
	40	[anon.]	*Monad in the Aeolian mode* [*Sic unda impellitur unda*]
	41	Obrecht	*Parce Domine*
	42	Adam von Fulda	*O vera lux et gloria* [*Ach hülf mich leid*]
	43	Damian a Goes	*Ne laeteris*
Hypophrygian	44	[anon.]	*Salvum me fac, Domine*
	45	Isaac	*Tota pulchra es*
	46	Josquin	*Magnus es tu Domine*
Hyperaeolian	47	Sixt Dietrich	*O Domine Jesu Christe*
	48	Pierre de la Rue	Christe eleison *from Missa S. Antonii*
Hypolydian	49	Gregor Meyer	*Monad in the Hypolydian*
	50	Gregor Meyer	*Dyad*
	51	Gerard a Salice	*Os justi*
	52	Fra Legendre	*Laudate Dominum omnes gentes*
Ionian	53	Josquin	*Ave verum (I)*
	54	Josquin	*"(II)*
	55	Adam Luyr	*Juppiter omnipotens*
	56	Johannes Richafort	*Christus resurgens*
Dorian	57	Gregor Meyer	*Monad in the Dorian*
	58	Brumel	Qui venit from *Missa Festivale*
	59	Thomas Tzamen	*Domine Jesu Christe*
	60	Jean Mouton	*Domine salvum fac Regem*
Hypomixolydian	61	Gregor Meyer	*Dyad in a monad*
	62	Josquin	Agnus Dei *from Missa de Nostra Domina*
	63	Johann Vannius	*Attendite popule meus*
Phrygian	64	Gregor Meyer	*Monad in the Phrygian*
	65	Paul Wuest	*Pleni sunt*
	66	Isaac [Pesenti]	*Tulerunt Dominum meum*

Table 5.1b (*cont.*)

Mode	Noª	Composerᵇ	Title
Hypoaeolian	67	Marbriano de Orto	*Monad in the Hypoaeolian* [Agnus Dei II from *Missa J'ay pris amour*]
	68	Josquin	Pleni sunt from *Missa Pange Lingua*
	69	Jean Mouton	*Miseremini mei*
	70	Nicolaus Craen	*Ecce video coelos apertos*
Lydian	71	Sixt Dietrich	*Servus tuus*
	72	Sixt Dietrich	*Erue, Domine, animam meam*
	73	Heinrich Isaac	*Loquebar de testimoniis tuis*
	74	Senfl	*Deus in adjutorium meum*
	75	Gregor Meyer	*Qui mihi ministrat* [Lydian]
Ionian	76	Gregor Meyer	" [Ionian]
Hyperphrygian	77	Sixt Dietrich	*Domine fac mecum*
	78	Sixt Dietrich	*Ab occultis meis*
Mixolydian	79	Brumel	*Benedictus*
	80	Josquin	*Per illud ave*
	81	Isaac	*Anima mea*
Hypoionian	82	Gregor Meyer	*Monad in the Hypoionian*
	83	Antoine de Févin	Pleni sunt from *Missa Ave Maria*
	84	Josquin	*O Jesu fili David* [*Coment peult haver joye*]
	85	Josquin	*Ave Maria*
Dorian/Hypodorian	86	Josquin	*Victimae paschali laudes*
Dorian/Phrygian	87	Josquin	*De profundis*
Phrygian/Hypophrygian	88	Josquin	*Liber generationis*
Lydian/Hypolydian	89	Josquin	Agnus Dei from *Missa Fortuna desperata*
Mixolydian/Hypomixolydian	90	Josquin	Et in terra pax from *Missa de nostra Domina*
Aeolian/Hypoaeolian	91	Gregor Meyer	*Connection of Aeolian and Hypoaelian* [*Kyrie de nostra Domina*]
Ionian/Hypoionian	92	Josquin	*Planxit autem David*
First Diapente: re la	93		*A furore tuo, Domine* [*Auss hertzen grund*]
Second Diapente: mi-mi	94	Andreas Sylvanus	Kyrie and Osanna from *Missa Malheur me bat*
Third Diapente: fa-fa	95	Gregor Meyer	*Confitebor Domino*
Ionian	96	[anon.]	*Ut sol in synemmenon* [*Ut queant laxis*]
Mixolydian	97	Nicolaus Listenius	*Jesu Christe*

Notes:

ª Numbering follows Miller's edition. Only examples actually printed in the treatise (as opposed to citations) are included in this table.

ᵇ Attributions follow Glarean (index and text); conflicting attributions, titles not identified by Glarean, and original text of contrafacta are provided in brackets.

Table 5.1c *Examples concerning the skill of* symphonetæ *(Dodecachordon, III: 26)*

No.	Composer	Title	Source
98	Josquin	Benedictus from *Missa L'homme armé super voces musicales*	Heyden 24; [*MunU 448*] [J1502]
99	"	" [Qui venit]	Heyden 23; [*MunU 448*] [J1502]
100	"	" [In nomine]	Heyden 22; [*MunU 448*] [J1502]
101	"	Agnus Dei II from *Missa L'homme armé super voces musicales*	Heyden 26; [*MunU 448*] [J1502]
102	Senfl	*Trium ex una*	?
103	Pierre de la Rue	*Quaternum vocum ex unica* [Agnus Dei II from *Missa L'homme armé*]	Heyden 27
104	"	Kyrie from *Missa O salutaris*	1516[1]
105–06	Josquin	Connected Modes [Pleni sunt from *Missa Mater Patris*]	Heyden 3; [J1514]
107–08	"	Connected Modes [Benedictus from *Missa Mater Patris*]	Heyden 4; [J1514]
109–10	"	Dorian [Agnus Dei II from *Missa Malheur me bat*]	Heyden 19; [J1505]
111	"	Fuga ad minimam [*De tous biens playne*]	*MunU 239* [1501]
112	Ockeghem	Fuga trium vocum in epidiatessaron [*Prennez sur moi*]	Heyden 10
113	"	Kyrie from *Missa ad Omnem tonum*	*MunU 448*
114	"	Benedictus from *Missa ad Omnem tonum*	*MunU 448*
115	Brumel	Pleni sunt from *Missa Dringhs*	*MunU 374* [=1509[1]]
116	"	Benedictus from *Missa Dringhs*	*MunU 374* [=1509[1]]
117	"	Agnus Dei from *Missa Dringhs*	*MunU 374* [=1509[1]]
118	Isaac	*Conceptio Mariae*	Heyden 28
119	Mouton	*Salve mater salvatoris*	[1520[2]]
120	"	*Nesciens mater*	[1521[7]]
121	Josquin	Song of Louis XII	*SGall 462*

The examples of polyphonic modality

Glarean is explicit about his reasons for including polyphonic compositions in the section on mode.[35] Resonances with Erasmus's *De copia* are not difficult to discern and I have attempted to highlight them with interpolations from Erasmus below.

(1) Glarean begins the chapter heading the discussion of the twelve modes in polyphony by stating that since he has already set forth the rules with clarity and brevity, it remains "to teach [this new art] by examples." He goes on to say that he will present "good, simple, clear, easily singable and unembellished songs . . . in which the essence" of the art of twelve modes is expressed.

---

[35] Miller, trans., 247–48. For a slightly different interpretation of Glarean's priorities in including examples, see Wiering, "The Language of the Modes," 186.

[E]nriching our style depends on the accumulation of proofs and arguments . . . Different reasons can be brought forward to confirm one and the same proposition, and the reasons themselves can be supported by further arguments . . . [T]he illustrative example properly so called . . . is a reference to a genuine or apparently genuine occurrence designed to induce people to accept what we are saying . . . (Erasmus, 605)

(2) Glarean limits himself to four-voice compositions, likening the four voices to the four elements.[36]

The four elements, so very unlike, even hostile one to another, are nevertheless the essence of primal matter. (Erasmus, 154)

(3) Glarean wants to contrast the examples of such superior *symphonetæ* as Josquin with the less beautiful songs of others, to aid the reader in judgments.

I shall indicate some of the ways [of enlarging and expanding examples]: first by "commendation," when we introduce a section in which we praise the incident, or the author, or the nation from which the illustration is drawn. If one quoted something done or said by a Spartan, for example, one could preface the anecdote by remarking that this people was always superior to the rest in wisdom and in military and civil organization, and abounded in splendid moral object-lessons . . .

One may invent little passages of commendation like this, making them long or short according to the requirements of the context; but one should take care to invent one that is appropriate; for example, if one is quoting something to illustrate faithfulness, one will commend one's source for seriousness and good faith, or if one wishes the audience to see something as an example of proper feeling, one will make proper feeling the subject of one's remarks. (Erasmus, 608–09)

(4) Glarean intends his examples to represent what he describes as "three ages" of composition: a few examples of the "old and simple" of seventy years before; examples of the art in its "early mature" stage forty years before; and the *ars perfecta* of the past twenty-five years.[37]

It is not enough to provide oneself with an enormous and very varied supply of illustrations . . .; one must also be able to handle them with variety. Variety can be provided by the very nature of the illustrative examples themselves. They can be things done or said in the past, or be derived from the customs of various nations . . . Or it may be a question of period: early times, then the subsequent periods of antiquity, recent history, and things in our own lives . . . (Erasmus, 607)

[36] The sole exception is Mouton's eight-voice *Nesciens mater*, canonically derived from four voices, at the very end of the *Dodecachordon*, for which Glarean apologizes. Five-voice works like Josquin's *Miserere* and *Stabat mater* are cited but not reproduced. Wiering, "The Language of the Modes," 186, comments on these examples.

[37] The "recent past" has to be understood here in relation to the period when most of the work on the *Dodecachordon* took place, probably between 1525 and 1539. The 1547 publication date, the result of difficulties in finding a publisher, reflects Glarean's insistence that the music examples be printed as part of the treatise. Thus, not surprisingly, most of Glarean's works come from sources from the first quarter of the century and his polyphonic repertory is much closer to that of Aron's *Trattato* published some twenty-two years earlier than to Zarlino's *Le istitutioni harmoniche* published a mere decade later. On the context of compositional eras, see Jessie-Ann Owens, "Music Historiography and the Definition of Renaissance," *Notes* 47 (1990), 305–30.

Glarean's stated criteria for including examples are remarkably consistent with the prescriptions of Erasmus's *De copia*. Most notable and directly parallel is Erasmus' injunction to teach by example, the subject of Glarean's first point. Indeed the *Dodecachordon* serves as a shining exemplar of a copious bounty of examples. That the examples are in musical notation is a reflection of the subject matter, but the approach is undeniably infused with the humanist's preoccupation with *exempla* and their authenticating power. Similarly, Glarean's other criteria (the natural elements, commendation and comparison, and chronological placement) are all given by Erasmus as ways of providing variety in the treatment of examples. I do not wish to suggest overt emulation of *De copia* on Glarean's part, but rather to highlight means and materials of humanist production that were so deeply ingrained as to cross disciplinary boundaries with ease. This perspective also suggests a previously unrecognized rationale for Glarean's insistence on including the examples in the treatise in the face of publication difficulties, for in this Erasmian frame of reference, the morally structured reading of *exempla* is the substance of the newly produced work; mere citation would not suffice. These music examples are part and parcel of a text that by design is a product of a true intertextuality of fragments.

A number of additional, but unstated, criteria also bear on Glarean's choice of examples. In keeping with his Catholic humanist stance, the texted polyphonic examples of the *Dodecachordon* have exclusively Latin texts, and almost all of those are central sacred texts which reinforce Glarean's theological position.[38] Secular compositions are either transmitted as contrafacts (e.g. Josquin "O Jesu fili David") or as textless "French songs" (e.g. Ockeghem's *Prenez sur moi*, Josquin's *De tous biens playne*). An even more nuanced understanding of this Catholic humanist agenda comes from a recognition of how Glarean compiled the examples for this section of the treatise. The role of teacher and writer as moral filter is omnipresent in the humanist confrontation of (potentially dangerous) pagan texts of antiquity and scriptural authority.[39] By examining manuscript notebooks and annotated prints associated with the repertory of this section of the *Dodecachordon* we are offered a glimpse into how Glarean compiled his examples as well as the way in which the process served as a moral filter on examples ultimately included in the *Dodecachordon*. This process is explored in detail in chapter 6.

[38] Fuller's recent work ("Defending the *Dodecachordon*") on the monophonic examples highlighted the complementary strands of Glarean's agenda, and a similar argument might be advanced for the polyphonic examples.
[39] Grafton and Jardine, *From Humanism to the Humanities*, 148, and Crane, *Framing Authority*.

THE POLYPHONY OF THE
DODECACHORDON

MUSICAL SOURCES OF MODAL EXAMPLES

I begin with the central and largest group of examples in the *Dodecachordon*: the illustrations of the twelve modes in polyphony. Glarean's ability to draw on other theorists for notated examples is extremely limited in this section of the treatise because there is almost no precedent for his venture, and what precedent there was was tied to eight-mode theory.[1] The congruences between Glarean's illustrations and a repertory represented by a number of music prints and manuscripts from the first decades of the sixteenth century has often been observed.[2] Most prominent among these are the first three of Petrucci's motet anthologies, *Motetti A*, *B*, and *C*,[3] a set of partbooks in Glarean's library in the hand of his student Martin Besard with Glarean's annotations and a date of 1527 (hereafter referred to as the Munich partbooks),[4] and the so-called "Tschudi Liederbuch," a notebook in the hand of another of Glarean's pupils, and its accompanying sketchbook.[5] The relationship of

[1] Sebald Heyden does include a set of examples for the eight modes at the end of his *Musicae* (1537) without comment (see the discussion in chapter 4), but these appeared after Glarean had apparently completed most of the work on this section of the treatise. The specific influence of Heyden's work on Glarean is discussed further below.

[2] Clement A. Miller ("The *Dodecachordon*: Its Origin and Influence on Renaissance Musical Thought," *Musica disciplina* 15 (1961)) discussed the shared content of the *Dodecachordon* and *MunU 322–25* and *SGall 463*; Clytus Gottwald (*Die Musikhandschriften der Universitätsbibliothek München* (Wiesbaden: Otto Harrassowitz, 1968)), highlighted the relationship of *MunU 322–25* and *RISM 1502¹* and *RISM 1503¹*; Donald Loach ("Aegidius Tschudi's Songbook," Ph.D. dissertation, University of California, Berkeley (1969)) considered the sources of *SGall 463* and shared materials of the *Dodecachordon*. George Warren Drake ("The First Printed Books of Motets, Petrucci's *Motetti A numero Trentatre A* (Venice, 1502) and *Motetti de Passione, de Cruce, de Sacramento, de Beata Virgine et Huiusmode B* (Venice, 1503): A Critical Study and Complete Edition," Ph.D. dissertation, University of Illinois (1972)) noted the number of motets from Petrucci's *Motetti A* and *B* which appeared in the *Dodecachordon*, *MunU 322–25*, and *SGall 463*, but was concerned with the dissemination of the Petrucci repertory rather than the interrelationship of these last three sources.

Similarly, Harry B. Lincoln's inclusion of the *Dodecachordon* in *The Latin Motet: Indexes to Printed Collections, 1500–1600*, Musicological Studies 59 (Ottawa: The Institute of Mediaeval Music, 1993) points to a number of concordances, but only for printed sources of the motet examples and must be used with caution.

[3] *Motetti A. numero trentatre. A* (Venice, 1502) = RISM 1502¹; *Motetti De passione De cruce De sacramento De beata virgine et huius modi. B* (Venice, 1503) = RISM 1503¹; and *Motetti C* (Venice, 1504) = RISM 1504¹.

[4] Munich, Universitätsbibliothek der Ludwig-Maximilians-Universität, MS 8° 322–25 (*MunU 322–25*).

[5] Saint Gall, Stiftsbibliothek, MS 463 ("Tschudi Liederbuch") and MS 464 (sketchbook). (*SGall 463* and *SGall 464*).

these sources with the *Dodecachordon*, however, has usually been described in terms of one-to-one relationships of concordances. Likewise, the survival of a portion of Glarean's library, including several of these sources, has long been taken as an indication of his sources for the compilation of the *Dodecachordon*.[6] Studies of this group of sources, too, have never considered the evidence that the complicated interplay of these prints and manuscripts *taken all together* along with the contents of Glarean's library (and with an understanding of the way Glarean produced his other, non-musical, books) offers for understanding the production of the *Dodecachordon*.

Previous studies that discussed these examples have tended to consider them in indexical fashion by composer, by genre, by modal indication, and so forth.[7] The extensive indices of the treatise itself might seem to support such an approach. Certainly the focus has been on the repertory as it is reproduced in these chapters of the treatise; little attempt has been made to re-create the larger repertory from which Glarean compiled his examples – a seemingly impossible task. Ironically, for Glarean's later readers even the need to compile a source list is mitigated because the examples are, after all, printed in the treatise.[8] Thus through the very printing of examples in full, Glarean veils the means by which they reached his treatise. In doing so, he stands firmly in the humanist tradition of gathering and framing by means of selection, rearrangement, and assimilation in the production of a new work. It is easy for modern readers to be lulled into a sense of complacency about the nature of Glarean's sources since many of the examples he included are common to central Petrucci and Antico prints from the first quarter of the century. It is also easy to make assumptions about Glarean's surviving books in reference to his working method without a real exploration of the information that what we know of his library does and does not offer *vis-a-vis* the production of the *Dodecachordon*.

In Table 6.1, the list of Glarean's polyphonic examples in the chapters which exemplify the twelve modes (outlined earlier in Table 5.1b) now includes a list of source concordances. Each chapter begins with works labeled "monads" that were either newly commissioned from composers like Gregor Meyer and Sixt Dietrich or were associated with Sebald Heyden's *Musicae* of 1537.[9] The list of examples in

---

[6] As I will discuss below in connection with examples borrowed from Heyden's *Musicae*, books not in Glarean's collection were often the source of his examples, even when such examples also appear in other works within his collection.   [7] As described in chapter 5; see especially the introduction and citations in nn. 11–12.

[8] As discussed in chapters 3 and 7, in the cases of Aron and Zarlino, the references are merely citations, so modern scholars found it necessary to establish sources for the works cited.

[9] This process of soliciting new works is necessarily distinct from the kind of gathering and framing that is my primary concern. These works and the evidence of their commissions are discussed by Miller, in his "Introduction" to the English Translation of the *Dodecachordon*, 31. For a detailed study of two of the works Glarean commissioned, see Powers, "Music as Text and Text as Music," in *Musik als Text*, ed. Hermann Danuser and Tobias Plebuch (Kassel: Bärenreiter, 1998), Part II. On the text and musical provenance of Sixt Dietrich's *O Domine Jesu Christe*, see Fuller, "Defending the *Dodecachordon*: Ideological Currents in Glarean's Modal Theory," *Journal of the American Musicological Society* 49 (1996), 214–16. The role of Heyden's treatise is discussed in greater detail below.

Table 6.1 is presented in two columns in recognition of this special group of works; I will postpone discussion of the "monads" momentarily.

For the remaining works (represented in the right half of the divided columns), I have deliberately restricted the list of concordances to give prominence to works known to be from, or associated with, Glarean's library in an effort to show how a relatively small number of material texts mediated a larger printed musical repertory. Thus the right portion of Column I of the primary sources in Table 6.1 contains only sources from the Munich collection. These are identified by the manuscript number of that collection even when they are simply binder's copies of prints with annotations. For example, Manuscript 374 contains two Petrucci prints bound as a single volume: *Motetti C* (RISM 1504[1]) and *Missarum diversorum auctorum* (RISM 1509[1]).[10] Column II lists a larger number of prints, representing a reading out from the sources cited in Column I. This representation comprises three distinct possibilities: (1) a print which served as the source for a particular work found within a manuscript collection; (2) the individual print in which a work appears from a binding that consists of two or more individual printed sources; or (3) printed sources not directly related to Glarean's library which textual evidence suggests are related to Glarean's source for the example. Column III supplies a concordance for those examples with no entries in Columns I or II as an indication of the wider range of sources in which these works appear. Finally, the pair of columns on the right indicates concordances with the Tschudi manuscripts (*SGall 463* and *464*) discussed below.

A glance through this delineation of types of examples and sources shows a distinction: sources that Glarean (almost) certainly used; sources he may or may not have had access to; and sources which simply share concordances with examples in the *Dodecachordon*. The distinction is crucial to understanding how he chose and framed his *exempla*. I am graphically representing a reading that moves "out" from the *Dodecachordon*, paying attention to the order of material in the original sources, considering what Glarean does *not* use from those sources as well as what he does, and how those sources served as a basis for the collection of examples. It is precisely the knowledge of what the theorist *omitted* that often points to the real significance of what is included and an understanding of the multiplicity of meanings which examples may carry. Thus a treatise may become a pointer to a repertory, a theoretical tradition, a political event, or a theological position, among other possibilities. In some cases the most significant sources are not at first glance the "obvious" ones, nor the earliest, but I suggest that the relatively small (and easily managed) collection of bound books that appears in Column I of Table 6.1 circumscribed the larger

---

[10] Such compilations were usual for sixteenth-century prints that were normally purchased unbound and grouped together by their owner for binding. The other prints from Glarean's library in Column I of Table 6.1 are: *MunU 322*, the Munich partbooks described above; *MunU 239*, Glarean's copy of Gaffurio's *De harmonia* with manuscript bifolios bound in the back; and *MunU 448*, Glarean's copy of *Liber quindecim missarum* (Nuremberg: Petreius, 1539).

group of sources listed in Column II that in one form or another represented the corpus from which Glarean chose his examples.

The starting point from which I began to understand the examples of the *Dodecachordon* from the perspective of the procedure of collecting *exempla* and the use of notebooks was the recognition of the role that the Munich partbooks (*MunU 322–25*) represent in this process. This set of motet partbooks copied by Glarean's pupil Martin Besard has modal annotations in Glarean's hand and an autograph preface at the beginning of the tenor partbook signed by Glarean and dated 1527.[11]

Taken as a whole, the motets that accompany this preface in the Munich partbooks present a more homogeneous collection of composers and liturgical associations than suggested by the profiles of the prints from which they are drawn through overt liturgical associations of text, music, or both. Well known, but not usually connected to the *Dodecachordon*, are the number of concordances between this manuscript and Petrucci's *Motetti A* and *B* outlined in Table 6.2. I have taken the prints rather than the Munich partbooks or the treatise as a starting point in order to demonstrate the selection process recorded in the relationship of these sources. The first six items of the partbooks come from *Motetti A* and were copied in order from that source. Items 7–11 of the partbooks comprise three motets attributed to Josquin followed by an untexted trio and duo.[12] Items 12–16 are again copied in order from a Petrucci print: *Motetti B*. The manuscript concludes with three Latin-texted works,[13] the last Senfl's *Crux fidelis*. The inclusion of Glarean's letter in the tenor partbook – dated 1527, just when he appears to have been seriously engaged in work on the *Dodecachordon* – offers the tantalizing possibility that the manuscript represents an intermediary notebook that facilitated the assembling of the theory treatise. Physical evidence discussed below confirms the relationship. The manuscript functions in this context like a commonplace book – a preliminary distillation of the *Motetti A* and *B* prints, with a notable emphasis on Josquin and on central liturgical texts (in other words, not on mode, *per se*). The final winnowing in the *Dodecachordon* – three of six selections from *Motetti A*, four of five from *Motetti B* – further heightens the emphasis on Josquin and on four-voice compositions, two explicit selection criteria of the *Dodecachordon* discussed in chapter 5.

Glarean's preface in the tenor partbook (reproduced in Fig. 6.1 and in the text translation discussed in detail below) also points to an understanding of the Munich partbooks from the perspective of the humanist's notebook. This letter, from Glarean, the teacher, heightens (indeed prescribes) the moral *raison d'être* for the

---

[11] Besard is identified as the copyist in Arnold Geering, "Die Vokalmusik in der Schweiz zur Zeit der Reformation," *Schweizerisches Jahrbuch für Musikwissenschaft* 6 (1933), 36, 92.

[12] Although two of these items do have concordances with Petrucci prints, the collecting method of the manuscript (i.e. copying a group of items in order from a single source) suggests they were copied from another (manuscript) source which probably contained all three items in this order.

[13] These are concordant with the *Odhecaton* and *Canti B*.

Table 6.1 Sources for Glarean's polyphonic examples of the modes (Dodecachordon, III: 13–25)

Mode	No.[a]	Composer[b]	Title	I: Primary source[c]	II: Print[d]	III: Other[e]	Tschudi[f]	SGall 464[g]
Hypodorian	30	Josquin	Pleni sunt	Heyden 8	J1505			
	31	Pierre de la Rue	Pleni sunt	Heyden 39	1516[l]			
	32	Bertrand Vaqueras	Domine non secundum	MunU 322	1503[1]		98	
	33	Josquin	Domine non secundum	MunU 322	1503[1]		97	
	34	Josquin	Adjuva nos	MunU 322	1503[1]			
	35	[anon.]	Deus meus	?		SGall 462	13	
	36	Antonius a Vinea	Ego dormio	?		[VatS 15]	103	
Aeolian	37	Obrecht	Monad in Aeolian mode	Heyden 9	1503[1]			
	38	Josquin	Monad in Aeolian mode	Heyden 5	J1514			
	39	Josquin	Pleni sunt from Missa Sine nomine	Heyden 38	J1514			
	40	[anon.]	Monad in the Aeolian mode	Heyden 6				
	41	Obrecht	Parce Domine	MunU 322	1503[1]		128	
	42	Adam von Fulda	O vera lux et gloria	?			163	x
	43	Damian a Goes	Ne laeteris	?				
Hypophrygian	44	[anon.]	Salvum me fac, Domine	?				
	45	Isaac	Tota pulchra es	MunU 322	[1504[1]]	[CorBC 95–6]	110	x
	46	Josquin	Magnus es tu Domine		1503[1]		112	
Hyperaeolian	47	Sixt Dietrich	O Domine Jesu Christe	commission				
Hypolydian	48	Pierre de la Rue	Christe eleison from Missa S.Antonii	MunU 374	1509[1]			
	49	Gregor Meyer	Monad in the Hypolydian	commission				
	50	Gregor Meyer	Dyad	commission				
	51	Gerard a Salice	Os justi	MunU 239				
	52	Fra Legendre	Laudate Dominum omnes gentes	?				
Ionian	53	Josquin	Ave verum	Heyden 43 / MunU 322	1503[1]		27	
	54	"	" (II)	Heyden 18 / MunU 322	1503[1]			
	55	Adam Luyr	Juppiter omnipotens	?			26	
	56	Johannes Richafort	Christus resurgens	commission	1520[2]			
Dorian	57	Gregor Meyer	Monad in the Dorian	commission				
	58	Brumel	Qui venit from Missa Festivale	MunU 448	1539[1]			
	59	Thomas Tzamen	Domine Jesu Christe		1520[2]		8	
	60	Jean Mouton	Domine salvum fac Regem		[Josquin]			

Mode	No.	Composer	Title	Source	Date / print	Index	x
Hypomixolydian	61	Gregor Meyer	*Dyad in a monad*	commission			
	62	Josquin	*Agnus Dei from Missa de Nostra Domina*	*MunU 448*	1539[1] [1516[1]]	111 [Josquin]	x
Phrygian	63	Johann Vannius	*Attendite popule meus*	*MunU 239*			
	64	Gregor Meyer	*Monad in the Phrygian*	commission			
	65	Paul Wuest	*Pleni sunt*	?			
	66	Isaac [Pesenti]	*Tulerunt Dominum meum*	*MunU 322*	[1503[1]]	136 [Mouton]	x
Hypoaeolian	67	de Orto	*Monad in the Hypoaeolian*	Heyden 7			
	68	Josquin	*Pleni sunt from Missa Pange Lingua*	[*MunBS 260*]	[1539[2]]		
	69	Mouton	*Miseremini mei*		1520[2] [Josquin]	20	
Lydian	70	Nicolaus Craen	*Ecce video coelos apertos*	*MunU 322*	1502[1]		
	71	Sixt Dietrich	*Servus tuus*	commission			
	72	Sixt Dietrich	*Erue, Domine, animam meam*	commission			
	73	Heinrich Isaac	*Loquebar de testimoniis tuis*		?		
	74	Senfl	*Deus in adjutorium meum*		?		
Ionian	75	Gregor Meyer	*Qui mihi ministrat [Lydian]*	commission			
	76	Gregor Meyer	*" [Ionian]*	commission			
Hyperphrygian	77	Sixt Dietrich	*Domine fac mecum*	commission			
	78	Sixt Dietrich	*Ab occultis meis*	commission			
Mixolydian	79	Brumel	*Benedictus*	?			
	80	Mouton [Josquin]	*Per illud ave*	[*MunBS 260* anon.]			
	81	Isaac	*Anima mea*	?			
Hypoionian	82	Gregor Meyer	*Monad in the Hypoionian*	commission			
	83	Antoine de Févin	*Pleni sunt from Missa Ave Maria*		1516[1]		
	84	Josquin	*O Jesu fili David*		1502[2]		
	85	Josquin	*Ave Maria*	*MunU 322*	1502[1]	148	x
Connected Modes	86	Josquin	*Victimae paschali laudes*	*MunU 322*	1502[1]	100	x
	87	Josquin	*De profundis*				
	88	Josquin	*Liber generationis*	*MunU 374*	1504[1]	127	
	89	Josquin	*Agnus Dei from Missa Fortuna Desperata*	*MunU 448*	1539[1] [J 1502]		
	90	Josquin	*Et in terra pax from Missa de nostra Domina*	*MunU 448*	1539[1] [1516[1]]	15	x

Table 6.1 (*cont.*)

Mode	No.ᵃ	Composerᵇ	Title	I: Primary sourceᶜ	II: Printᵈ	III: Otherᵉ	Tschudiᶠ	SGall 464ᵍ
	91	Gregor Meyer	*Connection of Aeolian and Hypoaelian*	commission				x
	92	Josquin	*Planxit autem David*		*MunU* 374 1504¹		146	
1st Diapente	93	[anon.]	*A furore tuo, Domine*	?			75	
2nd Diapente	94	Andreas Sylvanus	Kyrie and Osanna from *Missa Malheur me bat*	?				
3rd Diapente	95	Gregory Meyer	*Confitebor Domino*	commission				
Ionian	96		*Ut sol in synemmenon*	?				
Mixolydian	97	Nicolaus Listenius	*Jesu Christe*	Heyden 15				

Notes:

ᵃ Numbering follows Miller.

ᵇ The composer column is divided to reflect the different functions of the examples. Those to the left are often labeled "monads" and were excerpted from theoretical sources or commissioned by Glarean. Most appear to have been the last examples put into the treatise, sometime after 1537–39.

ᶜ The division of this column follows the principles outlined for composers. These are sources that either still form part of Glarean's library or that undoubtedly provided his example. Books from his library are given by the *MunU* sigla, even when these are simply annotated prints.

ᵈ This is a printed source which was (a) owned by Glarean and represented in his library; (b) appears to be the exemplar for a primary source listed in column I; or (c) appears to have been known to Glarean in some form.

ᵉ Concordances for works with no entries in Columns I and II.

ᶠ Concordances with the Tschudi Liederbuch (*SGall 463*) identified in Loach, "Aegedius Tschudi's Songbook."

ᵍ Works cited on the modal sketch of *SGall 464*, the sketchbook that was the basis of ordering Tschudi's Liederbuch.

Table 6.2 *Petrucci prints,* MunU 322–5, *the* Dodecachordon, *and* SGall 463

Motetti A		MunU 322	Mode	Dodecachordon	SGall 463
1	—	[*Misericordia et veritas*]			
2	Josquin	*Ave Maria gratia plena*	1	Hypoionian	85	148
3	[Compère]	*O genetrix gloriosa mater Dei*				
4	J. Pinarol	*Surge propera amica mea*				
5	Josquin	*Virgo prudentissima*	2	Hypodorian	—	99
6	Compère	*Crux triumphans*				94
7	Compère	*Propter gravamen*				
8	—	*Descendi in hortum meum*				118
9	Agricola	*O quam glorfica luce*				
10	Weerbecke	*Adonai sanctissime*				104
11	Josquin	*Victimae psachale laudes*	3	Dorian/Hypodorian	86	100
12	—	*Benedicta sit creatrix*	4	Hypomixolydian	—	125
13	Brumel	*Regina caeli laetare*				
14	Weerbecke	*Virgo Maria*				
15	Ghiselin	*O florens rosa mater*				18
16	N. Craen	*Ecce vidi celos apertos*	5	Hypoaeolian	70	20
17	Compère	*Sile fragor ac verborum*				
18	Compère	*Ave Maria gratia plena*				
19	Ghiselin	*La Spagna*				
20	[Craen]	*Ave Maria gratia plena*				
21	Brumel	*Ave stella matutina*				
22	Weerbecke	*Ibo mihi ad montem myrrhe*				
23	Weerbecke	*Ave Domina sancta Maria*				
24	Weerbecke	*O pulcherrima mulierum*				
25	—	*Stella caeli extirpavit*				
26	Weerbecke	*Vidi speciosam*				
27	—	*Ave vera caro Christi*				
28	—	*Da pacem Domine*				
29	Compère	*Quis numerare queat*				192
30	Tinctoris	*Virgo Dei throno digna*	6	Hypodorian	—	14
31	Weerbecke	*Christi mater Ave*				
32	Weerbecke	*Ave stella matutina*				
33	Ghiselin	*Anima mea liquefacta est*				
34	[Weerbecke in index]	*Mater digna dei*				
35	Josquin	*De tous biens*				
—	Josquin	*Memor esto verbi tui*	7	Licentious Dorian	[cited]	88
—	Josquin	*Magnus es tu domine*	8	Hypophrygian	46	112
—	Josquin	*Tulerunt dominum meum*	9	Phrygian	66 [att. Isaac]	111
—	—	*Trium* (untexted)	10	Hypodorian		
—	—	*Duum* (untexted)	11	Dorian		

Table 6.2 (*cont.*)

	Motetti B		MunU 322	Mode	Dodecachordon	SGall 463
1	Stappen	*Non lotis manibus*				
2	Josquin	*O Domine Jesu Christe*				
3	Josquin	*Qui velatus facie fuisti*				
4	—	*Secundum multitudinem*				
5	Weerbecke	*Tenebrae factae sunt*				
6	Josquin	*Ave verum corpus natum*	12	Ionian	53	27
7	Weerbecke	*Verbum caro factum est*				
8	Orto	*Domine non secundum*				
9	Vaqueras	*Domine non secundum*	13	Hypodorian	32	98
10	Josquin	*Domine non secundum*	14	Dorian/Hypodorian	33	97
11		*Tulerunt Dominum meum*	[9]		66 [att. Isaac]	111
12	Obrecht	*Parce Domine*	15	Aeolian [tenor hypoaeolian]	41	128
13	—	*Pange lingua gloriosi*				
14	—	*Ave Domina sancta Maria*				
15	—	*Parce Domine*				
16	Brumel	*Lauda Sion*				122
17	Weerbecke	*Panis angelicus*				
18	Weerbecke	*Ave verum corpus natum*				
19	Biaumont	*Aspice Domine*				134
20	Weerbecke	*Anima Christi*				
21	Compère	*In nomine Jesu*				
22	Gregoire	*Ave verum corpus natum*				
23	—	*Adoro te devote*				
24	Josquin	*Tu solus qui facis mirabilia*				95
25	Regis	*Ave Maria gratia plena*	16	[no modal ascription] —		9
26	Agricola	*Ave pulcherrima regina*				
27	—	*Sancta Maria*				
28	Martini	*Ave decus*				
29	—	*Haec est illa dulcis rosa*				
30	Stappen	*Ave Maria gratia plena*				
31	—	*Gaude virgo mater Christi*				
32	—	*Salve regina*				
33	—	*Quis dabit meo aquam*				
34	—	*Secunda impellitur*			[40]	
[1502²]	[Brumel]	*Ave ancilla trinitatis*	17	[no modal ascription] [39]		
[1501]	[Brumel]	*Mater patris*	18	[no modal ascription] —		
—	Senfl	*Crux fidelis inter omnes*	19	[no modal ascription] —		

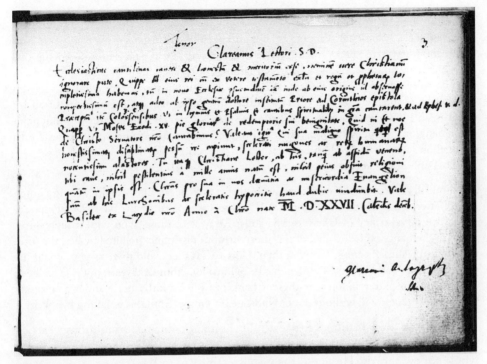

6.1 Glarean's letter in the tenor partbook of *MunU 324* (Munich University Library, 8° Cod.Mus. 324. Reproduced by permission.)

collection of his student. The letter is an integral part of the manuscript, not a later addition to the notebook.[14] Glarean's modal annotations throughout the tenor partbook, too, added *after* the selection and copying of the motets, fit a pattern of reading and annotation that seeks to put *exempla* in the appropriate pigeon-holes for later use.

Glarean's preface frames the interpretation of the motets contained in the part-books. Although normally described as a defense of plainsong against the attacks of Zwingli and the Basle reformers,[15] it is possible to read it as not merely a defense of plainsong, but of Latin sacred song generally (i.e., including polyphony). The placement of the letter in a notebook of motets copied by one of Glarean's students is not coincidental; it is the teacher's responsibility to supply exactly this kind of moral guidance:

---

[14] The superius, altus, and tenor partbooks of the set each consist of two gatherings with a flyleaf wrapper. The bassus book follows the two initial gatherings with two further gatherings on heavier paper with different preparation. Glarean's letter appears on the first page of the first gathering in the tenor partbook. This page serves as a title page in the other partbooks (with titles in Besardos' hand), with a second title page added on the flyleaf that encloses the gatherings. It is unclear when these notebooks were bound. As Fenlon, "Heinrich Glarean's Books," in *Music in the German Renaissance*, ed. John Kmetz (Cambridge: Cambridge University Press, 1994), 74–102, discussed, the binding on this set belongs with those of Glarean's first books, most of which appear to have French bindings that coincided with his stay in Paris. [15] Miller, "Introduction," 33.

Glareanus Lectori S.D.

Ecclesiasticas cantilenas canere et honestum et meritorium esse neminem uere
Christianum ignorare puto. Quapropter ut Moses Exodi XV pie gloriatur de redemptoris
sui benignitate, quidni et nos de Christo seruatore nostro cantabimus? Valeant igitur qui suo
maligno spiritu quidquid est honestissimarum disciplinarum pessum ire cupiunt, scelerati
nugones ac rerum humanarum nocentissimi alastores. Tu itaque Christiane lector ab his
tanquam ab aspidum veneno tibi caue, nihil pestilentius a mille annis natum est, nihil peius
obfuit religioni quantum in ipsis est. Christus pro sua in nos clementia ac misericordia
Euangelion suum ab his lurchonibus ac sceleratis hypocritis haud dubie uindicabit.

Vale. Basileae ex Lacydio nostro a. a Cho. nato MDXXVII Cal. Decembr.[16]

I think that no true Christian is unaware that it is virtuous and worthy to sing church
songs. Therefore as Moses in Exodus XV reverently gloried in his blessed redemption,
should we not also sing of Christ our Saviour? Away with those, who with malign spirits
desire in their anger the downfall of this most virtuous discipline, polluted by lies, the most
poisonous of human things. Do you, then, Christian reader avoid these as you would the
poison of asps. Nothing more pestilent has been born for a thousand years, nothing has been
a worse hindrance to religion than these. Christ for us in his forbearance and even more in
his loving-kindness will without doubt vindicate his Gospel from this polluting hypocrisy.

This is the exclamation of a Catholic humanist during tumultuous years in
Protestant Basle. By 1529, Erasmus would leave Basle for Freiburg, and Glarean
would follow shortly. He likens the events of his day to the schism of the eastern
and western church a thousand years before. When he implores his student to sing
as Moses did in Exodus 15, he evokes themes of exile, triumph, and redemption.[17]

Exodus 15: 1–21 (Douay–Rheims translation)

1. Then Moses and the children of Israel sang this canticle to the Lord: and said: Let us
   sing to the Lord: for he is gloriously magnified, the horse and the rider he hath thrown
   into the sea.
2. The Lord is my strength and my praise, and he is become salvation to me: he is my God
   and I will glorify him: the God of my father, and I will exalt him.
3. The Lord is as a man of war, Almighty is his name.
4. Pharao's chariots and his army he hath cast into the sea: his chosen captains are drowned
   in the Red Sea.
5. The depths have covered them, they are sunk to the bottom like a stone.
6. Thy right hand, O Lord, is magnified in strength: thy right hand, O Lord, hath slain the
   enemy.
7. And in the multitude of thy glory thou hast put down thy adversaries: thou hast sent thy
   wrath, which hath devoured them like stubble.
8. And with the blast of thy anger the waters were gathered together: the flowing water
   stood, the depths were gathered together in the midst of the sea.
9. The enemy said: I will pursue and overtake, I will divide the spoils, my soul shall have
   its fill: I will draw my sword, my hand shall slay them.

---

[16] The text is transcribed in Otto Fridolin Fritzsche, *Glarean, sein Leben und seine Schriften* (Frauenfeld: Verlag J. Huber, 1890), 129.

[17] These themes are discussed in chapter 9 in relation to *Magnus es tu Domine*, one of the motets in the collection.

10. Thy wind blew and the sea covered them: they sunk as lead in the mighty waters.

11. Who is like to thee, among the strong, O Lord? who is like to thee, glorious in holiness, terrible and praiseworthy, doing wonders?

12. Thou stretchedst forth thy hand, and the earth swallowed them.

13. In thy mercy thou hast been a leader to the people which thou hast redeemed: and in thy strength thou hast carried them to thy holy habitation.

14. Nations rose up, and were angry: sorrows took hold on the inhabitants of Philisthiim.

15. Then were the princes of Edom troubled, trembling seized on the stout men of Moab: all the inhabitants of Chanaan became stiff.

16. Let fear and dread fall upon them, in the greatness of thy arm: let them become unmoveable as a stone, until thy people, O Lord, pass by: until this thy people pass by, which thou hast possessed.

17. Thou shalt bring them in, and plant them in the mountain of thy inheritance, in thy most firm habitation which thou hast made, O Lord; thy sanctuary, O Lord, which thy hands have established.

18. The Lord shall reign for ever and ever.

19. For Pharao went in on horseback with his chariots and horsemen into the sea: and the Lord brought back upon them the waters of the sea: but the children of Israel walked on dry ground in the midst thereof.

20. So Mary the prophetess, the sister of Aaron, took a timbrel in her hand: and all the women went forth after her with timbrels and with dances:

21. And she began the song to them, saying: Let us sing to the Lord, for he is gloriously magnified, the horse and his rider he hath thrown into the sea.

The outer verses of this song from Exodus 15 proclaim Glarean's theme: "Sing to the Lord, for he is gloriously magnified." As he does elsewhere in the *Dodecachordon*, Glarean points from an Old Testament text to a New Testament context by the injunction to readers to sing to Christ as Moses sang.[18] And he is writing for the Erasmian reader of Scripture, the reader who always reads as a philologist would, who has framed excerpts of biblical texts in theological *loci*.[19]

But the Munich partbooks also stand apart from the commonplace tradition by the lack of *loci* and the inclusion of complete works rather than excerpts. Complete motets were gathered from other sources and entered in the notebook, itself a very specific sort of collection, and then further annotated. It is also a notebook that differs in marked ways from other musical compilations, for this is neither a "composer's notebook" nor a notebook in which someone mastered the grammar of composition by collecting phrases from the works of others. Instead, this collection is an exhortation for the moral edification of students and a source of *exempla* for a written text. The motets are excerpts in the sense that each is taken from a larger work – a printed book that in its material form defines a "whole" – but each is also

---

[18] The first song in the Bible, Exodus 15, often served this prophetic function as symbolically represented by its placement as the first canticle in the liturgy of the Easter Vigil.

[19] The reference to Exodus 15 cannot be seen in this view as an idle reference, yet to my knowledge, no previous study of the letter even mentions the subject of the scriptural reference. See Anthony Grafton and Lisa Jardine, *From Humanism to the Humanities: Education and the Liberal Arts in Fifteenth- and Sixteenth-Century Europe* (Cambridge, MA: Harvard University Press, 1968), 145–49, for a discussion of Erasmus's *Methodus*, the treatise that accompanied his new Latin translation of the New Testament and his approach to biblical exegesis.

complete within itself, indeed must be self-contained if it is ultimately to serve the purpose of representing the best compositions and demonstrating modality.

Physical evidence confirms that the Munich partbooks were the direct source for the examples that found their way into the *Dodecachordon*. Not only are the readings congruent. In the case of a work that extended beyond an opening when trans-ferred from partbook to choirbook format, the page turns have been indicated by *signa congruentiae* in the manuscript. While coordinated page turns are unnecessary in partbooks, they are essential for choirbook format. Compare the tenor of Josquin's *Ave Maria . . . virgo serena* in the Munich partbooks (Fig. 6.2) and the tenor as it appears in the choirbook format of the *Dodecachordon* (Fig. 6.3).

The relationship of the Munich partbooks and the Petrucci prints outlined in Table 6.2 is suggestive of the way Glarean worked with two printed sources (not now in his library) and the way in which a manuscript compilation mediated those prints and the final examples contained in the *Dodecachordon*. The basis for the manuscript notebook was not modal in its organization, but rather, as Glarean's preface in the tenor partbook suggests, as a collection of sacred song.[20] From that preliminary collection, examples were then selected for the treatise after the manu-script had been modally analyzed. While it seems reasonable to assume that such (now lost or unidentified) notebook collections may have furnished many of the polyphonic citations for the *Dodecachordon*, annotated printed sources in Glarean's library also offer evidence of the ways in which he both did and did not work more directly from printed sources when compiling the examples of the treatise.

PRINTED SOURCES IN GLAREAN'S LIBRARY

A source of particular interest is Glarean's composite binding of *Motetti C* (RISM 1504[1]) and the *Missarum diversorum auctorum liber primus* (RISM 1509[1]). Table 6.3 outlines the contents of *Motetti C*, the direct source for only two works that appeared in the *Dodecachordon*. The table includes the modal annotations that appear in Glarean's hand in the tenor partbook. In addition, attributions have been noted in the index for works that Glarean ultimately cites in the *Dodecachordon*. Both the tenor and bassus include indications of division into *partes* of the two genealogies Glarean cites (*Liber generationis* and *Factum est autem*) and these annota-tions occur only for these works, suggesting a direct relationship to the copying in the treatise or an intermediary notebook. Even more conclusive are the use of *signa congruentiae* to mark the places where page turns would occur in the choirbook format into which the music from these partbooks was transferred, as in the case of *Ave Maria . . . virgo serena* described above. Although in most cases, a complete *pars* or motet fits into a single opening on the *Dodecachordon*, a few longer works had to run across openings, necessitating an indication of the coordination of page turns in the parts from which the choirbook transcriptions were made. *Signa congruentiae* that correspond to the page breaks of the *Dodecachordon* appear in both the Munich partbooks and *MunU 374*. In both sources, *signa* like those encircled in Figure 6.4

---

[20] While I am arguing that the selection was on theological and musical grounds, the ordered copying also suggests an element of convenience in the mediation of print to manuscript.

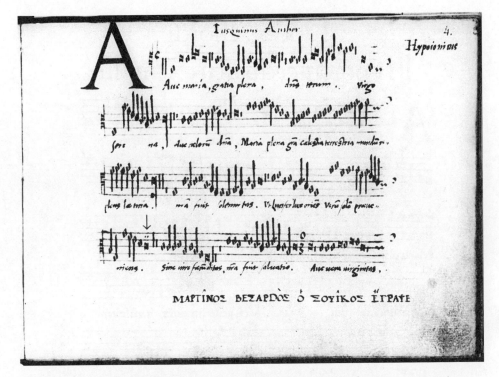

6.2 Josquin, *Ave Maria . . . virgo serena*, tenor, *MunU 324*, with *signum congruentiae* indicating placement of page break in the *Dodecachordon* (Munich University Library, 8° Cod. Mus. 324. Reproduced by permission.)

offer direct physical evidence of the use of these sources in the production of the *Dodecachordon*.[21]

Yet while the genealogies and *Planxit autem David* (33) appear to have come to the *Dodecachordon* directly from *Motetti C*, the version of *Magnus es tu Domine* (32) that appears in the Munich partbooks suggests at the very least mediation via the manuscript (and perhaps a different source entirely).[22] As indicated on Table 6.1, fewer works were drawn from the *Motetti C* repertory than those of *Motetti A* and *B*, even though the *Motetti C* print was part of Glarean's library. This point bears emphasis because it suggests a note of caution: one of the prints that Glarean actually owned and annotated supplied significantly fewer *exempla* for his treatise than a pair of prints for which no evidence of his ownership survives.[23] But more to the

---

[21] Thus, *signa congruentiae* appear in all voices of Josquin's *Ave Maria* in the Munich partbooks, and in his *Liber generationis* and the *prima pars* of *Planxit autem David* in Glarean's copy of *Motetti C*. (*Signa* are not present in any other works.) Glarean also corrected a minim rest in the tenor of *Planxit autem*.

[22] Were one unaware of the relationship of the Munich partbooks, *Motetti A* and *B*, and the *Dodecachordon*, this means of transmission would be less obvious. *Magnus es tu Domine* is discussed in detail in chapter 9.

[23] There is, of course, no way of knowing what percentage of the books that he owned are actually represented in the present collection in Munich and books associated with Glarean continue to be discovered in the collection. It is unlikely that any music books belonging to Glarean have not yet been identified, but his annotation of other books, such as Erasmus's *Adagia*, often have connections to the materials of the *Dodecachordon* through the series of intricate cross-referencing that characterized Glarean's pattern of annotation.

6.3 Josquin, *Ave Maria . . . virgo serena* (*Dodecachordon*, 358–59)

Liber III.

Idem Iodocus Pratesis author.

6.3 (cont.)

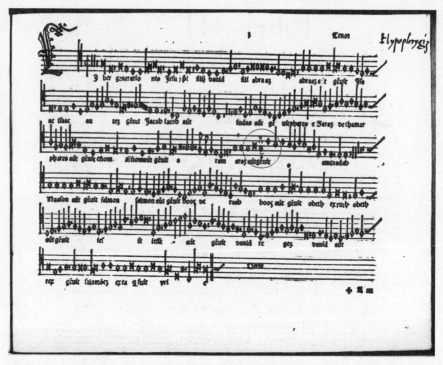

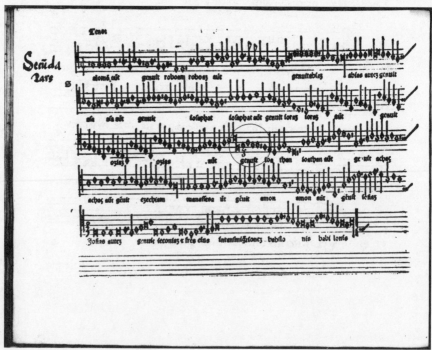

6.4 Josquin, *Liber generationis*, tenor from *MunU 374* (*Motetti C*), with annotations indicating mode and division into sections, and *signa congruentiae* marking page divisions in the *Dodecachordon* (Munich University Library, 4° Liturg. 374. Reproduced by permission.)

6.4 (*cont.*)

point is the kind of possession represented by the humanist's notebook. Physical possession of the material object was far less significant than the intellectual possession of the wealth of material acquired and ready for (re)use in the manuscript entries obtained from printed books.

Exemplars of two motets that were to appear in the *Dodecachordon* suggest the intermediate stage between annotated partbooks such as *Motetti C* and the Munich partbooks, on the one hand, and the theory treatise, on the other. Now bound at the end of Glarean's copy of Gaffurio's *De harmonia musicorum instrumentorum opus* are eighteen folios of music.[24] Iain Fenlon described the binding of this book as not one of Glarean's bindings, but "contemporary." I can now identify it specifically as a binding from the end of the sixteenth century associated with the library at Ingolstadt by the binder known as Perlschnur-Meister.[25] When the music was first bound with the treatise is unclear. The trimming has cropped annotations in the *Harmonia* as well as parts of the music manuscript. Various crease marks suggest that

[24] MunU 2° Art. 239.
[25] This binder is described in Ladislaus Buzás, *Geschichte der Universitätsbibliothek München* (Wiesbaden: Otto Harrassowitz, 1972), 67. When I began to attempt to identify the binding, Dr. Wolfgang Müller indicated that the half leather–half board binding was characteristic of bindings from the Ingolstadt library. With Irene Friedl's assistance, I was able to identify the specific binder through the tracings and descriptions of many of the early prints of the university library collection ("Buchbinderei" 4° Cod.ms. 996/ 14, 5). The scrolls on the Gaffurio binding match those of 2° Cod.ms.29 (= Cim 1). The flyleaf also contains the characteristic watermark associated with the Perlschnur-Meister bindings: a miter over a shield beneath which appear the initials B. F. Like all such books bound in the Ingolstadt collection, any indication of earlier ownership has vanished, but the annotations are without doubt by Glarean.

Table 6.3 *Motetti C*, Munich Partbooks, *Dodecachordon*, and Tschudi Liederbuch

Motetti C	Composer	Title	Annotations in Glarean's *Motetti C*	Munich partbooks	*Dodecachordon*	Tschudi Liederbuch
1	Josquin	*Ave Maria [. . . benedicta tu]*	Dorian out of Aeolian			
2	[Brumel]	*Ave celorum domina*	Dorian			
3	[Josquin]	*Liber generationis*	Hypophrygian [Josquin in index]		88	
4	[Josquin]	*Factum est autem*	"Ex Luca Ca. 3" [no mode]		[cited after 88]	
5	[Nico. Craen]	*Tota pulchra es*	Hypophrygian			
6		*Davidica stirpe*	Ionian			
7		*Beata Dei genitrix*	Hypomixolydian			
8	Josquin	*Missus est*	Aeolian / Hypodorian			
9		*Ergo sancti martires*	Aeolian			
10		*Concede nobis Domine*	Hypodorian			
11	[Obrecht]	*Requiem eternam*	Ionian to Phrygian			
12	[Ninot]	*Psallite noe*	Hypoionian			
13	[Ninot]	*Si oblitus fuero*	Hypodorian			
14		*Civitatem istam*	Hypoaeolian / Hypodorian			
15	[Ockeghem]	*Ut hermita*	[no annotation]			
16	[Josquin]	*O bone et dulcis / Pater noster*	[no annotation]			
17		*Missus est*	Hypodorian			
18	[Isaac]	*Alma redemptoris*	[att. Isaac] Ionian			
19		*Miles mire probitatis*	Hypoionian			
20		*Ave regina / O decus innocentie*	Ionian			
21		*Virgo precellens*	Hypodorian			

No.	Composer	Title	Mode			
22		*O sacrum convivium*	Ionian			
23		*O admirabile*	Hypoionian			
24	[Mouton]	*Sancti Dei omnes*	[Ninot Petit in index] Ionian / Hypoionian			
25		*Confitemini*	Hypodorian			
26		*Respice me in felicem*	Hypodorian			
27		*Trinitas deitas*	Hypodorian			
28	[Compère]	*Profitentes unitatem*	Dorian			
29		*Filie regum [In honore tuo]*	Phrygian			
30		*Miserere mei*	Dorian / Hypodorian			
31		*Si bona suscepimus*	Hypodorian to Hypoaeolian			
32	[Josquin?]	*Magnus es tu*	Hypophrygian	8 [Josquin, different mensuration]	46 [Josquin, mensuration as *MunU 322–5*]	112 [Josquin, mensuration as *MunU 322–5*]
33	[Josquin?]	*Planxit autem*	Ionian / Hypoionian [Josquin in index]	92 [att. Josquin]	146	
34	[Isaac]	*Rogamus te / O Maria*	Dorian / Aeolian			
35		*Inviolata*	Hypoionian			
36		*Gloria laus*	Dorian			
37		*Gaudeamus*	Hypodorian			
38		*Huc omnes pariter*	Hypoionian			
39		*O dulcissima*	Hypodorian [Petrus de Therache]			
40	[Josquin]	*Mittit ad virginem*	Hypoionian			
41		*Salvatoris mater pia*	Dorian			
42		*In lectulo*	Hypodorian			

that manuscript existed independently for some time as loose bifolios that were
independently folded as quartos. Three types of paper are represented in four gatherings with watermarks all dating from about 1515.[26] Although no specific date can
be offered for the copying and annotation of these gatherings, it seems plausible
that they were copied and annotated during the 1520s, that is, during the same
period of Glarean's study of *De harmonia* and his most intensive work on the
Dodecachordon. Whether this group of manuscripts was gathered together and
appended to the treatise by Glarean, or added to it when parts of his surviving
papers were bound in Ingolstadt is less clear. From the distribution of blank pages, it
is certain that each of these gatherings began life as individual, loose bifolios, copied
in choirbook format. The works are copied in four hands, one of which belongs to
Petrus Tschudi, a Glarean pupil, another of which is found in Glarean's copy of
Motetti C, and one of which appears to be Glarean's own hand (see Fig. 6.5).
Although separated in the present binding structure, two of the gatherings that
share paper type contain motets that appeared in the *Dodecachordon*. In both cases,
the readings and page turns match, suggesting that these may have served as exemplars for the production of the *Dodecachordon*; they have been preserved only coincidentally through binding with another treatise.

AN INTERTEXTUALITY OF THEORETICAL FRAGMENTS

An equally important printed source, of which there are no direct traces in
Glarean's library, is Sebald Heyden's *Musicae* (1537). Like others before me, as I
studied the examples of these chapters, I recognized concordances with Petrucci
prints from the first part of decades of the century, prints that I assumed were
Glarean's sources. As I have shown above, however, the actual situation involves a
complicated mediation of printed sources. Although I was aware of Glarean's ownership of the *Liber quindecim missarum* (1539, *MunU 448*) (which contains, for
example, Josquin masses that appear in a number of earlier sources, including some
owned by Glarean),[27] I discounted its significance for the *Dodecachordon* for two
reasons. Firstly, documentary evidence indicated that Glarean had finished most of
the work on the *Dodecachordon* by 1539, and secondly Glarean's annotations in this
print seem unrelated to the modal emphasis of the treatise. Yet understanding the

---

[26] The watermarks (but not the gathering structure) are described and identified in Gottwald, *Musikhandschriften*,
100. The first gathering (fols. 1^r–10^v) signed by Petrus Tschudi consists of Pierre de la Rue, *Missa Puer natus est*,
an unidentified four-voice *Pange lingua*, and Obrecht's *Missa Fors seulement*. Modal indications (not given in
Gottwald) are supplied for the two masses. The second and fourth gatherings (fols. 11^r–14^v and 17^r–18^v) contain
two motets that also appeared in the *Dodecachordon*: Vannius, *Attendite popule meus* and Gerard a Salice, *Os justi
meditabitur*. They are on the same paper in different hands. The first, unidentified, hand appears to be the same
one that added an attribution to Petrus de Therache in Glarean's copy of *Motetti C*. The second hand appears to
be Glarean's. The single bifolio, in yet another hand, inserted between these works contains Hayne van
Ghizeghem's *De tous biens pleine* without text, title, or attribution.

[27] *Liber quindecim missarum* (Nuremberg: Petreius, 1539) [RISM 1539^1]. Glarean's copy is Munich,
Universitätsbibliothek der Ludwig-Maximilians-Universität, MS 4° 448 (*MunU 448*). See the discussion of this
print in chapter 4.

compilation process points to a central role for Heyden's treatise and the *Liber quindecim missarum*. The relationship is pivotal to understanding the way Glarean collected his examples in the chapters surrounding those on mode in polyphony.

As discussed in chapter 4, there is a notable relationship between the untexted, and for the most part unidentified, examples in Heyden's treatise and the contents of the 1539 mass print. They were issued within two years of each other by the Nuremberg house of Petreius and the mass print preceded the publication of the enlarged edition of Heyden's treatise as *De arte canendi* (1540) by only months. Thus from the vantage point of the *Dodecachordon*, the treatise and mass print might be seen as forming a source pair. Although no copy of Heyden's treatise survives in Glarean's library, the concordances with the *Dodecachordon* along with annotations on his copy of the *Liber quindecim missarum* suggest that he at least recognized such a relationship.

At the beginning of each of the chapters on mode, Glarean has supplied examples either taken from Heyden or newly composed works commissioned from other composers for the pedagogic examples that he himself might traditionally have been expected to supply.[28] This subset of examples suggests that Glarean modified his original compilation in 1539 after acquiring Heyden's treatise and *Liber quindecim missarum*. The annotations to this latter print are quite unlike those of the other music books in Glarean's collection. There are no indications of modal names anywhere in the partbooks. Instead, Glarean has singled out the duos and trios, as the list in the tenor partbook indicates, identifying the part of the mass that is set for reduced voices (e.g. "Pleni in Prima Missa") and listing those voices which are silent with the indication "tacent" (see Fig. 6.6). Unfortunately, the placement of Knöringen's bookplate has obliterated part of the list.[29] Nonetheless, it is clear that this list would have supplied Glarean with the summary that he needed to locate duos and trios for use as the "monads" that begin chapters and as a cross-reference for locating works which appeared as textless examples in Heyden and texted when reproduced in the *Dodecachordon*.[30]

Tables 5.1a and 5.1c (pp. 132–35) provide a list of Glarean's sources for the examples in the chapters that begin and end Book III of the treatise. These sections reveal two distinct ways in which the writings of earlier theorists provided musical as well as textual material that served as the source for Glarean's new text. Several patterns emerge from a study of the chapters of the treatise that deal with mensuration. As

---

[28] That is, it is common for theorists to supply newly composed examples in support of the principles they elaborate and the *Dodecachordon* is exceptional for the lack of such examples. That absence may be explained in two ways: first, it is unclear that Glarean was able to compose such polyphony; but, second, whether or not he was capable of producing them, such newly composed examples would lack the necessary authority conveyed by examples in the tradition in which he was writing.

[29] The bookplate is pasted in the front cover of the tenor partbook. With the assistance of ultraviolet light, I was able to reconstruct a large portion of the covered section, although not the very central part of the page behind the darkest part of the plate.

[30] Although in cases where Heyden indicated the part of the mass excerpted (e.g. Benedictus), adding text was no great challenge.

6.5 Gerard a Salice, *Os justi* in Glarean's hand (manuscript appended to his copy of Gaffurio's *De harmonia*) (Munich University Library, 2° Art. 239. Reproduced by permission.)

6.5 (*cont.*)

6.6 Glarean's index of duos and trios in *Liber quindecim missarum* (*MunU 448*) (Petreius, 1539) (Munich University Library, 4° Liturg. 448. Reproduced by permission.)

Table 5.1a illustrates, Glarean's examples are drawn almost entirely from the writings of earlier theorists: Franchino Gaffurio's *Practica musicae* (Milan, 1497), Sebald Heyden's *Musicae* (Nuremberg, 1537),[31] and Cochlaeus's *Tetrachordum musices* (Nuremberg, 1511).[32] Miller identifies most of these borrowings in the mensural section without realizing how extensively Glarean borrowed from Heyden. He comments only briefly on the mensural examples, under the heading "Pedagogical Examples," noting that Glarean does not set himself up as an authority on mensural music, is careful to acknowledge his authorities, and in light of his synoptic treatment of the subject, avoids the more "abstruse" pieces from the *Practica musicae*.[33] While such an assessment is accurate as far as it goes, classifying the examples as merely "pedagogical" not only blurs the sense in which they functioned for Glarean, but potentially misrepresents them.

The mensural section of the treatise is divided into three sections. The first, an

[31] The enlarged edition of the treatise as *De arte canendi* in 1540 omits some of the examples of the 1537 edition which appear in the *Dodecachordon* while adding others. See the discussion of Heyden's and Cochlaeus's examples in chapter 4.

[32] The apparent reference to Georg Rhau's *Enchiridion utriusque musicae practicae* (Wittenberg: Georg Rhau, 1532) is in fact an example quoted directly from Heyden that retains Heyden's caption.

[33] Miller, "Introduction," 27–28.

elementary introduction, takes its demonstrative examples from Gaffurio, with two supplementary examples which may have been supplied by Glarean himself (Table 5.1a, 1–9; the last of these is attributed to Josquin in the Tschudi Liederbuch.). The reordering of Gaffurio's examples reflects Glarean's distillation of the sixteen chapters of Book II of the *Practica musicae*. The notated music examples are thus excised from a context in which they had already been framed by text. In other words, Glarean is treating them much like any other textual material, as is clear from his annotated copy of the *Practica*.

Although Glarean's copy of the *Practica musicae* is lightly annotated in comparison to many of his books, his glosses are revealing, as hinted at in the discussion of Figure 6.5. Glarean outlines topics in the margins (with headings like "declaratio," "questio solo," "exceptio") and underlines text, often providing the verbiage that will ultimately appear in the *Dodecachordon* (compare Figs. 6.7 and 6.8). Annotations are added to music examples at the specific points of illustration; aspects of difficult examples are often worked out in the margins in various notations (sometimes involving the doubling of note values).[34] In three instances, Glarean has scored the conclusion of the examples on a ten-line staff in the margin (see Fig. 6.9). Glarean was clearly a selective reader, skipping over the more obscure proportions that appeared between Gaffurio's discussion of quadruple proportion and sesquialtera (only one annotation appears between these sections). That he seems to have been reading the *Practica* with the *Dodecachordon* in mind is suggested not only by the way the annotations lead directly to the text as it appears in the *Dodecachordon*, but also by the reference on sig. gg[v] to the incipit "Ego dormio." This is the beginning of Antonius a Vinea's motet which appears as an example in the *Dodecachordon*.

The concluding three examples (Table 5.1a, numbers 10–11a) from this section of the *Dodecachordon* are all drawn from "real music" that appears as textless examples in Heyden's 1537 *Musicae*. Glarean acknowledges the authorship of two, Ghiselin and Josquin. The first example he attributes to Heyden, apparently unaware that it was taken from Isaac's *Missa Quant j'ay au cueur*. Its anonymous transmission in Heyden's treatise seems to have suggested to Glarean that, like the previous examples from Gaffurio, it was composed by the theorist himself. He was clearly aware of the different nature of Heyden's examples when compared to Gaffurio's, however, or at least made a distinction because of the attributions provided by Heyden. (See the Appendix to chapter 4, pp. 109–14.) This "real," if textless, music marks the end of the section.

An interpolated discussion of the *voces* follows in the *Dodecachordon*. Although a majority of these examples are texted in the *Dodecachordon*, they, too, occur without text in Heyden's treatise. The first (Table 5.1a, no. 12) is a second-hand borrowing from another theorist, Georg Rhau, which had been appropriated by Heyden.[35] The next three excerpts from Josquin masses (13–15) were known to Glarean in other sources that he owned, but I believe their appearance in Heyden is what drew

---

[34] This was a strategy advocated by Heyden for simplifying difficult passages with short note values.

[35] There is no evidence to suggest that Glarean knew Rhau's treatise at first hand.

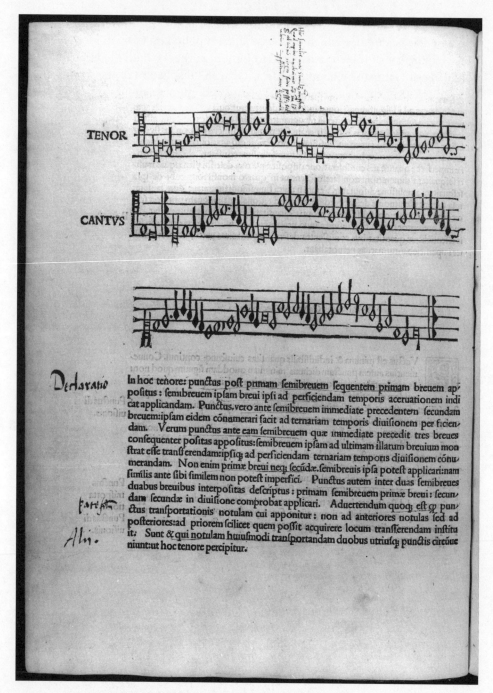

6.7 Glarean's annotations to mensural examples in his copy of Gaffurio's *Practica musicae* (Munich University Library, 2° Art. 239. Reproduced by permission.)

Exemplum puncti diuisionis

ex Franchino.

TENOR

CANTVS

R 4 In hoc

200 Dodecachordi

IN hoc tenore atcp adeo in prima notularum decade duæ sunt breueis, quarum prior imperfecta fit propter sequentem semibreuem, quod pū: ctum semibreui postpositum facit, Sequens autem imperficitur à præcedē te semibreui, atcp id quocp ob punctū quod præcedit, ut ternaria perfectio obseruetur. At punctum quod eam præcedit semibreuem, quæ proxime treis anteit breueis, innuit eam semibreuem ad tertiam breuium perferēdā, non ad primam, quia similis an te similē non imperficitur, ut postea dicet. Et quoties id fit, semper ad primam quācp sequentem, cui applicari potest refertur, nunquam ad præcedentem. Porro deinde inter duas semibreueis punctūm ita eos separat, ut alteram priori, alteram sequenti breui annume= randas significet. Quod autem hic de tempore exemplo docemus, hoc idē in modo, ac prolatione obseruandum censemus. Perfectionis item puncti apud eundem exemplum est, in quo & additionis, quod ipse augmenti uo cat, species est.

6.8 Parallel passage from the *Dodecachordon*, reproducing Gaffurio's example and incorporating Glarean's annotation

them to his attention, resulting in their appearance here. Of particular interest in this light is Glarean's copy of the *Liber quindecim missarum* from 1539. Heyden is not mentioned in the *Dodecachordon* as the source for these examples because the examples have been "re-read" – turned to a purpose other than that for which they were originally intended – and in that sense Glarean treats them differently from the examples that precede them from Heyden and Gaffurio.[36]

---

[36] Glarean makes no mention that Heyden's treatise overtly reflects Reformation ideologies for which he else-where has nothing but contempt. One can only wonder what he would have thought had he been acquainted with the 1532 version of the treatise. Unlike his use of Gaffurio's treatise, Glarean relies on Heyden solely for music, not the discourse that accompanies it.

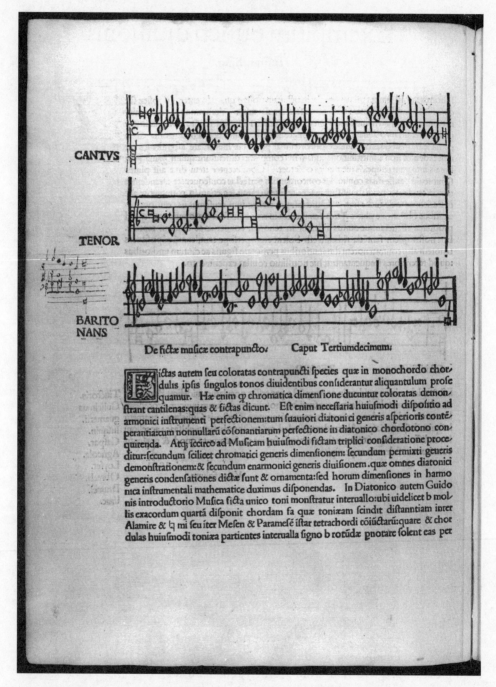

6.9 Glarean's use of a ten-line staff for scoring the conclusion of a mensural example in his copy of Gaffurio's *Practica musicae*
(Munich University Library, 2° Art. 239. Reproduced by permission.)

The final section of Glarean's mensural chapters deals with the proportions and is a conflation of excerpts from Gaffurio and Cochlaeus. Here, too, a clear pattern of borrowing occurs. After the opening two examples from Gaffurio (Table 5.1a, nos. 17–18), an example from Cochlaeus (19) is followed by one from Gaffurio (20). The end of this section, too, is marked by "real" music: examples from Obrecht's *Missa For seulement* (27–28). Again it is real music that is associated at least indirectly with a theoretical text. It appears as one of the six works bound in with his annotated copy of Gaffurio's *Harmonia musicorum instrumentorum* (*MunU 239*).[37]

Thus three theorists provide the examples for these chapters. The examples tend to be arranged in pairs. The opening section draws on Gaffurio and Heyden, examples from Heyden provide a transition, and the concluding section is based on examples taken from or associated with Gaffurio and Cochlaeus. Although examples from Gaffurio pervade this section of the treatise as a whole, and Glarean extols his writings,[38] the framework for the treatise is actually provided by Heyden and Cochlaeus, whose order Glarean follows when presenting examples from their treatises. These are supplemented and framed with selections from Books II and IV of Gaffurio's *Practica musicae* (seven of 111 examples in book IV) which are selectively chosen as the essential and most basic demonstrations. The role of Cochlaeus and Heyden is not surprising, for both supplied models for Glarean in his treatment of *exempla*. Although his copies of these treatises do not survive, the way he uses Heyden's examples suggests that his own copy (or excerpts from the treatise in a notebook) would have been heavily annotated with the addition of attributions and text or cross-references to the *Liber quindecim missarum*.[39]

Even in the process of taking over these examples, Glarean's role is not relegated to simple selection and ordering, but one shaped by annotation and collection in the commonplace tradition, as the discussion of his copy of the *Practica musicae* suggested. A direct demonstration within the *Dodecachordon* is his renotation of an example from Cochlaeus, shown in Figure 6.10, about which he says:

Here is an example from Cochlaeus. We have presented examples of this proportion [*proportio quadrupla*] and of *proportia dupla* more for the reason that they are easy to learn than because we believe them very important to the subject to the necessary practice of music. It is an exercise of ingenuity, but not so useful as it is in other subjects. For if one wishes to present the same example in the following way, what prevents him from doing it correctly? (Miller, Translation, 245)

Glarean presents the example in a more modern and fixed notation, a pedagogical strategy that he employs elsewhere,[40] removing the ambiguity of signs and ratios.

---

[37] See the discussion of *MunU 239* on p. 155–58.

[38] "[W]e have no writers of antiquity whom we may imitate here, and excepting one, as I believe, we have had for a century absolutely no distinguished men, few of whom have left us monuments of any importance, so that Franchinus, a man most worthy of perpetual memory, stands out almost alone in this subject" (Miller, trans., 224).

[39] There is ample precedent for Glarean's addition of attributions in his copy of *Motetti C* and in the addition of attributions to some copies of the *Dodecachordon* in his hand.

[40] See the discussion of *Magnus es tu Domine* in chapter 9.

Quadrupla proportio.

Quadrupla proportio est ꝯum maior numerus continet minorē qua
ter ut 4.1. Cæterum in cantu quoties numeri ad hunc modū ⦂⦂⦂
præfiguntur, notularum ualor quadruplo minuitur, Ita longa ſemibreui
ualet, breuis minima, & de reliquis eodē modo. Exemplū eſt hoc Coclęi.

CANTVS   **TENOR**

Cæterum & huius proportionis, & duplæ exempla poſuimus, magis
quia addiſcētibus facilia ſunt, quā quod ea magnopere ad rem ſiue ad
neceſſariū muſices uſum pertinere arbitremur, Ingenij eſt exercitatio, ſed
non perinde atꝗ in alijs rebus utilis. Nam quid prohibet, ſi quis ita hoc ex
emplum ponere uolet, quin id tuto liceat?

CANTVS   **TENOR**

Deſtruitur autem per ſubquadruplam, nullo interturbāte ſigno, ut ex
iam dicto exemplo atꝗ item ex hoc Franchini exemplo pateſcet.

                                    V 2   **CANTVS**

6.10 Glarean's renotation of an example by Cochlaeus in the *Dodecachordon*

This section of the *Dodecachordon* might be best described as an intertextual narrative woven from theoretical fragments. The examples themselves are integral to
the theoretical sources that Glarean selectively excerpts and reinterprets in his new
text. They offer authoritative examples from the theorists who composed them
along with the words which frame them. The exception to this sort of reading
relates to the Heyden examples which Glarean recognizes as being drawn from a
printed repertory with which he was familiar. To these he adds text and attribution,
and appropriates them in contexts other than those in which they originally
appeared. Heyden's text provides not only a theoretical model for Glarean but in
selection from Heyden's treatise provides an anthology of sorts – a model collection.

This is not the usual view of Glarean's relationship to Heyden, but it is sustained
and refined by an examination of the examples in the concluding chapter of
Glarean's treatise. This is the chapter, on the skill of *symphonetæ*, which Glarean sug-

gests is an addendum. In it, he offers observations on the composers Josquin (with an interpolation on Senfl and Pierre de la Rue), Ockeghem, Obrecht, Brumel, Isaac, and Mouton, describing mensural and modal features of the works he reproduces. As Table 5.1c (p. 135) illustrates, the twenty-four examples in this section are taken from only twelve compositions; the majority consists of small sections from masses. Almost all are found in Petrucci prints from the first decades of the century, some of which are in Glarean's library, as indicated in the source column. Perhaps because of this, it has apparently gone unnoticed that almost all of these excerpts also appear in Heyden's treatise, although in a very different context.

In explaining his decision to add this chapter, Glarean justifies his addition, introducing it with the following words:

This was to be the end of the book, certainly of monstrous size if one considers the examples, but of no great size at all if one looks at the text. But I wished to add only a single chapter on the skill of *symphonetae* . . .

[A] few words should be spoken about certain composers in so far as we, by instructive listening, have received prior information from trustworthy men (Miller, Translation, 271).

It does not seem too far-fetched to suggest that Heyden is that trustworthy man, or at least that his treatise represented such a trustworthy man. The composers, with the exception of Mouton, are those whom Heyden highlighted by means of examples. Although Glarean does provide modal designations for many of these works, he also reveals a particular fondness and admiration for the creation of several voices from one, part of Heyden's focus. He has also reshaped the materials, inserting examples that belong with Heyden's. Thus Glarean's Examples 98–104 are drawn from Heyden's *Musicae* of 1537. (For the original context of these works, see the Appendix to chapter 4.). The order of the first three (98–100) is reversed in the *Dodecachordon*, returning the segments from the Benedictus of Josquin's *Missa L'homme armé super voces musicales* to their proper order. Glarean then elaborates Heyden's examples with the insertion of a trio from Senfl (102) and an additional illustration from Pierre de la Rue (104). The next group of Josquin examples from Heyden is again expanded with Glarean's addition of *De tous biens playne* (111) as an illustration of *fuga ad minimam*. Like the Obrecht mass cited in the mensural section, this work is preserved in the manuscript bifolios appended to Glarean's copy of Gaffurio. The Ockeghem examples (112–14) come from Heyden and the 1539 mass print, reinforcing the sense that Glarean recognized these as related books. For Brumel, he substitutes examples from the *Missa Dringhs* (115–17), found in the other mass collection in his library. He returns to Heyden for his Isaac example (118).[41] The Mouton examples (119–20) represent Glarean's addition to the composer preferences reflected in Heyden.

---

[41] Heyden's caption for this excerpt reads: "Tertium Argumentum Henrichi Isaac est, ex Prosa historiae de Conceptione Mariae, in quo Tripla Proportio promiscue nunc Diminuto, nunc integro Notularum valori opponitur."

Thus the framing sections of Book III reflect a compilation of other theorists' examples which have been reordered and supplemented in a number of ways to fit the uses to which Glarean is turning them. This is not altogether surprising when one considers that both of these sections are in a sense outside the central concerns of the treatise (modal theory) and in the absence of classical authority for specifics, Glarean necessarily has to appropriate contemporary authority. Although he overtly gestures to Heyden with the first example from his treatise, this reflects Glarean's apparent assumption that Heyden was the composer of the example. Heyden's name in fact only appears twice in the *Dodecachordon*.[42] The examples which are most critical to Glarean's enterprise, the large group of examples illustrating the modes in polyphony, were chosen by different criteria. Understanding how Glarean's use of Heyden's examples both fits in with and contrasts with these provides the context for recognizing the impetus behind Glarean's appropriations from the theorist. There is a further and final visual connection between Heyden's treatises and Glarean's *Dodecachordon*: the music font that Petri used for the examples of the *Dodecachordon* was obtained from Petreius; it was the font that Petreius had cut for producing the examples of Heyden's *Musicae* and later used for *De arte canendi*.[43]

GLAREAN'S READERS: THE "TSCHUDI LIEDERBUCH" AND ITS SKETCHES

The relevance of the commonplace model of musical notebooks that I outlined in relation to the Munich partbooks may be readily seen in the manuscript collection of one of Glarean's students, Aegidius Tschudi. The "Tschudi Liederbuch" and its companion sketchbook also came from Glarean's circle and contain modal annotations, although several competing scenarios have been advanced for their direct or indirect relationship to the *Dodecachordon* and Glarean.[44] Table 6.1 (pp. 142–44) illustrates the remarkable degree of overlap between the two. However, the intertextuality would seem to result from the shared sources of the Petrucci prints, as Table 6.2 (p. 145) demonstrates. The Tschudi Liederbuch contains several works from these prints that appear in neither the Munich partbooks nor the *Dodecachordon*. Tschudi's modal indications suggest that he knew or discussed some preliminary version of the *Dodecachordon* with Glarean because there appears to be

---

[42] The two passages are: "Some, as Sebald Heyden, a distinguished musician in our time, call them characteristic letters, and this naming would not be unsatisfactory if it should become accepted in usage" (Miller, trans., 46), and "There will be three examples, the first of which has the tenor in the Hypodorian mode, and which is notated in two ways in the four voices, first in *prolatio triplex*, namely, *integra, diminuta, proportionata,* second in *tempus triplex*, namely *integrum, diminutum*, and *proportionatum*. Sebald Heyden, whom we mentioned in the first book, has distinguished these in this way" (Miller, Translation, 239).

[43] Petreius had been apprenticed to Petri and there were family connections. He frequently sold his fonts. His music fonts (and its use by Petri) are discussed in Teramoto, *Die Psalmmotettendrucke des Johannes Petrejus Nürnberg*, Frankfurter Beiträge zur Musikwissenschaft 10 (Tutzing: Schneider, 1983), 87–88.

[44] Miller, "Introduction," 28, seems to suggest that the Saint Gall manuscripts were sources for the *Dodecachordon*.

an attempt to adjust the modal assignments of some works that are concordant between the Liederbuch and the *Dodecachordon*. The Liederbuch also provides insight into the ways in which Glarean's modal theory influenced Tschudi's reading. Unlike the Munich partbooks and the *Dodecachordon*, Tschudi's collection contains works in various genres and for various numbers of voices. Tschudi arranges his compilation to reflect these features, grouping works under the headings of mode, which function as *loci communes* for musical discourse.

The sketchbook (*SGall 464*) that belongs with the Tschudi Liederbuch offers evidence of the way in which Tschudi "read" other sources, establishing the mode by writing down the opening phrase, concluding notes, and extreme pitches of the tenor. From this information, he ascertained which works would be included in the Liederbuch and the order in which they would occur.[45] These sketches were based on the summary of the modes, in Glarean's hand, included in the notebook that is reproduced in Figure 6.11.[46] The summary includes citations of works for each mode, many of which appeared in the *Dodecachordon*, whose date of publication was after the compilation of Tschudi's notebook.

The summary is remarkable in its concise illustration of the main precepts adumbrated in the *Dodecachordon*. Midway down the page the seven octave species are laid out under the headings of authentic and plagal:

Sketchbook (*SGall 464*)				*Dodecachordon* title page			
Authentæ		Plagij		Plagij			Authentæ
Dorius	1	Hypodorius	2	A	Hypodorius	D	Dorius
					Hypermixolydius Ptolemæi		
Phrygius	3	Hypophrygius	4	B	Hypophrygius	E	Phrygius
					Hyperæolius Mar. Cap.		
Lydius	5	Hypolydius	6	C	Hypolydius	F	Lydius
					Hyperphrygius Mar. Cap.		
Mixolydius	7	Hypomixolydius	8	D	Hypomixolyd.	G	Mixolydius
					Hyperiastius vel		Hyperlydius
					Hyperionicus Mar. Cap.		Mart. Cap.
Aeolius	9	Hypoæolius	10	E	Hypoæolius	A	Aeolius
Hyperlydius	11	Hyperphrygius	12	G	Hypoionicus	C	Ionicus
							Porphyrio Iastius
							Apuleius & Mar. Cap.
Ionicus	13	Hypoionicus	14	*F	Hyperphrygius	*B	Hyperæolius
					Hyperlydius Politia. sed		
					est error		

[45] The relationship of *SGall 463* and *SGall 464* is described in detail in Loach, "Aegidius Tschudi's Songbook," 35–52, and *passim*.

[46] Loach, "Aegidius Tschudi's Songbook," 63–67, reproduces this sketch and provides a detailed discussion of its examples. In many particulars, my discussion follows Loach's conclusions. Understandably, he does not draw attention to the specific points of contact with the *Dodecachordon* with which I am concerned.

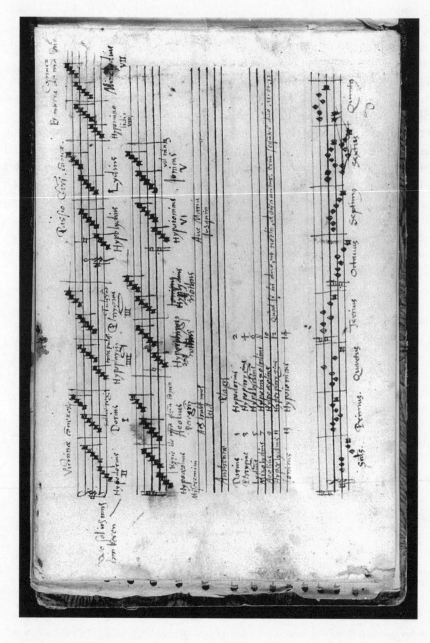

6.11 Summary of the modes in Tschudi's sketchbook (Stiftsbibliothek St. Gallen, Cod. Sang. 464. Reproduced by permission.)

Two contrasts with the *Dodecachordon* merit comment. The *Dodecachordon* identifies the octave species by final, while the sketchbook uses numbers beginning with the eight from chant theory. Yet the sketchbook retains the order of the octave species while the *Dodecachordon* transposes the order of the final two pairs and marks by asterisk the modal pair ultimately omitted from Glarean's dodecachordal scheme because of the problematic B final and imperfect octave division it occasions. The sketchbook notes the problem of this pair with the annotation: "Quod si hi duo, ut nothi, dejiciantur, erunt seguentes duo 11 et 12" ("If however these two, as spurious, are discarded, the following two will be 11 and 12"). The sketchbook also mistakes the names of the pair, using the alternative "Hyperlydius" attributed as an error of Politia on the title page of the *Dodecachordon* for the plagal and erroneously substituting Hyperphrygius for the authentic Hyperæolius.

The schema on the top two staves of the sketch represents a distillation of the central features of Books II and III of the *Dodecachordon*.[47] The division of the octaves, plagal followed by authentic, corresponds with the title page of the *Dodecachordon* in order, while corresponding in style with the examples from Book II that were reproduced in chapter 5 (pp. 123–25). The cautionary quadro (♮) sign draws extra attention to the *b mi* that characterizes the modes labeled here as Hypolydian and Hyperphrygian. The Hyperphrygian-Hyperlydian [Hyperaeolian] pair is designated as "spurious." The anomalous nature of the Lydian pair represented here is further highlighted by the absence of those Roman numerals of chant theory that are added under the names of other octave species. The opening pairs are assigned the usual numbers (I–IV [IIII]), with odd numbers for authentic and even for plagal, and match the table that follows. But no Roman numeral appears beneath the Hypolydian and Lydian pair; instead V and VI appear beneath the "traditional" representations of this pair which occur directly below (traditional in eight-mode theory which routinely used B♭ for the "f-modes"): the Ionian-Hypoionian pair. The additional annotations point to a "core repertory" of chants and polyphonic works by which these modes could be recognized and indeed, most of these works appear as examples in the *Dodecachordon*.[48]

Dorian:	*Salve regina* [chant]
Hypodorian:	*Wo sol ich mich*
Commixed Dorian-Hypodorian:	*Victimae* [*paschali laudes*] [chant and Josquin motet]
Phrygian:	*Tulerunt* [*Dominum meum*] [Pesenti, att. Isaac in the *Dodecachordon*]
Hypophrygian:	*Tota pulchra es* [Isaac]

[47] Interestingly, the bottom stave of the sketch, in Tschudi's hand was distilled from the *Isagoge*, suggesting an attempt on his part to reconcile the two.

[48] Loach, "Aegidius Tschudi's Songbook," 63, suggests the sketch must postdate Glarean's commission to Meyer, if the indication of the *Kyrie de nostra Domina* for the commixed Aeolian-Hypoæolian pair points to Meyer's setting (rather than the chant on which it is based).

Commixed Lydian-Hypolydian:[49]	*Passio Christe* [chant]
Commixed Mixolydian-Hypomixolydian:	**Et in terra de nostra Domina* [Josquin]
Aeolian:	**Peregrinus, Ach hulf mich leid* [Adam von Fulda, contrafact text *O vera lux et gloria* in the *Dodecachordon*]
Hypoæolian:	**Miseremini* [*mei*] [Mouton]
Commixed Aeolian-Hypoæolian:	**Kyrie de nostra Domina* [Gregor Meyer]
Ionian:	*Vil täntz*
Hypoionian:	*Josquin *Ave Maria*

* indicates work that appears in the *Dodecachordon*

In both method and content, the Tschudi Liederbuch and its companion sketches offer striking parallels with the manuscript commonplace book. These sources suggest that recollection also played a role in drawing together the examples of the *Dodecachordon*. The citations on the modal summary suggest a kind of "core repertory" for Glarean's teaching that may or may not have been recorded in a note-book along the lines of Tschudi's, grouped under the *loci* of modal labels. They also point to a repertory that Glarean either expected his students to know or to which they at least had access.

The list of "core" works on the modal summary in Tschudi's sketchbook suggests that the group of cited motets have been distanced from the context in which they are found in the Munich partbooks. Modal identity was a feature that was identified in the Munich partbooks only after the collection had been put together. The process appears to have been reversed in Tschudi's case: he chooses which works to include in his Liederbuch precisely on the basis of their modal identity and the structured order planned for the Liederbuch.[50] This is actually not a surprising turn in an Erasmian understanding of the *Dodecachordon*, because with its implicitly moral basis, Glarean's modal theory confers moral status upon exemplars which are read by means of his model.

The perspective of the commonplace-book tradition suggests that the musical examples that went into the *Dodecachordon* had been viewed by Glarean as constituting matter (*res*) subject to collection and manipulation, to be embedded in a discursive and rhetorical framework which structured their meaning. This turns back, then, to the question of how such examples were expected to be "read" and the degree to which musical notation can function as a text within a text.

While Erasmus describes no discipline as too far removed from rhetoric to provide *exempla*, his incorporation of musical references in *De copia* necessarily takes

---

[49] Loach, "Aegidius Tschudi's Songbook," 63, erroneously transcribes this as "Connexorum [Lÿdii Hÿpodo-riique].

[50] This process is discussed in relation to Tschudi's categorization of *Magnus es tu Domine* in chapter 9.

the form of descriptions *about* music.[51] Specialized commonplace books existed for the disciplines of medicine, law, and theology, yet none of these poses the difficulties inherent in discourse about music and the representation of music within that discourse. The Munich partbooks and Tschudi's Liederbuch share certain features of commonplace books, but cannot be commonplace books *per se* because while modal indicators can function as *loci* they must, of necessity, stand outside the *loci communes* tradition.

The scenario of the notebook offers insights into how and why the music examples of the *Dodecachordon* came to be there and the place they occupied in Glarean's mindset, but sidesteps the question of how (and if) they functioned *as music*. The Munich partbooks, Tschudi's sketchbook, and Glarean's annotated prints suggest at least what the reader represented by this small group of humanists might have been like. First and foremost, he was a reader who understood the significance of *exempla* in rhetoric. He may well have been a reader who was "glancing" for particular landmarks, modal or otherwise – outside of any sense of musical time or sonic simultaneity – that were easily apparent in the regularized format in which the music examples are presented. Indeed, such landmarks are often more easily observed when reading individual parts.[52] Such a reader may have also been a performative reader, and we must not exclude the possibility that he was reading only an individual part, even when all were available. At a more generalized level, at a time when music treatises in the vernacular were becoming increasingly the norm, white mensural notation could serve the function of the *lingua franca*, acting as a graphic or pictorial representation.[53] For many readers, for whom Glarean's Latin might be difficult, if not prohibitive, his instantiations of the modes with notated polyphony provides the means for understanding the text. At a most basic level, notated examples point to the *sound* of music in a generalized sense, even for the reader who will never realize the specific sounds represented on the page. But beyond that, Glarean's discussion of the examples in the *Dodecachordon* does seem to suggest that the notation functions as a reminder of a whole, and that the skilled reader was able to conceive (or recall) these works, transferred to choirbook format from partbook. Indeed, Glarean frequently introduces the examples with references to hearing and sound, for example:

---

[51] E.g., Erasmus's citation from Lucian's *Harmonides*: "You have by now taught me to tune the flute accurately and breathe into the mouthpiece gently and tunefully, to put the fingers down flexibly and in time with the constant rise and fall of the melody, to move with the beat and play in unison with the chorus, and to observe the characteristics of the different modes, the sublime frenzy of the Phrygian, the Dionysiac storming of the Lydian, the solemnity and dignity of the Dorian, the elegance of the Ionian" (*De copia*, 574). And when "music" is included as a heading in commonplace books, it is description *about* music, rather than notation as representative *of* music, that is included under such a heading.

[52] It is worth emphasizing that Glarean's modal annotations appear almost exclusively in tenor partbooks, while Tschudi's seem to have been added to all the parts.

[53] See the discussion of the changing role of images in printed texts in Elizabeth L. Eisenstein, *The Printing Press as an Agent of Change* (Cambridge: Cambridge University Press, 1976). Although Eisenstein's thesis is problematic in many aspects, especially when applied to music printing, she offers a useful consideration of the iconic implications of print culture.

Now let us hear the songs which we have discussed. . . .
Therefore, the Benedictus of *Missa L'homme armé VI toni* sounds thus. . . .

Such introductions serve as an invitation to view the examples of the text as an attempt to create the impression of verisimilitude. The reading that achieved such an effect may well have been a "prepared" one, not unlike the kind of prepared reading necessary for Latin texts in which the reader can make sense of a sentence or grammatical unit only after having studied its different parts – a situation in which the kind of beginning-to-end reading that we take for granted is inconceivable. The reading may also have been a communal one. The physical size of the *Dodecachordon*, while marking it as a "prestige" publication, also lends itself to performance of the works it contains by four singers gathered around the book. The choirbook format provides the visual clues necessary to the skilled individual or the group through the convenience of a single opening and coordinated page turns. The partbook format in which the examples were originally transmitted supplied a physical object that was easily manipulated in the compilation process.[54]

While the remarkable printed achievement represented by the incorporation of these examples has long been acknowledged, the purpose of their inclusion has been taken for granted in an assessment that fails to recognize the ways in which Glarean's treatise not only radically changed the expectations of the way a theorist related to a repertory but also manifests a specific intellectual environment which valued exemplarity above all else. The means by which the *Dodecachordon*, as immaterial theory and material musical object, was removed from that context of exemplarity – first by subsequent early modern and then by more recent readers – forms the basis of the final two parts of this book.

---

[54] That humanist-compilers were adept at manipulating multiple books in making their notebooks is attested by the various devices developed to allow them to do so.

PART IV

GIOSEFFO ZARLINO'S *LE ISTITUTIONI HARMONICHE* (1558)

COMPOSITION AND THEORY
MEDIATED BY PRINT CULTURE

> [T]he musician cannot perfect himself solely by reading and rereading books; ultimately to understand the things I have been demonstrating and others to be shown, he must consult with a person skilled in counter-point . . .
>
> Theory without practice, as I have said before, is of small value, since music does not consist only of theory and is imperfect without practice. This is obvious enough. Yet some theorists, treating of certain musical matters without having a good command of the actual practice, have spoken much nonsense and committed a thousand errors. On the other hand, some who have relied only on practice without knowing the reasons behind it have unwittingly perpetrated thousands upon thousands of idiocies in their compositions . . .
>
> *Le istitutioni harmoniche*, III: 226.[1]

This epigraph highlights three themes that shape my assessment of Gioseffo Zarlino's *Le istitutioni harmoniche*: first, an understanding that while books are to be read and reread as sources of knowledge, they are ultimately insufficient; second, as a corollary, a teacher has the ability to impart knowledge by authoritative means that (apparently) surpass what can be gleaned by an individual solely from reading; and third, an exposition of the symbiotic relationship of musical theory and practice that is central to all of Zarlino's activities. These form the central themes highlighted in this chapter as the music examples and citations of *Le istitutioni harmoniche* are examined for the pointers they offer to Zarlino's interaction with the world of printed music specifically and printed books more generally. The authority of *Le istitutioni harmoniche* for both its contemporary and modern readers rests in part in its codification of the teachings of a venerated master, Zarlino's own teacher,

---

[1] "Cosí quello non potrà esser perfetto, per haver letto, & riletto molti libri: ma li sarà disibogno alla fine, per intender bene quello, che hò mostrato di sopra, et molte altre cose, che son per mostrare; che si riduchi alle volte a ragionare con alcuno, che habbia cognitione della Prattica; cioè del Contrapunto . . .

Et se la Speculativa senza la Prattica (come altre volte hò detto) val poco; atteso che la Musica non consiste solamente nella Speculativa; cosi questa senza la prima e veramente imperfetta. Et questo e manifesto: conciosia che havendo voluto alcuni Theorici trattare alcune cose della Musica; per no havere havuto buona cognitione della Prattica, hanno detto mille chiachiere, & commesso mille errori. Simigliantemente alcuni, che si hanno voluto governare con la sola Prattica, senza conoscere alcuna ragione, hanno fatto nelle loro compositioni mille, & mille pazze, senza punto avedersene di cosa alcuna." (1558 III: 65, 261).

Adriano Willaert. Yet, underlying this overt gesture to Willaert's authority is the citation of authors of both antiquity and more recent times known to Zarlino through printed editions.[2] These, coupled with references to musical compositions and the inclusion of numerous newly composed musical examples, play a crucial role in establishing Zarlino's authority to transmit Willaert's teachings. Zarlino's personal relationship with Willaert (and the implicit understanding that a book such as this carried Willaert's *imprimatur*) will have lent credibility to the volume for Zarlino's mid-sixteenth-century readers. Zarlino has deliberately blurred the boundaries of his own contribution to the volume. On the one hand, he is cast as facilitator or transmitter of another's teachings, yet, on the other, we are clearly intended to recognize the breadth and originality of his theoretical speculations and interpretations. The epigraph shows Zarlino pointing his reader to a skilled contrapuntist. We understand Willaert to be the idealized representation of such a contrapuntist but also infer that Zarlino represents its embodiment in his generation. Through the medium of print, Zarlino creates and codifies his own place in history.[3] In the sense that he overtly codified Willaert's teaching, Zarlino provided in the *Istitutioni* – with its synthesis of theoretical and practical concerns – instruction of a kind never before available so directly from a book, all the while proclaiming the insufficiency of books as a means for obtaining such knowledge.

Zarlino's *Istitutioni* was one of the most influential theory treatises of the sixteenth and seventeenth centuries. It marks the culmination of the art of presenting musical examples in printed treatises within an intellectual culture in which musical theory had achieved its own place. Zarlino also operated within a manuscript musical culture in his affiliations with choirs and his studies with Willaert, though printed music had largely eclipsed that culture in interesting and significant ways. In the quarter-century since Aron had published his treatises, the availability and role of printed music had changed dramatically. Zarlino's position was also markedly different from Aron's. The *Istitutioni* stands in the Italian theoretical tradition of Aron's treatises, but is also deeply indebted to Glarean's *Dodecachordon*, even as it reflects specific mid-century Venetian intellectual currents, most notably the influence of Pietro Bembo. First published in 1558, a new title page was printed in 1561 and 1562. It appeared in an extensively revised edition in 1573.[4] With minimal

---

[2] Included among these are translations and editions that he commissioned, such as Antonio Gogava's translation of Ptolemy's *Harmonics*. See Claude Palisca, *Humanism in Italian Renaissance Musical Thought* (New Haven: Yale University Press, 1985), 133.

[3] There is an extensive literature on "self-fashioning" through print in the Renaissance. See especially Stephen Greenblatt, *Renaissance Self-Fashioning: From More to Shakespeare* (Chicago: University of Chicago Press, 1980) and Lisa Jardine, *Erasmus, Man of Letters* (Princeton: Princeton University Press, 1993).

[4] Gioseffo Zarlino, *Le istitutioni harmoniche* (Venice: [Pietro Da Fino], 1558; facsimile, New York: Broude Brothers, 1965); reissue, Venice: Francesco Franceschi Senese, 1561; second reissue, Venice: Francesco Franceschi Senese, 1562; enlarged, revised edition, Venice: Francesco Franceschi Senese, 1573 (facsimile, Ridgewood, NJ: Gregg Press, 1966); Slight revision of 1573 edition as volume 1 of *De tutte l'opere del r.m. G. Zarlino* (Venice: Francesco Franceschi Senese, 1588). Facsimile and transcription in Gioseffo Zarlino, *Music Treatises*, ed. Frans Wiering, Thesaurus Musicarum Italicarum 1 [Utrecht: Universiteit Utrecht, 1997]. German translation and commentary on Parts I and II (1573 ed.) in Michael Fend, *Theorie des Tonsystems*, Europäische

further revisions, it formed the first volume in Zarlino's complete writings, published a year before his death.

BOOK CULTURE IN VENICE

Despite his assertion that book knowledge was insufficient in and of itself, Zarlino was an individual for whom books were clearly valued objects. The inventory of his house at the time of his death lists in his studio more than 1,100 volumes: 290 printed folios; 294 printed quartos; 354 printed octavos; 206 printed duodecimos; and 1 parchment folio.[5] Like most such inventories, this one lists volumes only by size; there is no indication of titles or organization by content. Even so, the mere size of Zarlino's collection makes it stand out. The library merited mention in Francesco Sansovino's contemporary chronicle, *Venetia Città Nobilissima*, under the heading "Librerie."[6] While Sansovino singles out specific aspects of some of the libraries that he cites (for example subject

Hochschulschriften 36: 43 (Frankfurt am Main: Peter Lang, 1989). English translation of Part III (1558 ed.) by Guy Marco, *The Art of Counterpoint* (New Haven: Yale University Press, 1968). English translation of Part IV (1558 ed.) by Vered Cohen, *On the Modes* (New Haven: Yale University Press, 1983). Unless otherwise indicated, all translations follow Marco and Cohen, with page references to the translated text. References to the original texts are indicated by year of the edition, part, and chapter, followed by page reference.

[5] Among other items in the studio were included a clavicembalo cromatico, a lute, an astrolabe, and two globes. The inventory is reproduced in facsimile and transcribed in Isabella Palumbo-Fossati, "La casa veneziana di Gioseffo Zarlino nel testamento e nell'inventario dei beni del grande teorico musicale," *Nuova rivista musicale italiana* 20 (1986), 633–49. The presence of only one manuscript book is astonishing. Compare the inventory of the library of Aldo Manuzio the Younger, much of which probably belonged to his father. The library contains several manuscript treatises on music and he was neither a composer nor a theorist. (Bonnie J. Blackburn, Edward E. Lowinsky, and Clement A. Miller, *A Correspondence of Renaissance Musicians* (Oxford: Clarendon Press, 1991), 28–31.)

[6] Francesco Sansovino, *Venetia, città nobilissima, et singolare, descritta in XIIII libri . . . Con aggiunta di tutte le cose notabili della stessa città, fatte, & occorse dall'anno 1580. Sino al presente 1663. das d. Giustiniano Martinioni . . .* (Venice: S. Curti, 1663 (facsimile ed. Farnborough: Gregg International Publishers, 1968)): "Ci sona parimente Librerie particolari, di singolar stima & veramente meriteuoli d'esser ricordate & vedute. Et frà queste (tacendo delle publiche & comuni de monisteri, di San Giouanni & Paulo, di San Francesco, de Frati Minori di San Stefano, de Serui, di San Giorgio Maggior, di San Domenico, di Santo Antonio, che la hebbe per lascio del Cardinal Marin Grimani, essendo prima stata di Giouanni Pico dalla Mirandola) è notabile quella di Iacomo Contarini a San Samuello. Il quale con spesa indicibile, ha posto insieme quasi tutte le historie stampate & le scritte à penna, non pure vniuersali, ma particolari delle città, con diuersi altri libri & in gran copia nelle scienze.

Con quali sono àccompagnati disegni, stromenti mathematici, & altre cose di mano de i più chiari artefici nella pittura, nella scoltura, e nell'architettura, che habbia hauuto l'età nostra. I quali tutti egli hà sempre, come amante de i virtuosi fauoriti & accarezzati. E anco degnissima la Libreria di Daniello Barbaro Eletto d'Aquilea. Di Giouanni Delfino Vescouo di Torcello. Di Monsignor Valiero Vescouo di Ciuidale. Del Delfino Vescovo della Canea. Del Violmo Vescouo di Città Noua, & di Rocco Cataneo Auditor Generale di diuersi Legati del Papa in questa città. E nobile etiandio per Libri Greci, & Latini, lo studio di Sebastiano Erizo, di Luigi, & di Marc'Antonio, di Iacomo Marcello, di Luigi Lolino, di Francesco Soranzo, di Luigi Malipiero hauuta dal Cardinale Amulio, & di molti altri nobili studiosi delle lingue & delle scientie. S'annouera frà queste la Libreria di Luigi Balbi oratore & causidico facondissimo. Nella quale, oltre I libri teologici, historici, & di leggi, ridotti à facilità con sommari & repertorij in ogni materia, si nota una singolarissima sfera fatta con marauiglioso artificio. E anco copiosissima quella di Aldo Manutio Iuniore & piena di cose elette & singolari. Et quella di Monsignor Gioseppo Zarlino Maestro di Cappella di San Marco, del Medico Rino, di Agostino Amai, & di molti altre appresso, de quali non mi souiene al presente" (VIII: 370–71).

matter or type of collection: Greek and Latin volumes, or theology, etc.),
Zarlino's collection is included in a simple list. Its addition at the end of the list
would seem to suggest that it was not among the "premier" libraries of Venice,
but that a *maestro di cappella* of neither noble birth nor exceptional means should
appear among this list at all is striking and an indication of the social and intellectual circles in which Zarlino had ingratiated himself. Although direct comparisons are hard to come by, there is no doubt that Zarlino's library was
exceptionally large for a man of his status.[7] Zarlino's will also highlighted the significance of his library, in his specification that it was to go to his great-nephew
Iseppo, son of Vincenzo Colonna.[8] Yet despite the apparent vastness of his
library, few books containing Zarlino's annotations are known to have survived:
one is Stefano Vanneus's *Recanetum*.[9] The size of Zarlino's library is corroborated
by the breadth of his reading and apparent through his citations of both classical
and post-classical authors in his published works.[10]

---

[7] For a general comparison, see Giulio M. Ongaro, "The Library of a Sixteenth-Century Music Teacher," *Journal of Musicology* 12 (1994), 357–75. On German humanists' libraries, see Iain Fenlon, "Heinrich Glarean's Books," in *Music in the German Renaissance*, ed. John Kmetz (Cambridge: Cambridge University Press, 1994), 83–84.

[8] As transcribed in Isabella Palumbo-Fossati, 638, "La casa veneziana": "Voglio che tutta la libraria che io mi ritrovo sia di Iseppo mio nipote figliuolo di Marta mia nezza e di messer Vincenzo Colonna; la qual gli lasso con patto che voglia studiare; perché altrimenti voglio che sia de' Frati Zoccolanti di S. Francesco, al qual Iseppo lasso anco tutto il restante del mio, che mi ritrovo et commissario lasso detto mio. Vicenzo padre di detto Iseppo."

Iseppo must have been very young: the library was to be given to him only if he wished to become a scholar; otherwise, the books were to be given to the Observant Friars of San Francesco (presumably *San Francesco alla Vigna*). Vincenzo Colonna built a new organ for the parish church of San Marziale in 1573 and was salaried as the organ tuner for the Scuola Grande di San Rocco from 1560 to 1590. He repaired the organ at San Stefano in 1577 and worked for the parish church of San Giovanni in Bragora as a tuner from 1581 to 1584. When he assumed the San Rocco job in 1569, he identified himself as a student of the famous organ builder Vicenzo Colombo. (I am grateful to Jonathan Glixon for this information on Colonna. See also Don Gastone Vio, "Documenti di storia organaria Veneziana," *L'Organo* 17 (1979), 181–206.) I have not attempted to trace any records of Zarlino's sister or heirs although this might provide clues to the ultimate location of his library.

[9] Cited in Cohen, *On the Modes*, 47 n.7. The copy is in the Newberry Library, Chicago. The book is minimally annotated, but contains three pages of Latin manuscript at the end in Zarlino's hand. Although this has usually been presumed to have been the start of a treatise in Latin by Zarlino, I have identified a large section as an extended quotation from Guillaume Guerson, *Utilissime musicales regule* (Paris: Michel Thouloze, [c. 1495]). According to a note on the flyleaf written in a nineteenth-century hand, the *Recanetum* was originally bound with Zarlino's copy of Boethius, *De Arithmetica, Musica* (Paris: Scotto, 1492). The current location of this book is unknown. Beyond these, Zarlino's signature appears in a copy of Francesco Venturi, *Dionisio Halicarneseo delle cose antiche della Citta di Roma* (Venice: Bascarini, 1545), cited with facsimile of the signature in a sale catalog: Georg Kinsky, ed., *Versteigerung von Musiker-Autographen as dem Nachlaß des Herrn Kommerzienrates Wilhelm Heyer* (Cologne: Karl Ernst Henrici, 1926), 107. Irving Godt mentions that Zarlino's copy of *Julii Caesaris Scaligeri . . . Poetices libri septem* ([Lyons], 1561) is in the library of the University of Bologna (Irving Godt, "Italian *Figurenlehre*," in *Music and Language*, Studies in the History of Music 1 (New York: Broude Brothers, 1983), 192 n.21. Frans Wiering informed me in a personal communication that Zarlino's copy of Francisco de Salinas, *De musica libri septem* (Salamanca: Matthias Gastius, 1577) is in the collection of the Bibliothèque nationale in Paris.

[10] See for example the "Index of Classical Passages Cited," in Cohen's translation of Part IV of *Le istitutioni harmoniche* (113–14) and Claude Palisca, *Humanism in Italian Renaissance Musical Thought*, esp. 244–54 and 298–301. Additionally, Frans Wiering has compiled a list of forty-five post-classical books to which Zarlino makes reference ("The Language of the Modes," Ph.D. dissertation, University of Amsterdam (1995), 199).

As with Heinrich Glarean, a knowledge of the books Gioseffo Zarlino owned provides a glimpse into the intellectual and material life of the theorist. But the evidence of Zarlino's library contrasts starkly with that of Glarean's. While the survival of a core portion of Glarean's library provided the point of departure for the previous chapter, one can only speculate as to what percentage of Glarean's library it actually represents. Conversely, the size of Zarlino's library at the time of his death is precisely known, but its contents remain a matter of speculation. Nevertheless, the distribution of volumes by format suggests something of its content. The folios were almost certainly learned treatises with a few music books among them, while the quarto volumes in all likelihood included numerous printed partbooks.[11]

There is tantalizing evidence, albeit scant, that Zarlino's involvement in book culture extended not just to traditional pursuits of collection, consumption (reading), and production (writing), but to aspects of physical production and design,[12] as well as the financial interests in his publications that went hand-in-hand with book production in the sixteenth century. Also, the extravagant, but short-lived and ill-fated, Accademia Veneziana of which Zarlino was a member may be seen in its commercial and intellectual interests as an emblem of the melding of pragmatic and more elevated concerns represented by the material objects that were Zarlino's books.

Zarlino stands in a long and venerable line of writers who produced theory treatises and were employed as a *maestro di cappella* of a major religious institution. But unlike writers such as Gaffurio, Zarlino's first major treatise and the book for which he is most remembered, *Le istitutioni harmoniche*, was not a product of his years as *maestro di cappella* at San Marco: its publication preceded his employment there by some seven years. Indeed, I will argue that among Zarlino's reasons for publishing the volume was an attempt to position himself for an appointment like the one at San Marco. Its date of publication neatly coincided with the advent of the Accademia Veneziana but also, more significantly, with the declining health of

---

[11] It is difficult to offer a very specific assessment based simply on number because individual prints may well have been bound together thus representing more titles than extant volumes. At the same time, the number of quartos might also represent fewer individual prints because of the separate binding of partbooks. No information is available on whether or not Zarlino was in the habit of having multiple titles bound together. Certainly, however, the folios will have included treatises like Gaffurio's *Practica musicae*, Boethius's *De musica* (possibly as part of the complete works in either Scotto's edition or Glarean's 1546 edition) and music prints like the *Liber selectarum musicarum* (1520) (folio choirbook) and Willaert's *Musica nova* (1559) (oversize upright quarto). These last two are discussed in greater detail below. The portion of the quartos that were music prints probably included Venetian publications like those listed in Table 7.2 below. The "parchment folio" of the inventory is probably one of the two manuscripts that Zarlino mentions in the *Sopplimenti musicali*, 17–18, cited by Jessie Ann Owens, "Music Historiography and the Definition of 'Renaissance'," *Music Library Association Notes* 47 (1990), 318 n.49. On formats, see Mary Lewis, "Formats, Paper, and Typography," in *Antonio Gardano: Venetian Music Printer, 1538–1569: A Descriptive Bibliography and Historical Study* (New York: Garland, 1988), I: 35–62.

[12] Zarlino's connections to the Venetian printer Gardano are discussed in more detail below. Although a woodcut, *Vergine della Navicella* (1579), was attributed to Zarlino by Alfredo Bonaccorsi ("Zarlino, Gioseffo," *Enciclopedia italiana di scienze, lettere ed arti* (Rome: Treccani, 1937)), this attribution must be viewed with skepticism. The woodcut is reproduced in Loris Tiozzo, *Gioseffo Zarlino: Teorico musicale* (Venice: Veneta Editrice, 1992), 23.

Willaert and his extended absence from his duties at San Marco. Yet unlike Gaffurio or any of the theorists discussed in this book, or other humanist writers about music for that matter, Zarlino's earliest publication was not a treatise, but a book of music. As I will elaborate, it was a book that conveys in numerous (non-musical) ways that its author was not *merely* a practitioner but a true *musicus*, a theorist of great erudition steeped in humanistic learning. With remarkable canniness, Zarlino masterfully and meticulously manipulated his public image through the medium of print over a forty-year period beginning with this first publication in 1549. Although the composer/theorist conjunction this represents might seem a modern preoccupation, it is a dichotomy that recurs throughout Zarlino's printed works as he attempts to present himself with a foot planted firmly (and successfully) in each camp. These printed traces shape the narrative which follows: his first publication, a book of motets, contains a number of telling allusions to the world of humanist learning; his first theory treatise highlights Willaert, the foremost composer of his day, while implicitly promoting Zarlino as his worthy successor; his next publication of motets refers back to his theory treatise; his revised version of the treatise cites the recently published motets.

ZARLINO'S BIOGRAPHY AND THE RECEPTION OF HIS WORKS

Zarlino would, no doubt, have taken great pleasure in an assessment like Robert Wienpahl's:

The most important advances in 16th-century harmonic theory were made primarily by one man, Gioseffo Zarlino (1517–90), and it is safe to say that probably no theorist since Boethius was as influential upon the course of the development of music theory.[13]

While this stands among the grandest of modern assessments of Zarlino's influence, the signal importance of his theoretical *oeuvre* has long been acknowledged. Einstein, for example, described Zarlino as "the theorist of his century and maybe of all centuries."[14]

Zarlino would, I suspect, take less kindly to the reception of his musical compositions, works which Palisca describes as, "learned and polished, [but] of secondary interest."[15] More damning in some ways, but also typical, is Reese's faint praise that

---

[13] Robert Wienpahl, "Zarlino, the Senario, and Tonality," *Journal of the American Musicological Society* 12 (1959), 27. The bibliography on the *Istitutioni* is extensive; see David Damschroder and David Russell Williams, *Music Theory from Zarlino to Schenker*, Harmonologia 4 (Stuyvesant, NY: Pendragon Press, 1990), 391–95.

[14] Alfred Einstein, *The Italian Madrigal*, trans. Alexander H. Krappe, Roger H. Sessions, and Oliver Strunk (Princeton: Princeton University Press, 1971), I: 453.

[15] Claude Palisca, "Zarlino, Gioseffo," *New Grove Dictionary of Music and Musicians*, ed. S. Sadie (London: Macmillan, 1980), 648. Only a handful of Zarlino's motets have appeared in a modern edition: three in *Gioseffo Zarlino: Drei Motetten und ein geistliches Madrigal*, ed. Roman Flury, Das Chorwerk 77 (Wolfenbüttel: Möseler Verlag, 1960); one in *Thomas Crequillon und andere Meister: Vier Motetten*, ed. Bernhard Meier, Das Chorwerk 121 (Wolfenbüttel: Möseler Verlag, 1976); and two in *L'arte musicale in Italia*, ed. Luigi Torchi (Milan: Ricordi, 1897/R1968). Nine of the thirteen madrigals are edited in *G. Zarlino: Nove madrigali a cinque voci tratti da varie*

Zarlino was an "estimable composer."[16] From the interpretation of Zarlino's prints that I offer below, one senses that despite his self-promotion, he spent his early career at San Marco responding to precisely this perception: that while he was a man of great learning, he was but a second-rate composer.

Despite Zarlino's fame, his biography remains sketchy, with the outlines taken from Baldi's account of 1595 supplemented by a handful of archival documents.[17] An ordained priest, he left Chioggia Cathedral – where he was employed first as a singer and then as organist – for Venice in 1541.[18] In 1565, he was appointed *maestro di cappella* at San Marco. Although Baldi lists Zarlino's studies and teachers in Venice – music with Willaert, logic and philosophy with Cristoforo da Ligname, Greek with Guglielmo Fiammingo, Hebrew with a nephew of Elia Tesbite – his employment and whereabouts before his appointment at San Marco are scantily documented.[19] Since Baldi's 1595 account relied on Zarlino's personal recollection, it seems entirely reasonable to suspect that here as elsewhere Zarlino shaped his public image by means of selective recollection. That is, although his teachers (and thus his intellectual pedigree) are prominently identified, there is no mention of his Venetian employment before his appointment as *maestro di cappella* of San Marco.

Zarlino began to publish music in 1549: one madrigal in an anthology, three motets in anthologies, and his own book of nineteen five-voice motets. Typically, in two of the anthologies (RISM 1548[9] and 1567[16]), he is among the "other excellent composers" whose works are included along with the prominently named Cipriano de Rore and Orlando di Lasso. Table 7.1 offers an overview of Zarlino's singly authored works along with a list of his contributions to anthologies.

This overview reveals a publication history with three notable features. There is a regular alternation between the publication of compositions and theoretical works that ultimately favors the theory treatises: motets in 1549; *Le istitutioni harmoniche* in 1558–62; a book of motets in 1566 and several madrigals in anthologies in 1562–67;

raccolte, ed. S. Cisilino (Venice: Istituto per la collaborazione culturale, 1963). Roman Flury, *Gioseffo Zarlino als Komponist* (Winterthur: Verlag P. G. Keller, 1962), provides a brief overview of Zarlino's compositional *oeuvre*, but the assessment is problematic since Flury had access to only a partial set of the partbooks of Zarlino's largest motet print from 1549.   [16] Gustave Reese, *Music in the Renaissance* (London: J. M. Dent, 1954), 379.

[17] Bernardino Baldi, ed. Enrico Narducci, *Vite inedite di matematici italiani* (Rome: Tip. delle scienze matematiche e fisiche, 1887). Also published in *Bulletino di bibliografia e di storia delle scienze matematiche e fisiche* 19 (1886), 335–406, 437–89, 512–640. I am grateful to Benito Rivera for sharing with me a copy of the original "corrected" manuscript version of Baldi's biography of Zarlino.

[18] Although Zarlino is frequently described as a Franciscan (e.g. by Palisca, "Zarlino, Gioseffo," *New Grove*, XX: 646), Rivera has shown that he was a secular priest.

[19] According to Giulio Ongaro, he a "capellanus curatus" of the parish church of San Severo and a chaplain at the monastery of San Lorenzo (these latter two with Daniele Grisonio, a singer at San Marco), "The Chapel of St. Mark's at the Time of Adrian Willaert (1527–1562): A Documentary Study," Ph.D. dissertation, University of North Carolina at Chapel Hill (1986), 196. An archival document shared with me by Benito Rivera lists Zarlino's place of residence in 1557 as in the district of San Benedetto. Rivera has filled in a number of gaps in the Chioggia biography and has verified and filled out much of Baldi's account of Zarlino's early studies. Jonathan Glixon (personal communication) informed me that Zarlino served as a mansionario at the Scuola Grande Santa Maria della Carità at their altar in the church of Santa Maria della Carità from 1558 to 1565. His resignation, dated August 1565, appears in ASV, Scuola Grande di Santa Maria della Carità, Registro 258, 8.80v. His successor was Grisonio.

Table 7.1 Zarlino's publications

Date	Title	Printer	Dedicatee	Comments
1549	Musici quinque vocum	Gardano	Alvise Balbi Prior of Sancto Spirito	Motet print for five voices; modal attributions printed in tenor partbook; unusually careful text underlay
1558	Le istitutioni harmoniche	[da Fino][a]	Vincenzo Diedo Venetian patriarch	
1561	"	Francesco Franceschi Senese	"	reissue of 1558 with new title page
1562	"	Francesco Franceschi Senese	"	reissue of 1558 with new title page
1566	Modulationes per Philippum Iusbertum . . . collectae	Rampazetto	the procurators of San Marco	6 vv motets with dedication by Philippo Zusberti, a singer at San Marco
1571	Dimostrationi harmoniche	Francesco Franceschi Senese	Alvise Mocenigo, Doge of Venice	
1573	Le istitutioni harmoniche	Francesco Franceschi Senese	[Vincenzo Diedo]	enlarged and revised edition
1588–89	De tutte l'opere del r.m. G. Zarlino	Francesco Franceschi Senese	Pope Sixtus V	4 vols., revised eds. of Istitutioni and Dimostrationi; Sopplimenti musicali; and non-musical writings[b]

Entire publications credited to Zarlino's authorship are listed above. In addition:
Several motets appeared in anthologies:

RISM 1549[3] Primo libro de Motetti a sei voci diversi eccellentissimi Musici composti (Scotto, 1549): Victimae paschali (6vv, revised in 1566);

RISM 1549[7] Primo libro de Motetti a cinque voci da diversi eccellentissimi Musici composti (Scotto, 1549): Si ignoras (5vv) and Nemo potest (5vv, also published in Zarlino 1549);

RISM 1549[8]: Il terzo libro di motetti a cinque voci di Cipriano de Rore e de altre excellentissimmi Musici . . . A cinque voci (Gardano, 1549): Adiuro vos, filie (5vv);

RISM 1563[4]: Motetta D. Cipriani de Rore et aliorum auctorum quatuuor vocibus paribus decanenda (Scotto, 1563): Ecce iam venit (4vv). Parce mihi, Domine [Three lessons pro defunctis] (4vv);

RISM 1567[3]: Primo libro degli eterni Mottetti di Orlando di Lasso, Cipriano Rore et d'altri eccel. musici a cinque e sei voci (Scotto, 1567): Parcus Estenses (5vv).

One motet survives only in manuscript: *Amavit eum Dominus* (6vv) *I-TVca(d)*

Thirteen madrigals were published in seven anthologies:

RISM 1548[9] *Di Cipriano Rore et di altri eccellentissimi musici il terzo libro di madrigali a cinque voci* (Scotto, 1549): *Lauro gentile* (5vv);

RISM 1562[5] *I dolci et harmoniosi concenti fatti da diversi eccellentissimi musici sopra varii soggetti, a cinque voci* (Scotto, 1562): *Amor mentre dormia* (5vv), *Cantin' con dolc'e gratios' accenti* (5vv), *E questo il legno* (5vv), *I'vo piangendo* (5vv), *Spent'era gia l'ardor* (5vv);

RISM 1562[6] *I dolci et harmoniosi concenti . . . libro secondo* (Scotto, 1562): *E forse el mio ben* (5vv);

RISM 1566[23] *Di Hettor Vidue et d'Alessandro Striggio e d'altri eccellentissimi Musici Madrigale a V. e VI. voci* (Rampazetto, 1566): *Donna che quasi cigno* (5vv);

RISM 1567[16] *Tertio libro del Desiderio. Madrigali a quattro voci di Orlando Lasso et d'altri eccell. Musici* (Scotto, 1567): *Come si m'accendete* (4vv), *Quand'il soave* (4vv), *Si mi vida es* (4vv);

RISM 1568[16] *Corona della morte dell'illustre Signore il Sig. Comendator Anibal Caro al nobile et generoso cavaliero il Signor Giov. Ferro da Macearta* (Scotto, 1568): *Mentre de mio buon* (5vv);

RISM 1570[15]. *Raccolta di Cornelio Antonelli. I dolci frutti, primo libro de vaghi et dilettevoli Madrigali de diversi Eccellentissimi Autori a cinque voci* (Scotto, 1570): *Si ch'ove prim* (5vv) [= third stanza of *Questo si ch'è felice*, a multi-part "canzone di diversi."]

Notes:

[a] No printer is listed and the book is usually described as "self-published." However, the printer's mark that appears on the title page belongs to Pietro da Fimo, as discussed below.

[b] The final volume of Zarlino's *Tutte l'opere* of 1588–89 contains a number of non-musical works: *Trattato della patientia, Discorso intorno il vero anno, et il vero giorno, nel quale fu crucifisso il nostro Signor Giesu Christo, Informatione intorno la origine della congregatione de I Reverendi Frati Cappucini, Resolutioni d'alcune dimande sopra la correttione dell' anno di Giulio Cesare.* Each book within the volume retains its original dedication. The *Sopplimenti*, first published here, is dedicated to Pope Sixtus V.

the *Dimostrationi* and a revision of the *Istitutioni* in 1571–73; and the *Sopplimenti* and complete works in 1588–89,[20] a year before Zarlino's death. Zarlino's compositions appear primarily in two groups that cluster around his single-author motet prints of 1549 and 1566. And finally, Zarlino's non-musical writings appear only after he is employed at San Marco and long after his reputation as a humanist writer on music is established. By following his printed traces, I will illustrate how Zarlino used publication as a means of not only enhancing, but shaping, his public image; the evidence suggests that he was a masterful manipulator of his printed persona.

LE ISTITUTIONI HARMONICHE: AN OVERVIEW

Of Zarlino's publications, *Le istitutioni harmoniche* is generally agreed to be the most significant and the publication to which his name is routinely linked, no matter the context. First issued in 1558, new title pages and errata lists were printed in 1561 and again in 1562 and it was revised extensively and expanded in 1573. Finally, it was slightly revised and modernized as the first volume in Zarlino's complete works of 1588. Paradoxically, it stands simultaneously as perhaps the best- and least-known theoretical treatise from the sixteenth century. Magisterial in scope, the *Istitutioni* brings under one cover areas of music study that had always before merited not just discrete sections, but separate and distinctly defined volumes. Much modern-day study has reinforced those boundaries as it attempts to come to grips with the *Istitutioni*.[21] Indeed one must look some half a century or more before Zarlino to Tinctoris and Gaffurio to find theorists who write so widely on both speculative and practical matters. Zarlino surely stands as the culmination of this branch of the Italian theoretical tradition, but his writing in the vernacular and his immersion in print culture also set his work apart from these earlier theorists in important ways.[22] He is openly contemptuous of the works of his Italian predeces-

---

[20] Musical compositions, of course, were not included among the complete writings.

[21] Thus the Yale Music Theory Translation Series includes the "Prattica" sections of the treatise, Parts III and IV. Palisca argued in his introduction to the translation: "The monumental *Istitutioni* deserves to be read in its entirety. It documents the thought of a brilliant mind at a key moment of music history. A good case could be made for including the entire volume in the Music Theory Translation Series. Yet Part III has a clear priority over the rest. The *Art of Counterpoint*, with only rare excursions into speculation, presents a living method of composition" (xiii). In the subsequent introduction to Part IV, Palisca reiterated the significance of the practical aspects of the treatise: "Of the four books of Gioseffo Zarlino's *Le Istitutioni harmoniche*, Part III, on counterpoint, and Part IV, on the modes, are oriented toward the practicing composer and musician, while Parts I and II establish the theoretical foundation on which the later books are built" (vii). Michael Fend's German translation of Parts I and II and accompanying commentary (*Theorie des Tonsystems*) serves a similar function for the *Speculativa*. The boundaries between the two large sections of the treatise are also reinforced in the present chapter since musical citations and examples appear exclusively in Parts III and IV of the treatise.

[22] In Zarlino's case, writing in the vernacular reflects a specifically Bembist impulse of the 1530s that attempted to set up Italian as a learned language in its own right. Bembo and Speroni urged translators and authors to write in the vernacular without fear of being thought ignorant; Galileo's scientific writings are usually cited as the most significant manifestation of this trend. (Paul Rose, "The Accademia Venetiana: Science and Culture in Renaissance Venice," *Studi veneziani* 11 (1969), 201.) Zarlino is, of course, not the first music theorist to write in Italian; see the discussion of Aron in chapter 3. Unlike Aron, however, the choice to write in Italian is not a reflection of Zarlino's ability but of specific Venetian intellectual initiatives.

sors Vanneus, Aron, and Lanfranco, dismissing them as the "sophists of their time."[23] After Boethius (whose mistakes Zarlino does not hesitate to highlight either), only three writers on music – Gaffurio, Faber Stapulensis (both described as commentators on Boethius), and Fogliano – seem to meet with Zarlino's approval, albeit conditional.[24]

Intellectual framework and publication history of the *Istitutioni*

In a recent examination of the *Istitutioni*, Martha Feldman persuasively argued that it "tacitly embraced Bembo's single-model theory of imitation as argued in *De imitatione*."[25] Feldman points out that the title page of *Le istitutioni harmoniche* glosses that of Quintilian's *Istitutio oratoria* and sets out the broad framework of the treatise with its reference to poets, historians, and philosophers in an overtly Ciceronian gesture. Doing so solidifies an impression of Zarlino as a widely educated author. (See the title page in Fig. 7.1.) Feldman's interpretation provides the broad intellectual framework, indebted to Bembo, within which to understand the *Istitutioni*, much as I attempted to argue that the framework for Glarean's *Dodecachordon* was intellectually indebted to Erasmus. Yet numerous questions remain about the specific nature in which such a Bembist agenda is realized in the *Istitutioni*. A study of the use of musical examples and citations along with an understanding of the publication history of the volume provides insight into the role examples and citations play in this Bembist framework.

   Although the first edition of the *Istitutioni* is usually described as "self-published," presumably because no printer is overtly identified on the title page and because of the lack of a colophon,[26] recent studies of publishing and printing suggest that such

---

[23] "As regards theoretical or speculative music, few have taken the right path. Apart from Boethius, who wrote in Latin about our science and whose work is also imperfect, there has been no one who has gone beyond him into speculation on things pertaining to music, discovering the true proportions of the intervals – leaving aside Franchino and Fabro Stapulensis, for one might call them commentators on Boethius – except Lodovico Fogliano of Modena . . . The other theorists, leaning on what Boethius wrote on these matters, were unwilling or unable to go further, and occupied themselves by writing of the things mentioned. These things, which they said belonged to the quantitative genus, have to do with modus, tempus, and prolation, as may be seen in the *Recaneto di musica*, the *Toscanello*, the *Scintille*, and in a thousand books like them. In addition there are on such matters a diversity of opinions and lengthy disputations without end. There are also many tracts and apologies, written by certain musicians against others, which, were one to read them a thousand times, the reading, rereading, and study would reveal nothing but vulgarities and slander rather than anything good, and they would leave one appalled. But actually we should excuse these writers, for they were the sophists of their time" (*Art of Counterpoint*, 266–67). This dismissal should not be taken as an indication that Zarlino did not read and incorporate ideas from these treatises when they suited his purpose. See the parallel passages from *Le istitutioni harmoniche* that Bonnie J. Blackburn identified with Spataro's *Honesta defensio*, another book Zarlino dismissed (Bonnie J. Blackburn, "On Compositional Process in the Fifteenth-Century," *Journal of the American Musicological Society* 40 (1987), 230–31).

[24] The writings of two of these men – Faber Stapulensis and Fogliano – appeared among the list of authors to be published by the Accademia Veneziana. In the end only twenty of the some three hundred books that the Academy intended to publish were actually printed and none of the music books (listed in note 42 below) was published under their auspices.

[25] Martha Feldman, *City Culture and the Madrigal at Venice* (Berkeley: University of California Press, 1995), 172.

[26] E.g., Palisca, introduction to *The Art of Counterpoint*, xxiv.

LE ISTITVTIONI

HARMONICHE

DI M. GIOSEFFO ZARLINO DA CHIOGGIA;

Nelle quali; oltra le materie appartenenti

ALLA MVSICA;

Si trouano dichiarati molti luoghi

di Poeti, d'Hiſtorici, & di Filoſofi;

Si come nel leggerle ſi potrà chiaramente vedere.

¶ Θεῦ διδόντος, οὐδὲν ἰσχύει φθόνος.
Καὶ μὴ διδόντος, οὐδὲν ἰσχύει πόνος.

Con Priuilegio dell'Illuſtriſſ. Signoria di Venetia,
per anni X.

IN VENETIA MDLVIII.

7.1 Zarlino, *Le istitutioni harmoniche*, 1558, title page (Bayerische Staatsbibliothek,
2° Mus.th. 568. Reproduced by permission.)

a designation has little meaning in mid-century Venice. There *is* an identifiable printer's mark on the title page (the emblem on Fig. 7.1) that belongs to Pietro Da Fino, although it lacks the characteristic inclusion of his name.[27] But even though Da Fino can be identified as the printer of the *Istitutioni*, his role in the publication of the treatise is obscure, at best, and a number of questions remain including where Da Fino obtained the music font for the examples of the treatise.[28] Da Fino's mark does appear on at least two other music prints without his name and with another printer clearly identified.[29] In the case of the *Istitutioni*, one might speculate that Da Fino printed the work or supplied the type for its printing, but had no direct financial stake in the publication. Zarlino himself held the privilege, dated 16 October 1557 and granted for ten years.[30] It may be that the absence of Da Fino's name, despite the presence of his printer's mark, indicates that Zarlino (and possibly unnamed partners) financed the edition. A folio volume of 347 pages with over seventy figures and diagrams and more than 200 music examples, many extensive, cannot have been an inexpensive undertaking, regardless of the size of the print run.[31] *Le istitutioni harmoniche* reappeared in 1561 and again 1562, now under the imprint of Francesco Franceschi (see Figs. 7.2 and 7.3).[32] Although often described as a reprint, strictly speaking both must be classed as distinct issues of the first edition. The outer leaf of the first gathering has been replaced with a new title page

---

[27] At least three scholars have independently recognized the presence of Da Fino's mark in the *Istitutioni* in recent years. I am grateful to Jane Bernstein for first pointing it out to me and for several discussions of the possible significance of its presence (Jane Bernstein, *Music Printing in Renaissance Venice: The Scotto Press (1539–1572)* (New York: Oxford University Press, 1998), 144 n.25). Benito Rivera and Frans Wiering both recognized the mark as Da Fino's in their work on the *Istitutioni*. Wiering noted that the printer's mark, type, and watermark of the 1558 *Istitutioni* was the same as that of *Theoremata Marci Antonii Zimarae . . .* (Venice, 1556) which identifies Da Fino beneath the printer's mark on the title page and has the colophon: "Venetiis, Ioan. Gryphius excudebat, sumptibus Petri de Fine. MDLVI." Wiering was also able to match initials of the *Istitutioni* with others of Da Fino's prints (Personal communication, 13 July 1998).

[28] I can only say at this stage that the font was not borrowed from Scotto, Rampazetto, or Gardano, the most active publishers of music in mid-century Venice.

[29] See the facsimile of the title page of Scotto's *Canzone alla Napolitana a cinque voci dell'eccellentissimo musice giovan ferretti* (Venice, 1567), edited by Bonagiunta, in Bernstein, *Scotto*, 85. Here the presence of his mark seems to suggest that Da Fino had a financial interest in the print and that his subsidy allowed his mark to be placed on the title page, even though Scotto was the printer. I am grateful to Professor Bernstein for sharing a pre-publication version of this material with me.

[30] "Il Privilegio della Illustrissima Signoria di Venetia. 1557 Die 16 Octobris in Rogatis. Che sia concesso a M.P. Gioseffo Zarlino da Chioza, che niuno altro, che egli, ò chi haverà causa da lui, non possa stampare in questa nostra città, ne in alcun luogo della nostra Signoria, ne altrove stampata in quella vendere l'opera titolata Istitutioni harmoniche, latina, ne volgare, da lui composta, per lo spacio di anni dieci prossimi, sotto tutte le pene contenute nella sua sopplicatione: essendo obligato di osseruare tutto quello, ch'è disposto in materia di Stampe. Iosephus Tramezinus Duc. Not" (printed on the verso of the title page in 1558 and on the verso of the errata sheet in 1561/1562).

[31] Unlike the *Dodecachordon*, not all of the examples are extensive, and none compares to the extent of the complete pieces that characterized Glarean's work. Yet Zarlino's examples may have posed more difficulties of layout for the printer since they are incorporated into the text in varying formats, often occurring within a paragraph, rather than appended at the end of a section as are Glarean's. See the discussion below of the ways in which the examples are set.

[32] These issues are usually conflated and only the 1562 date is mentioned. Only two copies of the 1561 reissue are extant and my observations are based on the copy held by the Bayerische Staatsbibliothek, Munich.

(lacking the privilege on the verso) and a new errata list that replaces the original "Ai Lettori." The privilege now appears on the verso of the errata list. Otherwise there are no signs that any other part of the treatise was reset, despite the presence of a new printer's mark.[33] This suggests that after four years, Zarlino still held a considerable number of copies of the 1558 edition which were made to appear "new" by the addition of a new title page. Franceschi's first imprints date from 1562.[34] However he came by right to place his printer's mark on the treatise, the issue was advantageous to Franceschi because it allowed him to add a title under his imprint at minimal expense and effort – indeed, in what appears to have been among his first books he is actually responsible for printing only a single bifolio. Franceschi's subsequent revised and expanded edition of the treatise in 1573 is much more elegantly printed than the original (compare the title page in Fig. 7.4) and has very different orthography. The "house style" between the two editions is markedly different.

This discussion of the intellectual framework and publication history of the treatise obscures more basic questions of how and why Zarlino came to publish such a book at all, why it appeared when it did, and why he would reissue the work in 1561 and again in 1562. These questions impinge upon understanding the physical format and presentation of the book as well as many of the details of its contents. Circumstantial evidence suggests that Zarlino may well have used this publication, as I believe he used all his publications, as a means to career advancement and to cultivate and enhance his image as both a practical musician and learned composer. As Zusberti, the author of the dedication of Zarlino's 1566 motet print, phrased it:

all should understand that this same artist is able to discourse learnedly on the theoretical aspects of music and to produce the most lovely of all compositions.[35]

As mentioned above, Baldi's biography is extraordinarily vague about Zarlino's activities beyond his studies during the years in Venice before his appointment at San Marco. The appearance of a number of Zarlino's motets and a madrigal in 1549 along with those of a number of Willaert's protégés (among whom Cipriano de

---

[33] These observations are based on a comparison of the 1558 edition of the Library of Congress with the 1562 copy held by the Sibley Library at the Eastman School of Music and a direct comparison of the 1558, 1561, and 1562 issues in the Bayerische Staatsbibliothek, Munich, as well as examination of the 1562 issues in the Gesellschaft der Musikfreunde, the Österreichische Nationalbibliothek, and the Musikwissenschaftliches Institut, Vienna. In all cases, the title page bifolios of the 1561 and 1562 editions share the same watermarks which are distinct from those in the body of the treatise (including the gathering framed by the title page). Except for the title page of the 1561 and 1562 issues, the watermarks are the same for all three editions (that is, including the 1558 title page) – further confirmation that the title page was replaced in extant copies of the works rather than that the edition had been newly printed from old formes. The addition of a new title page is immediately obvious in the copy of the Musikwissenschaftliches Institut; instead of being placed around the first gathering, the bifolio of the title page was bound in front of the first gathering. Benito Rivera independently came to similar conclusions regarding the 1558 and 1562 issues based on his comparison of copies in the Marciana, in the Correr, in the University of Padua, and in the Newberry Library (personal communication), as did Frans Wiering from comparisons of still other copies (personal communication).

[34] D. W. Krummel and Stanley Sadie, eds., *Music Printing and Publishing* (New York: W. W. Norton, 1990).

[35] The full dedication is reproduced and discussed below, pp. 247–49.

LE ISTITVTIONI
HARMONICHE

DEL REVERENDO M. GIOSEFFO ZARLINO
DA CHIOGGIA

Nelle quali; oltra le materie appartenenti

ALLA MVSICA;

Si trouano dichiarati molti luoghi
di Poeti, d'Hiftorici, & di Filofofi;

Si come nel leggerle fi potrà chiaramente vedere.

¶ Θεῦ διδόντος, οὐδὲν ἰχύει φθόνος.
Καὶ μὴ διδόντος, οὐδὲν ἰχύει πόνος.

Con Priuilegio dell'Illuftriff. Signoria di Venetia,
per anni X.

IN VENETIA,
Appreffo Francefco Senefe, al fegno della Pace.
M D LXI.

7.2 Zarlino, *Le istitutioni harmoniche*, 1561, title page (Bayerische Staatsbibliothek, 2° Mus.th. 571. Reproduced by permission.)

LE ISTITVTIONI
HARMONICHE

DEL REVERENDO M. GIOSEFFO ZARLINO
DA CHIOGGIA;

Nelle quali; oltra le materie appartenenti

ALLA MVSICA;

Si trouano dichiarati molti luoghi
di Poeti, d'Hiſtorici, & di Filoſofi;

Si come nel leggerle ſi potrà chiaramente vedere.

Θεῦ διδόντος, οὐδὲν ἰχύει φθόνος.
Καὶ μὴ διδόντος, οὐδὲν ἰχύει πόνος.

Con Priuilegio dell'Illuſtriſſ. Signoria di Venetia,
per anni X.

IN VENETIA,

Appreſſo Franceſco Seneſe, al ſegno della Pace.
M D LXII.

7.3 Zarlino, *Le istitutioni harmoniche*, 1562, title page (Bayerische Staatsbibliothek, 2° Mus.th. 572. Reproduced by permission.)

ISTITVTIONI
HARMONICHE
DEL REV MESSERE
GIOSEFFO ZARLINO
DA CHIOGGIA,

Maeſtro di Capella della Serenissima Signoria di Venetia: di
nuouo in molti luoghi migliorate, & di mólti belli ſecreti
nelle coſe della Prattica ampliate.

*Nelle quali; oltra le materie appartenenti alla Musica; ſi trouano dichiarati
molti luoghi di Poeti; Hiſtorici, & di Filoſofi; ſi come nel
leggerle ſi potrà chiaramente vedere.*

Con due Tauole; l'vna che contiene le Materie principali : & l'altra
le coſe più notabili, che nell'Opera ſi ritrouano

¶ Θεῦ διδόντος, οὐδὲν ἰσχύει φθόνος ;
Καὶ μὴ διδόντος, οὐδὲν ἰσχύει πόνος .

PER ME SI GODE IN CIELO

PACE.

ET REGNA IN TERRA.

Σημεῖον τῦ εἰδότος καὶ τὸ δὑναϑαι διδάσκειν ἰςὶ.

IN VENETIA,
Appreſſo Franceſco de i Franceſchi Seneſe.
M. D. LXXIII.

7.4 Zarlino, *Le istitutioni harmoniche*, 1573, title page (Bayerische Staatsbibliothek,
2° Mus.th. 580. Reproduced by permission.)

Rore most quickly established an international reputation) suggests that these works may have stemmed from Zarlino's time as an active pupil of Willaert. The *Istitutioni* provided the means for Zarlino to position himself as the heir apparent to the ailing Willaert and to establish his reputation as a *musicus* in the fullest sense. Through the *Istitutioni*, the reader is intended to recognize Zarlino not merely as a practitioner, but as one who commanded a true – that is, mathematical – understanding of the subject. Circumstantial evidence links the date of publication to Willaert's health and events at San Marco. Willaert had been in ill-health for a number of years and his first will was recorded in 1542. A subsequent will, recorded in 1549 – perhaps not coincidentally the year of the publication of Zarlino's first compositions – mentioned that Willaert suffered seriously from gout. Willaert was granted leave from the chapel on 8 May 1556 to return to Flanders. There was clearly concern on the part of the *procuratori* that he would not return from this trip and they offered various gestures of appreciation as well as enticements to return. Willaert overstayed his leave and the date of his return is uncertain, but he filed a new will on 26 March 1558.[36] This was the first of six wills and codicils he was to file between this date and November 1562.[37] The privilege for the *Istitutioni* is dated October 1557. Although the treatise contains no colophon with the exact date of publication, its preparation appears to coincide with Willaert's absence and its publication to have taken place shortly after his return. There can be no doubt that it was widely known that it was only a matter of time until a search for a successor to the *maestro* would be undertaken. That Zarlino was a trusted associate of Willaert may be inferred from Willaert's naming of Zarlino as an executor of his estate in his wills of 1561 and 1562.[38] This suggests that at the very least he had Willaert's informal approval of the *Istitutioni*, if not his actual imprimatur. The dates of the reissues of the *Istitutioni* with a new title page coincide with these wills and Willaert's ultimate death and the time when the position at San Marco actually stood vacant.

Two other occurrences may also have played a role in the timing of the publication of the *Istitutioni*: the appearance of Vicentino's *L'Antica musica ridotta alla moderna prattica* and the advent of the Accademia Veneziana. Vicentino, also a pupil of Willaert, had applied for a privilege to publish his *L'Antica musica* in Venice in 1549 although it was not published until 1555, and in Rome, not Venice.[39] As Michael Fend has shown, the relationship between the two works is close and Zarlino's must be viewed in part as a direct response to *L'Antica musica*, all the more so as Vicentino's name never appears in the *Istitutioni*.[40] There is little doubt that

---

[36] Recent evidence suggests that he was already back by October 1557. See Ignace Bossuyt, "*O socii durate*: A Musical Correspondence from the Time of Philip II," *Early Music* 26 (1998), 436.

[37] The documents pertaining to Willaert's leave and wills are described in Ongaro, "The Chapel of St. Mark's," 141–44.

[38] The wills are transcribed in Ongaro, "The Chapel of St. Mark's," Document 492, pp. 461–66.

[39] Rome, 1555/R1557. Translated with introduction and notes by Maria Rika Maniates as *Ancient Music Adapted to Modern Practice* (New Haven: Yale University Press, 1996), xvii, xxxii.

[40] Fend, *Theorie des Tonsystems*, 397–99 and 429–33. Frans Wiering, "The Language of the Modes," 72–78, discusses the reasons why names and sources may be obscured in Renaissance treatises.

there was more than a small measure of competition between the two to establish an authoritative reading of ancient practice. Equally, it is clear that Zarlino was the "better" scholar of the two, but that Vicentino may well have been the more creative musician, whatever the ultimate virtues of the chromatic art he promulgated.

The initial publication date of the *Istitutioni* also neatly coincides with Zarlino's membership in the Accademia Veneziana, also known as the Accademia della Fama. Zarlino appears as one of four *musici* on the membership rolls within the mathematics section of the academy.[41] The members in the various sections comprised the intellectual and social elite of Venice. The Academy printed an ambitious list of some 300 books they intended to publish, and Zarlino's hand is much in evidence in the music list – the ancients and moderns are those writers whose works are influential in the *Istitutioni*, particularly in the *Speculativa*.[42] Yet while the *Istitutioni* may well have provided an admission ticket of sorts for Zarlino to the Accademia Veneziana, it seems unlikely that membership in this group was his primary

[41] The others are "Il Reverendo P. Fra Francesco da Venezia ai Crocechieri," "Il Magnifico M. Hieronimo Orio," and "Il Magnifico M. Alessandro Contarini." Although Francesco Caffi lists Andrea Gabrieli as a member ("Il Magnifico M. Andrea Gabriel" appears under the "Reggenti" of the "Mathematici"), Martin Morell has shown that this was not the musician (Francesco Caffi, *Storia della musica sacra nella già cappella ducale di San Marco Venezia dal 1318 al 1797* (Venice: Antonelli, 1854), and Martin Morell, "New Evidence for the Biographies of Andrea and Giovanni Gabrieli," *Early Music History* 3 (1983), 101–22). The full membership list appears in D. Pellegrini, "Breve dissertazione previa al Sommario dell'Accademia Veneta della Fama," *Giornale dell'Italiana Letteratura* 22–23 (1808), 115. There have been numerous studies of this academy in recent years including most recently Lina Bolzoni, "L'Accademia Veneziana: splendore e decadenza di una utopia enciclopedica," *Università, Accademie e Società scientifiche in Italia e in Germania dal Cinquecento al Settecento*, ed. Laetitia Boehm and Ezio Raimondi (Bologna: Il mulino, 1981), 117–67. The most extended study of the Academy in English is Paul Rose, "The Accademia Venetiana." The earliest mention of the Academy is dated September 1557 (Rose, "The Accademia Venetiana," 191 n. 4), a month before the privilege for the *Istitutioni* was issued. Its first constitution was published in November 1557. The exact date at which Zarlino joined is uncertain, although his membership is always one of the ones highlighted by modern commentators on the Academy. In 1560, the founder of the Academy, Federico Badoer, successfully petitioned the *procuratori* of San Marco for permission to transfer the daily meetings from his house to the vestibule of the newly completed Biblioteca Marciana (Rose, "The Accademia Venetiana," 209–10). By August 1561, however, after a series of extraordinarily dubious financial transactions, the academy was suppressed and Badoer and his close associates imprisoned (Rose, "The Accademia Venetiana," 212).

[42] The entire list is reproduced in Pellegrini, "Breve dissertazione." The music books, appearing on the list between those on perspective and astrology, are:

Ptolomaei musices theorice graeca nondum impressa, cum latina interpretatione, et Porphyrii commentariis.
Cantus liber novus theoricus.
Ptolemaeus de harmonia cum Porphyrii commentariis graecus, et latinus recens factus.
Aristidis Quintiliani musica.
In Ptolamaei musicen Aristidis explicatio.
Euclidis musice.
Ludovici Folliani musices theorice e latino in italicum sermonem versa cum quibusdam annotationibus ad confirmandam auctoris sententiam.
Iacobi Fabri musicae demonstrationes italico sermone expressae.
Disputatio in qua per demonstrationem ostenditur, an musice & geometria, vel arithmetica pendeat.
Qualitates, ac circumstantiae, quibus uti debet is, qui musicos cujusque generis concentus velit componere, ubi perspicuum fit, quantum posse intersecationem illam intervallorum chromaticorum, atque enharmonicorum in genere diatonico.
Mundi harmonia, e qua colligitur, qui soni musici de sphaerarum caelestium conversione, atque itidem de reliquis naturalibus procedere soleant.

motivation for writing and publishing the treatise. The visibility of the Academy's activities in Venice, on the other hand, may well have lent a certain prestige to publications by its members and also supplied an instant audience for their works.

Format and citations

The *Istitutioni* positions Zarlino as Willaert's successor not just by its overt references to Willaert and his teaching, but by tying the work specifically (although not by name) to the contents of Willaert's *Musica nova* and Zarlino's own motet prints through its citations of printed music. Not surprisingly, the musical examples and citations which are broadly my focus appear in the *Prattica* sections of the *Istitutioni*, Parts III and IV; thus, like many of Zarlino's subsequent readers, but for rather different reasons, I focus on these sections of the treatise. Part III contains nearly 200 music examples, almost all of which appear to be newly composed in support of its contrapuntal precepts,[43] and Part IV contains twenty-seven examples and figures, most of which comprise duos demonstrating each of the twelve modes. Zarlino's examples are often brief and appear in a number of formats, ranging from a single part, to quasi score, to individual parts of a multi-voice example. Score-like notation appears primarily in the discussion of cadence and consonances, as may be seen in Figure 7.5.[44] Most of the examples, however, are for two voices, usually written as separate parts with no concern for alignment; the same holds true for the examples for three and four voices. As may be seen in Figure 7.6 from Part III, the tenor voice (and *soggetto*) usually appears uppermost, with other voices beneath it. Text is included only in those few examples where a voice is borrowed from an extant composition; there is nothing approaching the elegant choirbook layout of Glarean's *Dodecachordon*. It seems reasonable to assume that the user of this part of Zarlino's treatise was able to read (i.e. study) these examples in this format by the time he reached this stage in the *Istitutioni*. There is a steady progression from two-part examples, to the addition of a third voice, and finally four-voice examples.[45]

As a preliminary overview of the relationship of the treatise to a printed musical repertory, Table 7.2 provides a list of Zarlino's citations of monophonic and polyphonic music in Parts III and IV of the *Istitutioni*. Although I have cited a potential source for most of the works listed in Table 7.2, I do not mean to suggest that these *were* Zarlino's sources, but rather to show the easy availability of most of these works in printed format, many in Venetian prints from the 1540s and 1550s.[46] As will become apparent in the discussion which follows, the contents of four of the publications cited on this table had particular importance in shaping the musical and printed world of the *Istitutioni*: Grimm and Wyrsung's *Liber selectarum cantionum*

---

[43] It is possible, of course, that Zarlino was reproducing here some of Willaert's actual teaching materials and examples rather than his own newly composed exercises.

[44] Quasi score or ten-line staves were traditionally used for illustrating this type of material.

[45] It is also possible, of course, that such examples were played at the keyboard or scored for study.

[46] Thus manuscript sources are not included on Table 7.2.

Parte. 223

mouimenti tra le prime, & le seconde figure : percioche facendo le figure della parte acuta i loro mouimenti sempre congiunti , quelle della parte graue alcune volte potranno procedere per mouimenti separati , discendendo alcuna volta insieme ; tuttauia , siano accommodate in qual maniera si vogliono, le seconde figure della Cadenza si porranno sempre distanti l'vna dall'altra , per l'interuallo di Sesta maggiore , & le vltime finiranno in Ottaua . Et ciò sempre tornerà bene , quando vna parte farà il mouimento del Semituono , o nel graue , oueramente nell'acuto ; & l'altra quello del Tuono , così in queste come in ogn'altra sorte di Cadenza , sia semplice , o diminuita . E ben vero che le Cadenze diminuite hanno la Sincopa , nella quale si ode la Settima sopra la sua seconda parte , cioè nel battere : Ma la Cadenza semplice è tutta consonante : percioche le sue figure sono tra loro equali ; si come ne i sotto posti essempi si può vedere .

Si può etiandio vedere, in qual maniera spesse volte si può cambiar le parti della Cadenza tra loro, & porre quel passaggio , che fa la parte posta nel graue , nella parte acuta ; & per il contrario , quel che fa la parte acuta , porlo nella parte graue , che corrispondino per vna Ottaua : percioche tali mutationi sono molto commode alli Compositori . Oltra queste due sorti di Cadenza , ve n'è vn'altra terminata per Ottaua , ouero per Vnisono , la qual si fa , quando si pone le seconde figure della parte graue , & quelle della parte acuta distanti tra loro per vn Ditono , facendo discendere la parte graue per mouimento di Quinta , ouero ascendere per quello di Quarta ; & ascendere la parte acuta per mouimento congiunto ; come si vede .

7.5 Zarlino, *Le istitutioni harmoniche* (1558), p. 223, showing "pseudo-score" and
placement of music examples

Et benche in ogni compofitione perfetta quattro parti folamente fiano baſteuoli, fi come il Soprano, l'Alto, il
Tenore, & il Baſſo; tuttauia quando fi vorrà paſſare più oltra, & hauer maggior numero departi, baſtarà
folamente raddoppiare (come hò detto altroue) vna delle Quattro nominate; & cotal parte ag giunta fi chia
merà medeſimamente Soprano, o Tenore, ouero Alto, o Baſſo; fecondo la parte, che fi hauerà doppiata; ag-
giungendoli Secondo, o Terzo fecondo'l numero di quelle parti, che fi troueranno in tale cantilena. Et fi fanno
le chorde eſtreme della parte ag giunta, equali a quelle della parte, che viene raddoppiata; ancora che non fa-
rebbe errore, quando non fuſſero equali, & le chorde della parte ag giunta fi eſtendeſſero più verſo'l graue, o
verſo l'acuto, che quelle della raddoppiata; cioè della parte principale. Si debbe però auertire, che alle volte fi
                                                                                              coſtuma

7.6 Zarlino, *Le istitutioni harmoniche* (1558), p. 262; four-voice example notated in parts

(1520 = RISM 1520[4]); Zarlino's two motet prints *Musici quinque vocum* (1549 = Zarlino 1549) and *Modulationes sex vocum* (1566 = Zarlino 1566); and Willaert's *Musica nova* (1559 = Willaert 1559). Taken together, these four prints account for well over half of the 140 citations of polyphonic compositions in the treatise. Although at least one of these prints, and possibly two, appeared after the *Istitutioni*,[47] they are intimately tied to the theories it espouses, its reception, and its publication history.

ZARLINO'S *MUSICI QUINQUE VOCUM* (1549)

As the first stage in understanding the citations and music examples of the *Istitutioni*, an examination of Zarlino's initial publication, his own motet print of 1549, as a print in its own right is in order.[48] A detailed understanding of this publication is essential not only to the argument being pursued here about Zarlino's relationship to print culture but also as a means of comprehending his compositional interaction with musical theory, particularly modal theory, in the decades preceding the publication of the *Istitutioni*. Unlike any of the other theorists studied in this book, Zarlino was a published composer and prided himself on being so. By recognizing the clues that this print offers about his interaction with music print culture, one begins not only to understand the significance of his citations of printed music in the *Istitutioni* but also to understand the ways in which the theory espoused in the *Istitutioni* relates to the practice it documents. That is, the 1549 motet print is significant from the viewpoint I advance *not only* for the intertextuality implied by references to it in the *Istitutioni*, but as a primary document itself through which one can gain insight about a number of Zarlino's intellectual and theoretical concerns as well as assess his compositional and professional ambitions in the decade preceding the publication of the *Istitutioni*.

Table 7.3 provides an overview of the contents of the *Musici quinque vocum*;[49] its dedication follows:

R[everendo] D[omino] Aloysio Balbo almae sancti spiritus Venetiarum religionis Priori Gen[erali] Dig[nissimo]
Iosephus Zarlinus S[alutem] P[lurimam] D[icit]
Cum tantae apud veteres dignitatis Musices disciplina fuerit Aloysi R[everende]. ut optimus quisque sacerdos aeqyptius nefas duceret absque ea sacroru[m] ritus apprehendere, censui

---

47 Despite its date of 1559, the *Musica nova* may have been published in 1558 and possibly before Zarlino's treatise. See the discussion of this work on p. 234.

48 It is interesting to note how frequently the *Istitutioni* is referred to as Zarlino's "first" publication (e.g. Feldman, *City Culture*) with no mention of his published compositions. This reflects a tendency to view printed music as a separate category from printed books that is not always borne out in contemporary accounts. For example, the inventory of Zarlino's house distinguishes among printed materials not by content but by format, as noted above.

49 *Musici Quinque Vocum Moduli, Motetcta vulgo Nuncupata Opus nunquam alias typis Excusum, ac Nuper accuratissime in Lucem aeditum. Liber Primus* (Venice: Gardano, 1549). This print will be referred to by short title (*Musici quinque vocum*) or simply as Zarlino's 1549 print. The sigla "Z1549" and "Zarlino 1549" are used in tables.

Table 7.2 Le istitutioni harmoniche *(1558): musical citations and sources*

Composer	Title	1558	Source[a]
Part III			
Josquin	*Missa L'homme armé*	III: 5	[Josquin 1502]
Rore	*Hellas coment*	III: 25	[Rore 1550]
Josquin	[no specific work cited]	III: 28	—
Mouton	[no specific work cited]	III: 28	—
Willaert	*Laus tibi sacra rubens*	III: 28	[1546[6]]
Zarlino	*Osculetur me osculis*	III: 28	**Zarlino 1549, 5**
Zarlino	*Ego rosa Saron*	III: 28	**Zarlino 1549, 6**
Zarlino	*Capite nobis vulpes parvulas*	III: 28	**Zarlino 1549, 18**
La Rue	*Pater de coelis deus*	III: 28	**1520[4], 7**
Zarlino	*Virgo prudentissima*	III: 28	**Zarlino 1566, 5**
Zarlino	*Pater noster / Ave Maria*	III: 28	**Zarlino 1549, 19**
			[Zarlino 1566, 13]
Willaert	*Scimus hoc nostrum*	III: 43	[Willaert 1542a]
Josquin	*Inviolata, integra*	III: 46	**1520[4], 6**
Willaert	*Aspro core*	III: 46	**Willaert 1559, 41**
Josquin	*Benedicta es coelorum regina*	III: 64	**1520[4], 6**
Willaert	*Nil postquam sacrum*	III: 66	[lost?]
Willaert	*Victor io salve*	III: 66	[Willaert 1539]
Willaert	*Inclite sfortiadum*	III: 66	[Willaert 1529]
Willaert	*Verbum supernum*	III: 66	**Willaert 1559, 26**
Willaert	*Praeter rerum seriem*	III: 66	**Willaert 1559, 23**
Jachet	*Descendi in ortum meum*	III: 66	[1539[3]]
[replaced in 1573 by Zarlino, *Misereris omnium Domine* **Zarlino 1566, 10**]			
Zarlino	*Miserere mei Deus*	III: 66	**Zarlino 1566, 6**
Zarlino	*Pater noster / Ave Maria*	III: 66	**Zarlino 1549, 19**
			[Zarlino 1566, 13]
Willaert	*Veni sancte spiritus*	III: 66	**Willaert 1559, 11**
Zarlino	*O beatum pontificem*	III: 66	**Zarlino 1549, 2**
Zarlino	*Salve regina*	III: 66	**Zarlino 1566, 12**
Zarlino	*Litigabant Iudaci*	III: 66	**Zarlino, 1566, 2**
Jachet	*Murus tuus*	III: 66	[1539[3]]
Willaert	*Salve sancta parens*	III: 66	**Willaert 1559, 15**
Willaert	*Venator lepores*	III: 66	[1542[10]]
Zarlino	*In principio Deus antequam*	III: 66	**Zarlino 1566, 8**
Josquin	*Alma redumptoris mater / Ave regina ceolorum / Inviolata integra et casta / Regina coeli*	III: 66	?
Gombert	*Salve regina / Alma redemptoris / Inviolata / Ave regina*	III: 66	[Gombert 1541]
C. Festa	*Exaltabo te Domines*	III: 66	—
Zarlino	*Ecce tu pulchra es*	III: 66	**Zarlino 1549, 7**
Mouton	*Nesciens mater*	III: 66	[1521[7]; Glarean]
Gombert	*Inviolata integra et casta*	III: 66	[Gombert 1539]
Willaert	*Salve sancta parens*	III: 66	**Willaert 1559, 15**
Willaert	*Sur l'hesrbe brunette*	III: 66	?

Table 7.2 (*cont.*)

Composer	Title	1558	Source
Willaert	*Sancta et immaculata*	III: 66	[1520³]
	Petite camusete	III: 66	[1520³]
La Rue	*Missa O salutaris hostia*	III: 66	[1516¹]
Willaert	*Missa Mente tota*	III: 66	?
Josquin	*Missa La sol fa re mi*	III: 66	[Josquin 1502; 1539¹]
Josquin	*Missa Hercules dux Ferrariae*	III: 66	[Josquin 1502]
Josquin	*Missa Pange lingua*	III: 66	[1539²]
Josquin	*Missa Gaudeamus*	III: 66	[Josquin 1502; 1539¹]
Josquin	*Missa Ave maris stella*	III: 66	[1539²]
Brumel	Requiem	III: 66	[1516¹]
Moulu	*Missa Duorum facierum*	III: 66	[1539¹]
Ockeghem	*Missa Prolationum*	III: 66	[Glarean]
Willaert	*Confitebor tibi Domine*	III: 66	Willaert 1550¹
Willaert	*Laudate pueri Dominum*	III: 66	Willaert 1550¹
Willaert	*Lauda Ierusalem Dominum*	III: 66	Willaert 1550¹
Willaert	*De profundis*	III: 66	Willaert 1550¹
Willaert	*Memento Domine David*	III: 66	Willaert 1550¹

[1573 edn adds Willaert *Dixit Dominus, Laudate pueri, Laudate Dominum, Lauda anima mea Dominum, Laudate Dominum,* and *Lauda Jerusalem,* all from Willaert 1555]

Zarlino	*Magnificat* (three choirs)	III: 66	?
Morales	*Verbum iniquum et dolosum*	III: 77	—
Willaert	*Aspice Domine*	III: 77	**Willaert 1559, 17**

Part IV

	Rorate coeli desuper	IV: 13	chant
	Vultum tuum deprecabuntur	IV: 13	chant
	Iustus es Domine	IV: 13	chant
	Puer natus est nobis	IV: 13	chant
	Victimae paschali laudes	IV: 14	chant
	Salve regina	IV: 14	chant
	Duo Seraphin	IV: 14	chant
	Sint lumbi vestri	IV: 14	chant
	Spiritus in Domini	IV: 14	chant
	Gaudete in Domine	IV: 15	chant
	Suscepimus Deus	IV: 15	chant
	Magnificat	IV: 15	chant
Jachet	[psalms]	IV: 15	1550¹
Lupus	*In convertendo Dominus*	IV: 15	[1539¹²]
Lupus	*Beati omnes*	IV: 15	[1539¹²]
Willaert	*Laudate pueri Dominum*	IV: 15	Willaert 1550¹
Willaert	*Laude Hierusalem*	IV: 15	Willaert 1550¹
	In sanctitate [ex.]	IV: 16	chant
	Amplius lava me [ex.]	IV: 16	chant
Mouton	*Missa Argentum*	IV: 16	?
Willaert	*Veni sancte spiritus*	IV: 18	**Willaert 1559, 11**
Willaert	*Victimae paschali laudes*	IV: 18	**Willaert 1559, 19**

[replaced in 1573 with Zarlino, *Victimae paschali laudes,* **Zarlino 1566, 9**]

Table 7.2 (*cont.*)

Composer	Title	1558	Source[a]
Willaert	*Giunto m'ha Amor*	IV: 18	**Willaert 1559, 38**
Zarlino	*O beatum pontificem*	IV: 18	**Zarlino 1549, 2**
[replaced with Zarlino, *Hodie Christus natus est* and *Salve regina*, **Zarlino 1566, 3, 12**]			
Zarlino	*Nigra sum*	IV: 18	**Zarlino 1549, 6**
[Morales	*Sancta et immaculata*]	IV: 18	[1541[4]]
[1573 adds Jachet, *Spem in alium*, [1539[15]]]			
Josquin	*Praeter rerum seriem*	IV: 19	**1520[4], 2**
Willaert	*Praeter rerum seriem*	IV: 19	**Willaert 1559, 23**
Willaert	*Che fai alma, che pensi?*	IV: 19	**Willaert 1559, 51**
Willaert	*Avertatur obsecro Domine*	IV: 19	**Willaert 1559, 12**
Willaert	*Ove ch'i posi*	IV: 19	**Willaert 1559, 47**
Zarlino	*Pater noster (a7)*	IV: 19	**Zarlino 1549, 19**
Zarlino	*Ego rosa Saron*	IV: 19	**Zarlino 1549, 16**
Zarlino	*Capite nobis vulpes*	IV: 19	**Zarlino 1549, 18**
Isaac	*O Maria mater Christi*	IV: 20	**1520[4], 21**
Willaert	*Te Deum patrem*	IV: 20	**Willaert 1559, 27**
Willaert	*Huc me sidereo*	IV: 20	**Willaert 1559, 22**
Willaert	*Haec est domus Domini*	IV: 20	**Willaert 1559, 21**
Willaert	*Io mi rivolgo*	IV: 20	**Willaert 1559, 40**
Zarlino	*Ferculum fecit sibi*	IV: 20	**Zarlino 1549, 14**
Josquin	*De profundis clamavi*	IV: 21	**1520[4], 18**
Willaert	*Peccata mea*	IV: 21	**Willaert 1559, 14**
Willaert	*Rompi de l'empio core*	IV: 21	[1541[16]]
Willaert	*L'aura mia sacra*	IV: 21	**Willaert 1559, 35**
[replaced in 1573 with *In qual parte del Ciel*, **Willaert 1559, 45**]			
Zarlino	*Miserere mei, Deus*	IV: 21	**Zarlino 1566, 6**
[1573 adds *Misereris omnium Domine*, **Zarlino 1566, 10**]			
Zarlino	*Missa [quarti toni]*	IV: 21	?
Willaert	*Spoliatis aegyptiis*	IV: 22	[Willaert 1542a]
Rore	*Di tempo in tempo*	IV: 22	[Rore 1550]
Rore	*Donna ch'ornata sete*	IV: 22	[Rore 1550]
Viola	*Fra quanti amor*	IV: 22	[Nuovo Vogel 1010 (1550)]
Mouton	*Ecce Maria genuit nobis*	IV: 23	[1514[1]]
Willaert	*In convertendo*	IV: 23	1550[1]
Willaert	*Pater, peccavi*	IV: 24	**Willaert 1559, 18**
Willaert	*I piansi, hor canto*	IV: 24	**Willaert 1559, 43**
Josquin	*Benedicta es, celorum regina*	IV: 25	**1520[4], 6**
Willaert	*Audite insulae*	IV: 25	**Willaert 1559, 16**
Willaert	*Verbum supernum*	IV: 25	**Willaert 1559, 26**
Willaert	*Liete e pensose*	IV: 25	**Willaert 1559, 50**
	Pater noster	IV: 26	chant
	Credo in unum Deum [ex.]	IV: 26	chant [Glarean]
	Ave Maria gratia plena [ex.]	IV: 26	chant [Glarean]
La Rue	*Missa Ave Maria*	IV: 26	?
	Gaudeamus omnes in Domino	IV: 26	chant
Josquin	*Missa Gaudeamus*	IV: 26	[Josquin 1502]
	In exitu Israel	IV: 26	chant [Glarean]
	Nos qui vivimus	IV: 26	chant [Glarean]

Table 7.2 (*cont.*)

Composer	Title	1558	Source
Jachet	*Spem in alium*	IV: 26	[Jachet 1539]
Morales	*Sancta et immaculata*	IV: 26	[1546²]
Zarlino	*Si bona suscepimus*	IV: 26	**Zarlino 1549, 12**
Zarlino	*I'vo piangendo*	IV: 26	[1562²]
[1573 adds Mouton, *Missa Benedicam Dominum*]			
Verdelot	*Gabriel archangelus*	IV: 27	[1539¹²]
Willaert	*Flete oculi, rorate genas*	IV: 27	[Willaert 1545]
	Missa De angelis	IV: 28	chant
	Alma redemptoris mater	IV: 28	chant
	Regina coeli laetare	IV: 28	chant
Josquin	*Stabat mater*	IV: 28	**1520⁴, 13**
Willaert	*O salutaris hostia*	IV: 28	[Willaert 1542]
Willaert	*Alma redemptoris*	IV: 28	**Willaert 1559, 13**
Willaert	*Pien d'un vago pensier*	IV: 28	**Willaert 1559, 48**
Jachet	*Descendi in hortum meum*	IV: 28	[1539³]
Gombert	*Audi filia et vide*	IV: 28	[1541³]
Zarlino	*Ego veni in hortum*	IV: 28	**Zarlino 1549, 8**
	Ave regina coelorum	IV: 29	chant
Josquin	*Inviolata, integra et casta es*	IV: 29	**1520⁴, 10**
Willaert	*Inviolata integra*	IV: 29	**Willaert 1559, 24**
Willaert	*Mittit ad virginem*	IV: 29	**Willaert 1559, 20**
Willaert	*Quando nascesti Amor*	IV: 29	**Willaert 1559, 49**
Willaert	*I vidi in terra*	IV: 29	**Willaert 1559, 46**
Willaert	*Quando fra l'altre donne*	IV: 29	**Willaert 1559, 34**
Jachet	*Decantabat populus*	IV: 29	[1541³]
Zarlino	*Nemo venit ad me*	IV: 29	
	[*Nemo potest venire*		**Zarlino 1549, 3?**]
[replaced in 1573 with *Litigabant Iudaei*, **Zarlino 1566, 2**]			
Zarlino	*O quam gloriosum*	IV: 29	**Zarlino 1566, 7**
Verdelot	*Si bona suscepimus*	IV: 30	[1539⁶]
Willaert	*O invidia nemica di virtute*	IV: 30	**Willaert 1559, 32**
	Kyrie de apostolis	IV: 30	chant
	Domine fac mecum	IV: 30	chant
	Tollite hostias	IV: 30	chant
	Per signum crucis	IV: 30	chant
Willaert	*I vidi in terra angeli costumi*	IV: 32	**Willaert 1559, 46**
Willaert	*Aspro core e selvaggio*	IV: 32	**Willaert 1559, 41**
Willaert	*Ove ch'i posi gli occhi*	IV: 32	**Willaert 1559, 47**
Willaert	*Quando fra l'altre donne*	IV: 32	**Willaert 1559, 34**
Willaert	*Giunto m'ha amor*	IV: 32	**Willaert 1559, 38**
	Credo cardinale	IV: 33	chant
Willaert	*Verbum bonum et suave*	IV: 36	[Willaert 1545]

Note:

[a] Only printed sources are given in this table. The lack of any printed source is indicated by "—". Unidentified compositions are indicated by "?". Sources closest to the *Istitutioni* are in bold type. Those which may or may not have been known to Zarlino are enclosed in brackets. Individual composer prints are indicated by composer and publication date (e.g. Zarlino 1549). Anthologies are identified by RISM sigla.

ego quoque mihi non iniurium fore, si meorum laborum huic studio partem aliquam tri-
buissem. Quae licet ad animi mei satisfactione[m] optime collocata fuerit, tamen an aliquid
assequutus sim, nescio. Quare ut aequissimarum aurium iudicio id probetur, hosce ingenij
mei praecoces fructus emitto, quos ad te quem omnes ob egregiam virtutem, ob miram
animi probitatem, ob summam modestiam, ob singularem deniq[ue] morum integritatem
venerantur, dirigere volui. Quo una cum dilectis fratribus tuis eos degustare, atq[ue] harmonica suavitate defessos interdum spiritus oblectare valeas. Fretus tamen quod etsi no[n]
erit eiusmodi hic noster labor, ut dulce[m] purgatissimis auribus vestris sonum afferre queat,
ipsa saltem verba ex sacra presertim lectione deprompta, quae modulis decantanda subieci id
efficiant spero. Prodeat igitur in luce[m] sub tui nominis auspicio, atq[ue] eum R[everendis-
simus] D[ominum] V[ostrum] veluti fidei, amorisq[ue] mei, ac perpetuae in te tuosq[ue]
observantiae pignus accipiat. Quo fias certior & tu, a me plurimum observari, & quanti te
faciam apud omnes testatum relinquam. Vale.

Gioseffo Zarlino sends heartiest greetings to the Reverend Lord Alvise Balbi, most worthy
Prior General of the life-giving Order of the Holy Spirit of Venice.

Since the discipline of Music enjoyed such dignity in the eyes of the ancients, Reverend
Aloysius, that all the best Egyptian priests considered it sinful to undertake their sacred rites
in its absence, I decided that it would do me no harm to devote some part of my own energy
to this pursuit. And while this was admirably agreeable to the satisfaction of my spirit, I do
not know whether I have actually accomplished anything. So, that this may be tested by the
judgment of the most impartial ears, I am sending the first fruits of the orchard of my intel-
lect, which I have chosen to direct to you whom all venerate for your remarkable virtue,
your marvelous honesty of spirit, your unsurpassed modesty, your singular integrity of character, so that you might sample them together with your beloved brethren and from time to
time soothe your fatigued spirit with sweet harmony. But confident that even if this our
effort shall not prove of such kind as may be able to offer sweet sound to your most discern-
ing ears, I nevertheless hope at least that the words, particularly as they are taken from sacred
reading, which I have underlaid for singing beneath the music, may accomplish this. May it
then be published under the sign of your name, and may your most revered Lordship accept
them as a pledge of my loyalty and my love, and of my steady service to you and yours.
Whereby you too may learn that I do regard you most highly and I may leave a testament for
all of how much I esteem you. Farewell.

The contents of this print have normally been scrutinized from two points of
view: principles of text setting and underlay, and modal theory.[50] Examples from
the print are adduced primarily as concrete and authoritative illustrations of
Zarlino's teaching. There is a good reason for this emphasis: Zarlino includes
printed dodecachordal modal ascriptions in the tenor partbook of the set (listed in

---

[50] On text underlay, see Mary Lewis, "Zarlino's Theories of Text Underlay as Illustrated in his Motet Book of
1549," *Music Library Association Notes* 42 (1985), 239–67; on text setting in *Nigra sum sed formosa* (the third motet
in Z1549), see Don Harrán, *In Search of Harmony: Hebrew and Humanist Elements in Sixteenth-Century Musical
Thought* (n.p.: American Institute of Musicology, 1988), 163–66; and on modal analysis Benito Rivera,
"Zarlino's Motets (1549): Keys to Interpreting His Teachings on Counterpoint and Mode" (unpublished paper
read at the Conference on Medieval and Renaissance Music, London, August 1986) and *idem*, "Finding the
Soggetto in Willaert's Free Imitative Counterpoint: A Step in Modal Analysis," in *Music Theory and the Exploration
of the Past*, ed. Christopher Hatch and David W. Bernstein (Chicago: University of Chicago Press, 1993),
75–80.

Table 7.3 Zarlino, *Musici quinque vocum* (Gardano, 1549)

No.	Title	Clef	Tonal type[a] Sig.	Final	Mode	Text	Istitutioni harmoniche
1	*Veni sancte spiritus*	g2-c2-c3-c3-f3	♭	G	Dorian (also in Quintus)	Sequence (Pentecost)	III: 66; IV: 18
2	*O beatum pontificem*	g2-c2-c3-c3-f3	♭	G	Dorian	Vespers antiphon (St. Martin)	IV: 29
3	*Nemo potest venire*	c1-c3-c4-c4-f4	♭	C (F in Quintus; F in Bassus)	[no mode in tenor] Hypoionian (in Quintus)	John 6: 44–42	
4	*Ave regina celorum*	c3-c4-f3-f3-f4	♭	F	Hypoionian	Marian antiphon	IV: 28
5	*Osculetur me*	c1-c3-c4-c4-f4	—	D	Dorian	Song of Songs 1: 1–3	II: 28
6	*Nigra sum*	c1-c3-c4-c4-f4	—	D	Dorian	Song of Songs 1: 4–6	IV: 18
7	*Ecce tu pulchra es*	c1-c3-c4-c4-f4	—	D	Dorian	Song of Songs 1: 14–16	III: 66
8	*Ego veni*	g2-c2-c3-c3-f3	♭	F	Ionian	Song of Songs 5: 1–4	IV: 28
9	*Confitebor tibi (a voce pari)*	c2-c3-c3-c4-f3	♭	F	Ionian	Matthew 11: 25–30	
10	*Beatissimus marcus*	c2-c3-c3-c4-f3	♭	F	Ionian	Vespers antiphon (St. Mark)	
11	*O sacrum convivium*	c2-c3-c3-c4-f3	♭	F	Ionian	Vespers antiphon (Corpus Christi)	
12	*Si bona suscepimus*	c2-c3-c4-c3-f3	♭	D	Aeolian	Responsory	IV: 26
13	*Clodia quem genuit*	g2-c2-c3-c3-f3	♭	A	Hypophrygian	Civic motet (lament on the death of Marchesino Vacca)	
14	*Ferculum fecit sibi*	c1-c3-c4-c4-f4	—	E	Phrygian	Song of Songs 3: 9–11	IV: 20
15	*In lectulo meo*	c1-c3-c4-c4-f4	—	E	Phrygian (handwritten addition)	Song of Songs 3: 1–4	
16	*Ego rosa saron*	c1-c3-c4-c1-f4	♭	G	Hypodorian	Song of Songs 2: 1–7	III: 28; IV: 19
17	*Aptabo cythare modos*	c1-c3-c4-c4-f4	♭	G	Hypodorian (handwritten addition)	Newly composed text in Horatian style	III: 28; IV: 19
18	*Capite nobis*	c1-c3-c4-c1-f4	♭	G	Hypodorian	Song of Songs 2: 15–17	III: 28; IV: 19
19	*Pater noster (a7)*	c1-c3-c4-c2-c3-c4-f4	♭ / ♭♭	D (G in Bassus)	(no indication – canon printed where other citations appear)	Precis / Marian antiphon	III: 28; III: 66, IV: 19

Note:

[a] Tonal types are given following the format of Harold Powers, "Tonal Types and Modal Categories in Renaissance Polyphony," *Journal of the American Musicological Society* 34 (1981), 428–70, with the modification that the final of the tenor is indicated; finals in the bassus which are not the same pitch-class as the tenor are indicated parenthetically.

the column of Table 7.3 headed "mode") and calls out the care given to text in the dedication. Both the pseudo-Greek modal labels and the careful underlay are unprecedented in Gardano's output, or that of any other mid-century Venetian printshop for that matter.[51] The *Istitutioni* further encourages an *a posteriori* view of the print as exemplification of the treatise with its numerous citations of works from this print (listed by book and chapter in the column of Table 7.3 headed "*Istitutioni harmoniche*"). Further, these theoretical considerations – mode and text setting – are addressed in adjacent chapters in the fourth part of the *Istitutioni*.

It is important to recall that those in possession of the print before the publication of the *Istitutioni* could hardly be expected to connect these motets to an as-yet unwritten treatise. Nevertheless, I would argue, this print contains clear and deliberate indications of the intellectual status and theoretical ambitions of its composer – markers that have been overshadowed by our greater familiarity with the monumental *Istitutioni*. These provide a unique perspective on Zarlino's relationship to printed music collections and his subsequent references to them in the *Istitutioni*.

While the dedication is formulaic in its praises of the dedicatee, it also sets the "learned" tone of the volume with its opening remark on the status of music in the ancient world and an allusion to the classical belief in the superiority of Egyptian music.[52] Although Zarlino would have his reader believe that these are "hasty" or "early" fruits of his labors, the arrangement and content of the collection belie this disclaimer. There is a deliberate attempt to create an impression of learnedness and circumstantial evidence suggests that the book reflects works composed for a variety of occasions and venues over a period of years that coincided with his formal study with Willaert.[53] The print, dedicated to the Prior General of the Order of the Holy Spirit, opens with a direct gesture to the institution of its dedicatee: the first motet is a setting of the Pentecostal sequence *Veni sancte spiritus*. The convent of Augustinian Canons Regular known as Santo Spirito in Isola was founded in the fifteenth century by wealthy noblemen;[54] Alvise Balbi appears to

---

[51] Lewis, "Zarlino's Theories of Text Underlay."

[52] There are various classical references to Egyptians and music; as, for example, in Demetrius, *De elocutione*, 71: "In Egypt when the priests sing hymns to the gods, they sing seven vowels in succession, and the sound of these vowels has such euphony that men listen to it instead of the flute and lyre" (Trans. Doreen C. Innes in Loeb Classical Library, L199). I am grateful to Leofranc Holford-Strevens for this citation.

[53] The exact dates of Zarlino's study with Willaert are unknown. By Baldi's (erroneous) dating of Zarlino's birth in 1519, Zarlino was forty-six when he took up his appointment at San Marco and this might explain the reference to forty-six, the age at which he is said to have concluded his studies with Willaert. His formal study with Willaert must have concluded long before.

"Per affinarsi dunque, e dar perfettione à que' principii ch'egli s'havesse preparati in Chioggia, accostossi ad Hadriano Villaert, nato nel territorio di Bruggia, huomo eccellentissimo in quella professione, e padre, come tutti confessano, de la musica florida: la quale è si lodata à questi tempi perciochè da la sua scuola sono usciti Cipriano di Rore, Orlando di Lasso, e tutti gli altri migliori. Sotto la disciplina di questo grand'huomo si essercitò tre anni intieri; nel qual tempo essendo arrivato à gran termine, [fu] conosciuta l'eccellenza sua, essendo egli d'anni quarantasei. Morto Hadriano, e Cipriano, successore di lui, partito dal servitio de la Signoria, hebbe il carico di mastro di Capella di S. Marco" (Baldi, ed. Narducci).

[54] I am grateful to Jonathan Glixon for pointing me to Santo Spirito in Isola. The fullest description of the monastery appears in Flaminio Corner, *Notizie Storiche delle Chiese e Monasteri di Venezia e di Torcello* (Padua: Giovanni Manfrè, 1758; facsimile Bologna: Forni, 1990), 493–97 and *idem*, *Ecclesiae Venetae antiquis monumentis nunc etiam*

have been a member of a well-known patrician family.[55] The dedication further suggests that the "brethren" are to sample these motets along with Balbi, raising the possibility that Zarlino may have been seeking not only Balbi's patronage with this dedication, but potential employment with the Augustinians at Santo Spirito or at least performance of his music at their establishment.[56]

Unusually, the dedication also draws attention to the care which has been accorded to text underlay in this print and, more importantly, the origin of the text in "sacred reading."[57] The elegance and accuracy of that underlay may be seen in Figure 7.7, the tenor part of the first motet in the collection.[58] The emphasis on sacred readings reflects an academic and text-oriented moment in north Italian culture that is particularly evident in the turn towards textual engagement in religious life. Finally one may read a hint of Zarlino's greater Venetian aspirations in his choice of dedicatee.[59] Indeed, in his choice of dedicatees, one can mark Zarlino's social rise from his dedication to Balbi in his first publication, to the Venetian patriarch Vincenzo Diedo (the *Istitutioni*), and finally to Pope Sixtus V (*Sopplimenti*).

The contents and distribution of the motets in the print also offer biographical glimpses while highlighting Zarlino's humanist predilections, giving some sense of the compositional initiatives he was undertaking in the 1540s. As mentioned, the

primum editis illustratae ac in decadis distributae (Venice: Pasquali, 1749). The monastery is also mentioned in Francesco Sansovino, *Venetia città nobilissima, et singalore, descritta in XIIII libri . . . Con aggiunta di tutte le cose notabili della stessa città, fatte, & occorse dall'anno 1580. Sino al presente 1663. das d. Giustiniano Martinioni* (Venice: S. Curti, 1663; facsimile, Farnborough: Gregg International Publishers, 1968), 229–30, and Elena Quaranta, *Oltre San Marco: Organizzazione e prassi della musica nelle chiese di Venezia nel rinascimento* (Florence: Olschki, 1998), 124–46, 273–74, 309–10, 374–78. Robert Kendrick informed me (personal communication) that at the end of the century Geronimo Lombardi's massive settings of vespers antiphons for the church year were printed by the canons in choirbook format (1597–1600), suggesting a printing tradition.

55 Definite identification of Balbi has proved elusive. At least two contemporaneous Luigi Balbis can be identified from citations in Emmanuele Cicogna, *Delle inscrizioni Veneziane* (Venice: Guiseppe Picotti, 1830), III: 17–19, but neither is identified as a cleric. Similarly, several brief citations of an "Alvise Balbi" appear in the Sanudo Diaries beginning in 1530, but without any clerical titles. One of these Balbis, again without ecclesiastical identification, shows up on the membership list of the Accademia Veneziana with Zarlino, as the only "arithmetichi." None of these three Balbi is to be confused with the later musician Ludovico (Luigi) Balbi and his nephew Luigi.

56 The archive of Santo Spirito in Isola consists only of parchments regarding their income-generating property and there is nothing left that might give further information on Balbi or any musical activities. There is no indication of Zarlino's connection with this institution although there is a connection between Santo Spirito and San Benedetto (the church of the district in Venice of which Zarlino was resident in 1557, although he is not known to have been employed there). There are also some connections, albeit tenuous ones, between Santo Spirito and Chioggia. The island on which the monastery was located is midway between Chioggia and Venice. I have no doubt that Zarlino was seeking patronage or employment (or both) with this publication in 1549. It is clear that Willaert was already in ill-health (see the mention of gout in his will from this year, discussed above), but hard to imagine that a relatively unknown Zarlino would aspire to San Marco at this stage.

57 "I nevertheless hope at least that the words, particularly as they are taken from sacred reading, which I have underlaid for singing beneath the music, may accomplish this."

58 For a detailed discussion of underlay in this collection, see Lewis, "Zarlino's Theories of Text Underlay."

59 The circumstances of Zarlino's relocation to Venice in 1541 are unclear, although there is no evidence to suggest that he left Chioggia on the promise of new or better employment in Venice. Benito Rivera has suggested, following Baldi, that Zarlino was forced to leave Chioggia and went to Venice as the most likely place to gain employment and further education with his credentials (unpublished typescript).

7.7 Zarlino, *Veni sancte spiritus* (tenor) (*Musices quinque vocum*, 1549) (Biblioteca Casanatense, Mus 682². Reproduced by permission.)

dedication points to the words "taken from sacred reading"; seventeen of the nineteen motets are based on liturgical or biblical texts (see the "text" column of Table
7.3). The opening motet, the sequence *Veni sancte spiritus*, is not only particularly
apt in a collection intended for the Order of the Holy Spirit but also functions more
broadly as an invocation for divine inspiration. The impetus for the composition of
the rest of the collection is less obvious, giving a sense that Zarlino collected here
whatever he had available for publication in 1549.[60] Of the antiphons in the collection, two would be of use in almost any place where polyphony was sung: the
Marian antiphon *Ave regina celorum* and the vespers antiphon *O sacrum convivium*,
proper to the feast of Corpus Christi. The other two antiphons were rather less
commonly set.[61] *O beatum pontificem* is proper to the second vespers for St. Martin
and *Beatissimus Marcus* for the second vespers of St. Mark. Both were the patron
saints of institutions to which Zarlino was or would be affiliated (namely San
Martino in Chioggia and San Marco in Venice). At least two of the motets in addition to *Veni sancte spiritus* set texts that had been frequently used by earlier composers and for which there was a tradition of polyphonic settings. The seven-voice
Pater noster and *Ave Maria* that concludes the print is in the tradition that followed
Josquin's setting; the responsory *Si bona suscepimus* is in a tradition stemming from
Verdelot's motet.[62] These works may well represent directly or indirectly Zarlino's
studies with Willaert as they comprise obvious emulation of well-known motet tra-
ditions, including Willaert's own settings of *Veni sancte spiritus* and the *Pater noster* –
Ave Maria pair.[63] In addition, there are two settings of gospel texts. The remainder
of the sacred texts are primarily non-liturgical texts excerpted from the *Song of
Songs*.[64]

[60] Zarlino also published some motets individually in anthologies in the same year. The individual pieces may have
gone to press first. Then, when the opportunity for his own volume arose, Zarlino published what remained. As
will be shown below, there are musical and textual connections among a group of *Song of Songs* motets that are
obscured both by their placement in different prints and also by their ordering within the *Musici quinque vocum*.

[61] I base this assertion primarily of the number of occurrences of these texts in Harry B. Lincoln, *The Latin Motet:
Indexes to Printed Collections, 1500–1600*, Musicological Studies 59 (Ottawa: The Institute of Mediaeval Music,
1993); Lewis, *Gardano* I and II; and Bernstein, *Scotto*. Lincoln indexes only anthologies and includes neither
single-composer prints nor manuscripts. There is at present no comprehensive source for ascertaining with any
accuracy the frequency with which motet texts were set, but in most cases the number of settings of any one
text that appear in Lincoln's sources may be taken as a relative indication of the frequency with which it was set.
The Lewis and Bernstein indices do include a number of single-composer prints.

[62] For a partial list of settings of *Si bona suscepimus*, see James Haar, "Orlande de Lassus: *Si bona suscepimus*," in *Music
before 1600*, ed. Mark Everist (Oxford: Blackwell, 1992), 154–74. Zarlino cites Verdelot's motet as well as his
own in the *Istitutioni*. For a discussion of the relationship of Zarlino's motet to the *Si bona suscepimus* complex of
motets, see Cristle Collins Judd and Christopher Amos, "Multi-layered Borrowing: Zarlino's *Si bona suscepimus*
and a Complex of Motets," in *Early Musical Borrowing*, ed. Honey Meconi (New York: Garland, forthcoming).

[63] For a detailed discussion of Willaert's *Veni sancte spiritus*, see Benito Rivera, "Finding the *Soggetto* in Willaert's
Free Imitative Counterpoint," 75–80.

[64] It should be remembered that what constitutes a non-liturgical text in 1549, outside San Marco, is not entirely
clear, in part because of the promulgation of the *Quinones Breviary*. Taken with two other motets that appeared
in anthologies of 1549 (*Si ignoras* and *Adiuro vos filie*) there is a complete setting of chapter 1 of the *Song of Songs*
(*Osculetur me, Nigra sum, Si ignoras, Ecce tu pulchra es*), a partial setting of chapter 2 (*Ego rosa* and *Capite nobis*; no
setting of *Song of Songs* 2: 8–14, *Vox delicti mei*, is known by Zarlino), and all of chapter 3 (*In lectulo meo, Adiuro
vos filie*, and *Ferculum fecit sibi*). Flury, *Gioseffo Zarlino als Komponist* (Winterthur: Verlag P. G. Keller, 1962), had

Two texts stand apart from this remarkably diverse but apparently somewhat motley sacred collection: *Clodia quem genuit* and *Aptabo cythare modos*. The first of these is a civic motet that can be related to a specific occasion: the death of Marchesino Vacca of Chioggia in 1546.[65]

Clodia quem genuit nereia carmine dignum	He whom Chioggia, daughter of Nereus,
Legibus et musis is quoque dignus erit.	begot worthy of song will also be
	worthy of laws and the muses.
Crudelis fato iuvenem immaturo peremit	By untimely fate the cruel Parca cut him
Decem bis annos tam sibi parca dedit.	down in youth, giving him only twice
	ten years.
Felix cui circum fundent sua iura napee	Happy is he whom the Wood nymphs
Et tumulum ex omni parte dolore colunt.	surround with their protection and whose
	grave they tend on every side with
	mourning.
Ips[a]e et castalio charites de fonte liquorem	The very Graces drip water from the
Aureaque Eridano rorat ab amne Venus.	Castalian spring and golden Venus
	sprinkles waters from the river Po.
Vacce Marchesini mestis lugere camenis	One may mourn with sad poems and
Perpetuis lachrymis funera acerba licet.	unending tears the bitter death of
	Marchesino Vacca.
Cesareo requies equiti pax ocia cantus	Oh may rest, peace, tranquility, and
O sint cineribus scilicet usque piis.	song accompany the noble knight, even
	unto the grave.[66]

The motet was certainly composed between 1546 (the date of Vacca's death) and 1549 (its date of publication). Its inclusion in this collection might be understood in a number of ways. First and foremost, its opening word – "Clodia," i.e. Chioggia – points to Zarlino's roots in Chioggia; indeed, in subsequent publications he is usually identified as "Gioseffo Zarlino da Chioggia" rather than the latinized Iosephus Zarlinus of the title page of this print.[67] This motet text suggests not only that Zarlino maintained connections with Chioggia after moving to Venice, despite

---

footnote 64 *(cont.)*

access only to an incomplete version of Z1549 and makes only a partial identification of the texts set, and some are misidentified. The incipient *Song of Songs* cycle contained in these prints has not previously been recognized. The modal ordering that appears to characterize the set is discussed below. For a full discussion of the cycle, the musical relationships of the motets, and its textual source, see Cristle Collins Judd, "A Newly-recovered Eight-Mode Motet Cycle: Zarlino's *Song of Songs* Motets," in *Theory and Analysis 1450–1650*, ed. Anne-Emmanuelle Ceulemans and Bonnie J. Blackburn (Louvain-la-Neuve, forthcoming).

[65] Marchesino Vacca, son of Messer Antonio who was *cancellier grande* of Chioggia from 1517 to 1563, was delegated in 1545 to deliver the town's congratulations to Francesco Donato on the occasion of his election as doge (1545–53). During that visit, the Venetian senate conferred on the twenty-year-old Marchesino the order of *Cavalier di San Marco*. At that time he was attending the University of Padua (and thus, presumably, the reference to his worthiness of the law and the muses). His death occurred in the following year (1546). I am grateful to Benito Rivera for sharing this information from his forthcoming study of Zarlino and for allowing me to summarize it here.   [66] This translation is based on Rivera's with slight modifications.

[67] See, for example, the title pages of the *Istitutioni* in Figures 7.1–4.

the apparently unfavorable situation which forced him to leave there in 1541,[68] but also, that even in this print he is styling himself as "Zarlino da Chioggia" by his inclusion of this text.

The other non-sacred text is a setting of a newly composed text in the style of a Horatian epode with a meter much like that of the Teucer ode to which its last line alludes. It consists of seven pairs of alternating lines of glyconic and hexameter with overt allusions to Horatian texts.[69]

Aptabo cythare modos[70]	I shall fit tunes to my cithara
prudentem nactus dominum semperque benignum	having obtained a wise lord who is always kind
qui musas colit impares	who worships the unequaled muses
qui patrie venete, qui nobis vivit amicus	who lives a friend to the Venetian homeland and to us
huius quis metuit fidem?	Who is afraid to trust him?
gratia iam nulla es si rerum inscitia vexat.	There is no beauty if ignorance disturbs us.
Nobis te duce te patre	May we, with you for guide, you for father
egypti colles placeant silueque virentes	be delighted by the hills of Egypt and the green woodlands
buxusque & berecynthie[71]	and may the boxwood (pipe) and the
delectet tube sonitus baccataque laurus	sound of the Berecynthian horn delight us, and the berried laurel
cantantes pede libero	Singing and with unencumbered feet
let cum satyris terram pulsemus alumnam[72]	let us happily stamp the life-giving
ducentes volucrem diem	earth with the satyrs spending the day that swiftly flies.
nil desperandum est Gauro duce & auspice Gauro.[73]	There is no reason to despair with Gaurus for leader, under the auspices of Gaurus.

---

[68] "Vestissi gli habiti clericali di ventidue anni, et indi à poco tempo trasferissi à Venetia; perciochè, havendo egli alcuni anni prima havuto l'organo del Domo di Chioggia, fu sforzato da persecutioni de'malevoli à lasciarlo, il che gli fu cagione di molto bene; perciochè quello che non havrebbe mai potuto imparare ne la patria sua, hebbe larghissima commodità d'apprendere in quella città nobilissima" (Baldi, ed Narducci).

Rivera attempted to relate the motet's inclusion to Santo Spirito, commenting that the community also administered the church of San Michele in the district of Brondolo in Chioggia. However, I believe that the only overt attempt to connect this print to Santo Spirito comes from the dedication and the selection of the first motet. The print simultaneously advances numerous agenda on Zarlino's part, of which noting or continuing Chioggia connections is but one.

[69] I am grateful to Joseph Farrell and Leofranc Holford-Strevens for their assistance in understanding this text and its Horatian allusions, which they identified for me.

[70] A blend of two Horatian tags: *Ode* 1.12.1/4 "bella aptari citharae modis," and *Epist.* 1.3.12–13 "fidibusque Latinis Thebanos aptare modos."

[71] Berecyntius, an epithet derived from a region of Phrygia, means "pertaining to Cybele," Mother of the Gods.

[72] Cf. Horace, *Odes* 1.31.1–2 ("Cleopatra" ode) "nunc pede libero pulsanda tellus."

[73] Horace, *Ode* 1.7.27 ("Teucer" ode) "nil desperandum Teucro duce et auspice Teucro." The Gauro (or Gavro) to whom this text refers remains a mystery at this time. In all likelihood, it is a member of the Venetian noble family known as "Guoro" or "Goro" and latinized as "Gauro," although I have not yet been able to locate a member of the family to whom this text might be addressed.

Whether or not an owner of this print is meant to recognize Zarlino as the author of this text – which he may well have been given his studies in Greek and Latin – the very inclusion of such a text, like the allusion to the Egyptian priests in the dedication, reminds the reader of the composer's connection to classical learning.

Zarlino's "compositional" learnedness appears in a number of ways, many visual as well as aural. Canons are given for four works; three are found in the tenor, one in the superius.[74] The most obvious of these is the motet *Nigra sum* which is entirely in black notation.[75] The superius is headed by the second verse of the text (*Song of Songs* 1: 5: "Nolite me considerare quod fusca sim quia decoloravit me sol" ("Do not look at me because I am dark for the sun has discolored me")) that draws further attention to the notation of the motet (see Fig. 7.8).

But undoubtedly the most "theoretical" aspect of this print – its many other indications of Zarlino's learning notwithstanding – is the inclusion of modal labels drawn from Glarean's *Dodecachordon*. The modal ascription may be seen in Figure 7.7 (p. 210), a reproduction of the tenor of the opening motet, *Veni sancte spiritus*. Modal ascriptions appear in the tenor for fifteen of the nineteen works; two more are handwritten in all extant copies in the same hand, and two appear in the quintus book (one duplicates the tenor; in the other the quintus, not the tenor, concludes with the modal final).[76] In addition to the modal ascriptions, the works are grouped by tonal type, as may be seen in Table 7.3 (p. 207). That the groupings are by tonal type, rather than mode, is confirmed by the two separate representations of "Dorian" (with a G final in *cantus mollis* and a D final in *cantus durus*). Several precedents exist from Gardano's press for such groupings, most notably his Willaert motet prints of 1545.[77] In addition, Bernhard Meier, Harold Powers, Frans Wiering, and others, have identified ordered modal cycles from Venetian presses in the 1540s.[78] There is also a Venetian precedent that stems from Scotto's didactic prints of his own madrigals that included modal labels (*primi toni* and so forth).[79] But the names

---

[74] Tenor: *O beatum pontificem* "Fuga sex temporum in diapason intensum"; *Ecce tu pulchra es* "Canon. Fuga trium temporum in diapason"; *Pater noster* "Fuga trium temporum in diapente & sex temporum in diatessaron"; *Ave Maria* (= *secunda pars* of *Pater noster*) "Primus erit novissimus & novissimus primus." Superius: *Nigra sum* "Canon. Nolite me considerare quod fusca sim quia decoloravit me sol."

[75] Zarlino later denounced the use of black notation as appealing only to the eye in the *Istitutioni*.

[76] Lewis, *Antonio Gardano*, 652, catalogues the handwritten additions in extant copies. I have seen first hand only the incomplete set of partbooks in the Music Collection of the Austrian National Library. The hand appears to match the known examples of Zarlino's handwriting and I believe that he was responsible for the insertions.

[77] On the groupings in the Willaert prints, see Anne Smith, "Willaert Motets and Mode," *Basler Jahrbuch für historische Musikpraxis* 16 (1992), 117–65. The modal ordering of a collection was clearly a secondary consideration for Gardano, however, as he willingly disrupted the modal order of some Scotto collections that he reprinted in an effort to give an appearance of "newness" to his collection. I am indebted to Jane Bernstein for this observation.

[78] Bernhard Meier, *Die Tonarten der klassischen Vokalpolyphonie*, trans. Ellen Beebe as *The Modes of Classical Vocal Polyphony* (New York: Broude Brothers, 1988); Harold Powers, "Tonal Types and Modal Categories," *Journal of the American Musicological Society* 34 (1981), 428–70; and Frans Wiering, "The Language of the Modes."

[79] Scotto, *Madrigali a tre voci* (1541) contains fifty-six madrigals which are labeled as *primi toni* (eighteen), *tertii toni* (sixteen), *quinti toni* (fourteen), and *septimi toni* (eight). They are not obviously grouped by tone within the collection although there are small clusters of madrigals in the same tone. Scotto's other print from the same year, *Primo libro dei madrigali a 2*, also contains indications of the tone in its forty-two madrigals. The beginning of the

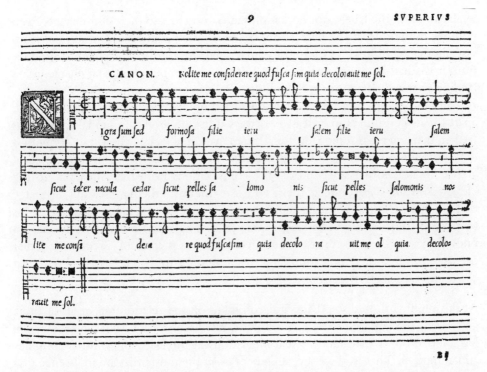

7.8 Zarlino, *Nigra sum sed formosa* (superius) (*Musices quinque vocum*, 1549) (Biblioteca
Casanatense, Mus 682². Reproduced by permission.)

attached to the eight tonal types represented in Zarlino's motet print mark a striking
departure from these traditions, for his nomenclature points to directly to Glarean's
Dodecachordon a scant two years after its publication. As Mary Lewis suggested,
circumstantial evidence about the unusual care given to text underlay, the inclusion
of the modal labels, and the handwritten addition of those labels which were inadvertently omitted, points to Zarlino's close involvement in the production of the
print.[80] This is, to my knowledge, the first printed collection (anywhere) to use
Glarean's nomenclature.[81] It is all the more striking that it appears in a context so
distant from the repertory of the *Dodecachordon*.

I can only speculate on the importance Zarlino attached to these labels, taking
care as he appears to have done to make sure that those which were inadvertently
omitted in the process of printing were added. Not only must we ask what Zarlino
intended by the inclusion of such labels, but also what he expected the prospective
owner of the print to understand by such indications. The dedication contains no

---

collection seems to be arranged by tone (the first sixteen madrigals are labeled *primi toni*, but this large grouping
breaks down as the book progresses. Unlike the collection of three-voice madrigals, there are also two works in
this print that are identified as plagal tones (*quarti toni*). The distribution by tone is as follows: *primi toni* (twenty-
one); *tertii toni* (five); *quarti toni* (two); *quinti toni* (eight); and *septimi toni* (six). There is no obvious answer to the
question of why these are almost exclusively in authentic modes. For fuller information on these prints see
Bernstein, *Scotto*, 270–74.   [80] Lewis, "Zarlino's Theories of Text Underlay," 242–43.

[81] Wiering, "Language of the Modes," also identifies this as the first dodecachordal collection.

explanation for the labels, nor does it provide overt clues to their significance. Even without the notice of the dedication, the print itself immediately makes obvious visually that Zarlino and Gardano have lavished extraordinary care on its production. It is a harbinger of a relationship to luxurious publications that characterizes Zarlino's printed persona over the whole of his career.[82]

The modal labels attached to the tenor partbook would have set Zarlino's print apart for its consumers in at least two ways. On one level, the modal indications (rather than mere grouping by tonal type) would associate these motets with a didactic tradition represented by prints like Scotto's madrigals. *But* the choice of Greek dodecachordal labels moves the compositions from the "didactic" to the "learned" realm *and* connects them with the "newest" theory, creating an image that associates Zarlino with learned theory nine years before the publication of his first theory treatise. Even the reader, or, perhaps, *especially* the reader who has no knowledge of Glarean's treatise would recognize via the use of Greek names that these are not the usual indications and thus point not to the ecclesiastical tradition but to the classical writers on music.

At this point, I should step back and comment on the relationship of all of these gestures to the "music itself." The whole of my discussion of *Musici quinque vocum* has focused on its visual and textual indications of the learnedness of its compiler and composer. That is, these are references *about* the music that are in essence discrete from the compositions as performable entities. These would be immediately obvious to *cognoscenti* regardless of their musical literacy while of less import to performers actually using the liturgical items of this print in a functional context.[83] They also suggest, I believe, the audience for whom this print is most directly intended – an audience who may (or may not) have possessed a high degree of musical literacy but who would have recognized and appreciated the theological implications of the texts, the social allusions to Vacca and Guoro, the Horatian allusions of *Aptabo cythare modos*, and the theoretical implications of the modal labels. These are readers who, like Baldi, would have proclaimed that Zarlino "was not only a singer but also a musician – that is to say, a mathematician and a theorist."[84]

This is perhaps clearest when the role of the modal labels in relation to the motets in the print is unraveled. While these modal labels may be what most sets this print apart for the modern reader, the modes of individual compositions are subordinate to textual and textural considerations in the ordering of the collection as a whole.

---

[82] The one notable exception is the *Modulationes* of 1566, discussed on pp. 242–50.

[83] That is not to say that the compositions do not also project "learnedness" in their manipulation of *soggetti* and so forth, but rather that these are not the qualities which set this print apart. A partial view of Zarlino's compositions as "sounding music" (rather than as printed artifact as I discuss them here) is available in Flury, *Gioseffo Zarlino als Komponist*. See also the discussion of *Nigra sum* in Harràn, *In Search of Harmony: Hebrew and Humanist Elements in Sixteenth-Century Musical Thought* (n.p.: American Institute of Musicology, 1988) and the discussion of *Capite nobis* in Rivera, "Zarlino's Motets (1549)."

[84] "Quella ragione che ci mosse a scrivere la vita di Aristosseno, ci move anco à stendere quella di Gioseffo Zarlino; poichè questi fu, non solo Cantore, ma Musico etiandio, cioè Matematico e Teorico in quella professione" (Baldi, ed. Narducci).

Veni sancte spiritus is the first motet in the collection because of its relevance to the dedicatee and its obvious function at the head of such a collection. If the works are to be grouped by tonal type (as Gardano was wont to do), this determines that *O beatum pontificem*, which shares its tonal type, will be the second motet. Were mode the primary means of organization, the second Dorian group (beginning with motet 5 *Osculetur me*) should follow, but the two representations of the Dorian mode are separated by a pair of Hypoionian motets. Just as the opening tonal type of the collection is determined by an individual work, so the conclusion of the collection with the Hypodorian group is predetermined, this time by textual and textural considerations. The concluding *Pater noster* and *Ave Maria* is a large-scale work for seven voices, two of which are generated canonically from the tenor. As is usual works (or in this case, the work) for a greater number of voices conclude the collection, and the *Pater noster* was clearly intended by Zarlino as a compositional *tour de force*.[85]

With a single exception, the modes actually identified in the collection would pose little challenge to a traditional eight-mode scheme, leading to further speculation about why Zarlino chooses to attach dodecachordal labels to these works. Like Glarean's own prints, the annotations appear primarily in the tenor partbook. As I will demonstrate below, the modal labels were grafted on to an extant repertory (or a repertory composed without consideration of dodecachordal theory in a prescriptive frame). The eight tonal types represent seven modes, three of which (Ionian, Hypoionian, and Aeolian) stand outside a traditional eight-mode scheme. The group of works labeled here as "Ionian" and "Hypoinian" would be identified as Modes 5 and 6 in traditional nomenclature. An examination of the contents of the print along with an understanding of Zarlino's later writings on modal theory suggests that at this stage his use of the labels represents a straightforward mapping of Glarean's terminology on to a collection of Zarlino's own compositions – nothing about the collection suggests that it was composed with any deliberate intention to "represent" Glarean's modes.[86] On the one hand, tonal types are predetermined by chants which serve as the *soggetti* for paraphrase compositions. This may be illustrated by a quick glance at *Veni sancte spiritus*, the first motet of the collection. The opening of the *prima pars* (Ex. 7.1) is typical of the paraphrase procedures used in this book; the chant is marked on Example 7.1 by crosses above the notes. Normally two voices state the chant either in alternation or as the basis of a quasi-imitative framework within a relatively dense contrapuntal texture. The modal indication appears in the quintus partbook in addition to the tenor, perhaps in recognition of the extensive appearance of the chant in this voice.[87]

---

[85] He refers to it repeatedly in the *Istitutioni* and his 1566 motet print concludes with a revised version of this motet.

[86] There is, to be sure, the possibility that the annotations were Gardano's, not Zarlino's, but this seems highly unlikely given the circumstantial evidence of Zarlino's close involvement in the print and later indications of Zarlino's connections to Gardano (discussed below).

[87] In the other instance in which the mode is indicated in the quintus (no. 3 *Nemo potest venire*), the quintus, not the tenor, concludes on the modal final.

Ex. 7.1 *Veni sancte spiritus*, opening, Zarlino 1549

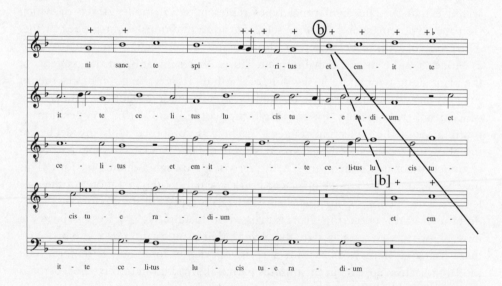

7.1 *(cont.)*

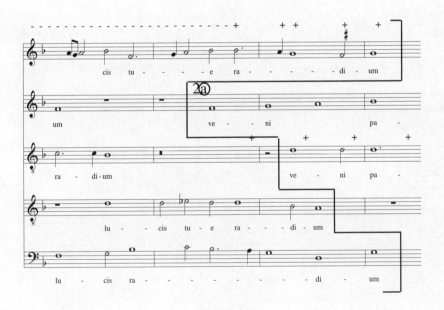

Ex. 7.2 *Si bona suscepimus*, opening and conclusion, Zarlino 1549

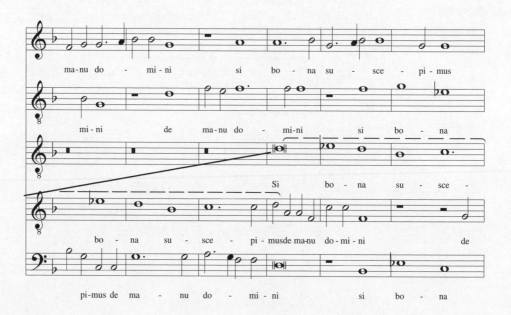

7.2 (*cont.*)

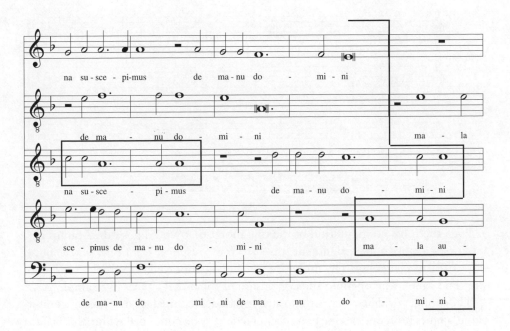

7.2 *(cont.)*

end of *secunda pars*

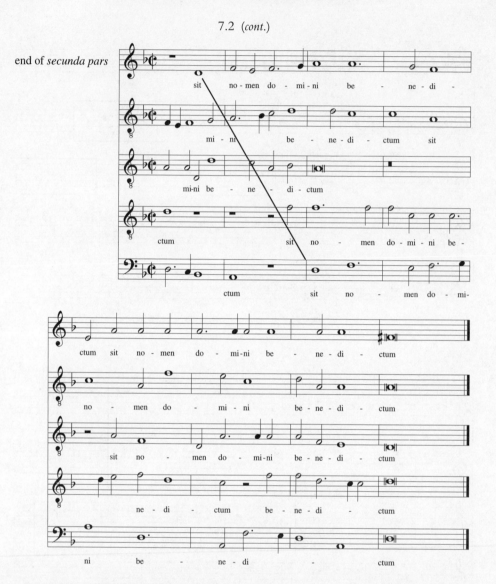

Even the tonal configuration of the one motet that would push the bounds of a traditional eight-mode assignment, the "Aeolian" responsory *Si bona suscepimus*, is not of Zarlino's making. The motet is one of many modeled on Verdelot's motet of the same name. The opening and conclusion of the motet appear in Example 7.2.[88]

The stronger evidence that Zarlino attached dodecachordal labels to extant compositions comes from uncovering part of an octenary cycle concealed within this print: a

---

[88] There is no doubt that Zarlino knew Verdelot's motet which he cites in the *Istitutioni*. The text and tradition of polyphonic settings of *Si bona suscepimus* is discussed in detail in James Haar, "Orlande de Lassus: *Si bona suscepimus*." Haar mentions Zarlino's motet, but does not actually discuss its relation to this tradition, which is a complicated one. The connection of Zarlino's motet to Verdelot's setting is mediated by a number of intervening settings, and raises questions about families of motet settings, rather than the direct one-to-one relationships that are often the focus of polyphonic borrowing. See Judd and Amos, "Multi-layered Borrowing."

Song of Songs cycle. The traces of this cycle offer new evidence not only of the way that Zarlino understood modal theory in relation to his own compositional endeavors, but also suggests he shifted from octenary to dodecachordal modal theory relatively shortly after his encounter with it sometime between 1547 and the publication of this motet print. I have assembled the remains of this hypothetical cycle in Table 7.4.

This is a remarkable venture on several counts. First, Zarlino is systematically setting these as biblical texts, not the more usual centonate liturgical texts derived from *Song of Songs*.[89] Secondly, he seems deliberately to have meant to set up a parallel between the eight chapters which comprise the *Song of Songs* and the eight modes. Thus, chapter one is divided into four parts and set as four motets with the same cleffing, signature, and final, as a though representation of Mode 1 on D; chapter 2 is set as though presenting Mode 2;[90] chapter 3 as though Mode 3. It is this correlation of evident modal number and chapter division that suggests that Zarlino was embarked upon an eight-mode cycle. The textual impetus for the collection may have been the same that motivated Cipriano de Rore's *Vergine* cycle from about the same period. Certainly the cycle would be comparable as a large-scale, ordered setting of sacred but non-liturgical texts.[91] The more obvious models may have been Rore's modally ordered motet and madrigal cycles published by Gardano earlier in the 1540s.[92] But this cycle differs in significant ways. First, it apparently dispenses with any notion of compositional concern with modal ethos:[93] the modal assignments are based not on textual content or affect but syntactic division by chapters. Yet with one important exception, work on the projected cycle appears to have ceased at the conclusion of chapter 3 (= Mode 3). Several reasons can be advanced for this, but the most likely appears to be that Zarlino's encounter with the twelve-mode theory of the *Dodecachordon* undermined the premises of the eight-mode cycle on which he was embarked.[94] Yet, Zarlino appears not to have

[89] This might explain why he draws attention to the setting of sacred texts in the dedication. The motivation for this cycle is discussed in Judd, "Zarlino's *Song of Songs* Motets."

[90] I can only speculate about the middle verses of this chapter, for which no setting by Zarlino is known. The publication of one motet each from the middle of chapters 1 and 3 in other prints suggests that Zarlino may also have completed a setting of *Vox delicti*, but deliberately withheld it from Z1549 with the intention of publishing it elsewhere.

[91] Despite Meier's interpretation, however, there is no evidence that the *Vergine* cycle was modally ordered. For the fullest discussion of this cycle, see Feldman, *City Culture* and Mary Lewis, "Rore's Setting of Petrarch's 'Vergine bella'," *Journal of Musicology* 4 (1985), 365–409.

[92] For an overview of these prints, see Lewis, *Gardano*. On tonal types and modal ordering generally, see Powers, "Tonal Types and Modal Categories." On Rore's madrigals, see Jessie Ann Owens, "Mode in the Madrigals of Cipriano de Rore," in *Altro Polo: Essays on Italian Music in the Cinquecento*, ed. Richard Charteris (Sydney: Frederich May Foundation for Italian Studies, University of Sydney, 1990), 1–16, and Harold Powers, "Monteverdi's Model for a Multi-modal Madrigal," in *In cantu et in sermone: For Nino Pirrotta on his 80th Birthday*, ed. Fabrizio della Seta and Franco Piperno (Florence: Olschki, 1989), 185–219.

[93] The same appears to be true of Rore's 1542 print, which was undoubtedly also assembled from pre-existing pieces arranged to fit an octenary plan.

[94] The cessation of the cycle at Mode 3 might also be a sign of the notorious difficulty in distinguishing between Modes 3 and 4 polyphonically. For example, see the extended discussion of the Palestrina offertories in Dahlhaus, *Studies on the Origins of Harmonic Tonality*, trans. Robert Gjerdigen (Princeton: Princeton University Press, 1990); Meier, trans. Beebe *The Modes of Classical Vocal Polyphony*, and Harold Powers, "Modal Representations in Polyphonic offertories," in *Early Music History* 2 (1982), 43–86.

Table 7.4 *Zarlino's modally ordered setting of the* Song of Songs

Mode[a]	Text[b]	Motet	Source[c]	Tonal type	Label[d]
1	1: 1–3	*Osculetur me*	Z1549, 5	c1–c3–c4–c4–f4 — D	Dorian
	1: 4–6	*Nigra sum*[e]	Z1549, 6	c1–c3–c4–c4–f4 — D	Dorian
	1: 7–13	*Si ignoras*	1549/7	c1–c3–c4–c4–f4 — D	—
	1: 14–16	*Ecce tu pulchra es*	Z1549, 7	c1–c3–c4–c4–f4 — D	Dorian
2	2: 1–7	*Ego rosa saron*	Z1549, 16	c1–c3–c4–c1–f4 ♭ G	Hypodorian
	[2: 8–14	*Vox delicti mei*	no setting]		
	2: 15–17	*Capite nobis*	Z1549, 18	c1–c3–c4–c1–f4 ♭ G	Hypodorian
3	3: 1–4	*In lectulo meo*	Z1549, 15	c1–c3–c4–c4–f4 — E	Phrygian
	3: 5–8	*Adiuro vos filie*	1549/8	c1–c3–c4–c4–f4 — E	—
	3: 9–11	*Ferculum fecit sibi*	Z1549, 14	c1–c3–c4–c4–f4 — E	Phrygian
4	[4: 1–11]			[— E]	
5	5: 1–4	*Ego veni*	Z1549, 8	g2–c2–c3–c3–f4 ♭ F	Ionian
	[5: 5–17]				
6	[6: 1–12]			[♭ F]	
7	[7: 1–13]			[— G]	
8	[8: 1–14]			[— G]	

Notes:

[a] Modal numbers reflect a hypothetical eight-mode classification of a modally ordered collection that corresponded to the eight chapters of the *Song of Songs.*

[b] Chapter and verses from the *Song of Songs.*

[c] Sigla: Z1549=Zarlino, *Musici quinque vocum* (Gardano, 1549); for other prints, see Table 7.1.

[d] Dodecachordal labels in the 1549 motet print.

[e] *Nigra sum* is in "black" notation throughout.

discarded these motets in light of Glarean's theories. Instead, he expediently culled and rearranged motets from the cycle in service of his publication ambitions in 1549. Among other results, this has the effect of obscuring the cyclic origins of the individual motets. The one motet that sets a text beyond chapter 3 supports these conclusions. *Ego veni* (Z1549, no. 8) is the opening of the fifth chapter of *Song of Songs.* If, as I have suggested, Zarlino had begun an eight-mode setting of the *Song* that corresponded to chapter divisions, a text from chapter 5 would thus be set to represent traditional Mode 5, as this motet does with its high clefs, F final, and B♭ signature. There is no reason to assume that he worked through the texts only in an ordered fashion (although the extant motets suggest that this was his primary approach). But in Glarean's nomenclature, of course, this configuration is no longer Mode 5 (or in his terminology Lydian) but a representation of Ionian, and the motet is so labeled in Zarlino's 1549 print. In the *Istitutioni* (1558), it is cited as Mode 11.[95]

Thus *Musici quinque vocum* stands as the first printed trace of Zarlino's interaction with modal theory in more far-reaching ways than its overt inclusion of dodeca-chordal labels. It documents, on the one hand, unprecedented compositional exper-imentation with a cyclic polyphonic representation of the eight modes of traditional theory and, on the other, a first engagement with, and pragmatic appropriation of, the nomenclature of Glarean's dodecachordal theory. Whether Zarlino had har-bored qualms about the internal contradictions of a system in which the true form of Mode 5 (F final in *cantus durus*) was a theoretical possibility while a practical impos-sibility or was simply persuaded by Glarean's presentation in the *Dodecachordon*, he seems readily to have adapted Glarean's framework to his own compositions, evi-dently conceived under quite different theoretical prescriptions, with remarkable facility. There is no doubt that the motets of the *Song of Songs* cycle, even in the par-tially finished state at which I have suggested Zarlino abandoned the cycle, repre-sented a significant commitment on his part.[96] It also represented an enterprise that was decidedly scholarly and wide ranging in its cast.

---

[95] For a more detailed discussion of this motet and its various modal assignments, see Cristle Collins Judd, "Renaissance Modal Theory: Theoretical, Compositional, and Editorial Perspectives," in *The Cambridge History of Western Music Theory*, ed. Thomas Christensen (Cambridge: Cambridge University Press, forthcoming).

[96] From his relatively small output, one can guess that the anecdote he relates regarding the slowness of Willaert's composition might also apply to his own work. In the *Sopplimenti musicali*, Zarlino recounts an incident which he dates as 5 December 1541 (i.e., shortly after his arrival in Venice). Some singers gave a reading of a five-voice piece by a "Messer Alberto." At its conclusion, Alberto turned to Girolamo Parabosco, a student of Willaert, and inquired how long it would take Willaert to compose a similar piece. Parabosco replied that a piece of that length would take Willaert at least two months. When Alberto reacted in surprise and offered that he had com-posed the piece in a single evening, Parabosco immediately responded that he was surprised that Alberto hadn't managed ten such pieces in that time, but that when Willaert composed he gave all his energies and pondered and studied a composition at great length, which is how he had gained his reputation (*Sopplimenti musicali* (Venice, 1588), VIII:13, p. 326).

8

"ON THE MODES"

THE CITATIONS OF *LE ISTITUTIONI HARMONICHE*, PART IV

The ease with which Zarlino apparently adopted Glarean's nomenclature in his first motet print is complicated by his subsequent engagement with modal theory in the *Istitutioni harmoniche* and its revisions – the next printed trace of Zarlino's engagement with modal theory. Powers has described the *Istitutioni* as "bringing polyphonic texture, modal structure, and modal ethos under the rule of a single unifying musical principle." For the moment, I will focus specifically on the chapters in which Zarlino describes the twelve modes individually.

He begins:

I shall [discuss] each mode separately, starting with the first mode and proceeding in order. In discussing each mode, I shall first show that it is in use not only among churchmen but also among the whole community of musicians. Then I shall show the notes on which one can regularly begin a mode and those on which one can make cadences. Having done this, I shall discuss to some extent the nature of the mode.[1]

He later adds:

In order that what I have said may be understood more easily, I shall present an example for two voices, by means of which the reader may know the proper places of the regular cadences and see the manner that should be adhered to in composing their melodic lines.[2]

And so he does, for each of his twelve modes.

Figure 8.1 reproduces the discussion of the third mode that appears on pages 323–24 of the 1558 edition of the *Istitutioni*. This excerpt highlights the usual format of each chapter (normally in the order followed here): species, cadences,

---

[1] "Verrò hora a dar principio al ragionamento di ciascun Modo separatamente, incominciando dal Primo, acciò procediamo con ordine; & mostrarò primieramente, che non solamente appresso gli Ecclesiastici; ma anche appresso tutta la scuola de i Musici è in uso. Dipoi mostrarò, dove regolarmente si possa dar principio ad esso Modo; & dove (tanto in questo, quanto in ciascuno de gli altri Modi) si possa far le Cadenze; il che fatto, ragionarò alquanto intorno la sua Natura" (1558 IV: 18, 320; trans. Vered Cohen, *On the Modes* (New Haven: Yale University Press, 1983), 54).

[2] "Ma acciò più facilmente si scorga quello, che si è detto, porro uno essempio a due voci, dal quale si potrà conoscere I proprij luoghi delle Cadenze regolari, & vedere il modo, che si hà da tenere nelle loro modulationi" (1558 IV: 18, 321; trans. Cohen, *On the Modes*, 55).

citations, irregularities (in this case the relationship to another mode), and, in some cases, a discussion of modal ethos.[3] The physical placement of the illustrative duo within the chapter is purely a convention of house style in the 1558 edition. It occurs either at the bottom or top of a text block. There is no discussion of the duos beyond the initial one explaining their function, but as has often been observed, they adhere (indeed quite slavishly) to Zarlino's prescriptions.

In these chapters, Zarlino draws on three strands of argument. Recognizing them as such clarifies both the role of his citations and his relationship to Glarean. First is the discourse of traditional modal theory as mediated by dodecachordal theory that informs the discussion of species and cadences.[4] The second, of most interest here, is a specifically Venetian strand of modal theory exemplified by Pietro Aron's *Trattato* (1525) with its instantiations from contemporary printed polyphonic repertories. The third is the *musica practica* tradition of Part III of the *Istitutioni* which now extends to the duos supplied for Part IV. The format in which these duos are presented is an immediate clue for the reader to their function and meaning. That is, their appearance corresponds to the numerous didactic duos of Part III, and the writing in these duos continues to display the various contrapuntal devices discussed in the earlier book. Thus, in the example of Mode 3, transcribed and annotated as Example 8.1, the points of imitation begin uniformly on the pitches which mark and divide the octave species of the mode: E and B. Primary cadences are to the "regular" cadential pitches, E, G, and B, while cadences to "irregular" pitches like D and A are elided or avoided. Imitation appears at the regular intervals of the octave (above or below) or at the fifth (above or below) at a variety of temporal intervals and with various treatments of *soggetti*.

Thus the substance – the discourse – of Glarean's twelve modes is now placed in a rhetorical and material context that renders them recognizable in name only. And even in name, Zarlino (however disingenuously) has distanced himself from Glarean's theory. While the 1549 motet print used Glarean's pseudo-classical modal nomenclature, including the "new" Aeolian and Ionian indicators, Zarlino abandons these names in the course of Part IV of the *Istitutioni* in favor of simple numerical designations when he actually comes to discuss individual modes.[5]

Modes 3 and 4 supply a representative point of departure for exploring the questions of the citations in the treatise as a whole, Zarlino's (likely) sources, the relationship of the treatise to printed repertories, and the nature of revisions in the later

---

[3] The inconsistency with which modal ethos is discussed may reflect Zarlino's own practical relationship with the concept as witnessed in the *Song of Songs* cycle discussed in chapter 7.

[4] The most detailed examination of Zarlino's borrowing from Glarean is found in Bernhard Meier, "Heinrich Loriti Glareanus als Musiktheoretiker," in *Aufsätze zur Freiburger Wissenschafts- und Universitätsgeschichte*, ed. Clemens Bauer *et al.* (Freiburg im Breisgau: Verlag Eberhard Albert Universitätsbuchhandlung, 1960), 65–112. Zarlino borrows most heavily and directly from Glarean in his description of the "new" modes, Modes 5 and 6 and 9 and 10.

[5] Palisca has suggested that Zarlino was forced to abandon Glarean's nomenclature by his reading of Ptolemy and the recognition that Glarean's nomenclature was incompatible with Ptolemy's. See his introduction to Cohen, trans., *On the Modes*.

Parte.   323

*no ; & dicono, che è Modo atto alle parole, che rapresentano pianto, mestitia, solicitudine, cattiuità, cala-
mità, & ogni generatione di miseria; & si troua molto in vso ne i loro canti; & le sue Cadenze principali, & regolari(per essere questo Modo dal Primo poco differente: percioche l'vno & l'altro si compongono
delle istesse specie) si pongono nelle chorde nominate di sopra, che sono a, F, D, & A; che si vedeno
nello essempio : l'altre poi, che si pongono ne i altri luoghi sono tutte Irregolari. Dicono li Prattici, che questo Modo si compone della Prima specie della Diapente a & D posta nell'acuto, & della Prima della Dia
tessaron D & A posta nel graue ; & lo chiamano Collaterale, ouer Plagale del Primo modo. Si trouano molte compositioni del Secondo modo, composte da molti Antichi, & da Moderni Musici ; tra le
quali è il motetto, Præter rerum seriem, composto a sei voci da Iosquino; & da Adriano a Sette voci ; col
madrigale, Che fai alma, similmente a sette voci ; il motetto Auertatur obsecro domine, & il madrigale,
Oue ch'i posi gli occhi; l'vno & l'altro a sei voci, con molti altri. Composi anche io in tal Modo la Oratio-
ne Dominicale, Pater noster ; con la Salutatione angelica, Aue maria, a sette voci ; & li motetti, Ego rosa
Saron, & Capite nobis vulpes paruulas a cinque voci. Si trouano etiandio molte altre compositioni fatte da
diuersi compositori, le quali per essere quasi infinite si lassano. Questo Modo rare volte si troua nelli Canti figurati nelle sue chorde propie : ma il più delle volte si ritroua trasportato per vna Quarta ; come si può vedere nelli Motetti nominati ; & questo: percioche si può trasporre; come anco si può trasporre il Primo modo,
con l'aiuto della chorda Trite synemennon, verso l'acuto. Et si come il Primo col Nono hà molta conuenienza, così questo l'hà veramente col Decimo.*

Del Terzo Modo.   Cap. 20.

 *L Terzo modo dicono, che nasce dalla Quinta specie della Diapason diuisa harmonica-
mente dalla chorda ♮ ; ouero dalla vnione della Seconda specie della Diapente E &
♮, posta nel graue, con la Seconda della Diatessaron ♮ & e, posta nell'acuto. Questo Modo hà la sua chorda finale E commune col Quarto modo; & gli Ecclesiastici hanno di questo Modo infinite cantilene, come ne i loro libri si può vedere. Le sue Cadenze*

SOPRANO.

TENORE.

S 2   *principali*

8.1   Zarlino, *Le istitutioni harmoniche* (1558) IV: 20: the third mode

324   Quarta

principali ſi fanno nelle chorde de i ſuoi principij regolari, i quali ſono le chorde moſtrate E, G, ♮, & e; che ſono le eſtreme della ſua Diapente, & della ſua Diateſſaron, & la mezana della Diapente; le altre poi, che ſono Irregolari, ſi poſſono fare ſopra l'altre chorde: Ma perche conoſciuto le Regulari, facilmente ſi può conoſcere le Irregolari; però daremo vno eſſempio delle prime, acciò veniamo in cognitione delle ſeconde. Si debbe però auertire, che tanto in queſto, quanto nel Quarto, nel Settimo, & nell'Ottauo modo, regolarmente ſi fanno le cadenze nella chorda ♮: ma perche tal chorda non hà corriſpondenza alcuna per Quinta nell'acuto, ne per Quarta nel graue; però è alquanto dura: ma tal durezza ſi ſopporta nelle cantilene compoſte a più di due voci: percioche ſi tiene tal'ordine, che fanno buono effetto; come ſi può vedere tra le Cadenze poſte nel Cap. 61. della Terza parte. Molte compoſitioni ſi trouano compoſte ſotto queſto Modo, tra le quali è il motetto, O Maria mater Chriſti a quattro voci di Iſac; & li motetti di Adriano, Te Deŭ patrem; Huc me ſydereo; & Hæc eſt domus domini, compoſti a ſette voci: & il Madrigale, I mi riuolgo indietro, compoſto da Adriano medeſimamente a cinque voci: alli quali aggiungeremo, Ferculum fecit ſibi rex Salomon, il quale gia compoſi inſieme con molti altri di tal Modo ſimigliantemente a cinque voci. Se queſto Modo non ſi meſcolaſſe col Nono, & ſi vdiſſe ſemplice, hauerebbe la ſua harmonia alquanto dura: ma perche è temperata dalla Diapente del Nono, & dalla Cadenza, che ſi fa in a, che in eſſo grandemente ſi vſa; però alcuni hanno hauuto parere, che habbia natura di commouere al pianto; la onde gli accommodarono volentieri quelle parole, che ſono lagrimeuoli, & piene di lamenti. Hà grande conuenienza col detto Nono: percioche hanno la Seconda ſpecie della Diateſſaron commune tra loro; & ſpeſſe volte i Muſici moderni lo traſportano fuori delle ſue chorde naturali per vna Diateſſaron più acuta, con l'aiuto del la chorda ♭; ancora che'l più delle volte ſi ritroui collocato nel ſuo propio, & natural luogo.

Del Quarto Modo.   Cap. 21.

 E G V E dopo queſto il Quarto contenuto tra la Seconda ſpecie della Diapaſon ♮ & ♮, mediata dalla ſua chorda finale E arithmeticamente. Queſto (come dicono li Prattici) ſi compone della Seconda ſpecie della Diapente ♮ & E, poſta in acuto; & della Seconda della Diateſſaron E & ♮, congiunta alla Diapente dalla parte gra ue. Queſto medeſimamente, ſecondo la loro opinione, ſi accommoda marauiglioſamente a parole, o materie lamenteuoli, che contengono triſtezza, ouero lamentatione ſupplicheuole; come ſono materie amoroſe, & quelle, che ſignificano otio, quiete, tranquillità, adulatione, fraude, & detrattione; il perche dallo effetto alcuni lo chiamarono Modo adulatorio. Queſto è alquanto più meſto del ſuo principale, maſſimamente quando procede per mouimenti contrarij, cioè dall'acuto al graue, con mouimenti tardi. Credo io, che ſe'l ſi vſaſſe ſemplicemente, ſenza meſcolarui la Diapente, & la Cadenza poſta in a, che ſerue al Decimo modo; che hauerebbe alquanto più del virile, di quello, che non hà coſì meſcolato: ma accompagnato in tal maniera, ſi vſa grandemente, di modo che ſi trouano molte cantilene compoſte ſotto queſto Modo, tra le quali ſi troua il motetto, Deprofundis clamaui ad te Domine a quattro voci di Ioſquino; & il motetto, Peccata mea Domine, col Madrigale, Rompi dell'empio cor' il duro ſcoglio di Adriano, l'vno, & l'altro compoſti a ſei voci; & il madrigale, Laura mia ſacra compoſto a cinque voci. Compoſi ancora io molte cantilene, tra le quali ſi troua a ſei voci il motetto, Miſerere mei Deus miſerere mei, & vna Meſſa, ſen za vſar le oſſeruanze moſtrate nella Terza parte; & ciò feci, non per altro, ſe non per moſtrare, che ciaſcu no il quale vorrà comporre ſenza partirſi dalle date Regole, potrà etiandio comporre facilmente ſenza queſte oſſeruanze, & aſſai meglio di quello, che fanno alcuni, che non le ſanno, quando lo vorrà fare. Si trouano di queſto Modo quaſi infinite cantilene eccleſiaſtiche, nelle quali rariſſime volte (anzi s'io diceſſe mai, non erra rei) ſi vede toccar la chorda ♮. Bene è vero, che paſſa nell'acuto alla chorda c, di maniera che quando'l Semituono douerebbe vdirſi nel graue, ſi ode nell'acuto; & coſì gli eſtremi di cotal Modo vengono ad eſſere le chorde c & C. Li ſuoi Principij irregolari appreſſo gli Eccleſiaſtici ſi trouano in molti luoghi: ma li regolari ſono nelle chorde ♮, E, G & ♮ ſolamente; ſi come ſi trouano anco le ſue Cadenze regolari, che ſono le ſottopoſte; ancora che molte ſiano le Irregolari. Il più delle volte li Prattici lo traſportano per vna Diateſſaron nell'acuto, ponendo la chorda ♭ in luogo della ♮, come ſi può vedere in infinite cantilene; il che fanno etiandio (come hò detto) ne gli altri Modi.

Del

Ex. 8.1 Duo Mode 3 (cf. fig. 8.1), Zarlino, *Le istitutioni harmoniche* (1558), IV: 20, 323

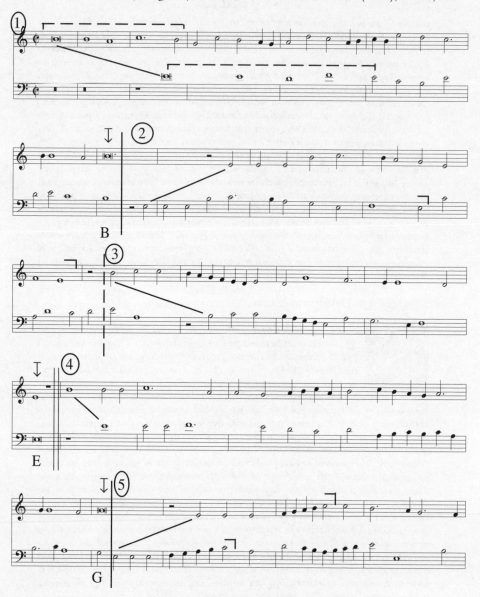

8.1 (*cont.*)

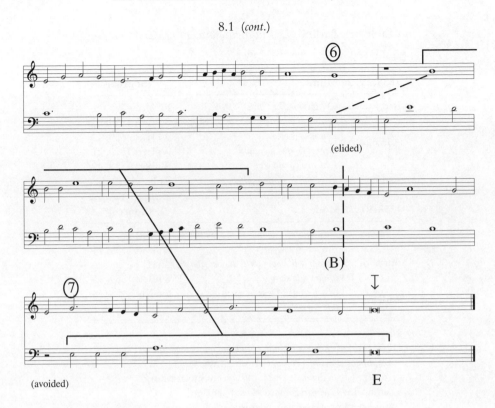

(elided)

(B)

(avoided)   E

Notes:

1 imitation down a fifth at 5 semibreves; cadence to B
2 imitation up an octave at 2 semibreves; cadence to (D) [weakened]
3 imitation down an octave at 2 semibreves; cadence to E
4 imitation down a fifth at 1 semibreve; cadence to G
5 imitation up an octave at 2 semibreves (elided into next phrase)
6 imitation up a twelfth at 2 semibreves, shifting to an octave at 3 semibreves; cadence to B, followed by an averted cadence to A
7 soggetto of sixth phrase down a twelfth; cadence to E

Table 8.1 Zarlino, *Le istitutioni harmoniche, Citations for
Modes 3 and 4 (1558)*

1558, IV: 20 Mode 3		(Source)[a]
Isac	*O Maria mater Christi*	1520⁴, 21
Adriano	*Tè Deum patrem*	Willaert 1559, 27
	Huc me sydereo	Willaert 1559, 22
	Hec est domus domini	Willaert 1559, 21
	I mi rivolgo indietro	Willaert 1559, 40
Zarlino	*Ferculum fecit sibi rex Salomon*	Zarlino 1549, 14

1558, VI: 21 Mode 4		(Source)[a]
Josquino	*De profundis clamavi ad te Domine*	1520⁴, 18
Adriano	*Peccata mea Domine*	Willaert 1559, 14
	Rompi dell'empio cor'il duro scoglio	[1541¹⁶]
	L'aura mia sacra	Willaert 1559, 35
Zarlino	*Miserere mei, Deus miserere mei*	1566/6
	une Messe	?

Note:

[a] RISM 1520⁴: *Liber selectarum cantionum quas vulgo Mutetas appelant
sex quinque et quatuor vocum* (Grimm & Wyrsung)
[1541¹⁶: *La piu divina . . . madrigali, a sei voce* (Gardano)]
Zarlino 1549: *Musici quinque vocum* (Gardano)
Willaert 1559: *Musica nova* (Gardano)
Zarlino 1566: *Modulationes sex vocum* (Rampazetto)

1573 edition.[6] Table 8.1 lists the citations for Modes 3 and 4 with Zarlino's composer and title indications, followed by a source. Zarlino follows an order that
moves from older to newer, concluding with himself. While the ancient/modern
distinction is an unremarkable formality, several aspects of its realization in the
Istitutioni merit mention.

First, while Josquin is Zarlino's usual choice of "ancient," a careful look at his
citations in the treatise as a whole suggests that a particular print, Grimm and
Wyrsung's *Liber selectarum cantionum* of 1520, defined the "ancient" for Zarlino,
serving as his source for Josquin, Isaac, and Pierre de la Rue.[7] Table 8.2 provides an
outline of the print and identifies the seven motets cited in the *Istitutioni* by part and
chapter of citation. This folio choirbook edited by Senfl appears to have defined
Zarlino's knowledge of the motet repertory from the Josquin generation. In addi-

---

[6] Frans Wiering, "The Language of the Modes: Studies in the History of Polyphonic Modality," Ph.D. dissertation, University of Amsterdam (1995) has taken what might be described as an "internal" view of the citations,
examining only those works actually cited in the treatise, while I am interested in the broader context that
frames them.

[7] Frans Wiering independently identified this as a source for Zarlino's citations ("Language of the Modes"). A
detailed study and transcription of this anthology (RISM 1520⁴) appears in Kenneth Creighton Roberts, "The
Music of Ludwig Senfl: A Critical Appraisal," Ph.D. dissertation, University of Michigan (1965; UMI
66–6687). The print is also discussed in Stephanie Schlagel, "Josquin des Prez and His Motets: A Case-Study in
Sixteenth-Century Reception History," Ph.D. dissertation, University of North Carolina at Chapel Hill (1996).

Table 8.2 *RISM 1520[4]* Liber selectarum cantionum *(Grimm & Wyrsung)*

No.	Composer	Title	clef	Tonal type sig.	final	Zarlino 1558
1	Isaac	*Optime divino date munere*	c1–c4–c4–c4–f4–f4	♭	G	
2	Josquin	*Praeter rerum seriem*	c1–c3–c3–c4–f4–f4	♭	G	IV: 19
3	Isaac	*Virgo prudentissima*	c1–c1–c3–c4–f3–f4	♭	G	
4	Josquin	*O virgo prudentissima*	c1–c3–c4–c4–c4–f4	♭	G	
5	—	*Anima mea liquefacta est*	c1–c3–c4–c3–f4–f4	♭	G	
6	Josquin	*Benedicta es caelorum regina*	c1–c4–c3–c4–f4–f4	—	G	III: 64; IV: 25
7	Pierre de la Rue	*Pater de caelis Deus miserere*	c1–c3–c3–c4–f4–f4	—	D	III: 28
8	Senfl	*Sancte pater divitas decus*	g1–c2–c3–c4–c4–f3	♭	A	
9	Josquin	*Miserere mei Deus*	c1–c3–c4–c4–f4	—	A	
10	Josquin	*Inviolata integra et casta*	c2–c3–c4–c4–f4	♭	F	III: 45; IV: 29
11	Obrecht	*Salve crux arbor vitae*	c2–c3–c3–c4–f4	♭	F	
12	—	*Lectio actuum apostolorum*	c1–c3–c4–c4–f4	—	E	
13	Josquin	*Stabat mater dolorosa*	g2–c3–c3–c4–f3	♭	F	IV: 28
14	Mouton	*Missus est Gabriel angelus*	g2–c1–c2–c3–f3	—	D	
15	—	*Anima mea liquefacta est*	c3–c4–c4–f4–f4	—	G	
16	Senfl	*Gaude Maria virgo*	c1–c3–c4–f4–f4	♭	F	
17	Isaac	*Ave sanctissima Maria*	c1–c3–c3–f4	—	C	
18	Josquin	*De profundis clamavi*	c2–c4–f3–f5	—	E	IV: 21
19	Isaac	*Prophetarum maxime*	c1–c3–c3–f3	—	G	
20	—	*Deus in adjutorium meum*	c1–c3–c4–f4	♭	F	
21	Isaac	*O Maria mater Christi*	c2–c4–c4–f4	—	E	IV: 20
22	Senfl	*Discubuit Jesu et discipuli*	c1–c4–c4–f4	—	E	
23	Senfl	*Usque quo Domine*	c1–c3–c4–f4	—	E	
24	Senfl	*Beati omnes*	g2–c2–c3–f3	—	D	
25	Senfl	*Salva sancta parens*	[c3–c3–f3–f3]	—	E	

tion to the works that he cites in the *Istitutioni*, some of these compositions appear to have provided models for Zarlino's own motet compositions.[8] Zarlino could hardly have chosen a more elegant material representation of the "ancient" art. Beyond the compositions it contained, this is a book that would have appealed to Zarlino as a model and object of study. It was a luxurious double-impression print with meticulous text underlay. It opens with a lengthy introduction that extols the Platonic role of music and concludes with a puzzle canon.[9] In many ways, it might serve as a companion to Glarean's *Dodecachordon* for a reader like Zarlino – it is of comparable layout, and it contains repertory by the composers Glarean most admired while extending beyond the self-imposed four-voice restriction of the *Dodecachordon* to the five- and six-voice works which obviously held greater interest for mid-century musicians like Zarlino.

[8] E.g., Isaac's *Virgo prudentissima*, and Josquin's *Miserere*.
[9] The preface is transcribed in Roberts, "The Music of Ludwig Senfl," Appendix D, 5–7.

CITATIONS FROM *MUSICA NOVA* (1559)

The second feature to observe about the citations illustrated in Table 8.1 is that, as often noted, the majority refer to music of Willaert.[10] More specifically, though, in the chapters on individual modes, the citations are almost exclusively to works that were to appear in Willaert's *Musica nova*.[11] I have thus far glossed over the apparent chronological disparity of citing as a primary "source" a publication which appeared after the *Istitutioni*, such as Zarlino's 1566 motet print, but above all Willaert's *Musica nova*, published only in 1559.[12] Table 8.3 outlines the content of *Musica nova*. The arrangement of the collection is by number of voices, not tonal type, with motets followed by madrigals. That Zarlino cites none of the five-voice motets while omitting only one of the six- and seven-voice works may suggest that he effectively substituted his own five-voice motet print of 1549 for these works. But it might also be suggestive of the pre-publication version of the collection he knew. As Newcomb and Agee/Owens have shown, *Musica nova* circulated long before its publication.[13] Zarlino is not just associating the *Istitutioni* with Willaert, but by citation very specifically with a collection that would come to have special connotations for one group of his potential readership, for upon the publication of *Musica nova*, the luxurious folio theory treatise could be implicitly connected with an equally luxurious music edition.

It appears that Zarlino was intimately acquainted with details and possibly directly involved in the publication of *Musica nova*. As Owens and Agee have shown, the publication history of *Musica nova* was fraught with conflict.[14] Briefly, Antonio Zantani and Juan Iacomo Zorzi obtained a privilege to publish a collection entitled *La eletta* in 1556. The collection was to include four four-voiced madrigals by Willaert. In April 1558, Prince Alfonso requested his ambassador to Venice, Faleti, to apply for a privilege for *Musica nova*, which he did in August 1558. It does seem that *La eletta* was already printed (although it did not appear until 1569),[15] but

---

[10] Compare also Table 7.2, pp. 202–05.

[11] *Musica nova di Adriano Willaert all'illustrissimo et eccellentissimo signor il signor Donno Alfonso D'Este prencipe di Ferrara* (Venice: Gardano, 1559). Cited hereafter simply as *Musica nova* or "Willaert 1559." Modern edition in *Adriani Willaert: Opera Omnia*, Corpus mensurabilis musicae 3/5: *Motets*, ed. Hermann Zenck and Walter Gerstenberg (Rome: American Institute of Musicology, 1957) and 3/13: *Madrigals*, ed. Hermann Zenck and Walter Gerstenberg (n.p.: American Institute of Musicology, 1966). For an examination of Zarlino's citation of Willaert's *Avertatur obsecro*, see Michele Fromson, "Zarlino's Modal Analysis of Willaert's 'Avertatur Obsecro'," in *Secondo convegno europeo di analisi musicale: atti*, ed. Rossanna Dalmonte and Mario Baroni (Trent: Dipartimento di storia della civiltà europea, Università degli studi di Trento, 1992), 237–48.

[12] Jessie Ann Owens and Richard Agee, "La Stampa della *Musica nova* di Willaert," *Rivista italiana di musicologia* 24 (1989), 213–305, suggest that some presentation copies of *Musica nova* may actually have been published in 1558 and point to the discrepancy of the dating of Viola's dedication (September 1558) and the apparent date of publication. For an overview of the history of the publication, see Katelijne Schiltz, "De 'Musica Nova' (1558–1559) van Adriaan Willaert: De muzikaal-historische context. Een analyse van de motetten," M.A. thesis, Katholieke Universtiteit Leuven (1996).

[13] Anthony Newcomb, "Editions of Willaert's *Musica nova*: New Evidence, New Speculations," *Journal of the American Musicological Society* 26 (1973), 132–35; Owens and Agee, "La Stampa della *Musica nova* di Willaert."

[14] Owens and Agee, "La Stampa della *Musica nova* di Willaert."

[15] On the printing history of *La eletta*, see Jane Bernstein, *Music Printing in Renaissance Venice: The Scotto Press (1539–1572)* (New York: Oxford University Press, 1998).

the documents testify to Faleti's efforts to have the four madrigals removed from Zantani's work at Gardano's behest. In Zantani's reply to Faleti in December 1558, he protests that so much attention has been paid to the petition of "certain tradesmen like Gardano and Father Gioseffe Zarlino" ("de certi mecanici come è il Gardana, Pre Isepo Zerlin") and that he has been ill-treated, even though his father was a consigliere. He then invokes the supplication of his privilege to make a selection from all the madrigals printed and unprinted.[16] This single mention of Zarlino is important for several reasons. Most obviously, it links him directly to Gardano and the efforts to publish *Musica nova*. But it may also shed light on Zarlino's social status in 1558. Zantani deliberately dismisses him as a tradesman like Gardano; there is no indication that he is an intellectual of any standing. While this might simply be a gesture on Zantani's part toward establishing his claims, this statement may also hint that Zarlino was directly involved in the music productions of Gardano's press.

The final feature of the list of citations in the *Istitutioni* is Zarlino's inclusion of his own works, perhaps the most interesting point from the present perspective. The references are to motets that appeared in the 1549 *Musici quinque vocum* discussed in chapter 7 and to works subsequently published in 1566.

Table 8.4 lists the citations for chapters 18–29 of Part IV (the chapters on the individual modes). The four principal sources I adduced with reference to the Mode 3 and 4 citations contain the bulk of the repertory cited in these chapters: the ancients are supplied by the Grymm and Wyrsung print of 1520, Willaert is represented by *Musica nova* and Zarlino is represented by his two motet prints.

The places of departure from these sources are revealing. First, the chapters on Modes 5 and 6: neither of these chapters invokes the four primary sources and two of the mere three works by Rore cited in the treatise appear here. Of the fifth mode, Zarlino comments that although it was widely found in sacred chant books, it "is not much in use among modern composers," which we might read more literally to mean "not in use by Willaert and Zarlino."[17] The sixth mode, he observes, was frequently used by churchmen, but now he excuses himself by saying: "I remember having *seen* many compositions written in this mode, but at present only the following come to mind."[18] I think that the use of *seen* here is not simply

---

[16] Owens and Agee, "La Stampa della *Musica nova* di Willaert," Document 45.

[17] Meier, "Heinrich Loriti Glareanus als Musiktheoretiker," 105 n.288, points out Zarlino's debt to Glarean in this chapter: Zarlino IV: 22, 325: "Molte cantilene si trovano ne I libri ecclesiastici di questo Modo; ancora che non sia molto in uso appresso li compositori moderni: percioche pare a loro, che sia Modo più duro, et più insoave di qualunque altro." Glarean II: 25, 127: "Porro hic Modus apud veteres Ecclesiasticos in magno fuit usu, ut ex cantibus vetustioribus stais liquet, sed tetricus videtur Modus . . ." More generally on this mode, see Powers, "Music as Text and Text as Music," in *Musik als Text*, ed. Hermann Danuser and Tobias Plebuch (Kassel: Bärenreiter, 1998), and "Monteverdi's Model for a Multimodal Madrigal," in *In cantu et in sermone: For Nino Pirrotta on his 80th Birthday*, ed. Fabrizio della Setta and Franco Piperno (Florence: Olschki, 1989), 193.

[18] Zarlino 1558 IV: 23, 327 "Molte cantilene mi ricordo hauer veduto composte in questo Modo: ma al presente mi soccoreno alla memoria solamente queste; Un motetto di Motone a quattro voci, Ecce Maria genuit nobis Salvatorem, & un Salmo a due chori spezzati di Adriano a otto voci, Inconvertendo Dominus captivitatem Syon."

Table 8.3 *Willaert*, Musica nova *(Gardano, 1559)*

No.	Title	clef	Tonal type[a] sig.	final	1558
1	*Domine, quid multiplicati*	c3-c4-c4-f4	♭	G	
2	*Dilexi, quoniam exaudiet*	c1-c2-c3-c4	—	C	
3	*Confitebor tibi Domine*	c3-c4-c4-f4	—	G	
4	*Recordare Domine*	c4-f4-f3-f5	—	E	
5	*O admirabile commercium*	c2-c3-c4-c4-f4	—	D	
6	*Miserere nostri Deus*	c3-c4-c4-f3-f4	♭	F	
7	*Sub tuum praesidium*	c3-c4-c4-f3-f4	♭	G	
8	*Beati pauperes spiritu*	c1-c3-c4-c4-f4	—	G	
9	*Sustinuimus pacem*	c2-c3-c4-c4-f4	—	G	
10	*Omnia quae fecisti*	c2-c2-c3-c3-f3	♭	A	
11	*Veni sancte spiritus*	g2-c1-c2-c3-c3-f3	♭	G	III: 66; IV: 18
12	*Avertatur obsecro*	c1-c3-c3-c4-c4-f4	♭	G	IV: 19
13	*Alma redemptoris mater*	g2-c1-c2-c3-c3-f3	♭	F	IV: 28
14	*Peccata mea*	g2-c2-c2-c3-c4-f4	♭	A	IV: 21
15	*Salva sancta parens*	c1-c2-c3-c4-c4-f4	♭	G	III: 28
16	*Audite insulae*	c1-c3-c3-c4-c4-f4	—	G	IV: 25
17	*Aspice Domine*	c4-c4-f3-f4-f4-f5	♭♭	C	III: 66; III: 77
18	*Pater, peccavi*	g2-c1-c2-c3-c3-c4	—	G	IV: 24
19	*Victimae paschali laudes*	g2-g2-c2-c3-c3-f3	♭	G	IV: 18
20	*Mittit ad virginem*	c2-c3-c3-c4-c5-f4	♭	F	IV: 29
21	*Haec est domus Domini*	c1-c2-c3-c4-c4-f4	—	E	IV: 20
22	*Huc me sidereo*	g2-c2-c2-c3-c4-f3	♭	A	IV: 20
23	*Praeter rerum seriem*	c1-c2-c3-c3-c3-c4-f4	♭	G	III: 66; IV: 19
24	*Inviolata, integra*	c1-c1-c2-c3-c4-c4-f4	♭	F	IV: 29
25	*Benedicta es coelorum*	c1-c1-c3-c3-c4-c4-f4	—	G	
26	*Verbum supernum*	c1-c2-c3-c4-c4-c4-f4	—	G	III: 66; IV: 25
27	*Te Deum Patrem*	g2-g2-c1-c2-c3-c3-f3	♭	A	III: 20

Notes:

[a] Tonal types are given by Martha Feldman, *City Culture and the Madrigal at Venice*, 225–26. I have arranged the motet and madrigal contents side by side to highlight the correspondences Feldman pointed out between tonal types of the opening and closing works of each section (i.e., works for four and seven voices).

Table 8.3 (*cont.*)

No.	Title	clef	Tonal type[a] sig.	final	1558
28	*Io amai sempre*	c3–c4–c4–f4	♭	G	
29	*Amor, Fortuna*	c1–c2–c3–c4	—	C	
30	*Quest'anima gentil*	c3–c4–c4–f4	—	G	
31	*Lasso, ch'i ardo*	c4–c5–f4–f5	—	E	
32	*O invidia*	c3–c4–c4–f3–f4	♭	D	IV: 30
33	*Più volte già*	c3–c3–c4–c4–f4	—	G	
34	*Quando fra l'altre donne*	c2–c3–c4–f3–f4	♭	F	IV: 29; IV: 32
35	*L'aura mia sacra*	c3–c4–c4–f3–f4	♭	F	IV: 21 [−1573][b]
36	*Mentra che'l cor*	c2–c2–c3–c3–f3	♭	A	
37	*Onde tolse Amor*	c1–c3–c4–c4–f4	—	G	
38	*Giunto m'ha Amor*	g2–c2–c3–c4–f3	♭	G	IV: 18; IV: 32
39	*I begli occhi*	c1–c3–c4–c4–f4	♭	G	
40	*Io mi rivolgo*	c2–c3–c3–c4–f4	—	E	IV: 20
41	*Aspro core*	c2–c3–c3–c4–c4–f4	—	G	III: 46; IV: 32
42	*Passa la nave*	g2–c2–c2–c3–c3–f3	♭	G	
43	*I piansi, hor canto*	g2–c1–c2–c3–c3–c4	—	G	IV: 26
44	*Cantai: hor piango*	c1–c3–c3–c4–c4–f4	—	E	
45	*In qual parte del ciel*	c2–c3–c3–c4–f4–f5	—	E	[+1573][b]
46	*I vidi in terra*	c1–c3–c3–c4–f3–f4	♭	F	IV: 29; IV: 32
47	*Ove ch'i posi gli occhi*	g2–c2–c2–c3–c3–c4	—	D	IV: 19; IV: 32
48	*Pien d'un vago pensier*	g2–c1–c2–c3–c3–f3	♭	F	IV: 28
49	*Quando nascesti, Amor*	c1–c2–c3–c3–c4–c4–f4	♭	F	IV: 29
50	*Liete e pensose*	c1–c1–c3–c3–c4–c4–f4	—	G	IV: 25
51	*Che fai, alma*	c1–c2–c3–c3–c4–f3–f4	♭	G	IV: 19
52	*Occhi piangete*	g2–c1–c2–c3–c3–c4–f3	♭	A	

[b] The only change in citations from *Musica nova* between the 1558 and 1573 editions of *Le institutione harmoniche* is the substitution of *In qual parte del ciel* for *L'aura mia sacra* which appears to have been cited in error.

Table 8.4 Zarlino, *Le istitutioni harmoniche, Book IV: 18–29,*
musical citations and sources (1558 and 1573)[a]

Composer	Title	1558	1573	Source
Mode 1				
Willaert	*Veni sancte spiritus*	IV: 18	IV: 20	Willaert 1559, 11
Willaert	*Victimae paschali laudes*	IV: 18	—	Willaert 1559, 19
Willaert	*Giunto m'ha Amor*	IV: 18	IV: 20	Willaert 1559, 18
Zarlino	*O beatum pontificem*	IV: 18	—	Zarlino 1549, 2
Zarlino	*Hodie Christus natus est*	—	IV: 20	Zarlino 1566, 3
Zarlino	*Victimae paschali laudes*	—	IV: 20	Zarlino 1566, 9
Zarlino	*Salve regina*	—	IV: 20	Zarlino 1566, 12
Zarlino	*Nigra sum*	IV: 18	IV: 20	Zarlino 1549, 6
[Morales	*Sancta et immaculata*]	IV: 18	IV: 20	[1541[4]]
[Jachet	*Spem in alium*]	—	IV: 20	[1539[13]]
Mode 2				
Josquin	*Praeter rerum seriem*	IV: 19	IV: 21	1520[4], 2
Willaert	*Praeter rerum seriem*	IV: 19	IV: 21	Willaert 1559, 23
Willaert	*Che fai alma, che pensi?*	IV: 19	IV: 21	Willaert 1559, 51
Willaert	*Avertatur obsecro Domine*	IV: 19	IV: 21	Willaert 1559, 12
Willaert	*Ove ch'i posi*	IV: 19	IV: 21	Willaert 1559, 47
Zarlino	*Pater noster (a7)*	IV: 19	IV: 21	Zarlino 1549, 19
Zarlino	*Ego rosa Saron*	IV: 19	IV: 21	Zarlino 1549, 16
Zarlino	*Capite nobis vulpes*	IV: 19	IV: 21	Zarlino 1549, 18
Mode 3				
Isaac	*O Maria mater Christi*	IV: 20	IV: 22	1520[4], 21
Willaert	*Te Deum patrem*	IV: 20	IV: 22	Willaert 1559, 27
Willaert	*Huc me sidereo*	IV: 20	IV: 22	Willaert 1559, 22
Willaert	*Haec est domus Domini*	IV: 20	IV: 22	Willaert 1559, 21
Willaert	*Io mi rivolgo*	IV: 20	IV: 22	Willaert 1559, 40
Zarlino	*Ferculum fecit sibi*	IV: 20	IV: 22	Zarlino 1549, 14
Mode 4				
Josquin	*De profundis clamavi*	IV: 21	IV: 23	1520[4], 18
Willaert	*Peccata mea*	IV: 21	IV: 23	Willaert 1559, 14
Willaert	*Rompi de l'empio core*	IV: 21	IV: 23	[1541[16]]
Willaert	*L'aura mia sacra*	IV: 21	—	Willaert 1559, 35
Willaert	*In qual parte del ciel*	—	IV: 23	Willaert 1559, 45
Zarlino	*Miserere mei, Deus*	IV: 21	IV: 23	Zarlino 1566, 6
Zarlino	*Misereris omnium Domine*	—	IV: 23	Zarlino 1566, 10
Zarlino	*Missa [quarti toni]*	IV: 21	IV: 23	?
Mode 5				
Willaert	*Spoliatis aegyptis*	IV: 22	IV: 24	[Willaert 1542a]
Rore	*Di tempo in tempo*	IV: 22	IV: 24	Rore 1550
Rore	*Donna ch'ornata sete*	IV: 22	IV: 24	Rore 1550
Viola	*Fra quanti amor*	IV: 22	IV: 24	[Nuovo Vogel 1010]
Mode 6				
Mouton	*Ecce Maria genuit nobis*	IV: 23	IV: 25	[1514[1]]
Willaert	*In convertendo*	IV: 23	IV: 25	1550[1]
Mode 7				
Willaert	*Pater, peccavi*	IV: 24	IV: 26	Willaert 1559, 18
Willaert	*I piansi, hor canto*	IV: 24	IV: 26	Willaert 1559, 43

Table 8.4 (*cont.*)

	Composer	Title	1558	1573	Source
	Mode 8				
	Josquin	*Benedicta es, celorum regina*	IV: 25	IV: 27	1520^{4}, 6
	Willaert	*Audite insulae*	IV: 25	IV: 27	Willaert 1559, 16
	Willaert	*Verbum supernum*	IV: 25	IV: 27	Willaert 1559, 26
	Willaert	*Liete e pensose*	IV: 25	IV: 27	Willaert 1559, 50
③	chant	*In exitu Israel*	—	IV: 27	
③	chant	*Nos qui vivimus*	—	IV: 27	
③	chant	*Martyres Domini*	—	IV: 27	
	Mode 9				
	chant	*Pater noster*	IV: 26	IV: 28	[Glarean]
	chant	*Credo in Unum Deum* [ex.]	IV: 26	IV: 28	[Glarean]
	chant	*Ave Maria gratia plena* [ex.]	IV: 26	IV: 28	[Glarean]
	La Rue	*Missa Ave Maria*	IV: 26	IV: 28	
	chant	*Gaudeamus omnes in Domino*	IV: 26	IV: 28	
	Josquin	*Missa Gaudeamus*	IV: 26	IV: 28	[Josquin 1502]
	chant	*In exitu Israel*	IV: 26	IV: 28	[Glarean]
	chant	*Nos qui vivimus*	IV: 26	IV: 28	[Glarean]
	Jachet	*Spem in alium*	IV: 26	IV: 28	[Jachet 1539]
	Morales	*Sancta et immaculata*	IV: 26	IV: 28	[1546^{9}]
	Zarlino	*Si bona suscepimus*	IV: 26	IV: 28	Zarlino 1549, 12
	Zarlino	*I'vo piangendo*	IV: 26	IV: 28	[1562^{2}]
④	Mouton	*Missa Benedicam Dominum*	—	IV: 28	
	Mode 10				
	Verdelot	*Gabriel archangelus*	IV: 27	IV: 29	[1539^{12}]
	Willaert	*Flete oculi, rorate genas*	IV: 27	IV: 29	[Willaert 1545]
	Mode 11				
	chant	*Missa de angelis*	IV: 28	IV: 18	
	chant	*Alma redemptoris mater*	IV: 28	IV: 18	
	chant	*Regina coeli laetare*	IV: 28	IV: 18	
	Josquin	*Stabat mater*	IV: 28	IV: 18	1520^{4}, 13
	Willaert	*O salutaris hostia*	IV: 28	IV: 18	Willaert 1542
	Willaert	*Alma redemptoris*	IV: 28	IV: 18	Willaert 1559, 13
	Willaert	*Pien d'un vago pensier*	IV: 28	IV: 18	Willaert 1559, 48
	Jachet	*Descendi in hortum meum*	IV: 28	IV: 18	ModE 314
	Gombert	*Audi filia et vide*	IV: 28	IV: 18	[1541^{3}]
	Zarlino	*Ego veni in hortum*	IV: 28	IV: 18	Zarlino 1549, 8
	Mode 12				
	chant	*Ave regina coelorum*	IV: 29	IV: 19	
	Josquin	*Inviolata, integra et casta es*	IV: 29	IV: 19	1520^{4}, 10
	Willaert	*Inviolata integra*	IV: 29	IV: 19	Willaert 1559, 24
	Willaert	*Mittit ad virginem*	IV: 29	IV: 19	Willaert 1559, 20
	Willaert	*Quando nascesti Amor*	IV: 29	IV: 19	Willaert 1559, 49
	Willaert	*I vidi in terra*	IV: 29	IV: 19	Willaert 1559, 46
	Willaert	*Quando fra l'altre donne*	IV: 29	IV: 19	Willaert 1559, 34
	Jachet	*Decantabat populus*	IV: 29	IV: 19	[1541^{3}]
⑤	Zarlino	*Litigabant Iudaei*	—	IV: 19	Zarlino 1566, 2
⑤	Zarlino	*Nemo venit ad me* [*Nemo potest venire*	IV: 29	—	Zarlino 1549, 3?]
	Zarlino	*O quam gloriosum*	IV: 29	IV: 19	Zarlino 1566, 7

Note:

[a] Numbered boxed areas highlight changes between the 1558 and 1573 editions of the treatises discussed on p. 256.

metaphorical, but also a reflection of the process by which Zarlino collected his examples and a suggestion of the meaning of the labels of his 1549 print. Zarlino's citations are not based solely, or even primarily, on aural recollection of a repertory, but physical and visual collection from a repertory circumscribed here by a remarkably small number of printed sources. Although Feldman expressed surprise that Cipriano de Rore was so infrequently cited by Zarlino, it is only the lack of examples for these modes in Zarlino's core repertory that results in Rore being cited at all.[19] Thanks to Rore, Zarlino is not in Glarean's position of having to commission examples for these modes, and he is perfectly capable of providing his own didactic duo. But neither the ancients at his disposal as represented by the 1520 print, nor Willaert, nor Zarlino in his composer's hat used these modes. That Francesco dalla Viola, editor of Willaert's *Musica nova*, is also represented here points to Willaert's circle as the context of the citations generally.

Modes 9 and 10 also offer a contrast to the prevailing pattern of citation and, again, his reliance on Glarean's rhetoric is greatest here. Zarlino asserts the "ancientness" and long-standing use of the ninth mode, changing his pattern to attest that ancientness by citing a series of chants (and printing partial examples of them).[20] He moves from these chants which he believes (following Glarean without acknowledgment) properly to be Mode 9 (including the Credo and *Ave Maria*) to masses based on those chants, then to two motets cited in the chapter on Mode 1 as being altered to Mode 9 and thence to his own motet and madrigal.[21]

From the *Musica nova* citations as well as from the self-references to his *Musici quinque vocum*, one can see that Zarlino actually documents almost exclusively an eight-mode system, although not the usual one: Modes 1–4, 7–8, and 11–12. This suggests a striking cognitive dissonance between his promulgation of twelve-mode theory and his documentation of that theory through citations from prints that appear to represent only eight modes.[22] Indeed, Zarlino's citation style differs little from that of his predecessor Pietro Aron. Zarlino relies on even fewer sources and a more circumscribed repertory. But unlike Aron, Zarlino's citations must function within the Bembist framework of the treatise and its realization via Willaert as

[19] Martha Feldman, *City Culture and the Madrigal at Venice* (Berkeley: University of California Press, 1995). One cannot help but wonder, too, if Rore's exclusion was deliberate. If Zarlino was, as I suggested, using these prints to establish himself as Willaert's successor, he is hardly likely to feature the student of Willaert who had already established a far greater compositional reputation. On these madrigals, see Powers, "Monteverdi's Model."

[20] Of the chants Zarlino cites (and prints), the *Pater noster*, *Credo*, *Ave Maria*, *Nos qui vivimus*, and *In exitu Israel* are all taken from Glarean, II, 104. Glarean does not cite *Gaudeamus omnes* although he does cite the Benedictus from the *Missa Gaudeamus*. On Zarlino's use of Glarean's rhetoric in this chapter, see Meier, "Heinrich Loriti Glareanus als Musiktheoretiker," 105.

[21] Although he does not include his own *Si bona suscepimus* among the list of works whose modes are transformed from the first to the ninth, this may well be how he understood the motet in the context of his 1549 motet collection.

[22] Zarlino's *Song of Songs* cycle discussed in the previous chapter is a case in point. Conceived as an eight-mode cycle, Modes 5 and 6 are replaced by Modes 11 and 12, but the role of Modes 9 and 10 is less clear. As suggested above, his single Mode 9 motet, *Si bona suscepimus*, would have fallen under the traditional heading of Mode 1.

model. The authorities to whom Zarlino points and his relationship to them is clear both by the order and nature of the citations: Josquin, the ancient master (but Josquin as materially represented in the Grimm and Wyrsung anthology of 1520), Willaert, the modern master, and Zarlino. It is the "and Zarlino" that adds the interesting quirk to this case. By and large, Aron's citations were to well-known prints to which he might well have expected his readers to have access. Glarean eliminates the necessity of such common sources by reprinting examples as necessitated by the Erasmian intellectual framework of the *Dodecachordon*. Zarlino's citations are much more problematic in this sense. Long experience with Josquin sources led me to recognize the relevance of the Grymm and Wyrsung anthology to Zarlino's citations, a connection that seems hardly likely on the part of mid-century Venetian readers. The "ancient" works he cites from this collection were for the most part available individually in other sources. Yet the indications of Zarlino's own use of sources would seem to suggest that it is highly unlikely that a reader of the *Istitutioni* would either own or have access to – or, more to the point, attempt to collect – these works from a large number of printed sources. For the *cognoscenti* – readers perhaps like members of the Accademia Veneziana – the *Musica nova* citations would be obvious, the Zarlino citations possibly less so, the Grimm and Wyrsung, not at all.

That Zarlino would tie the *Istitutioni* so closely not just to Willaert, but specifically to *Musica nova* merits comment. *Musica nova* was an extraordinary and enigmatic print on every account: in its content, format, and publication history. There is nothing comparable among mid-century Venetian music prints from either Scotto's or Gardano's presses. By the time of its publication, the collection had been in circulation for a decade or more; the sense in which it remained "new" in 1559 is uncertain.[23]

Zarlino's heavy reliance on the collection may suggest that it served – for at least one community of its readers – primarily as material for study. At least it seemed to have furnished such an object for Zarlino. It certainly seems hardly coincidental that the two books of compositions (by composers other than himself) on which Zarlino relied most heavily were luxurious publications which may have recommended them as books for study. Partbooks offered convenience in size and expense for publishers and performers alike. There is no doubt that multiple partbooks could be, and were, "read" and used by individuals.[24] Choirbooks like *Liber selectarum cantionum* offered the significant advantage for Zarlino's purposes of coordination of page turns, not to mention the more general convenience of having to handle only one book instead of four or more. The large fonts employed in both 1520[4] and *Musica nova* necessitated frequent page turns which might also assist in the mental coordination of spatially separated parts.

---

[23] On the reception of *Musica nova*, see Mary Lewis, *Antonio Gardano, Venetian Music Printer, 1538–1569: A Descriptive Bibliography and Historical Study* (New York: Garland, 1988), II.

[24] This seems to have been especially true of keyboard players. See Robert Judd, "The Use of Notational Formats at the Keyboard," D.Phil. diss., Oxford University (1989).

There is only one point in the treatise at which Zarlino directly mentions a printed source. In his advice on composing for more than three voices, he says:

Especially because many other compositions are issued daily, composed by the most excellent Adriano which, in addition to being full of a thousand beautiful and graceful inventions, are eruditely and elegantly composed. There are innumerable others composed by other very excellent musicians, many of which can be found in an octavo booklet printed by Andrea Antico in Venice. Studying those can be of much help in devising similar effects, and with their light anyone can undertake larger and more difficult compositions creditably.[25]

Strikingly, this single print to which overt reference is made is not one of what I have cast as Zarlino's "main" sources, but probably Antico's *Motetti novi*, the source for only two citations in this treatise. The title of this volume, too, contains indications of its "newness," although it is a much less presupposing print than those to which Zarlino indirectly refers. It may be that Zarlino chose to highlight this print because it contained Willaert's first published works.

Feldman's recent assessment of *Le istitutioni harmoniche* asserts that:

Zarlino included no quotations of the repertory that he cited, so it seems he expected students either to know it or, if not, to learn it.[26]

The implication – that the cited works would have been essential for a "complete" understanding of the theory – is an interpretation that is open to question, however. How were readers of the book, outside Zarlino's immediate circle, to learn from Zarlino's self-citation of works that were not published until 1566?

MODULATIONES SEX VOCUM (1566)

Table 8.5 outlines that publication, Zarlino's *Modulationes sex vocum*,[27] the next trace in the narrative of Zarlino's assimilation of modal theory. Six motets that eventually appeared in this collection were cited in the 1558 edition of the *Istitutioni*. Unlike Zarlino's earlier motet print, there are no modal indications in 1566, works are not ordered by tonal type, and in over half the works, the tenor does not conclude on the modal final. In other words there are no overt clues about mode, although the number and nature of canonic inscriptions and resolutions would align the print

---

[25] "Massimamente perche ogni giorno si veggono molte altre compositioni, composte dallo Eccellentissimo Adriano Vuillaert, lequali, oltra che sono piene di mille belle, & leggiadri inventioni; sono anche dottamente, & elegantemente composte. Infinite altre etiandio ve ne sono, composte da altri Eccellentissimi Musici; delle quali molte se ne ritrovano in un libretto, ilquale gia fù stampato in Vinegia da Andrea antico in ottavo foglio; lequali vedute, potranno esser di grande aiuto per ritrouare altre simili inventioni: percioche da quelle, si havera un tal lume, che ciascuno dipoi si potrà porre a maggiori, & a più difficili imprese, & honoreuoli" (Zarlino 1558 III: 66, 266; trans. Guy Marco, *The Art of Counterpoint* (New Haven: Yale Univesity Press, 1983), 240–41. I have slightly modified Marco's translation.   [26] Feldman, *City Culture*.

[27] Iosephi Zarlini Clodiensis musici celeberrimi, atque illustriss. et excellentiss. Dominii Venet. musices D. Marci moderatoris *Modulationes sex vocum*, per Philippum Iusbertum musicum Venetum collectae, ac per eundem nunc primum in publicum datae. Cum privilegio. (Venice: Rampazetto, 1566). Referred to hereafter by short title as *Modulationes* or with the siglum Z1566.

with a "learned" tradition. These canonic inscriptions harken back to Part III of the *Istitutioni*, the counterpoint book, where polyphonic citations occur with much less regularity in the counterpoint section of the treatise than in the section on mode. They are found primarily in two places: chapters 28 and 66 (see Table 7.2, pp. 202–05). Chapter 66 provides a compendium of contrapuntal practice that supplements the didactic examples printed within the text (see Table 8.6).

Canonic instructions that accompany the contents of the 1566 print are listed in Table 8.5. The prominence of such procedures connects the works directly to the compendium of chapter 66, leaving the strong impression that Zarlino might have composed those works while he was actively engaged in the writing of Part III of the *Istitutioni*. The actual publication of the motet print, however, appears yet again to have been motivated by career issues. Fully understanding the publication requires a momentary step outside the printed traces to events between the reissue of the *Istitutioni* in 1562 and the publication of the *Modulationes* in 1566.

In chapter 7 I argued that circumstantial evidence suggested that the publication of the *Istitutioni* might be tied to Zarlino's attempts to establish himself as Willaert's successor at San Marco. That he was "on the market" in this period is confirmed by documentation of his failed attempt to secure an appointment as *maestro di cappella* at Padua Cathedral in 1560. I am unaware of any records of the deliberations regarding the search for Willaert's successor at San Marco, but after a hiatus, Cipriano de Rore – undoubtedly the most renowned composer to have been associated with Willaert in the Veneto and beyond – was hired. The appointment proved troublesome from the beginning. Shortly before Willaert's death the procurators had significantly reorganized the cappella in a move that signaled a far greater degree of involvement on the part of the administration than for the entirety of Willaert's lengthy tenure.[28] The combination of this problematic new arrangement and Rore's temperamental personality proved unworkable and he vacated the post in 1564.[29] The two years of his tenure marked a period of extraordinary instability for the cappella.

Zarlino's appointment followed Rore's departure. In choosing Zarlino, the foremost concerns for the procurators appear to have been the restoration of the stability of the choir. The structure reverted to that of Willaert's tenure and the procurators praised Zarlino's administrative abilities and great learning:

Wishing to hire a *maestro* for the chapel of St. Mark's who should be not only learned and experienced in the art of music, but, as the one who must be above the other musicians, also prudent and modest in performing his duties, having had excellent reports on the modesty and ability of messer pre Iseppo Zarlino, and having conferred about this matter with His Serenity, [Their Lordships] have appointed him *maestro* of the said chapel.[30]

---

[28] This reorganization is described in detail in Ongaro, "The Chapel of St. Mark's at the Time of Adrian Willaert (1527–1562): A Documentary Study," Ph.D. dissertation, University of North Carolina at Chapel Hill (1986).

[29] See Owens, "Cipriano de Rore a Parma (1560–1565): nuovi documenti," *Rivista italiana di musicologia* 11 (1976), 5–26.   [30] Cited and translated in Ongaro, "Chapel of St. Mark's," 230–31.

Table 8.5 Zarlino, *Modulationes sex vocum* (Rampazetto, 1566)

No.	Title	Text	clef	sig.[b]	final	1558	1573	Canon
			Tonal type[a]					
1	*Ascendo ad patrem meum*	Responsory (John 20: 17)	g2-c2-c2-c3-c3-f3	—	G (d)	—	—	Quintus: Canon. Incipe in Unisono; post pausas deinde gradatim Voce una ascendas, id quatuorq[ue]; vices. [Sextus: Resolutio]
2	*Litigabant Iudaei ad in vicem*	John 6: 53–8	c1-c2-c2-c3-c4-f4	♭/–	F (c)	III: 66	III: 66; IV: 19	Quintus: Fuga quinque temporum in Diapente intensum. [Sextus: Resolutio.]
3	*Hodie Christus natus est*	Antiphon	g2-c2-c2-c3-c4-f3	♭/–	G	—	IV: 20	Tenor: Canon suo funcatur quisque officio. [Altus: Resolutio.]
4	*Exaudi Deus orationem meam*	Psalm 63	c1-c3-c3-c4-c4-f4	–/–	D	—	—	Sextus: Canon. Prima locum servat, thesin altera sentit & arsin: Octavam duo post tempora tertia habet.
5	*Virgo prudentissima*	Antiphon	c1-c2-c3-c3-c4-f4	♭/–	D	III: 28	III: 28	
6	*Miserere mei Deus*	Psalm / Antiphon	c2-c4-c4-f4-f4-f5	—	E	III: 66; IV: 21	III: 66; IV: 23	Tenor: Canon. Non quod tres cantent: sed ter renovetur hic ordo, Signa docent, quatuor prior incipe tempora linquens, Scande sed ad Quartam, dein bis canta in Diapente. [Sextus: Resolutio.]
7	*O quam gloriosam*	Antiphon	c1-c3-c4-f3-f3-f4	♭	F (c)	IV: 29	IV: 19	Sextus: Fuga quatuor temporum ad Diapente remissum. [Quintus: Resolutio.]
8	*In principio Deus*		c1-c3-c3-c3-c4-f4	–/♯	G (d)	III: 66	III: 66	Quintus: Alternis dicetis, amant alterna Camoenae. [Altus: Resolutio.]
9	*Victimae paschali* (Revised, first published in 1549)	Sequence	g2-g2-c2-c3-f3	♭	G (♭♭)	—	IV: 20	Sextus: Fuga quinque temporum ad Diapason remissum. Secunda pars: Fuga sex temporum ad Diapason remissum. [Quintus: Resolutio ex cantu.]

10	*Misereris omnium Domine*	Introit	c2–c3–c3–f3–f4–f5	—	E	—	IV: 23	Tenor: Canon. Clavibus ingreditor, caetera cuncta patent. Quintus: Qui canis haec, iteranda scias tibi saepius esse: Semper & in reditu, tempus te deserat unum. Ad Quartam in primo reditu descendere deges: Ad Quintam veniens terum, cane voce sub illa. Deinde ascendendum toties erit ordine eodem. [Altus: Resolutio.]
11	*Sebastianus Dei cultor*	Antiphon	c1–c3–c3–c4–f4	—	D (a)	—	—	Quintus: Regula. Consequens canitur in Diapente intenso, post tria tempora: ut patat. [Altus: Resolutio.]
12	*Salve regina misericordiae*	Antiphon	c1–c1–c3–c4–f3–f4	—	D	III: 66	III: 66; IV: 20	Tenor: Fuga in Diapason intensum post sex tempora. [*Secunda pars*: Resolutio secundae partis ex Cantu.] [*Tertia pars*: Resolutio tertiae partis ex Cantu.] Sextus: [*Prima pars*: Resolutio ex Tenore.] *Secunda pars*: Fuga trium temporum in Diapason remissum. *Tertia pars*: Fuga in Diapason remissum post quatuor tempora.
13	*Pater noster* (a7) (Revised, first published in 1549)	Preces / Antiphon	c1–c3–c3–c4–c4–f4	♭	G (d)	(see 1549, 19)	—	Quintus: Fuga duplex. Trium temporum in Diapente: Et sex temporum in Diatessaron. *Secunda pars*: Fuga duplex. videlicet, Trium temporum in Diatessaron remissum: Et sex temporum ad Tonum intensum. [Sextus: Resolutio.] [Septime: Resolutio.]

Notes:

a Indications for tonal type follow Powers, "Tonal Types." Concluding pitch is the lowest note of final sonority; concluding pitch of the tenor is indicated parenthetically when not the final.

b When two signatures are given the first is prevailing, the second necessitated by the *resolutio* of a canon, usually in a single voice.

Table 8.6 Zarlino, *Le istitutioni harmoniche, Counterpoint compendium (1558 III: 66)*

Cantus firmus in tenor

Willaert	*Nil postquam sacrum*	[lost?]
Willaert	*Victor io salve*	[Willaert 1539]
Willaert	*Inclite sfortiadum*	[Willaert 1529]

Cantus firmus in tenor; two or three voices in consequence

Willaert	*Verbum supernum*	Willaert 1559, 26
Willaert	*Praeter rerum seriem*	Willaert 1559, 23
Jachet	*Descendi in ortum meum*	[1539³]
Zarlino	*Miserere mei Deus*	Zarlino 1566, 6
Zarlino	*Pater noster/Ave Maria*	Zarlino 1549, 19 [Zarlino 1566, 13]

Consequent stops short of guide

| Willaert | *Veni sancte spiritus* | Willaert 1559, 11 |
| Zarlino | *O beatum pontificem* | Zarlino 1549, 2 |

Repetition

| Zarlino | *Salve regina* | Zarlino, 1566, 12 |
| Zarlino | *Litigabant Iudaei* | Zarlino, 1566, 2 |

Strict fugue of two or more voices

| Jachet | *Murus tuus* | [1539³] |
| Willaert | *Salve sancta parens* | Willaert 1559, 15 |

Inverted repetition

| Willaert | *Venator lepores* | [1542¹⁰] |
| Zarlino | *In principio Deus antequam* | Zarlino 1566, 8 |

Multiple cantus firmi

| Josquin | *Alma redemptoris mater/Ave regina coelorum/Inviolata integra et casta/Regina coeli* | ? |
| Gombert | *Salve regina/Alma redemptoris/Inviolata/Ave regina* | [Gombert 1541] |

Combines two clefs

| C. Festa | *Exaltabo te Domines* | ? |

Two parts in consequence without cantus firmus

| Zarlino | *Ecce tu pulchra es* | Zarlino 1549, 7 |

Voices in pairs; each in imitation

Mouton	*Nesciens mater*	[1521⁷; Glarean]
Gombert	*Inviolata integra et casta*	[Gombert 1539]
Willaert	*Salve sancta parens*	Willaert 1559, 15
Willaert	*Sur l'hesrbe brunette*	?

Parts in consequence, in imitation

| Willaert | *Sancta et immaculata* | [1520³] |
| | *Petite camusete* | [1520³] |

Four voices from one

| La Rue | *Missa O salutaris hostia* | [1516¹] |
| Willaert | *Missa Mente tota* | ? |

Table 8.6 (*cont.*)

Masses by the ancients on cantus firmi		
Josquin	*Missa La sol fa re mi*	[Josquin 1502; 1539¹]
Josquin	*Missa Hercules dux Ferrariae*	[Josquin 1502]
Josquin	*Missa Pange lingua*	[1539²]
Josquin	*Missa Gaudeamus*	[Josquin 1502; 1539¹]
Josquin	*Missa Ave maris stella*	[1539²]
Brumel	Requiem	[1516¹]
With or without rests in any prolation		
Moulu	*Missa Duorum facierum*	[1539¹]
Ockeghem	*Missa Prolationum*	[Glarean]
Chori spezzati		
Willaert	*Confitebor tibi Domine*	Willaert 1550¹
Willaert	*Laudate pueri Dominum*	Willaert 1550¹
Willaert	*Lauda Ierusalem Dominum*	Willaert 1550¹
Willaert	*De profundis*	Willaert 1550¹
Willaert	*Memento Domine David*	Willaert 1550¹ [1573 ed. adds six more psalms, all from Willaert 1555; see Table 7.2]
Three choirs		
Zarlino	*Magnificat* (three choirs)	?

Yet if those attributes recommended Zarlino to the procurators after Rore's fiery tenure, the expectation remained that one of the primary functions of the *maestro di cappella* was to compose for the choir of San Marco.[31]

It is in this context that Zarlino's motet volume of March 1566 appeared, less than a year after his appointment at San Marco. Philippo Zusberti, a choir member at San Marco, overtly connects this motet print and the *Istitutioni*, midway through the dedication of the volume. The print is much more modest in its intellectual claims, and its work-a-day nature corresponds to the duties of a *maestro di cappella*, much of which were as singing master, dealing with the integration of chant and polyphony:

Clariss[imis] D[ominis] Divi Marci Procur[atoribus] de supra nuncupatis.
Foelicitatem perpetuam.
Cum pulcherrimas quasdam musicas compositiones, Clarissimi ac Nobilissimi Senatores, A Iosepho Zarlino Clodiensi Musico Celeberrimo olim aeditas, sparsim collegissem, facturus opera praetium arbitratus sum, si eas in publicum darem. Nam autor ipse, ut est ab omni

---

[31] In disputes between singers and *procuratia* in 1589 and 1600 over the singing of the psalm *Confitebor angelorum*, the singers argued that if this psalm were to have been sung by the double choir, either Willaert, Rore, or Zarlino would have set it and none of them had. An outline of this event is recorded in Ongaro, "Chapel of St. Mark's," 90–91. A fuller description appears in James H. Moore, *Vespers at St. Mark's: Music of Alessandro Grandi, Giovanni Rovetta and Francesco Cavalli* (Ann Arbor: UMI Research Press, 1981), 133–35.

ambitione longe alienus, tantum abest, ut eas aliquando foras emitteret, ut periculum sit, ne mihi, hoc succenseat, quod fecerim. Sed utcunque erit, iuvabit tamen, et musicis omnibus, et in primis honori praeceptoris mei, pro viribus meis, consuluisse. Quippe qui ab eo, iam olim musicas artes ita edoctus sum, ut nunquam futurum est, ut me poeniteat: adde etiam quod (adeo est humanus et pius) ut hanc mihi offensam facile sit remissurus, praesertim cum noverit, me non, nisi pietatis causa, id fecisse. At neque hoc temere factum videre videor, nam post illum librum cui titulum indidit de Institutionibus Harmonicis, in quo de musica disciplina ita docte pariter et diserte disputare videtur, ut nemo hactenus (quod pace omnium dictum esto) rem ipsam dilucidius, et copiosius tractaverit, quis est qui hunc alterum modulationum librum, non desideret? idq; eo maxime, quod plurimum de iis in superiore libro illo meminerit? Huc accedit illud, quo intelligant omnes, eiusdem artificis esse, et de Theoricis musicae docte disserere, et modulationes quasque suavissimas efficere posse. Sed exiliet malevolorum turba, et (ut verius loquar) perniciosa pestis, quae quidem nunquam non promptu habet, ut de aliorum dignitate nihil non detrahat, quare ad vos con-fugiendum putavi Senatores optimi, ut cui hanc provinciam, non nisi Dei nutu, delegastis, ut musicis omnibus in Choro D. Marci praesit, eundem simul mecum ab eorum venenosis morsibus summa vestra autoritate vindicetis. Nam vobis patrocinatibus nihil est, quod huiusmodi sycophantarum latratibus terreamur. Porro autem nequis existimet plus me de aliis, quam de meipso laborare, propediem modulationes quasdam meas, quales quales erunt, in lucem dabimus, quae quidem, vestro quodam iure, vobis debentur, utpote quibus et meipsum, et mea omnia, ut ante hac, nunc etiam dedo, dicoq. Quem et patrocinio ut adiuvetis, et autoritate ut servetis, et rogo vos, et fore confid. Deus Opt. Max. ad vestram, ac Reip. utilitatem diu servet incolumes. Valete.

Venetijs Idib.Martij. MDLXVI.

Humilis seruus. Philippus Iusbertus musicus in Choro D. Marci.

To my most brilliant lord procurators of Saint Mark's concerning those matters broached above. [May you have] felicity everlasting.

Having collected from various places certain extremely beautiful musical compositions, Most Brilliant and Most Noble Senators, composed once upon a time by the Most Famous musician Gioseffo Zarlino of Chioggia, I thought it would be worth while to make them public. For the author himself, being an utter stranger to any form of ambition, was so far from ever letting them get out that there is danger he may become angry with me for doing so. But however that may be, it will nevertheless be beneficial to take thought, to the best of my ability, both for all musicians and especially for the reputation of my mentor; because long ago now he so taught me the arts of music as it will never come to pass that I could feel regret; besides which, so humane and pious is he that he will easily forgive me this offense, especially since he knows that I should not have done it except by reason of piety. But neither do I regard this as a rash deed, for after that distinguished book to which he gave the title *On the Institutes of Harmony* in which he seems to discourse on the discipline of music with such learning and eloquence that no one yet (and let this be said with the indulgence of all) has treated this particular subject more clearly or fully, who is there that would not long for the second book of compositions? And all the more so, because he very frequently makes mention of these matters in the earlier book? Another motive is that all should understand that this same artist is able to discourse learnedly on the theoretical aspects of music and to produce the most lovely of all composi-tions. But away with the rabble of backbiters and (to speak more truthfully) that pernicious pestilence that is never slow to detract from the fame of others; wherefore I thought it best to take refuge with you, excellent Senators, so that you might, by your unsurpassed authority, together with me protect from the venomous carping of these people the same man to whom you, not without God's will, assigned such an office as the leadership of all the musicians in the Choir of Saint Mark's. For with you as our patrons we shall have no fear of such barking syco-phants. And furthermore, lest anyone think that I am doing more on others' behalf than on my own, I shall very shortly publish certain compositions of my own, such as they are, which are to be presented to you as by your right, you to whom just as before I now dedicate and commit both myself and all my possessions. That you will aid me by your patronage and protect me by your authority I ask you and trust that it will be so. May God Almighty keep and protect you for your own good and that of the Republic. Farewell.

Venice, March 1566.

Your humble servant, Philippo Zusberti, musician of the choir of San Marco.

Zusberti had been hired as a singer at San Marco in 1562. Between 1557 and 1562, some nine singers had been hired as part of the reorganization of the chapel and Zusberti was among these.[32] The dedication deliberately and formulaically dis-tances the print from Zarlino,[33] but it is not hard to see Zarlino's hand in this extraordinary document. The specific occasion alluded to by the dedication's refer-ence to "backbiters" and their "venomous carping" is unknown; it may be no more than a literary flourish. But given the appearance of this print so shortly after Zarlino's appointment and its apparent preparation by one of the more recently hired singers of the choir, it seems entirely possible that he was being compared unfavorably to his predecessors. The very learnedness which seems ultimately to have garnered the appointment may have been a liability in his fulfillment of his day-to-day duties at San Marco, especially for the provision of music. By compari-son to his 1549 print, this is a smaller collection – only thirteen motets for six voices, two of which had already been printed in earlier versions in 1549.[34] The volume also lacks any of the hallmarks of "luxurious" printing that are associated with Zarlino's other publications. Published not by Gardano, but by Rampazetto (who had worked with Scotto in 1555–56),[35] the print is a work-a-day set of part-books, distinguished only by the canonic inscriptions and the title. Its close connec-tion with Part III of the *Istitutioni* is confirmed by the distribution of citations. Of the ten occasions on which six of the works appearing in this collection are cited in the *Istitutioni* in 1558, two are in Part III, chapter 28, five are found in Part III, chapter 66, and three are scattered across Part IV.[36] Thus, at the very most, only five of the motets in this collection post-date 1558: No. 1 *Ascendo ad patrem*; No. 3 *Hodie Christus natus est*; No. 4 *Exaudi Deus*; No. 10 *Misereris omnium Domine*; and No. 11 *Sebastianus Dei cultor*. Unlike the earlier motet collection, these are mostly "functional" liturgical items: antiphons, a sequence, an introit, a responsory, and a

---

[32] Ongaro, "Chapel of St. Mark's."

[33] "For the author himself, being an utter stranger to any form of ambition, was so far from ever letting them get out that there is danger he may become angry with me for doing so."

[34] The *Modulationes* concludes with a revised version of the seven-voice *Pater Noster–Ave Maria* that ended the earlier print and also includes a revised version of the sequence *Victimae paschali laudes* which had appeared in another print of 1549.   [35] Bernstein, *Scotto*.

[36] That balance changes subtly in the 1573 revision of the treatise discussed below.

psalm. Almost all were appropriate for the liturgy at San Marco, although it appears that few were likely to have been composed specifically for that venue or in the period between Zarlino's appointment and the publication of the collection. But here again the dedication sheds light. By dedicating this print full of motets appropriate for use at San Marco to the procurators, Zarlino (via Zusberti, a member of the choir) would seem to be using the publication as the most effective way of answering and silencing the unnamed critics who have questioned his capabilities, all the while reaffirming his relationship with his employers. The dedication does not distance the motets from the *Istitutioni*, but overtly connects them to it – reinforcing yet again the printed persona of Zarlino as both theorist and composer. If it was his learning and status among Venetian intellectuals that secured the appointment, it was his ability as a composer which was most at question in the early years following the tenure of such esteemed composers as Willaert and Rore.[37]

In the same period, a number of Zarlino's madrigals appeared in anthologies edited by Bonagiunta for Scotto. Like Zusberti, Bonagiunta was one of the more recently recruited singers to San Marco. This suggests that whatever difficulties Zarlino encountered may also have been a reflection of a division between the senior choristers and more recent additions to the choir.[38] Whatever the exact nature of the difficulties upon Zarlino's appointment, it seems ineluctable that the publication of motets and madrigals in 1566–67 via two members of the choir of San Marco will have been, at least in part, involved in a deliberate public relations campaign. Zarlino's own voice is only thinly veiled in Zusberti's dedication of the *Modulationes*. While a direct response to Zarlino's critics (in print or otherwise) would be beneath the dignity of the *maestro di cappella* of San Marco, it is beyond doubt that Zusberti published this collection with Zarlino's imprimatur. In its overt references to the *Istitutioni*, it fits a pattern established from Zarlino's first publication, the *Musici quinque vocum* (1549), of a constantly forefronted intertextuality of compositional and theoretical initiatives.

CHANGES IN CITATIONS IN THE 1573 REVISION OF *LE ISTITUTIONI HARMONICHE*

By the 1570s, Zarlino's publications shifted in favor of theoretical works. His last published composition, the madrigal *Si ch'ove prim'*, appeared in Scotto's 1570 *Raccolta di Cornelio Antonelli. I dolci frutti, primo libro de vaghi ed dilettevoli Madrigali de diversi Eccellentissimi Autori a cinque voci*. His next major theoretical work, *Le dimostrationi harmoniche*, appeared in 1571[39] and an extensive revision of the *Istitutioni*

---

[37] During Zarlino's tenure, perhaps in response to the unsatisfactory situation with Rore, the *maestro* became more of an administrator, while composition was placed more and more in the hands of organists, such as Buus, Merulo, and Annibale Padavano.

[38] Zarlino also appears to have had a connection with Daniele Grisonio, another of the recent appointees. See chapter 7, note 19.

[39] For the most recent detailed study of the *Dimostrationi* see John Emil Kelleher, "Zarlino's 'Dimostrationi Harmoniche' and Demonstrative Methodologies in the Sixteenth Century," Ph.D. dissertation, Columbia

appeared in 1573. Although I will not consider the *Dimostrationi* in any detail here, I must mention Zarlino's famous reordering of the modes in this treatise.[40] This reordering is responsible for the substantive changes in musical citations that occur between the 1558 and 1573 editions of the *Istitutioni*. Figure 8.2 highlights the reordering of the modes by reproducing Zarlino's tabular summaries from the *Dimostrationi*. Zarlino's rationale for renumbering the modes is not my primary concern here, but, briefly, the reordering he proposed correlates the order of hexachordal syllables and modal finals while establishing the superiority of harmonic division over arithmetic. Thus the modes are now ordered from C to a, with no gap in finals, and the "Ionian" mode becomes Mode 1, thoroughly distancing Zarlino's twelve modes from those of Glarean.

Table 8.7 again lists Zarlino's citations for Modes 3 and 4 (now Modes 5 and 6 in the new numbering) in the *Istitutioni* and adds the citations as they appear in the 1573 edition. A brief glance at the comparable pages (reproduced as Fig. 8.3) will highlight the general changes between the two editions in Part IV of the treatise. Most is usually made of the renumbering of the modes following the *Dimostrationi*. Thus old-style Modes 3 and 4 become new-style Modes 5 and 6. But equally significant, the 1573 edition is both more elegant and spacious in its layout: what had occupied roughly a page in the first edition now nearly fills two. The music examples are spaciously set with descriptive captions and citations are called out in the text. The text and citations for Mode 3 are unchanged between the two editions. For Mode 4, Zarlino corrects an erroneous citation, replacing Willaert's *L'aura mia sacra* with another madrigal from *Musica nova* that fits the modal category: *In qual parte*.[41] Apart from correcting such errors, the other change to the citations is the addition of more works. In many cases, as typified by the citations for Mode 4 (as seen in Table 8.7), the addition is a motet from Zarlino's 1566 print – an apparent "updating." Although the logical assumption might be that the citations to additional works from this print in the later edition mark works composed after the 1558 edition of the *Istitutioni*, a closer examination suggests a more tangled picture. In Table 8.5 (pp. 244–45) the citations from the two editions are listed. In 1558, there are seven citations which refer to works in this print; in 1573 there are twelve. But of the new citations, only three are actually to works that had not been cited elsewhere in the 1558 edition, and one of these, *Victimae paschali laudes*, had been published in 1549, long before the 1566 print. In all cases, moreover, such changes occur in Part IV of the treatise. Although the effect might seem to be an updating through the more frequent gestures to works in the 1566 print, at most two of the works cited (No. 3 *Hodie Christus natus est* and No. 10 *Misereris omnium Domine*) post-date 1558.

University (1993; UMI 9333801). The case that I have made for Zarlino's self-fashioning could be extended even further in the *Dimostrationi*, both in the ways that Zarlino manipulates the dialog format and also in the subsequent revisions to the treatise.

40   For a detailed discussion of the reordering, see Richard Crocker, "Perchè Zarlino diede una nuova numerazione ai modi?" *Rivista italiana di musicologia* 3 (1968), 49–58. In an error in Figure 8.2, Zarlino omits the final (G) of the ninth mode in his diagram of the new modes in the *Dimostrationi*.

41   The misreading is discussed in Wiering, "The Language of the Modes."

MODI PRINCIPALI ET AVTENTICI.

CH DE	C	D	E	F	G	a	♮	c	d	e	f	g	aa
Primo.	C	D	E	F	G	a	♮	c					
Terzo.		D	E	F	G	a	♮	c	d				
Quito.			E	F	G	a	♮	c	d	e			
Settimo.				F	G	a	♮	c	d	e	f		
Nono.						a	♮	c	d	e	f	g	
Vndecimo.						a	♮	c	d	e	f	g	aa

(interval labels between columns: Tuono, Tuono, Semituono maggiore, Tuono, Tuono, Tuono, Semituono maggiore, Tuono, Tuono, Semituono maggiore, Tuono, Tuono)

MODI NONPRINCIPALI, O PLAGALI.

CHORDE	Γ	A	♮	C	D	E	F	G	a	♮	c	d	e
Secōdo.	Γ	A	♮	C	D	E	F	G					
Quarto.		A	♮	C	D	E	F	G	a				
Sesto.			♮	C	D	E	F	G	a	♮			
Ottauo.				C	D	E	F	G	a	♮	c		
Decimo.					D	E	F	G	a	♮	c	d	
Duodecimo.						E	F	G	a	♮	c	d	e

(interval labels between columns: Tuono, Tuono, Semituono maggiore, Tuono, Tuono, Semituono maggiore, Tuono, Tuono, Tuono, Semituono maggiore, Tuono, Tuono)

8.2 Zarlino, *Dimostrationi harmoniche* (1571), renumbered modes

Table 8.7 Zarlino, *Le istitutioni harmoniche*, Citations for Modes 3 and 4 (1558 compared with 1573)

	1558, IV: 20	=	(Source)[a]	=	1573, IV: 22	
	Mode 3				**Mode 5**	
Isac	*O Maria mater Christi*		1520⁴, 21		*O Maria mater Christi*	Izac
Adriano	*Te Deum patrem*		Willaert 1559, 27		*Te Deum patrem*	Adriano
	Huc me sydereo		Willaert 1559, 22		*Huc me sydereo*	
	Haec est domus domini		Willaert 1559, 21		*Haec est domus domini*	
	I mi rivolgo indietro		Willaert 1559, 40		*I mi rivolgo indietro*	
Zarlino	*Ferculum fecit rex Salomon*		Zarlino 1549, 14		*Ferculum fecit sibi rex Salomon*	Zarlino

	1558, IV: 21	=		=	1573, IV: 23	
	Mode 4				**Mode 6**	
Josquino	*De profundis clamavi ad te Domine*		1520⁴, 18		*De profundis clamavi ad te Domine*	Giosquino
Adriano	*Peccata mea Domine*		Willaert 1559, 14		*Peccata mea Domine*	Adriano
	Rompi dell'empio cor' il duro scoglio		[1541¹⁶]		*Rompi dell'empio cor' il duro scoglio*	
	L'aura mia sacra		Willaert 1559, 35		—	
	—		Willaert 1559, 45		*In qual parte del ciel*	
Zarlino	*Miserere mei, Deus miserere mei*		1566, 6		*Miserere mei, Deus miserere mei*	Zarlino
	—		1566, 10		*Misereris omnium Domine*	
	une Messe		?		*une Messa*	

Note:

[a] RISM 1520⁴: *Liber selectarum cantionum quas vulgo Mutetas appellant sex quinque et quatuor vocum* (Grimm & Wyrsung) [1541¹⁶: *La piu divina ... madrigali, a sei voce* (Gardano)]

Zarlino 1549: *Musica quinque vocum* (Gardano)

Willaert 1559: *Musica nova* (Gardano)

Zarlino 1566: *Modulationes sex vocum* (Rampazetto)

400   # Quarta

Aue maria, *à sette voci, & li motetti*; Ego rosa Saron, *&* Capite nobis vulpes
paruulas; *à cinque voci*: Si trouano etiandio molte altre compositioni fatte da diuersi
compositori, le quali per essere quasi infinite si lasciano. Questo Modo rare volte si troua nelli canti figurati nelle sue Chorde propie; ma il più delle uolte si ritroua trasportato
per una Quarta; come si può vedere nelli Motetti nominati; & questo; percioche si
può trasporre; come anco si può trasporre il Terzo modo, con l'aiuto della Chorda Trite synemennon, verso l'acuto. Et si come il Terzo col Vndecimo hà molta conuenienza,
così questo l'hà veramente col Duodecimo.

Del Quinto Modo.   Cap. 22.

IL Quinto modo nasce dalla Terza specie della Diapason diuisa harmoni-
camente della Chorda ♮: ouero dalla unione della Terza specie della Dià
pente E, & ♮, posta nel graue, con la Terza della Diatessaron ♮ & e, po
sta nell'acuto. Questo Modo ha la sua Chorda finale E commune col Se-
sto & gli Ecclesiastici hanno di questo Modo infinite cantilene; come ne
i loro libri si può vedere. Le sue Cadenze principali si fanno nelle Chorde de i suoi principij
regolari, i quali sono le chorde mostrate E, G, ♮, et e: che sono le estreme della sua Diapete
& della sua Diatessaron, & la mezana della Diapente: le altre poi, che non sono Irrego-

SOPRANO della Cantilena del Quinto modo.

Tenore

8.3   Zarlino, *Le istitutioni harmoniche* (1573) IV: 22: The fifth mode
(= 1558, IV: 20, The third mode, cf. Fig. 8.1, pp. 228–29)

lari, ſi poſſono fare ſopra l'altre chorde . Ma perche conoſciuto le Regolari, facilmente
ſi può conoſcere le Irregolari ; però hò dato l'eſſempio delle prime ; accio veniamo in cognitione delle ſeconde . Si debbe però auertire , che tanto in queſto , quanto nel Seſto ,
nel Nono . & nel Decimo modo , regolarmente ſi fanno le Cadenze nella Chorda ♮ : ma
perche tal Chorda non hà corriſpondenza alcuna per Quinta nell'acuto, ne per Quarta
nel graue; però è chorda alquãto dura: ma tal durezza ſi ſopporta nelle cãtilene compoſte a più di due voci ; percioche ſi tiene tal ordine, che fanno ouono effetto : come ſi può
vedere tra le Cadenze poſte nel Cap. 51. della Terza parte. Molte compoſitioni ſi trouano compoſte ſotto queſto Modo , tra le quali è il motetto : O Maria mater Chriſti , à
quattro voci di Rac ; & li motetti di Adriano ; Te Deum patrem : Huc me ſydereo ; & Hæc eſt domus domini, compoſti à ſette voci ; & il Madrigale: I mi riuolgo in dietro, còpoſto da Adriano medeſimamente à cinque voci : alli quali aggiungeremo ; Ferculum fecit ſibi rex Salomon , il quale gia compoſi inſieme con molti altri ſimigliantemente à cinque voci . Se queſto Modo non ſi meſcolaſſe col Nono , & ſi
vdiſſe ſemplice, hauerebbe la ſua Harmonia alquãto dura ; ma perche è temperata dalla Diapente del Vndecimo , & dalla Cadenza, che ſi fa in a , che in eſſo grandemente ſi
vſa ; però alcuni hanno hauuto parere, che habbia natura di commouere al pianta ; la
onde gli accommodarono volentieri quelle parole , che ſono lagrimeuoli & piene di lamenti . Hà grande conuenienza col detto Vndecimo ; percioche hanno la Terza ſpecie
della Diateſſaron commune tra loro : & ſpeſſe volte: Muſici moderni lo traſportano fuori delle ſue Chorde naturali per vna Diateſſaron più acuta, con l'aiuto della Chorda b ,
ancora che l'più delle volte ſi ritroui collocato nel ſuo propiò & natural luogo .

Ll 3   Del

8.3 (cont.)

With the exception of removing the "erroneous citation" no other alterations are
made to citations from *Musica nova*. Thus the only attempt to "update" the repertory of the treatise creates another stage in the extraordinary self-referential citation
that alternates the publication of motet prints and editions of the treatise. This
pattern is borne out in the changes to the citations in the treatise as a whole, boxed
and numbered on Table 8.4 (pp. 238–39). The most extensive alterations occur at
(1) in the citations for Mode 1. There Zarlino substitutes his setting of *Victimae paschali laudes* for Willaert's, and replaces one citation from his 1549 motet book (*O
beatum pontificem*) with two from his 1566 book (*Hodie Christus natus est* and *Salve
regina*). In the citations for Mode 4 at (2), besides correcting the erroneous Willaert
citation, he adds his *Misereris omnium* which is clearly intended to be paired with his
Miserere mei Deus (they share a *soggetto*).[42] At (3), Zarlino mentions that these *tonus
peregrinus* chants are sometimes described as Mode 8, although they are properly
Mode 9, a simple clarification between editions. Mouton's *Missa Benedicam
Dominum* (4) is the only addition not taken from Zarlino's publications. And finally,
at (5), Zarlino replaces the enigmatic citation of *Nemo venit ad me* with a motet from
the 1566 collection (*Litigabant Iudaei*).[43]

In some ways, the picture that I have painted of Zarlino – his self-citation and ultimate "possession" of dodecachordal theory in the form of his reworkings over a
twenty-five-year period – may seem all too obvious. Only when viewed as one
piece of a larger picture of how music citations and musical notation function when
embedded in a discursive narrative does the significance of these citations for a
"thick" reading of the treatise emerge. Undoubtedly the printed (and manuscript)
sources that I have discussed were music for performance, but the question remains
of how they would have been used by a reader when evoked by a citation in a
theory treatise. Of course, most modern readers of Zarlino "know" or have had
easy access to at best only half Zarlino's citations – the *Musica nova* citations. There
is an enormous gap between these works and Zarlino's self-citation, not to mention
the didactic duos provided in each chapter, that is never articulated. The *Musica
nova* citations do not function in the treatise simply as "proof texts." By preferring
these works to others of Willaert, Zarlino is aligning himself directly with their
reception. It is a reception that predates the publication of both the *Istitutioni* and
Musica nova and one bound up with Zarlino's interaction with men like the
members of the Accademia Veneziana. These were by no means the only readers of
the *Istitutioni* but they were the ones for whom Zarlino's specific Willaert references
had greatest moment.

But if these readers were the "target audience," so to speak, they were certainly

---

[42] Similarly in Part III, chapter 66, Zarlino substitutes his *Misereris omnium Domine* for Jachet's *Descendi in ortum
meum*, also pairing the *Miserere* and *Misereris omnium* (see Table 7.2, p. 202).

[43] Wiering, "The Language of the Modes," discusses this substitution. The only other significant change in citations between the two editions comes in Part III, chapter 66, where Zarlino introduces the polychoral psalms
which would have become mainstays in his work at San Marco (see Table 7.2, p. 203).

not the only readers, as the dedication of the 1566 motet print attests. From these most informed readers, for whom Zarlino's citations may well have supplied authority through invoked recollection of a known and shared repertory, there is a continuum that reaches to the reader who approached the treatise without any knowledge and minimal access to the works cited. Somewhere in the middle were readers who had access to parts of Zarlino's repertories in various forms.

Table 8.8 distills from Zarlino's citations those works that also appear in Modena, Biblioteca Estense 313–314. These elegant manuscript motet partbooks, which Owens suggests were probably copied in the 1560s, have no direct connection to the *Istitutioni* but they contain a repertory remarkably similar in its outlines to that cited by Zarlino: primarily motets and psalms by Willaert, with a few psalms and motets by Jachet and Rore, four by Zarlino, two by Francesco dalla Viola, etc.[44] It is not difficult to imagine that a reader of the *Istitutioni* in possession of such a manuscript would be well aware of the common repertory represented by the two. The printed sources noted on Table 7.2 (pp. 202–05) also point to "common" repertory. As gathered here, it is Zarlino's repertory, but it is a repertory intimately connected to the materials issued from Venetian presses, specifically Gardano's, around mid-century. The citation of works from those prints without direct mention of them appears to work on the assumption of a reader who is already familiar with the music. No pointers are given for the reader who is not, but the other strands of the rhetoric of the treatise will stand as a self-contained and self-sufficient text.

To address that rhetoric is to address a fundamental question of the relationship of this treatise and Glarean's *Dodecachordon*. Nuanced versions of "Zarlino the plagiarist" have often characterized the modern reception of his book on modal theory. Undeniably, Part IV of the *Istitutioni* relies extensively and significantly on Glarean: the overlaps are many and unacknowledged.[45] Yet replication of text should not be interpreted as synonymous with transfer of content. The perspective on Zarlino's relationship to Glarean that I offer comes not primarily from the perspective of modal theory, its history, and Zarlino's borrowings, but from their musical examples and citations. Zarlino's citations of music and his appropriation of Glarean's dodecachordal theory are inextricably entwined. Reading "out" from the citations of the *Istitutioni* to the manuscripts and printed sources to which they implicitly point and in turn back to subsequent editions of the treatise provides a remarkable window on Zarlino's engagement with modal theory from compositional, editorial, and theoretical perspectives over a twenty-five-year period that ranges from his first motet print of 1549 through the definitive edition of the *Istitutioni* in 1573. Zarlino's work provides a specific instance of the significance of citations and notated music exam-

---

[44] Jessie Ann Owens, "An Illuminated Manuscript of Motets by Cipriano de Rore: München, Bayerische Staatsbibliothek, Mus. Ms. B," Ph.D. dissertation, Princeton University (1979), 66–68. An inventory of the manuscripts appears in Pio Lodi, *Catalogo delle Opere Musicale Città di Modena R. Biblioteca Estense* (Parma: Fresching, 1923), 18–20.

[45] Zarlino does acknowledge Glarean in the *Sopplimenti*. The extent of his borrowings is detailed in Meier, "Heinrich Loriti Glareanus als Musiktheoretiker." Wiering, "The Language of the Modes," discusses authors whom Zarlino has deliberately not acknowledged, including Glarean and Vicentino.

Table 8.8 *Modena, Biblioteca Estense, Mus. C.313*
and Mus. C.314

Composer	Title	*Istitutioni*
ModE 313		
[Motets for 4 voices]		
Willaert	*Aule lucide*	
Jachet	*Audi dulcis*	
Willaert	*Confitebor tibi domine*	III: 66
Willaert	*Congratulamini*	
Willaert	*Dic nobis*	
Willaert	*Dilexi quoniam*	
Willaert	*Domine quid multiplicati*	
Willaert	*Intercessio quesumus*	
Willeart	*Nunc pio corde*	
Jachet	*Spem in alium*	IV: 26
Willaert	*Tota pulchra es*	
[Motets for 5 voices]		
Willaert	*Ave maris stella*	
Rore	*Ad te levavi*	
Jachet	*Aspice domine*	
Continus	*Angelus domini*	
Continus	*Alleluia surrexit*	
Continus	*Ave vivens hostia*	
Willaert	*Beati pauperes*	
Willaert	*Benedictus redemptor*	
Nicolaus	*Benedictus deus*	
Rore	*Beatus homo*	
Rore	*Benedictum*	
Willaert	*Creator omnium*	
Animucius	*Cantate domino*	
Willaert	*Christus resurgens*	
Jachet	*Dixit autem dominus*	
Viola	*Dilectus meus*	
Jachet	*Domine secundum actum*	
Willaert	*Domine Jesu Christe*	
Rore	*Domine deus*	
Rore	*Da pacem*	
Willaert	*Ecce Maria*	
Willaert	*Ecce dominus veniet*	
Viola	*Et filius*	
Willaert	*Germinavit*	
Willaert	*Hodie Christus natus es*	
Jachet	*In die tribulationis*	
Rore	*In convertendo*	
Rore	*In die tribulationis*	
Rore	*Justus es domine*	

Table 8.8 (*cont.*)

Composer	Title	*Istitutioni*
Willaert	*Locuti sunt*	
Jachet	*Locutus est*	
Continus	*Laetare hierusalem*	
Rore	*Laudem dicite*	
Willaert	*Laus tibi*	III: 28
Willaert	*Laetare sancta mater*	
Willaert	*Mirabile misterium*	
Willaert	*Magnum hereditatis*	
Willaert	*Mane prima sabati*	
Jachet	*Mirabile misterium*	
Willaert	*Miserere nostri*	
Willaert	*Ne projicias*	
Jachet	*Nigra sum*	
Willaert	*O admirabile*	
Viola	*Oia que fecisti*	
Rore	*O altitudo*	
Continus	*Omnes in domino*	
Jachet	*O quam praeclara*	
Morales	*O sacrum convivium*	
Willaert	*Prolungati sunt*	
Jachet	*Pater noster*	
Willaert	*Peccavi super numerum*	
Willaert	*Quando natus es*	
Willaert	*Rubum quem viderat*	
Jachet	*Rex babilonis*	
Jachet	*Repleatur os meum*	
Jachet	*Salvum me fac*	
Jachet	*Surge petre*	
Jachet	*Si vera*	
Willaert	*Salva nos domine*	
Verdelot	*Si bona suscepimus*	IV: 30
Zarlino	*Si bona suscepimus*	IV: 26
Willaert	*Sub tuum*	
Rore	*Tribularer*	
Willaert	*Veni redemptor*	
Animucius	*Venit lumen*	
Willaert	*Verbum iniquum*	
Rore	*Vado ad eum*	

ModE 314

[Motets for six voices]

Willaert	*Audite insule*	IV: 25
Zarlino	*Ascendo ad patrem*	
Willaert	*Ave virgo sponsa dei*	
Willaert	*Alma redemptoris*	IV: 28

Table 8.8 (*cont.*)

Composer	Title	*Istitutioni*
Jachet	*Ave regina coelorum*	
Continus	*Benedictus deus*	
Willaert	*Beata viscera*	
Willaert	*Creator omnium*	
Willaert	*Domine Jesu Christe*	
Viola	*Domine deus iustorum*	
Viola	*Descendit hodie*	
Jachet	*Descendi in ortum*	III: 66; IV: 28
Continus	*Hodie completi sunt*	
Rore	*Hodie Christus natus est*	
Willaert	*Huc me sidereo*	IV: 20
Willaert	*In diebus illis*	
Willaert	*Infelix ego*	
Continus	*Miseremini mei*	
Jachet	*Murus tuus*	III: 66
Willaert	*Mittit ad virginem*	IV: 29
Zarlino	*Miserere mei deus*	III: 66; IV: 21
Zarlino	*Misereris omnium*	III: 66; IV: 21
Continus	*Nativitas tua*	
Willaert	*O gloriosa domina*	
Willaert	*O proles hispaniae*	
Willaert	*O salutaris hostia*	IV: 28
Willaert	*O beatum pontificem*	
Willaert	*Pater peccavi*	IV: 24
Willaert	*Pater noster*	
Willaert	*Peccata mea*	IV: 21
Willaert	*Regina coeli*	
Willaert	*Salve sancta parens*	III: 66
Willaert	*Vocem iocunditatis*	
Willaert	*Victimae paschali*	IV: 18
Willaert	*Veni sancte spiritus*	III: 66; IV: 18

[Motets for 7 voices]

Composer	Title	*Istitutioni*
Rore	*Ave regina coelorum*	
Willaert	*Benedicata es*	
Rore	*Descendi in ortum*	
Willaert	*Inviolata*	IV: 29
Willaert	*Preter rerum*	III: 66; IV: 19
Rore	*Quem vidistis*	
Willaert	*Te deum*	IV: 20
Willaert	*Verbum supernum*	III: 66; IV: 25

ples embedded in discursive writing about music that is emblematic of a reflexive intertextuality of theory and repertory.

Glarean and Zarlino exhibit strongly differentiated relationships to notated music that reflect the traditions in which they write, their social status, the function of their treatises and the audience to whom they are addressed, the agendas each is attempting to advance, and the role of the treatise in the sum of each man's output. The most obvious distinction in the two treatises is the repertories they treat, but this is perhaps the least significant. What is more important is the role that repertory plays in the larger context of the treatise as a text. Zarlino self-consciously embraced Pietro Bembo's single-model theory of imitation in a demonstration of how and why Willaert's method of composing had restored music to its ancient status. At the simplest level, the citations of the treatise function to support this agenda as proof texts, but the process is complicated by Zarlino's self-citation and the way this insinuates him in the picture.

Glarean's treatise, by contrast, relies not on citation but on printed music examples. I argued in Part III that his inclusion of polyphonic examples is central to *his* underlying agenda – one quite different from Zarlino's and strongly influenced by Erasmus and the commonplace book. Glarean provides, through his examples, a selective moral digest of a repertory. The musical notation becomes a text to be read within a text as Glarean circumscribes a repertory. Citation will not suffice for Glarean because of the rhetorical tradition in which he participates.

Thus it is not simply the chronological distance separating the repertories to which they refer that is significant, but rather the roles those repertories play and the larger agenda they are intended to support. The *Istitutioni* and the musical context which frames it as filtered to us through the traces of Zarlino's citations marks an extraordinary intersection of music theorizing and musical print culture. As composer and theorist, Zarlino operates as both consumer and agent. The citations of the *Istitutioni* offer a picture of how a repertory shaped (and was shaped by) theoretical discourse. Zarlino masterfully manipulated the associations of his works and image – to the "newest" modal theory in 1549, to the "newest" music in 1558, to his own theory in 1566, and again to his own music in 1573. Indeed his self-citation may have provided for his music a shelf-life (or at least the chimera of a shelf-life) that it would otherwise never have attained as the citations and didactic duos were repeated by subsequent theorists in strikingly new contexts.[46] Most of all, the printed traces to which these citations direct us suggest the subtly changing balances that characterize Zarlino's appropriation, assimilation, and ultimate possession of a theoretical concept.

---

[46] Wiering, "The Language of the Modes," catalogs other theorists' appropriation of Zarlino's examples.

PART V

READINGS PAST AND PRESENT

9

EXEMPLI GRATIA

A RECEPTION HISTORY OF *MAGNUS ES TU DOMINE/TU PAUPERUM REFUGIUM*

This penultimate chapter shifts the focus of examination from localized modes of production that characterized the preceding case studies to wide-ranging reception, taking a single piece attributed to Josquin, the motet *Magnus es tu Domine*, as a point of departure. Through the reception history of *Magnus es tu Domine*, I will extend the specific claims of earlier chapters and offer an example of the ways this study relates not only to the ongoing process of history of music theory but to the disciplines of music theory and analysis as practiced today. Thus I now depart from a narrow focus on the sixteenth century – while examining the reception of a composition first published in that century – and explore more broadly the nature and significance of musical exemplarity and the intersections of music theory and print culture by tracing the reception of the motet to the present day.

Magnus es tu Domine poses obstacles that might make it seem an unusual choice as the subject of such a reception exercise. Several aspects of the transmission of this motet since its first appearance in print in 1504 are problematic. Firstly, its earliest source is anonymous; in later versions it is attributed variously to Josquin and Heinrich Finck. One source even recognized the attribution to both.[1] Secondly, the work is transmitted in essentially three versions. The first is that of the earliest source, *Motetti C* (1504). A second group of sources, which may have derived from *Motetti C*, stems from the version of the motet found in the Munich partbooks associated with Glarean's circle (1527). The third group of sources, derived from the *Secundus tomus* (Nuremberg, 1538), shares features of both *Motetti C* and the Munich partbooks, but represents a parallel line of transmission.[2]

---

[1] The sources of the motet are: *Motetti C* (Venice: Petrucci, 1504) = RISM 1504[1] [anon.]; Munich University Library MS 322–325 (1527) = *MunU 322–24* "Munich partbooks" [Josquin]; *Secundus tomus novi operis musici, sex, quinque et quatuor vocum* (Nuremberg: Formschneider, ed. Ott, 1538) = RISM 1538[3] [Finck]; Regensburg Bischöfliche Zentralbibliothek B.211–5 ["Josquin, alii H.F."] = "Regensburg Partbooks"; St. Gall Stiftsbibliothek MS 463 = "Tschudi Liederbuch" [Josquin]; Vienna, Österreichische Nationalbibliothek, MS SM 15500 (1544) [anon.] = "Vienna Partbooks"; Glarean *Dodecachordon* (Basle: Petri, 1547) [Josquin]

[2] Brown connects the Vienna and Regensburg partbooks to *Motetti C* (Howard Meyer Brown, "Hans Ott, Heinrich Finck and Stoltzer: Early Sixteenth-Century German Motets in Formschneider's Anthologies of 1537 and 1538," in *Von Isaac bis Bach: Studien zur älteren deutschen Musikgeschichte*, ed. Frank Heidlberger (Kassel: Bärenreiter, 1991), 83 n.14). However, the Vienna partbooks were clearly copied directly from the *Secundus tomus* although the attribution to Finck is not reproduced. The Regensburg partbooks also follow the *Secundus tomus* in many important details including the ending of the first part and acknowledging the attribution to Finck. A number of variants suggest that the motet in Regensburg was copied from a source related to that used by Ott, not from *Motetti C*.

Sources of *Magnus es tu Domine*

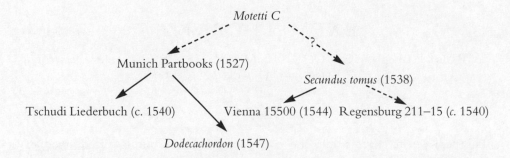

In the group of sources stemming from the Munich partbooks, the note values of Part I have been doubled and the mensuration sign changed from **O** to **₵**, changing the motet from Petrucci's *tempus perfectum* to *tempus imperfectum diminutum prolatio minor*.[3] Ott's *Secundus tomus* and the sources related to it retained the mensuration of *Motetti C* but contain notable text variations (some shared with the Munich partbooks) and alter the ending of the first part (see below, p. 279).

Magnus es tu Domine has been problematic for Josquin scholars in this century not only because of its varied attributions and exemplars, but also because the two parts of the motet appear hardly to belong together.[4] In Osthoff's words:

The main problem lies in the stylistic discrepancy between the two parts. The first – with its severe linear diction, complicated rhythm, narrow dovetailing from phrase to phrase, repeated intricate voiceleading with frequent octave leaps, archaic duo episodes, and blurred text–music relationship – accords with the late Burgundian style, whereas the second part – with its predominently chordal sense, formal sectionalization in small parts (twelve general pauses!) and clear correspondence between text and music – betokens clear Italian influence. The stylistic contrast can be accounted for neither by the text nor the overall musical form, allowing the supposition that Josquin combined two early works from different periods. Without a doubt, the second chordally beautiful part (*Tu pauperum refugium*) is superior to the first in musical quality.[5]

Osthoff goes on to quote Glarean's enigmatic judgment of the entire motet – one of the only such assessments in the literature:

The third example [*Magnus es tu Domine*] is truly complete in all respects, even as music, already established in the highest rank for 20 years, has become celebrated. But as the song is

---

[3] This change is the most remarked upon aspect of the motet in the literature, as in Reese's comments, *Music in the Renaissance* (London: J. M. Dent, 1954), 258. The differences between the two versions are discussed further below.

[4] *Illibata Dei virgo nutrix* is another motet which has been similarly problematic because of the apparent stylistic discrepancies of its two parts. For radically divergent views on the stylistic implications of *Illibata*, see Richard Sherr, "Illibata Dei virgo nutrix and Josquin's Roman Style," *Journal of the American Musicological Society* 41 (1988), 434–64, and Thomas Brothers, "Vestiges of the Isorhythmic Tradition in Mass and Motet ca. 1450–1475," *Journal of the American Musicological Society* 44 (1991), 1–56.

[5] Helmuth Osthoff, *Josquin Desprez*, 2 vols. (Tutzing: Hans Schneider, 1962, 1965), II: 84–85.

more ingenious [*ingenium*], so it is far more unrestrained [*licentium*]; this is my opinion, and the reader is free (as we everywhere suggest) to judge as he wishes.[6]

Osthoff's aesthetic privileging of *Tu pauperum refugium*, the second part of the motet, rests on a reception history from at least the early nineteenth century which isolated this section for study and performance. Figure 9.1 offers starkly juxtaposed notational representations of the two parts of the motet from the sixteenth and twentieth centuries. Figure 9.1a is the opening of the *Dodecachordon* that contains Part I of the motet. Figure 9.1b is Part II of the motet as published in the *Historical Anthology of Music (HAM)*, almost exactly 400 years later. *Magnus es tu Domine* appeared in the *Dodecachordon* as one of a number of its polyphonic examples drawn ultimately from published music anthologies but mediated by collection in a manuscript notebook (the Munich partbooks).[7] Through the examples of the *Dodecachordon*, which served as a self-contained musical world, numerous generations came to know the motet across several centuries. Excerpted from Petrucci's anthology for inclusion in a treatise, the work subsequently came full circle, moving from treatise back to anthology as it appeared in works like *HAM*. Just as Petrucci's motet books shaped the theorizing of a generation by the convenience an anthology offered, so too did *HAM* shape the theorizing of a generation of Americans through the repertory it conveyed. The journey of *Magnus es tu Domine* from *Motetti C* to the *Dodecachordon* to *HAM* and beyond is a circuitous one that offers valuable insights on the ways in which theory shapes, as it is shaped by, the music it conveys. Tracing the route from the motet's first appearance in 1504 to its various present-day guises will involve a number of detours into questions of the transmission and availability of musical texts, the role of attribution in musical analysis, changing aesthetic priorities, and the nature of reception history.

GLAREAN AND TSCHUDI

From its appearance in the *Dodecachordon*, *Magnus es tu Domine* might be read as a "neutral" example of Glarean's Hypophrygian mode; it is the third of three such examples. As was his practice in Book III, Glarean provides a brief overview of the mode and concludes with a discussion of the examples that follow the text in choirbook format.

A comparison of Glarean's text of the motet with the version that appeared in *Motetti C* shows that, apart from the changes in mensuration, the differences between this version and those of the *Dodecachordon* and the Munich partbooks from which Glarean derived many of his examples are minor. Figures 9.2 and 9.3 reproduce the tenor parts from *Motetti C* and the Munich partbooks, respectively.

[6] Trans. Miller, II: 254. Although Osthoff provides no context for this quotation, its opening only makes sense when one realizes that Glarean places his three examples as chronological representations: the first from a simpler age, the second from a more erudite era, and the third from a time when music had reached its peak (i.e., twenty years before in the compositions of Josquin).

[7] See discussion of these partbooks in chapters 5–6.

9.1a *Magnus es tu Domine*, third example of the Hypophrygian mode
(*Dodecachordon* III: 14, 272–73)

Liber III.

273

Iodocus a Prato author.

9.1a *(cont.)*

90. Josquin des Près

Tu pauperum refugium   Motet

9.1b *Tu pauperum refugium* (= Part II of *Magnus es tu Domine*) (*Historical Anthology of Music*)

Glarean annotated both as "Hypophrygian." The mensural alteration appears to be a simple pedagogical one that in essence "modernizes" the representation of Part I by doubling the note values which are then interpreted under simple ₵.[8] The opening of the tenor from all three sources is provided in a parallel transcription in Example 9.1. While the ₵, notation may have been more "modern" and easier to read, it has the effect (at least in a transcription with bar lines) of obscuring the underlying triple mensuration.[9] The few changes beyond the doubled note values are the substitutions of two notes for one (marked a and b on Ex. 9.1), changes in text underlay, and occasional textual alteration. While the tenor of *Motetti C* begins with the second word of text, "es," the Munich partbooks begin one word further along ("tu") and the *Dodecachordon* starts with the second phrase ("et magnum . . ."). The first change in Munich seems to be the division of one note into two that matches the changed text underlay (for the first two syllables of "Domine"). Otherwise text underlay follows the general outlines of *Motetti C*, which itself represents only a rough approximation of text placement (compare Figs. 9.2 and 9.3). The *Dodecachordon* reproduces the alterations of the Munich partbooks (including the change from "uberrime" to "uberrimus") but reflects greater care in text placement.

The provenance of *Magnus es tu Domine* remains a mystery. Although texts of this type are common in Books of Hours, no source is known for the text of the motet.[10] And although the text contains biblical allusions, it is not a scriptural text.[11] The text as it appears in *Motetti C* follows:

Magnus es tu, Domine,	Thou art great, O Lord,
et magnus nomen tuum	and great is thy name,
uberrime[12] fons omnium[13] gratiarum,	an abundant fount of all grace,
inclyta proles summi Dei,[14]	the illustrious offspring of God the most high
et Deus summe[15] bonus,	and God supremely good,
languentis animae suave refrigerium[16]	gentle refreshment to the weary soul,
lacrymantis[17] dulce solatium	sweet solace to those who weep,
unica merces supernorum civium.	the only reward of heaven's citizens.

---

[8] Glarean adopted this procedure of renotation with doubled note values in his annotations to Gaffurio's *Practica musicae*, as well as in his manuscript copy of the *Missa Si dedero* in the flyleaf of *MunU 374*. Sebald Heyden advocated this practice as a way to eliminate small note values which would prove too difficult for less experienced singers unfamiliar with them.

[9] More common would have been an interpretation of this notation under the sign **O2**.

[10] Brown, "Hans Ott," provides a brief overview of the text of the motet.

[11] Loach, "Aegidius Tschudi's Songbook (St. Gall MS 463): A Humanistic Document from the Circle of Heinrich Glarean," Ph.D. dissertation, University of California, Berkeley (1969) is in error when he classes the motet as a biblical motet. He was perhaps misled by the annotation "Jeremiah 10" in the cantus part of the Tschudi Liederbuch, discussed below.   [12] *Dodecachordon* and Regensburg 211: uberrimus.

[13] *Dodecachordon* and Regensburg 211: "omnium" omitted except in bassus.

[14] 1538³, Regensburg 211, and Vienna 15500 omit this line of text.

[15] Regensburg 211 omits "summe."   [16] 1538³ and Vienna 15500: languentium suave refugium.

[17] 1538³, Regensburg 211, and Vienna 15500: lachrymatium.

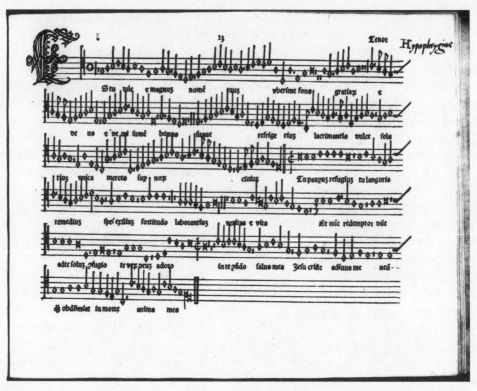

9.2 *Magnus es tu Domine*, tenor (*Motetti C*) (Munich University Library, 4° Liturg. 374. Reproduced by permission.)

Tu pauperum refugium,
tu languorum remedium,
spes exulum,
fortitudo laborantium,
via errantium,
veritas et vita.[18]
Et nunc, redemptor Domine,[19]
ad te solum confugio,
te verum Deum adoro,[20]
in te spero,[21]
in te confido[22]
salus mea,[23] Jesu Christe, adiuva me,
ne umquam obdormiat
in morte anima mea.[24]

Thou are the refuge of the poor,
thou the relief of all weariness,
hope of exiles,
strength of those that labor,
the way of those that have gone astray,
truth and life.
And now, Redeemer, Lord,
to thee alone I fly,
thee the true God I adore,
in thee I hope,
in thee I trust,
my salvation, Jesus Christ, help me,
that my soul may never fall
asleep in death.

[18] 1538[3] and Vienna 15500: veritas vita et via errantium; Regensburg 211 omits "veritas et vita."
[19] 1538[3] and Vienna 15500: Et nunc redemptor optime.
[20] 1538[3], Regensburg 211, and Vienna 15500: te Deum verum adoro.
[21] 1538[3] and Vienna 15500: line omitted.   [22] Regensburg 211: line omitted.
[23] 1538[3] and Vienna 15500: nostra.
[24] 1538[3] and Vienna 15500: anima mea omitted. Thus both references to *anima* are omitted in this text.

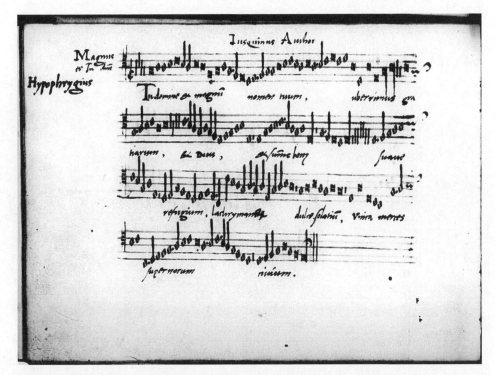

9.3 *Magnus es tu Domine*, tenor (Munich partbooks) (Munich University Library, 8° Cod. Mus. 324. Reproduced by permission.)

The motet is the eighth work in the Munich partbooks, the means by which, in all probability, it reached the *Dodecachordon*. From this source, it is possible to highlight the ways in which Glarean's choice of example operated. As I argued in chapters 5–6, such motets held the potential to function in a powerfully emblematic way for readers who understood exemplarity in a moral framework. *Magnus es tu Domine* is one of the few motets in the Munich partbooks without overt liturgical associations of text, music, or both. Yet its themes are exactly those Glarean invoked in the letter which heads the collection (see pp. 147–49). There he implores the student to sing as Moses did in Exodus 15: a canticle that highlights themes of exile, triumph, and redemption. These were themes – the very themes of *Magnus es tu Domine* – that spoke with pertinence to a Catholic audience during the upheavals of Protestant Basle, as did Glarean's reference in his letter to the schism of the Church a thousand years earlier.

The opening line of the motet text evokes the psalms in its parallel construction and alludes to a verse from Psalm 85:

Motet:	Thou are great, O Lord/and great is thy name
	Magnus es tu, Domine/et magnum nomen tuum
Psalm 85: 6	quia magnus tu et faciens mirabilia/tu Deus solus
	For thou art great and do wondrous things/Thou alone art God

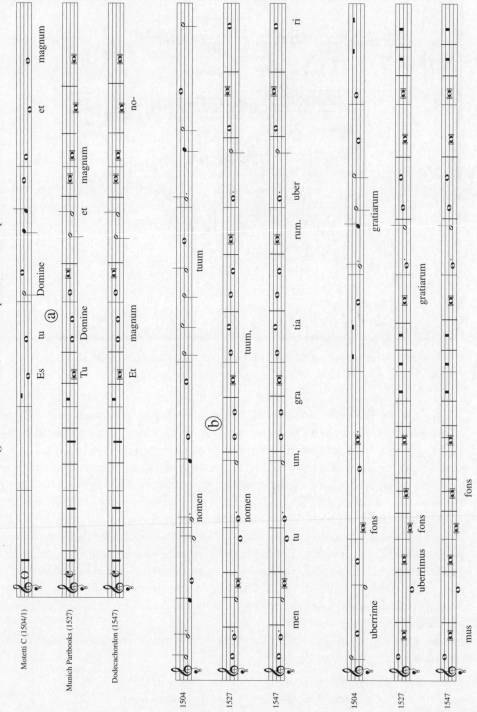

Ex. 9.1 *Magnus es tu Domine*, tenors in parallel transcription

While the similarity might seem hardly to merit mention, a reading of the entire psalm suggests that it is an allusion of just the sort Erasmian readers like Glarean and his students would recognize. Glarean could well have expected his knowledgeable readers to appreciate the relationship, for Psalm 85 in turn includes a well-known quotation from Exodus 15. (See pp. 148–49 for the full text of the canticle.)

Ps 85: 5   Among the gods there is none like unto thee, O Lord
              non est similis tui in diis Domine

Ex 15: 11   quis similis tui in fortibus Domine
              Who is like unto thee, O Lord, among the gods?

Such associations, which speak to Glarean's initial interest in the motet, are entirely veiled when the example is removed from the context of the Munich partbooks and the focus of Glarean's letter and placed in the new framework of modal theory of the *Dodecachordon*.

This can be seen in the reading of the motet by Glarean's pupil, Aegidius Tschudi. As I argued in chapter 6, Tschudi's means of organizing his Liederbuch relies upon the *loci communes* tradition with modal categories acting as commonplaces. Tschudi clearly had difficulty with *Magnus es tu Domine*. His version of the motet stems from the Glarean circle, but he is less certain than Glarean of its appropriate modal classification.

Figure 9.4 reproduces the page from the sketchbook in which Tschudi outlined his examples for the Phrygian, Mixolydian, and Hypomixolydian modes. As was his habit, he writes out the opening phrase of the tenor and final for a number of works. He then decided upon the order of the pieces for inclusion in the Liederbuch and numbered them accordingly.[25] But the groups of works listed as "Phrygian" proved problematic. *Magnus es tu Domine* appears in the top row, third from the left. Sketches appear for six motets: *Tulerunt* [*Dominum meum*], *Tota* [*pulchra es*], *Magnus es tu* [*Domine*], *Beatus auctor*, *Nova veniens*, and *Rex autem David*. Above the staff, four are labeled "connexorum," indicating the connection of the authentic and plagal modal pairs: *Tulerunt*, *Tota*, *Magnus es tu*, and *Nova veniens*. But the numbering underneath suggests three groups of three ordered as (1) *Tota*, (2) *Tulerunt*, (3) *Magnus es tu* || (1) *Nova veniens*, (2) *Beatus auctor*, (3) *Rex autem David*. And this is indeed the order Tschudi adopts in the song book. Underneath the system the additional indications "Hyp" point to *Tota pulchra* and *Magnus es tu* as the first and third motets in the Hypophrygian group, perhaps following Glarean's categorization of these motets. Yet the uncertainty witnessed in the sketchbook recurs in the Liederbuch, for above the Hypophrygian designation in the superius, Tschudi adds: "Phrygius in media sedes i[d. est] Quartus tonus" ("Phrygian in the middle seat, that is, the fourth tone [Hypophrygian]"[26] (see Fig. 9.5). Tschudi also includes

---

[25] This process is discussed in detail in Loach, "Aegidius Tschudi's Songbook."

[26] Unfortunately only the superius and altus of the Liederbuch survive. Unlike Glarean, however, Tschudi appears to have placed modal indications in all voices even though his modal assignment was clearly based on a cursory examination of the tenor. Tschudi frequently moves between modal numbers and dodecachordal labels, although this is one of the few places where he directly combines the two and the only use of the phrase "in media sedes" to indicate a plagal mode.

a biblical reference, to Jeremiah 10, the other biblical text besides Psalm 85 that includes the opening words of the motet.

Motet: Thou are great, O Lord/and great is thy name
         Magnus es tu, Domine/et magnum nomen tuum

Jer 10: 6 non est similis tui Domine magnus tu et magnum nomen tuum in fortitudine
           Forasmuch as there is none like unto thee, O Lord; thou art great and thy name is great in might.

Tschudi was apparently not the only one somewhat perplexed by features of this motet, perhaps those features that led Glarean to describe it as "ingenious" and "unrestrained."[27] Ott's edition of the motet in his *Secundus tomus novi operis musici* (1538) obviously predates the *Dodecachordon*, although not the manuscript edition in Glarean's partbooks. Apparently unknown (or at least unpersuasive) to Ott was the ascription of the motet to Josquin. Given Ott's proclivity for Josquin attributions, his ascription to Finck suggests that the work came to him with an ascription.[28] The musical differences from the motet as found in *Motetti C* are for the most part relatively minor – often simple rhythmic alterations – although divergences in the text are more frequent.[29] Nevertheless, Ott's edition does contain one telling musical change: the ending of the first part is altered to match that of the second (see Ex. 9.2). This change suggests discomfort – not unlike present-day reactions – with the apparent ambiguity of endings on A in "E-Phrygian" pieces. Other "mi" works in German anthologies from this period suggest a priority of tonal closure reflected here.[30]

[27] Both "ingenium" and "licentium" are terms that appear frequently in the *Dodecachordon*, especially in connection with Glarean's assessments of Josquin's music. "Ingenium" refers to compositional invention while "licentium" refers to exceeding the boundaries of the mode. This is the only place in which the two terms are coupled together and among the only occurrences of the superlative forms.

[28] Lothar Hoffmann-Erbrecht, *Henricus Finck – musicus excellentissimus (1445–1527)* (Cologne: Gitarre und Laute Verlagsgesellschaft, 1982), 188, 219, lists *Magnus es tu Domine* as a doubtful composition and assigns it to Josquin. His description of the motet is strongly reminiscent of Osthoff's in its evaluation of the motet's style. As Hoffmann-Erbrecht notes, the Jena copy of RISM 1538³ has the ascription changed from Finck to Hellinik. This is impossible since Hellinck was born in 1494. Finck is possible as the composer of the motet on chronological grounds, but the attribution has generally been discounted not least because so few German composers appear in Petrucci's prints. Brown, "Hans Ott," 75, outlines a series of stylistic reasons to doubt the attribution to Finck.

[29] Ott's general assessment of the motets in the *Secundus tomus* also invoked the virtue of *ingenium*, when in the preface he said: "As regards the *cantiones* which we now publish, we hope that we will satisfy even learned musicians. We did not choose them for their ready availability but after careful listening and consideration, chose those which stood out for their *suavitas* and *ingenium*." The entire preface is reproduced and translated in Royston Gustavson, "Hans Ott, Hieronymus Formschneider, and the *Novum et insigne opus musicum* (Nuremberg 1537–38)," Ph.D. dissertation, University of Melbourne (1998), 573.

[30] See Cristle Collins Judd, "Aspects of Tonal Coherence in the Motets of Josquin," Ph.D. dissertation, King's College London (1993), 263–69.

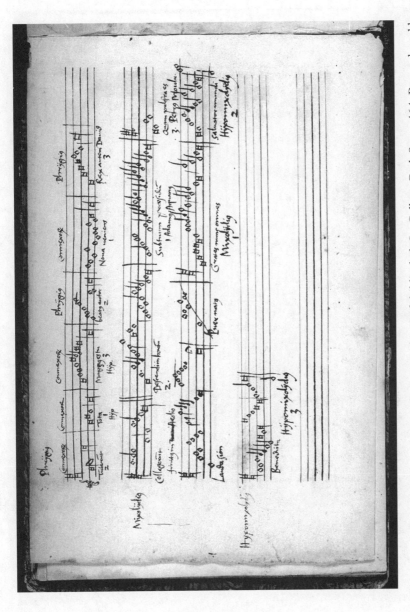

9.4 Tschudi's sketches for the Phrygian and Mixolydian modes (Stiftsbibliothek St. Gallen, Cod. Sang. 464. Reproduced by permission.)

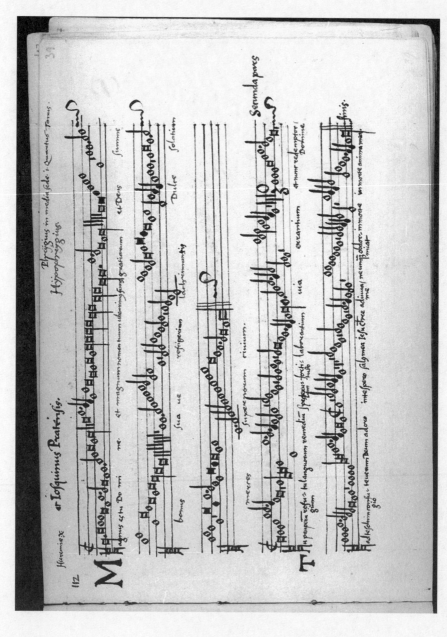

9.5 *Magnus es tu Domine*, superius (Tschudi Liederbuch) (Stiftsbibliothek St. Gallen, Cod. Sang. 463. Reproduced by permission.)

Ex. 9.2 Endings of *Magnus es tu Domine*

Motetti C, end of *prima pars*

1538/3, Vienna 15500, Regensburg 211, end of *prima pars*

End of *secunda pars* (all sources)

FROM THE *DODECACHORDON* TO MODERN
MUSICOLOGY

Although copies of both *Motetti C* and the *Secundus tomus* appear to have been relatively common in European collections and were known to writers on music from
the eighteenth and nineteenth centuries, it was primarily by means of the
Dodecachordon that *Magnus es tu Domine* was known to later generations. This was
due in no small part to Glarean's attribution of the work to Josquin: anonymous
works such as those in *Motetti C* and similar anthologies generally garnered less
attention in the process of recovering a repertory. More importantly, Glarean's "life
and works" of Josquin as extracted from the *Dodecachordon* dominated later accounts
of the composer's *oeuvre*. Copies of the *Dodecachordon* were widely available in all
the major collections, and Glarean's treatise offered an apparently authoritative
source on the music of the generations preceding Palestrina.[31]

Reading (and transcribing) the music of the *Dodecachordon* posed difficulties for
its later users. Annotations in the copy of the treatise in the Munich University
Library open a window to the reception of *Magnus es tu Domine*. The pages are
reproduced in Figure 9.6. The annotator has carefully indicated every tactus with
penciled-in numbers and barlines, even adding up the rests of the bassus in the
margin. This is the only example so thoroughly annotated in this copy of the treatise. Such marks are far more precise than the marks of congruence, sometimes
found in theory treatises, by which readers have aligned spatially separated parts
with each other.[32] For this particular reader, using the book when it was already
part of a library collection, Glarean's notation required extensive mediation. His
interest lay in Part I of *Magnus es tu Domine*; this hand appears only a few times in
the treatise and nowhere else so extensively.[33] With only numbers and barlines it
would be nearly impossible to identify the annotator,[34] but August Wilhelm
Ambros's notebooks and editions of many early works illustrate the process by
which one known reader of the *Dodecachordon* demonstrably employed similar editorial and working methods in making an edition of *Magnus es tu Domine*.[35]
Although Ambros's transcriptions were not ultimately published in the anthology

---

[31] That availability may have stemmed from the many presentation copies Glarean appears to have sent to biblio-
philes whose collections were highly prized by subsequent owners (see the discussion in chapter 5).

[32] See, for example, the annotations to Morley's treatise discussed in chapter 1, p. 14.

[33] I have encountered similar partial annotations where barlines and numbering have been used in an attempt to
right an edition that has obviously gone wrong in the process of transcription but nothing that approaches the
thoroughness of this annotator. It may be that this represents an attempt to compare Glarean's version with that
of *Motetti C*.

[34] Although I have received wildly different suggestions about the provenance of this hand, the consensus seems to
be that it is probably nineteenth-century German.

[35] Ambros's surviving papers are in the Austrian National Library. For an overview of his editions of Josquin's
music, see Don Harrán, "Burney and Ambros as Editors of Josquin's Music," *Josquin des Prez*, ed. Edward
Lowinsky (New York: Oxford, 1976), 148–77. The outlines Harrán presents in this useful article are accurate,
although some details of his interpretation are open to question. He appears not to have made a distinction
between the two kinds of books in the collection: working notebooks and fair copies in the hand of professional
copyists.

he envisaged for the final volume of his *Geschichte der Musik* (1862–68), they formed the basis of his discussion of Josquin's music in volume III.[36] The first page of Ambros's edition of *Magnus es tu Domine* is reproduced in Figure 9.7.[37] In his *Geschichte*, however, *Magnus es tu Domine* merits only a single sentence that emphasizes the beauty of its second part, linking it to the style of another homorhythmic motet, *Tu solus qui facis mirabilia*.[38] Although *Motetti C* is prominently indicated as a source both in Ambros's edition and in his *Geschichte*, the notation and attribution to Josquin follows Glarean. The motet is bound in one of two manuscript volumes that comprise Ambros's edition of Josquin motets, several of which appear to have been prepared for possible publication. The additional barlines of the first two systems in the superius correspond to the mensuration of the Petrucci incipit provided in the upper left-hand corner. Although he supplied the information on the *Secundus tomus* concordance, Ambros dismissed its attribution to Finck.

A comparison of the barlines in this edition by Ambros with the annotations in the Munich *Dodecachordon* shows the similarity of editorial principles.[39] Breves across barlines are not tied, but placed with the barline squarely bisecting them (e.g. superius mm. 8–9 and 11–12); in the case of dotted notes across barlines, the dot follows the barline (e.g. superius, m. 8). That Ambros himself worked in this way is apparent from the notebooks from which his editions were made.[40] When in his travels Ambros encountered a printed or manuscript source that was otherwise unavailable to him, he apparently copied the source, often in its entirety, into a notebook that preserved its original notation and format. From these notebooks, he then transcribed and scored selected pieces. For sources more readily available, he may have simply transcribed the work directly. Figure 9.8 presents two pages from such a notebook.[41] Ambros seems to have encountered particular difficulty with works in *tempus perfectum*. His solution here is like that of the reader of the Munich *Dodecachordon*: he introduced barlines and measure numbers.[42]

As far as I have been able to determine, the first published edition of *Magnus es tu Domine* to appear after the *Dodecachordon* predated Ambros's *Geschichte* by nearly half

---

[36] The final volume of the history was prepared by Otto Kade in 1888, who used only twenty-six of Ambros's transcriptions. The situation is described in detail in Harrán, "Burney and Ambros," 157 n.37. More generally on Ambros, see Philipp Naegele, "August Wilhelm Ambros: His Historical and Critical Thought," Ph.D. dissertation, Princeton University (1954).   [37] A-Wn Ms. Supp. 1556, 55^v-56^r, dated 1863.

[38] Ambros, *Geschichte der Musik* (Leipzig: F. E. C. Leuchart, 1887–1911), III: 229.

[39] Harrán discusses Ambros's editorial procedures in some detail. Kade's practice in volume 5 of the *Geschichte* departs from Ambros in a number of significant details even where he based his edition on one of Ambros's scores.

[40] Only a fair copy of *Magnus es tu Domine* survives, and this version was professionally copied for Ambros. That it was copied into this book from a score, not parts, is obvious from the erasure in the altus at the end of Part I where two measures of the tenor were accidentally copied originally.

[41] A-Wn Suppl. Mus. 1595, 12^v-13^r.

[42] Another of Ambros's books, not mentioned by Harrán, his heavily annotated copy of Heinrich Bellermann, *Die Mensuralnoten und Taktzeichen* (Berlin: Walter de Gruyter, 1858) (A-Wn Mus. Hs. 36846), offers extraordinary insight into his editorial policies and the breadth of his reading, with frequent extended glosses from Tinctoris, Heyden, Coclico, Gaffurio, Finck, Ornithoparcus, Praetorius, and Glarean. All of the music which is transcribed by Bellerman comes from the examples of Heyden's *De arte canendi* and Glarean's *Dodecachordon*.

9.6 *Magnus es tu Domine*, annotations in the Munich University Library *Dodecachordon*
(Munich University Library, 2° Art. 127. Reproduced by permission.)

9.6 (*cont.*)

9.7 *Magnus es tu Domine*, Ambros's transcription (Österreichische Nationalbibliothek Musiksammlung, Ms. Supp. 1556, 55ᵛ. Reproduced by permission.)

9.8 Annotations in Ambros's notebook (Österreichische Nationalbibliothek Musiksammlung, Supp. Mus. 1595, 12ᵛ–13ʳ. Reproduced by permission.)

a century, although Ambros appears not to have made reference to it. *Tu pauperum refugium* was one of the examples attributed to Josquin in Friedrich Rochlitz's *Sammlung vorzüglicher Gesangstücke* of 1835.[43] This two-volume anthology was intended as a supplement to his *Für Freunde der Tonkunst*, which appeared in four volumes between 1830 and 1832. Volume I of the anthology, covering the period 1380–1550, includes three examples by Josquin. The editor of *Allgemeine musikalische Zeitung* from 1798–1818, Rochlitz was one of the most highly respected writers on music in the German-speaking world.[44]

In his introduction to the contents of the anthology (in parallel French and German texts), Rochlitz explained that he tried to demonstrate the diversity of Josquin's style and his individuality. The opening of the motet as it appears in this edition is reproduced in Figure 9.9. He called *Tu pauperum refugium* a hymn taken from a larger piece. He gave no indication of his sources, but the unquestioned attribution to Josquin points to the *Dodecachordon*. Almost all of Rochlitz's examples are excerpted from larger works: individual Kyries, parts of motets and so on. For Josquin, in addition to *Tu pauperum refugium*, he provided an *Et incarnatus est* and the motet *Misericordias Domini*.[45] Most startling from our late twentieth-century perspective of the music of Josquin is the unabashedly "a-minor" character of *Tu pauperum refugium* as realized by Rochlitz. His heavy editorial hand consistently introduced g-sharps to make dominant chords in a minor; g-naturals remain in harmonic progressions to the relative major (e.g. mm. 6–7, where an e is misprinted for a g♮ in the canto, and 13–14). He also markedly increased the sectionalization of the piece with the addition of a double barline in m. 20 and the rewriting of the altus (here labeled tenor 1).

INTO THE TWENTIETH CENTURY

With Rochlitz's decision to excerpt Part II of the motet for his anthology, *Tu pauperum refugium* seems to have begun a life of its own.[46] It moved from its role as documentary evidence in overtly theoretical and historical writing back to a

---

[43] Friedrich Rochlitz, *Sammlung vorzüglichen Gesangstücke*, vol I. (Mainz, Paris, and Antwerp: Schott, 1835).

[44] For an overview, see Horst Leuchtmann, "Rochlitz, (Johann) Friedrich," *New Grove Dictionary of Music and Musicians*, ed. S. Sadie (London: Macmillan, 1980), 16, 83–84. It is difficult to ascertain how widely owned Rochlitz's anthology was, but, for example, a copy that belonged to Brahms (dated 1868) is in the archives of the Gesellschaft der Musikfreunde.

[45] The frequent appearance of *Misericordias Domini* in anthologies seems to stem from Burney. The motet also appeared, with Burney acknowledged as source, in Kiesewetter's anthology published in 1826. In my search for appearances of the motet before 1875, I have relied on Robert Eitner, *Verzeichniss neuer Ausgaben alter Musikwerke aus der frühesten Zeit bis zum Jahre 1800* (Berlin: Trautwein, 1871; supplement 1877); I have attempted to fill gaps in Eitner's survey and have not discovered any other nineteenth-century editions of *Magnus es tu Domine*.

[46] *Magnus es tu Domine* also appeared twice near the end of the century in *Publikation alterer praktischen und theoretischen Musikwerke*: once in Eitner's edition of the complete works of Finck (1879), where he discounted the attribution to Finck, and a few years later in Peter Bohn's translation and modern transcription of the *Dodecachordon* (1888).

9.9 *Tu pauperum refugium*, Rochlitz's edition

free-standing work in the practical context of editions and anthologies aimed at per-
formers. *Magnus es tu Domine* appeared as the nineteenth motet in Albert Smijers's
Werken van Josquin des Pres, published in the third fascicle of the edition (1924).[47]
The early fascicles of this scholarly edition systematically proceeded through the
Petrucci anthologies and the third fascicle was devoted to Petrucci's *Motetti C*. Four
of the five motets included here were also included in or mentioned in the
Dodecachordon, and two of the attributions to Josquin (*Magnus es tu Domine* and
Planxit autem David) were known only from Glarean. Smijers's solution to the problematic transmission of Part I of *Magnus es tu Domine* was to publish both mensural
versions: version A followed *Motetti C*, while version B followed the *Dodecachordon*.
Although the impulse to provide both editions is understandable, particularly in the
context of Smijers's attempt at comprehensive representation of his sources, the
decision may have had the effect of making *Magnus es tu Domine* appear inaccessible,
even though, as scholars often remarked, the two versions were simply different
notational representations of the same aural phenomena. At the least, the appearance
of the first part of the motet in two versions routinely led to observations on questions of mensuration and reinforced a notion of its "archaic" style.

At about the same time as the publication of the critical edition, three editions of
Tu pauperum refugium targeted at segments of the performing market appeared.[48] A
Schirmer octavo edition, in a series aimed at church choirs, first appeared in 1924.
More significantly for the present reception history, Heinrich Besseler included *Tu
pauperum refugium* in his *Altniederländische Motetten* (1929) (fig. 9.10a) which preceded his monumental history of medieval and Renaissance music.[49] Like the series
Das Chorwerk (of which the first volume appeared in the same year and with which it
shared aims, editorial procedures, and layout) Besseler's edition presented in concise
form the information needed by the scholar as well as that required for a modern
performance while retaining the practical format of a performing edition. Besseler
offered four motets by Ockeghem, Compère, and Josquin as documents of the
highest art of Netherlandish music in the half century between 1460 and 1510. He
identified his source for *Tu pauperum refugium* as Smijers's edition from a few years
before, but Besseler transposed the motet up a tone, transcribed it in modern clefs
and halved note values, and made use of *mensurstriche*. In his preface to the edition,
he held up *Tu pauperum refugium* not only as an example of Josquin's Italian chordal
style, but as a triumph of symmetrical order. The immediate audience for such an
edition were members of the relatively recently revived *collegia musica*, amateur academic music groups associated with German universities interested in early music.

Tu pauperum refugium also appeared two years later, in 1931, in the enlarged and
revised edition of Franz Wüllner's enormously popular didactic *Chorübungen* series.

---

[47] Smijers, the first to hold a position in musicology at any Dutch university, worked on this edition from 1921
until his death in 1957; the *Werken* was completed by his pupils Antonowycz and Elders.

[48] A similar history can be charted for *Tu solus qui facis mirabilia*, the motet Ambros linked stylistically with *Tu pauperum refugium*.

[49] *Die Musik des Mittelalters und der Renaissance* (Potsdam: Akademische Verlagsgesellschaft Athenaion, 1931).

First published in 1875, the original three-volume version of the *Chorübungen* went through at least twenty printings as well as translations into English and French. These books were intended for training of and performance by large amateur choirs (in the original preface Wüllner states that his own choir numbered 150). In 1895, Wüllner added a new volume containing works for five to eight voices.[50] The effect of musicological scholarship of the last quarter of the nineteenth century is immediately obvious, for in the new series Wüllner listed for the first time the sources of the works he included. The major revision of the first three-volume series by Eberhard Schwickerath in 1931 introduced two notable alterations reflecting the changing competencies of the users of the volume: two versions of Book III were available, one with original clefs and note values and a newer version with fewer c-clefs and halved note values.[51] Additionally a number of pre-Palestrina works were added to the revision. Among these is *Tu pauperum refugium* (fig. 9.10b). The didactic nature of the edition is brought home by the comments provided for the choir director to offer his choir when they begin work on this piece:

Words! – Serious. Dark color. Phonetics: all e's and i's have to be adapted to the neighboring dark vowels (refugium, remedium, fortitudo, errantium). Take note of the melodic direction of "errantium" (of those going astray). 27 in tenor and bass, natural declamation. 34 with full organ sound. 57 peaceful, devoutly prayerful, from 62 gently die away.

The inclusion of only Part II of the motet in such an edition stems from both practical and aesthetic concerns, but it also reflects emerging choral and early music traditions that regarded *Tu pauperum refugium* as a free-standing motet. The mensural and melodic difficulties of its first part, as well as its contrapuntal intricacies, were surely inappropriate for most of the ensembles for whom this anthology was aimed and well beyond the didactic exercises of the *Chorübungen*. The difference in orientation of Besseler's edition and the version of the *Chorübungen* is immediately apparent in a comparison of Figures 9.10a and 9.10b. Ironically, although the *Chorübungen* is more faithful to the text of the original notation in terms of note values and clefs than Besseler's edition, the score is loaded with numerous dynamic and chromatic inflections while Besseler avoids any such performance indications and indicates accidentals editorially, presenting a "clean" transcription.

These three editions of *Tu pauperum refugium* appearing between 1924 and 1931, and the priorities they reflect, served as the antecedents of a number of subsequent editions and Part II of *Magnus es tu Domine* was recorded for the first time in the late 1930s by Strasbourg Cathedral Choir. The editions ultimately stemmed from the *Dodecachordon* and Glarean's attribution of the motet to Josquin. Both the authority of the *Dodecachordon* and the authorship of Josquin were crucial to the central place the motet would achieve in both choral and academic circles. In Rochlitz's,

---

[50] The Berkeley library copy of the *Chorübungen* bound with the new series belonged to Alfred Einstein (dated 1901), suggesting that its audience was not limited to directors and members of amateur choirs.

[51] A further revision (of Book III) with English and German prefaces, retaining the earlier contents and adding later music through Hindemith, was published by Sikorski in 1954.

9.10a *Tu pauperum refugium*, Besseler's edition

Du, der Armen Zuflucht, du der Schwachen Heilung, Hoffnung der Verbannten, Stärkung der Arbeitenden, Weg der Irrenden, Wahrheit und Leben. Und nun, du Erlöser und Herr, zu dir allein nehme ich meine Zuflucht; dich, wahren Gott, bete ich an, auf dich hoffe ich, auf dich vertraue ich, mein Heil, Jesus Christus; hilf mir, daß nicht entschlafe im Tode meine Seele.

9.10b *Tu pauperum refugium*, Wüllner/Schwickerath's edition

Besseler's, and Wüllner's anthologies, *Tu pauperum refugium* succinctly stood as an illustration of what the nineteenth century had termed the Italian chordal style that was most often represented by similar excerpts of the music of Palestrina and his contemporaries.

With the proliferation of Collected Editions in the late nineteenth and early twentieth centuries, sources like the *Dodecachordon* might seem to have become less influential in the transmission of repertory. Yet Glarean's book had so profoundly shaped seventeenth-, eighteenth-, and nineteenth-century evaluations of Josquin's *oeuvre* that its influence continued indirectly to be exerted even as Glarean as editor was faulted. Bohn's translation of the treatise and transcription of the examples just made the *Dodecachordon* accessible yet again to a wider audience. It hardly seems coincidental that Besseler, like earlier editors, chose *Tu pauperum refugium* as a freestanding example of Josquin's style, even though the Smijers edition and various other collected editions had made a far greater amount of repertory available to him than to the predecessors with whom he shared this example.

The influence of Besseler's edition on the musicological community, including his students who were to become important scholars in their own right, along with his assessment of Josquin's style as represented by *Tu pauperum refugium* can hardly be overstated. *Altniederländische Motetten* was reprinted numerous times in the ensuing decades, but equally significantly, *Tu pauperum refugium* was taken into another anthology only a few years after Besseler's: Apel and Davison's *Historical Anthology of Music* (fig. 9.1b, p. 270). They, too, mentioned that it was Part II of *Magnus es tu Domine* and cited Smijers's *Werken* as their source.

Along with the second Agnus Dei from the *Missa L'homme armé super voces musicales* and *Faulte d'argent*, *Tu pauperum refugium* became one of the representative works of Josquin's style for several generations of American music students. The influence of *HAM* as an arbiter of repertory was pervasive. Although Collected Editions were widely available, *HAM* often provided the point of entry into an *oeuvre*, genre, or compositional style, particularly in the case of early music. For non-specialists, its first volume provided convenient, affordable access to music from chant through the end of the sixteenth century; its short score format offered the ease of reading at the piano.

FROM ANTHOLOGY TO THEORIST: RECENT ASSESSMENTS OF *TU PAUPERUM REFUGIUM*

The importance of *HAM* for a group of music theorists writing in the 1950s, 1960s, and 1970s can be readily demonstrated. To cite just two representative cases, the penultimate chapter of Felix Salzer's *Structural Hearing*, "The Historical Development of Tonal Coherence," draws five of its examples from *HAM*.[52] Similarly, Salzer's article on early polyphony largely relied on *HAM* for its exam-

---

[52] Felix Salzer, *Structural Hearing: Tonal Coherence in Music* (New York: Charles Boni, 1952/R Dover, 1962, 1982).

ples.[53] Anthologies like *HAM* figured prominently in work like Salzer's by providing access to (presumably) representative works from repertories that stood outside the mainstream of music-theoretic writing. His gesture may be seen as part of a larger attempt to validate twentieth-century analytical methods (and particularly Schenkerian approaches) as universally applicable and thus relevant to both "pre-tonal" and "post-tonal" music. The use of *HAM* by Salzer and other theorists is remarkably similar to the role the Petrucci anthologies played in the writings of Aron and Glarean. The more direct parallels may be highlighted through an examination of a series of analyses of *Tu pauperum refugium*. In briefly highlighting aspects of these analyses, I will illustrate points of contact among their divergent interpretations that are ultimately traceable to the appearance and transmission of the motet in *HAM*. Among these are notions of segmentation, aesthetic value, historical continuity, the role of attribution in framing theoretical examinations, and how and why certain language is appropriated and reinterpreted – in this case, primarily the vocabulary of mode and *musica ficta*.

Three analyses of Part II of *Magnus es tu Domine* appeared within a decade of each other in quite divergent settings: an introductory theory textbook; a more rarefied theoretical exposition; and a specialized journal article.[54] Their common feature was that all may be seen as falling squarely within the discipline of music theory. While in some sense they stake out very different terrain, all embrace a historical perspective that locates in the year 1500 a watershed in the history of music, a moment when composers are supposed to have displayed a new awareness of harmonic possibilities and the organizing force of tonality.[55] And all accept Josquin as the bearer of that polyphonic tonality. While lip service may be paid to the conflicting attributions of the sources, a circular argument about the greatness of the motet ties it back to Josquin the great composer. Ironically, a mere twenty years after the last of these essays appeared, *Tu pauperum refugium* is hardly seen as representative composition.[56]

Salzer and Schachter's discussion of *Tu pauperum refugium* begins as follows:

> Example 10–3 [a graphic analysis reproduced in Figure 9.12 below] analyzes the second part of a motet generally ascribed to Josquin and certainly the work of a great master. This *secunda pars* forms a self-contained and intelligible whole and can be considered apart from the entire motet. It falls into two large sections, measures 1–33 and 34–69. Structural analysis reveals that the second section is an imaginative variation of the first. Each section divides into five phrases: measures 1–5 correspond to 34–37; 6–11 correspond to 38–46; 11–20 correspond to 46–56; 20–27 correspond to 56–60; and 27–33 correspond to 60–69. (pp. 402–03)

---

[53] Felix Salzer, "Tonality in Early Medieval Polyphony," *The Music Forum* 1 (1967), 35–98.

[54] Felix Salzer and Carl Schachter, *Counterpoint in Composition* (New York: Dover, 1969), 402–09; Wallace Berry, *Structural Functions in Music* (New York: Dover, 1976), 45–47, 236–41; and Charles Joseph, "Architectural Control in Josquin's *Tu Pauperum Refugium*," *College Music Symposium* 18 (1978), 189–95.

[55] This thesis was most passionately argued by Edward Lowinsky (a pupil of Besseler) in *Tonality and Atonality in Sixteenth-Century Music* (Berkeley: University of California Press, 1962).

[56] Given the current fractiousness of debates about who Josquin was views on his style have become understandably qualified.

In Figure 9.11 I have attempted to provide a graphic illustration of the parallel phrases of the varied reprise proposed by Salzer/Schachter, retaining the complete notation of their source (*HAM*). One senses underlying this parsing a desire to demonstrate the "triumphant symmetry" remarked upon by Besseler. While the pitch relationship of mm. 1–5 and mm. 34–37 is incontestable, it will be seen shortly that the nature and relevance of the structural variation proposed by Salzer/Schachter strongly reflect the Schenkerian premises that motivate their analysis. The salient features in the segmentation that go unremarked in Salzer/Schachter's commentary are the sonorities that mark beginnings and endings of their phrase groupings, summarized in Example 9.3. These appear far more consistent than local melodic and registral correspondences, as well as durational relationships, which might bring the suggested parallels into question. A discussion of these five phrase pairs along with a foreground graph of the entire work and a middleground graph of the first section follows. Salzer and Schachter conclude by observing that the "piece is an outstanding example of the polyphonic use of the phrygian mode."

Salzer and Schachter's middleground graph for the first thirty-three measures is reproduced in Figure 9.12. This neo-Schenkerian representation highlights the recurrence of framing sonorities and structural repetition of melodic contour while supporting the claims of a "polyphonic" phrygian mode with its neighboring cadential motion. While Glarean incorporated *Magnus es tu Domine* in his treatise by the inclusion of the choirbook representation of the entire motet accompanied by minimal explanatory commentary, Salzer/Schachter, by contrast, "possess" the motet by means of a graphic representation of an atemporal abstraction ordered left to right. Such examples rely either on a convention that assumes that the reader has sufficient access to the music so represented (hence the reliance on a widely available anthology) or make the reader cede the actual "hearing" to Salzer/Schachter and accept their abstraction as a true and meaningful representation of music that goes unheard, unseen, and unimagined. The reader partakes of a theoretical narrative that relies upon a relationship not only with practice, but with notation itself. The visuality of such a representation is undeniable, yet the use of notation points the reader to abstractly aural interpretation.[57]

Wallace Berry's discussion, appearing seven years later, also overtly relied on *HAM* as its source. His opening statement outlines his concerns and perspectives:

An example of Josquin, which can be seen in Vol. I of the *Historical Anthology of Music*, is the striking *Tu pauperum refugium*, Part 2 of the motet *Magnus es tu Domine*. It is a phrygian piece whose general form involves digression – very pronounced in textural contrast – and homorhythmic return in metric and other variation (m. 34) . . . Points of cadential arrival are in accord with phrygian usage: E, A, C (final, plagal cofinal, and authentic cofinal) and individual phrases can be analyzed as embellishments and prolongations of central "harmonic" factors. (45)

---

[57] Brian Hyer, "Picturing Music" (paper read at the Society for Music Theory, Tallahassee, November 1994) offered an illuminating discussion of the visuality of Schenkerian representations.

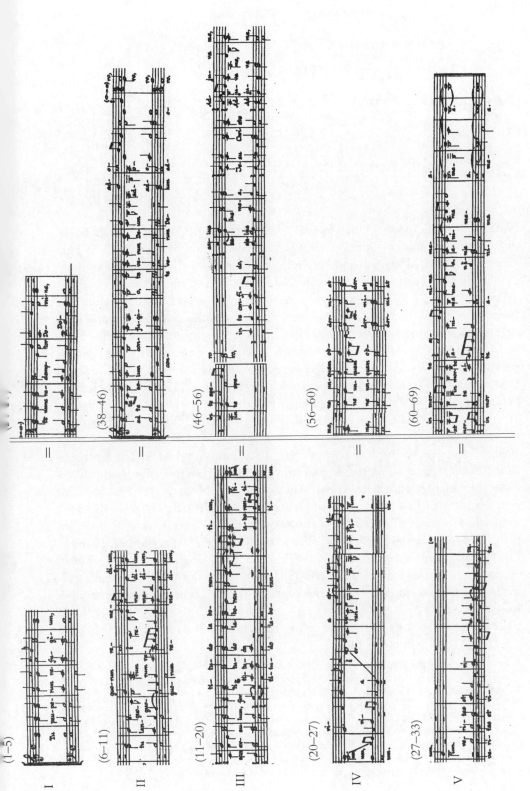

9.11 Parallel phrases in varied reprise proposed by Salzer and Schachter

Ex. 9.3 Sonority types (opening and closing of phrase groups)

Notable here is Berry's "neo-modal" language.[58] Like Salzer/Schachter, he describes the motet as "Phrygian." Glarean's distinction with which Tschudi labored – between Phrygian and Hypophrygian – no longer exists for these theorists, indeed had ceased to exist sometime in the eighteenth century.[59] Berry appropriates more than a simple modal classification, however, incorporating the language of modal theory – final, cofinal, plagal, authentic – while adumbrating a system that foreshadows the conventions of later tonality in its hierarchic tonal order. By so doing, he placed the motet firmly in the emerging tonality debate. Extensive discussion of cadences, leading tones, and *musica ficta* refers directly to Lowinsky's *Tonality and Atonality in Sixteenth-Century Music*. Like Salzer/Schachter before him, Berry is deliberately casting a wide net in his discussion of what he calls "the concept of tonality broadly defined." He highlights this through the hierarchical relationships and cadential plan of *Tu pauperum* reproduced in Figure 9.13. While Berry's representation corresponds at the large level of varied reprise to Salzer/Schachter's analysis, it differs in its segmentation because of its emphasis on cadential ordering and in its visual orientation and means of presentation. For Berry, a series of bass pitches represents an ordered cadential plan and carries the implications of sonorities built upon those pitches. The "hierarchic succession" of Berry's example 1–7b (Fig. 9.13b) realizes and verifies the abstraction projected in his synoptic example 1–7a (Fig. 9.13a). The three areas of elaboration – a primary "tonic" (e), a secondary area of "subdominant" (a) and a third level of a "submediant" (c) – are represented by their associated sonorities in a hierarchical pyramid of tonal relationships.

Berry goes on to mention "highly provocative sixteenth-century works," but it is

---

[58] Jessie Ann Owens coined the term "neo-modal" to refer to a twentieth-century abstraction of diatonic scale types corresponding to Renaissance modes ("Concepts of Pitch in English Music Theory, c. 1560–1640," in *Tonal Structures in Early Music*, ed. Cristle Collins Judd (New York: Garland, 1998), 186).

[59] There has been extended debate about the meaning of a distinction between plagal and authentic modes in polyphony. Following Carl Dahlhaus, many scholars adopted a concept of *Gesamtmodus*, in which the plagal and authentic were linked (Robert Gjerdingen, trans., *Studies on the Origin of Harmonic Tonality* (Princeton: Princeton University Press, 1990)). The counterview was argued by Bernhard Meier (Ellen Beebe, trans., *The Modes of Classical Vocal Polyphony* (New York: Broude Brothers, 1988)). An intermediate stance was proposed by Harold Powers, "Modal Representation in Polyphonic Offertories," *Early Music History* 2 (1982), 43–86.

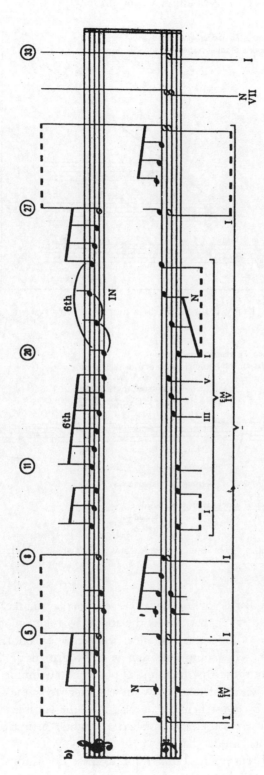

9.12 Salzer/Schachter middle-ground graph of first section of *Tu pauperum refugium*

Ex. 1-7a. Josquin, *Tu pauperum refugium.*
Synopsis of tonal system.

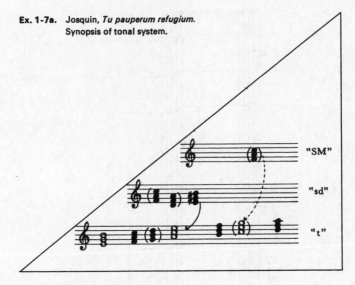

9.13a Berry, Example 1–7a "Synopsis of tonal system"

Ex. 1-7b. Josquin, *Tu pauperum refugium.*
Succession and hierarchic order of cadential centers.

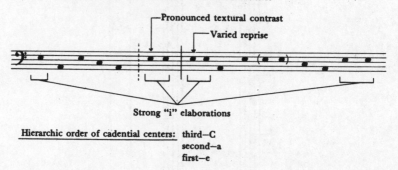

9.13b Berry, Example 1–7b "Succession and hierarchic order of cadential centers"

the extraordinary regularity of *Tu pauperum refugium* (again recalling Besseler's observation of "symmetry") that makes the motet so useful in his and Salzer/Schachter's discussions of tonal features. Sheer recurrence of sonorities on E leaves no doubt as to the motet's "tonic" and thus its "Phrygian-ness." Other repeated sonorities, particularly those that function as points of beginning and ending in accordance with the syntax of text, allow these writers to frame an abstract harmonic hierarchy that is comprehensible in relation to the vocabulary of functional harmonic theory, but nevertheless construed as slightly primitive or somehow exotic on account of its "modal" basis.

One also senses a latent political dimension to these discussions – an agenda in which historical antecedents are sought and in which "early music" must enter the mainstream of music-theoretic writing if a developmental theory of tonality is to be sustained. In yet another turn in the back-and-forth movement from anthology to theorist to anthology that has characterized the reception of this motet, Charles Burkhart, explicitly crediting *HAM* as his source, added *Tu pauperum refugium* to the second edition of his *Anthology for Musical Analysis* as the single example by Josquin. No doubt this was a reflection of Burkhart's personal and intellectual connection to Salzer and Schachter (he points his readers to their analysis); it also represented an expansion of his anthology to increase the coverage of "pre-tonal" repertories. For both Salzer/Schachter and Burkhart, *Tu pauperum refugium* serves an overtly pedagogic purpose in texts aimed at university undergraduates. In both instances, the primarily homophonic texture of the motet, the ease with which its tonal center can be identified – notwithstanding its Phrygian framework – and its clear division in two sections marked by a return of the opening material means that it serves as a comprehensible example and introduction for less experienced students as well as being receptive to analysis by tools formulated for the tonal repertory.

Close on the heels of Berry's book, Charles Joseph picked up where Berry left off in a 1978 article focusing on questions of form and pacing that appeared under the rubric "Fresh and Historical Approaches to Theory."[60] That rubric itself is a telling indication of the climate in which the article appeared. Like almost all the writers I have cited in this survey, Joseph's commentary begins with the obligatory gesture to Josquin's ingenuity:

The music of Josquin des Prez has long been admired for its compelling compositional logic. One marvels at the consummate integration of the simplest motivic cells into large musical structures of architectural perfection. Thus quite understandably, for centuries, teachers of composition and analysis have recommended to their students a detailed examination of Josquin's works. (189)

The language moves to a new analytic realm with its invocation of motive and the most spatial of structural metaphors: architecture. Joseph argues that while most examinations attempt to discover the means by which Josquin achieves "macroformal" coherence (an apparent reference to the overarching schemes of analyses like those of Salzer/Schachter and Berry), his own analyses of three excerpts "from the justly famous *Tu pauperum refugium*" will focus on "microformal aspects of Josquin's compositional technique [that have remained] largely unexplored." The three excerpts are from the "opening, reprise, and final cadence." Joseph's first example deliberately moves one away from the orbit of *HAM* and the world of anthologies. The typography is obviously that of Smijers's *Werken*, with its c-clefs and original note values (see Fig. 9.14). Note-for-note the same as *HAM* (which, after all, acknowledged the *Werken* as its source), the example instantly conveys visually the

---

[60] Charles Joseph, "Architectural Control in Josquin's *Tu pauperum refugium*," *College Music Symposium* 18 (1978), 189–95.

Ex. 1.

9.14 Joseph, Example 1 (Beginning of *Tu pauperum refugium* from Smijens, *Werken*.)

weight and authority of a scholarly edition.[61] Joseph's article is framed in decidedly different terms from those of Salzer/Schachter and Berry: it appears under the masthead of "historical" approaches to theory; it relies on a critical edition; it acknowledges in some detail the problem of ascription; and it avoids mention of the Phrygian mode apart from Joseph's suggestion that the motet has been harmonically analyzed to death.[62]

But on reading further in Joseph's article, it becomes clear that the "historical approach to theory" extends only to the preamble to the essay, with no discernible effect on the analysis that follows. The interesting tension of these approaches is never acknowledged, nor is the implicit "anachronism" charge which Joseph appears to be attempting to forestall by his comments on sources and attributions.[63]

---

[61] Joseph describes the source situation of the motet as follows: "Manuscript sources for this motet are listed in A. Smijers, *Werken van Josquin des Pres*, Volume 1, Bundel III, pp. xiv–xv (Amsterdam, 1922). Once only 'ascribed' to Josquin, the preponderance of source critical materials clearly indicates that the motet is Josquin's. There is, however, evidence to assign the *prima* and *secunda pars* to different periods of Josquin's compositional activity. As nearly as can be ascertained, both parts stem from the last quarter of the fifteenth century, certainly before the year spent in Ferrara (1503–04). For a detailed listing of the sources see Lowinsky [*Josquin des Prez* (New York: Oxford University Press, 1976)], pp. 267 ff."

[62] From this perspective, the information cited in the previous note is nothing short of bewildering. While presumably authoritative and persuasive to someone unfamiliar with the source history of the motet, it can make little sense to those who know it and suggests that the rest of Joseph's article would have been given little credence by any who worked closely on Josquin and his contemporaries. Smijers does list manuscript sources, but also three printed sources which he clearly favors. By what means the source materials indicate the motet as Josquin's is unclear: the ascription has always rested with the Glarean sources and stylistic analysis. The "evidence" assigning the two parts to different periods of Josquin's life is presumably Osthoff's stylistic speculation quoted at the beginning of this chapter. The "detailed list of sources" cited is in fact a partial listing of the "German" sources of the motet.

[63] Thus the opening of the article might be understood to be positioned generally as a response by a theorist to stances like Putnam Aldrich, "An Approach to the Analysis of Renaissance Music," *Music Review* 30 (1969), 1–21, and the highly charged "emerging tonality" debate.

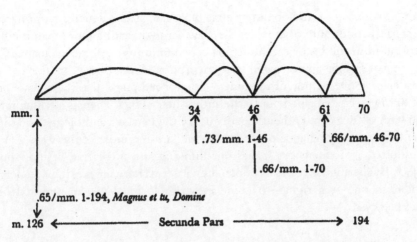

9.15 Joseph, Example 6 "Architectural levels of *Tu pauperum refugium*"

Joseph concludes with a schematic diagram of "architectural levels" which places his analysis in a larger context and relates Part II to the motet as a whole (see Fig. 9.15). Joseph's parsing differs significantly from Salzer/Schachter's and also Berry's, giving *a priori* preference to near-Golden Section proportions. Although the Golden Section is not mentioned explicitly in the article, the context of a number of analyses in this period, particularly of early music, which sought to demonstrate the relevance of such proportions, forms an evident backdrop for the essay. The reasoning by which the durational relationship of the two parts is posited proves problematic when the historical context that Joseph invokes at the beginning of the article is considered further. His abstract tabulation of measures, by which the relationship is figured, relies on Glarean's notation, offering in a note that "the fact that some manuscripts suggest an alternate notation does not affect the aural result regarding architecture." But this misrepresents Glarean's transformation of Petrucci's notation while begging the question of how the two parts of the motet are durationally related and what effect, if any, Glarean's notation would have had on performance.

With Joseph's analysis, the little analytical flurry around *Tu pauperum refugium* more or less ended. A number of factors were coincident in this ending, not least of which was the replacement of *HAM* with numerous other anthologies in the late 1970s and early 1980s. Equally important were the number of studies in which questions of authenticity and attribution had been brought to the fore. By the time of Burkhart's anthology, Josquin was still prominently listed as the composer, but a footnote qualified the authorship by saying that "the attribution of this work to Josquin, while traditional, is not certain." Equally, too, the analytic impulse to annex early examples to broad histories of tonality appeared to have been replaced in the 1980s by attempts to annex analytic strategies to discussions of examples grounded in a contextual framework.

Relatively few motets ascribed to Josquin have been the subject of such extended analytical discussion, and no other single piece has garnered such attention from the theoretical community (while, by the way, hardly meriting more than the briefest mention from the historical musicological community). All these "analyses" of *Tu pauperum refugium* appropriated and incorporated the motet in the service of broader narratives, a potent reminder – if we need one – that the agency belongs not to the piece described but to the author describing. There is a telling intersection with Glarean's and other theorists' use of the Petrucci anthologies and the mid-twentieth-century reliance on *HAM* – a salutary reminder of the ways that music transmitted as notated text shapes our thinking and theorizing of it as sounding object. By sharing Glarean's example, these later writers and we, their readers – and writers in our own right – become inextricably linked in an intertextuality of exemplarity.

EXCURSUS: *MAGNUS ES TU DOMINE/TU PAUPERUM REFUGIUM*, A DIALOGIC READING

Like others of my generation, I first encountered *Tu pauperum refugium* in *HAM* in the context of an undergraduate music history class. It was one of the first pieces ascribed to Josquin with which I had something approaching intimate acquaintance: I studied and annotated the score; I listened repeatedly to a recording; I sang it through with classmates; I played it at the piano. On encountering Salzer and Schachter's text a few years later, there was a comforting recognition that I already "knew" the work to be analyzed, that I could measure the veracity of the analytical observations against my own experiential knowledge of the piece and the annotated score within easy reach on my bookshelf. Even had I not been so positioned, the motet was easily accessible in a format less forbidding than that of the collected edition. And by the time Salzer and Schachter's text appeared, several recordings of Part II (and Part II only) of the motet were readily available. Only relatively recently has the first recording of the entire motet appeared, a stunning performance by a group not in the mainstream of early music performance.[64] Meanwhile, the second part continues to be featured regularly on new releases.[65]

This excursus presents aspects of my own evolving analysis of *Magnus es tu Domine* – a discussion that has been shaped in subtle ways by the process of writing this book. Yet the impossibility of standing outside my historical moment would make it presumptuous, if not impossible, to place this reading in a simple narrative

[64] *Factor orbis: Geistliche Vokalmusik der Renaissance*, Singer Pur, Ars Musici AM 1165–2 (1997).

[65] Most recently, *Tu pauperum refugium* appeared on a CD of decidedly "new-age" orientation entitled "Beyond Chant: Mysteries of the Renaissance" (Voices of Ascension, Dennis Keene, conductor, Delos DE 3165 1994). It is one of two motets representing Josquin (the other is *Ave Maria . . . virgo serena*) described as his "masterpiece." Josquin, compared in the liner notes by Dennis Keene to Beethoven, is credited "through the sheer strength of his musical personality" with "[breaking] from the limits of Medieval musical language to create his own individual, early Renaissance style. Although his two motets featured here were composed some five hundred years ago, their internal worlds are so strong that we feel an intense, direct link with the soul and vision of this great man."

continuum, as though I were not as susceptible to the contingencies of the materiality of the text and inherited conventions of exemplarity as my theoretical predecessors.

Although *Tu pauperum refugium* has had a life of its own – variously for aesthetic, practical, pragmatic, and didactic reasons – at least since the nineteenth century, the reception history of the first half of the sixteenth century testifies to a rather different perception: one in which the two parts together constituted the motet. An attempt to understand and balance nineteenth- and twentieth-century biases which treated the two parts as though they had nothing to do with each other became an important aspect of my analysis. Initially part of the *Motetti C* repertory, the transmission of the motet – insofar as the extant sources attest to it – appears to have been primarily Germanic. Both its Christological text and its modal assignment suited the needs of Glarean's collection. That Christological orientation also made it especially suitable for Ott's Nuremberg motet collection of 1538, with its multivalent intent of serving both a Catholic and Protestant audience.

Tonal features of the motet – specifically the divergent ending of its two parts – were problematic for at least some segment of the motet's audience, leading to the altered ending of the first part transmitted in Ott's 1538 version (see ex. 9.2, p. 274), which presumably created a desired effect of greater tonal closure. The "modality" of the motet has also preoccupied theorists over the centuries, with strikingly different results, beginning with Glarean's "Hypophrygian" designation and Tschudi's struggle with and modification of it. Tschudi's minimal summary in his sketchbook encapsulates the essence of such a Hypophrygian classification in its outline of the opening tenor melody and cadence to A and the conclusion of the motet on E.[66] Yet such markers, as a basis of classification, carry minimal information about internal musical behavior.

At a basic level, the reception history of this motet leads to questions of how an analysis should proceed when its function is neither to demonstrate stylistic features in the service of assessing attribution, nor to place a work in a historical continuum of musical style, nor to argue a specific music-theoretic point. Added to that is the question of where and how my own experience – my "hearing" of this motet – comes into play.

My discussion highlights musical evidence connecting the two parts of the motet and provides an extended discussion of Part I that balances the analytic attention Part II has received. The analytic framework is a creature of its era in its self-conscious historicism just as was Glarean's in its Erasmian assumptions or that of Salzer/Schachter or Berry in their formalist organicism. I have drawn on my earlier work based on study of treatises and repertory that attempts to place the motet in a context of a corpus of early sixteenth-century music, unlike Salzer/Schachter and Berry, who juxtapose *Tu pauperum refugium* with examples ranging over half a millennium of Western music history. And, not surprisingly in the context of this

---

[66] Both parts close on E in the tenor. It is only with emphasis on the bassus that the question of whether the two parts close on the same sonority even arises.

book, I have been preoccupied with questions of notational presentation and what I intend for my examples to "mean" and how they are to be "read."

An edition of the first part of the motet in modern score notation accompanies this essay as an appendix (pp. 314–17). The visual contrast of the two parts in this modern notation is far greater than that of its original choirbook or partbook format, as a glance back at Figures 9.1a and 9.3 will indicate, and of course it was from score notation that commentators from the nineteenth and twentieth century came to "know" the motet. The difficulties of apprehending the motet aurally from the printed page, especially Part I, are considerable for any but the most experienced score readers and I am now asking of my readers a competence that I have deliberately avoided for most of this book.

I will begin by re-engaging more recent discussions of *Tu pauperum refugium*. Salzer and Schachter's graph of the middleground of *Tu pauperum refugium* (first half) is reproduced again in Figure 9.16. Superimposed on the graph with dividing lines and roman numerals are the five sectional divisions they articulate in their formal parsing. Disjunctions of formal and structural articulation are unproblematic on Schenkerian grounds, yet they presume a notion of prolongation that is difficult to justify in relation to this motet: indeed, it is hard to imagine how Part I might be accounted for from this perspective. Both Salzer/Schachter and Berry articulate the relationship of E and A as tonic and subdominant (I and IV), reminding their readers of the impossibility of a true "dominant" in the Phrygian mode because of the B–F tritone.[67] Yet distinctions among "neo-modal" Phrygian, viewed through the lens of hierarchic theories of tonal function, Glarean's "Hypophrygian," and Tschudi's "Phrygian in the middle seat" should give us pause for thought.

I suggested above that Salzer and Schachter's segmentation relied on sonorities associated with points of beginnings and endings, an observation I would like to refine further. Recurrent framing sonorities, the chords with E and A as bass, act as tonal pillars in the sonic landscape of *Tu pauperum refugium*. Equally important for establishing closure however is the specific disposition of the voice parts and the melodic motion of the superius. Thus, the most frequently recurring and in a sense "neutral" sonority (*pace* Rochlitz) is that of the opening, labeled α in Example 9.4. Following from that sonority and signaling stronger, but still interior closure is β. More extended linear descents lead to χ, and closure is signaled by support in the bassus, δ. This framework points to a rather different parsing, which recognizes the "varied repeat" at m. 34 as resulting from what might be described as a modular approach to composition,[68] represented by the alternative reduction shown beneath Salzer and Schachter's graph in Figure 9.16. Relatively small units are connected

---

[67] See also Saul Novack's analysis of Josquin's *Miserere* ("Fusion of Design and Tonal Order in Mass and Motet," *Music Forum* 2 (1970), 187–263). Rochlitz, of course, solved the "Phrygian problem" in a rather different way: through his frequent editorial insertion of G-sharp, he implicitly offered an a-minor motet ending on its dominant (see Fig. 9.9, p. 287).

[68] On compositional modules, see Owens, *Composers at Work: The Craft of Musical Composition 1450–1600* (New York: Oxford University Press, 1997).

Salzer / Schachter parsing overlaid on graph

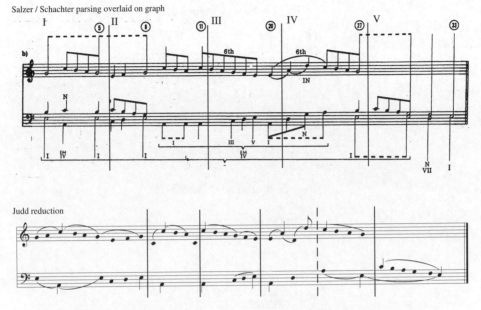

Judd reduction

9.16 Salzer/Schachter annotated graph with alternative reduction

with both textual syntax and meaning shaping the order of units. Those units are further shaped by the registral boundaries shown in Example 9.5. This may be seen in the opening gesture, articulated contrapuntally in the framework of outer voices in what I have described elsewhere as a "mi" modal type, shown in my reduction in Figure 9.16.[69] Thus melodic descents from c² are articulated variously at g, a, and e. In each case, the articulation coincides with the "pillar" sonorities outlined in Example 9.4. The basic contrapuntal module can be expanded or compressed to accommodate changing line lengths and internal articulation of texts as in the three-fold repetition of "salus mea, Jesu Christe, adjuva me" (see Fig. 9.1b, mm. 50–56). The next phrase begins with a further expansion and continuation. Example 9.6 represents these relationships schematically. In such a model, mm. 20–33 represent a clear "digression" and return motivated by text. Both texturally and tonally, mm. 21–27 are a vivid depiction of "via errantium" – a contrast that Rochlitz made even starker by the insertion of a double barline and alteration of the dovetailed phrase of the altus to delineate the syntactic division. (See the third system on Fig. 9.9, p. 287.) Yet the "digression" is nevertheless consistent within the tonal framework of *Tu pauperum*, relying as it does on *a la mi re* to move from emphasis on *mi* (e) to focus on *d re* and back again. The larger sense of a two-part form of *Tu pauperum refugium* is thus perhaps seen not so much as a structural variation of five phrases, but as a quasi-strophic treatment of the two large grammatical

---

[69] Cristle Collins Judd, "Modal Types and *Ut, re, mi* Tonalities: Tonal Coherence in Sacred Vocal Polyphony from about 1500," *Journal of the American Musicological Society* 45 (1992), 428–67, and *eadem*, "Aspects of Tonal Coherence in the Motets of Josquin."

Ex. 9.4 Sonority types

Ex. 9.5 Registral boundaries

units that make up the text relying on a limited number of melodic and contrapuntal modules that are reordered, compressed, and expanded to fit the needs of the individual phrases of text. The "reprise" of the opening melodic statement at m. 34 represents not only a return (motivated by the text: a return to the true way by those who have gone astray) but simultaneously functions metrically as a strongly contrastive discontinuity that emphatically marks a new beginning: "And now . . ."

Ironically, the very phrase that Rochlitz eliminated in his more direct segmentation of contrasting sections is the piece of internal evidence that suggests the strongest musical link between the two parts of the motet. As shown in Example 9.7, the altus–superius counterpoint of these measures appears in the same contrapuntal relationship between superius and tenor in Part I of *Magnus es tu Domine*. There, the dyad is part of the continuation of an imitative section of paired duos while in Part II it serves to dovetail at the point of textural alteration.[70]

Highlighting this shared material brings the discussion back to the question of the relationship of the two parts of the motet. While modern notation in score visually highlights the obvious textural differences, points of continuity are perhaps more easily seen (and heard) in the melodic material of individual voices. This is particularly evident from the layout and mensuration of Tschudi's superius partbook (Fig. 9.5).[71] The melodic contour of the phrase "et magnum . . . gratiarum"

---

[70] This relationship is most obvious in Glarean's sources, where the note values are identical.

[71] I am grateful to Richard Sherr for extended discussions of the Josquin motets in the Tschudi Liederbuch.

Ex. 9.6 Modular composition

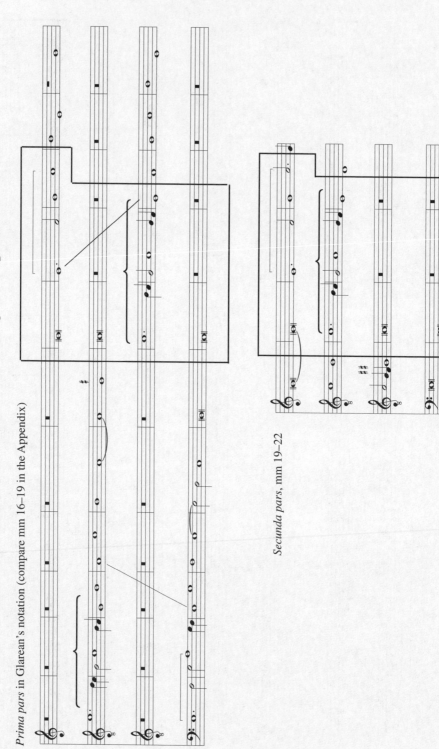

Ex. 9.7 Contrapuntal shared dyad between the two parts of *Magnus es tu Domine*

Prima pars in Glarean's notation (compare mm 16–19 in the Appendix)

Secunda pars, mm 19–22

in Part I is easily recognized as recurring in the phrase "venantium . . . laborantium" of the second. The recognition is aided by the similar placement, in which the two are almost vertically aligned (staves 1 and 5). Recurrent phrase endings of direct falling fifths (occasionally compressed to fourths) are seen in both parts (as at the conclusion of "et Deus," Part I, and "languorum," Part II). The pitch d^2 is only reached once in each part, both times as a semibreve, both times descending to g^1 (also a semibreve), and both times in approximately the same place, thus offering a larger context for the textual and tonal digression of *Tu pauperum refugium*. Such visual observations of relationships between parts are much more obvious in Tschudi's partbook notation than the choirbook of the *Dodecachordon*, which places the two parts on separate openings. While the *Dodecachordon* (and later score notation even more so) offers the possibility of a synoptic reading of all parts together, the partbook format allows exactly the kind of reading that was so useful for Tschudi in classifying his works, and highlights for the modern reader aural relationships such as those just noted between the two parts of the motet, relationships that may be less easily observed in other formats.

Part I of the motet articulates cadences to the same primary areas as Part II, namely E and A with momentary emphasis on D, but a hierarchic order of specific sonorities like that of *Tu pauperum refugium* is difficult to posit. Instead webs of contrapuntal modules lead to series of overlapped cadences in voice pairs moving from E to A, in which the "finality" of one over the other seems never clearly established. Example 9.8 illustrates the process at the opening of the motet. Cadential articulation to E is of necessity "Phrygian," while the contrapuntal framework prescribes that cadences to A are of the "leading tone" variety. This heightens the sense of contrast between the cadential points.

Although the individual vocal ranges of Part I are significantly larger than those of the second part, the tonal compass of the motet (i.e. the extremes of the superius and bassus ranges) is the same. And, as an abstraction, the "modal type" of the two parts is the same, encapsulated by the melodic similarities I highlighted from Tschudi's partbook (Ex. 9.9). But the articulation of that modal type is markedly different, most notably in the complete avoidance of g^1 as a major point of articulation in Part I (and with it an emphasis on sonorities on C) and the concomitant emphasis on A.

The text of Part I is articulated in three sections of similar length (mm. 1–15, 15–32, 32–42) marked by strikingly contrasted textures. The opening section is characterized by the long, cantus-firmus-like melody of the superius. The middle section consists of a series of overlapped duos, while the final section returns to the full texture of the opening. The beginning of each of these sections is further marked by the prominent appearance of the E–F–E (mi–fa–mi) motive so frequently associated with "phrygian" motets (Ex. 9.10). The segmentation is also readily apparent in Tschudi's notation of the superius. The opening section seems motivated by a contrapuntal working with the superius melodic type abstracted as

Ex. 9.8 Cadences to E and A (opening of *Magnus es tu Domine*)

mm 1–9

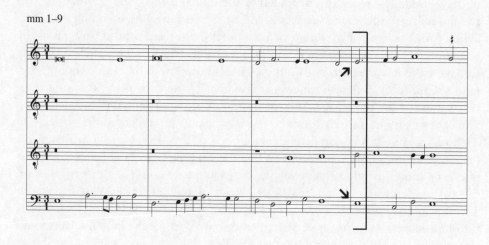

Example 9.11;[72] it also exhibits constructivist tendencies and melodic–rhythmic patterns that are exploited subsequently: (a) the descending fourth pattern with its characteristic formulation ♩. ♫ ♪; (b) the immediate repetition of melodic materials in the same voice at a new pitch level but otherwise unvaried of melodic materials (e.g. the bassus in mm. 9–10; see further mm. 18–20, 24–25, and 35–38); and (c) the pairing of voices together in thirds or sixths (e.g. m. 14, tenor and bassus).

The use of such constructivist techniques is combined in the middle section with

---

[72] Richard Sherr suggested to me that this might be based on a popular religious melody or hymn in triple time. This might have engendered a reinterpretation of **O2** (the doubled note values of Glarean's sources which are misrepresented as ¢), that was occasionally used to represent such melodies, so that the notation would look like the long–breve chant notation in which these tunes were known. Finding such a melody (if one exists) would be a near-impossible task since it is unlikely to have been associated with the text "Magnus es tu Domine."

Ex. 9.9 Modal type of *Magnus es tu Domine*

extended points of imitation as shown in Example 9.12, mm. 23–26. The end of this section encompasses the full superius range and the strictest extended imitation in conjunction with highly disjunct melodic writing. The final section of the motet is climactic in a number of ways. A consistent expansion of the motive introduced at the end of the first section culminates in the framing superius and bassus duo of mm. 38–40 (Ex. 9.13). The most intensive and motivically saturated segment of the motet precedes it. Again, the layout and alignment of Tschudi's superius highlights this motivic expansion. The phrases "et Deus" and "suave" follow extended periods of rests; the expansion of the motive of "suave" at the phrase beginning "supernorum" are conveniently aligned on the second and third staves. Glarean's observations of ingenuity and lack of restraint both seem aptly to apply to Part I of *Magnus es tu Domine*: the ingenuity of its constructivist counterpoint and the extraordinary lack of registral restraint in its melodic writing.

While the textural contrast of the two parts could hardly be starker, the allusion in the second to the contrapuntal dyad from the first represents an overt compositional gesture at connecting the two parts, a gesture that is all the more obvious in the doubled note values of Glarean's sources. Similarly, melodic gestures (both the descents from c^2 and the frequent use of falling fifths to mark phrase endings) connect the two parts. But one suspects that it never occurred to writers, scribes, editors, and musicians of the first half of the sixteenth century to view the two parts of the motet as separable in the way that later writers did, even if their uncertainty about both the composer and the tonal relationship of the parts was apparent. The appreciation of *Tu pauperum refugium* in more recent times has focused on and valued large-scale connections (in the form of symmetry, varied reprise, and durational relationships) as well as an affective interpretation that privileges its "chordal" style. Yet viewed in the context of the first part of the motet, it is perhaps not the large scale that holds greatest interest, but rather the way in which small units create highly complex music. Radically different on its surface, *Tu pauperum refugium* nevertheless represents an ingenious realization of the tonal, textural, melodic, and textual implications of Part I of *Magnus es tu Domine*.

Readings past and present

Ex. 9.10 "Mi–fa–mi" motive

Prima pars, beginning of first section

End of first section, beginning of second section

End of second section, beginning of final section

Ex. 9.11 Abstraction of melody

Ex. 9.12 Constructivist techniques

mm 23–26

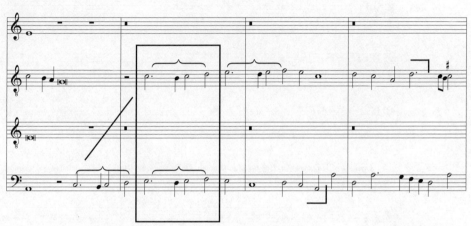

Ex. 9.13 Motivic expansion

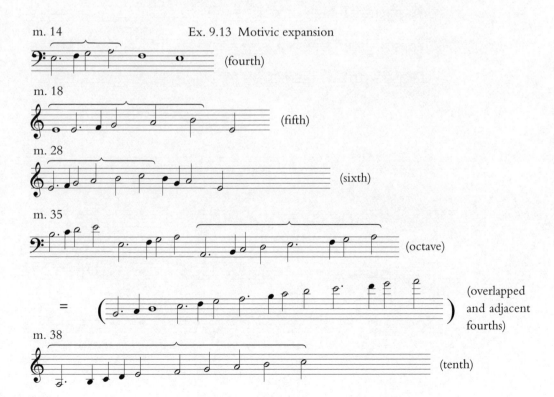

Appendix *Magnus es tu Domine*, edition of *prima pars*

Magnus es tu, Domine, prima pars.   Petrucci, *Motetti C* (Venice, 1504) [anonymous]

Opening of *Magnus es tu, Domine* after Glarean, *Dodecachordon* (Basle, 1547) [attribution Josquin]

Appendix (*cont.*)

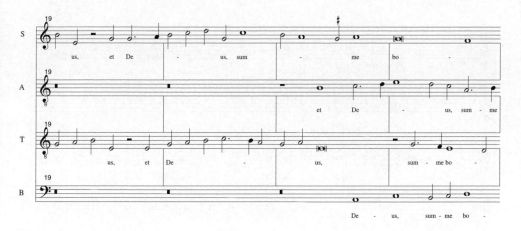

Appendix (*cont.*)

Appendix (*cont.*)

10

EPILOGUE
READING THEORISTS READING (MUSIC)

The case studies of this book have offered differing, at times strongly contrasting, perspectives on the intertextuality of theory treatises and a wider culture of printed books; the nature of the relationship is revealed through the material traces of printed music and its incorporation in a rhetoric of exemplarity. Pietro Aron appropriated the contents of recently published music anthologies to serve as instantiations from a repertory that was defined by its appearance and transmission in printed partbooks. The availability of printed music fundamentally altered the relationship of a theorist like Aron with the notated representation of sounding object. The printed musical page served simultaneously to exemplify and authenticate his theoretical claims while implying the general validity of his observations for the musical world encapsulated in anthologies like Petrucci's. Printed music – primarily in partbook, but also in choirbook, format – available in multiple, reproducible copies (which now also included the music contained in theory treatises), was associated with profound changes in the nature of writing about music. Thus an understanding of Nuremberg treatises like Sebald Heyden's apart from the broader context of a culture of book and music collectors and the music anthologies issued in the same city, often from the same publisher, is necessarily only partial.

Heyden also participated in a northern humanist rhetorical tradition of exemplarity. That tradition achieved its culmination in musical writing with Heinrich Glarean's *Dodecachordon*. Glarean deliberately contained and framed his examples within the material confines of his text as mandated by a conceptual framework of *paradeigmata*. By contrast, Gioseffo Zarlino constantly gestured outside his book to a musical world conjured up by mere citations of composer and title, like Aron, alongside his newly composed, completely internal examples. These gestures, so central to Zarlino's self-fashioning as composer, theorist, and heir to Willaert, are dependent for their meaning on the medium of print and conventions of print culture.

These studies of individual authors and treatises have by their very nature focused on production, with any discussion of reception keyed to an imagined audience who shared the author's cultural matrix to a greater or lesser degree. By invoking such contemporary expectations, I have suggested the complex picture that music examples and citations project of sixteenth-century print culture. Implicit in this view is an attempt to step outside twentieth-century ways of reading the music of such texts while simultaneously providing the groundwork that will move toward an understanding of the source of our own modes of reading – to question what music notation can "mean" when it is surrounded by words, framed by theory. This brings to the fore a sense of the varied layers of meaning such notation in its material guises of partbooks, notebooks, choirbooks, vernacular treatises, didactic volumes, and learned tomes, could carry to varied communities of readers.

One of the narrative threads that connects these case studies is the role of six-teenth-century treatises in the reception history of Josquin des Prez, the composer most shared among their examples and citations. Aron's citations of Josquin reflect chronological and geographical proximity as well as the composer's prominence in the Petrucci anthologies on which Aron relied. The editors of the Nuremberg anthologies in the late 1530s and early 1540s highlight Josquin's prominence in their prefaces and are responsible for the transmission of numerous posthumous attribu-tions of works to the composer. These publications established the "German" Josquin described in chapter 4. They testify to the reception of non-German reper-tory of the previous generation and suggest compositional and theoretical priorities reflecting the reception, assimilation, and imitation of that repertory. Glarean's *Dodecachordon*, compiled at the same time as these anthologies, but published a decade later, solidified the German-speaking view of Josquin as "classic," through the number of examples he attributed to the composer as well as his description of them and their composer. For Zarlino, Josquin represented the most venerable of the "ancient" composers, whose torch of greatness had passed to Willaert and (Zarlino's readers are implicitly to understand) was now carried by Zarlino.

From those narrowly situated case studies, the Josquin connection suggests a much wider-ranging exploration of the ways music examples and citations shape music theorizing as they are simultaneously shaped by it, from the sixteenth century to our day. The details of the historical narrative of the reception of *Magnus es tu Domine* highlight the grounding of individual interpretation in the intellectual foundations and social context of the ideologies by which it is framed. But this reception history also demonstrates the ways in which such interpretation is depen-dent upon the material means by which music is transmitted and the role it plays in the way music theory is practiced. The interconnectedness of music anthologies, theory treatises, and print culture points to the centrality of the music (as captured by notation) that theorists know and choose to write about within an intertextual-ity of exemplarity.

By means of my own analysis of *Magnus es tu Domine*, I suggested that such a reception history might point us toward a web of interpretation and the possibility of extrapolating from this web a convergence on an ideally cogent view. In learning from theorists of the past, we learn not solely from their pronouncements but from their practice. We enter their enterprise in an attempt to partake of a continuity of theoretical praxis. It is hardly surprising, given where I started, that this book should end with a detailed discussion of a motet attributed to Josquin, yet that was not part of my original plan. Rather I came to see in the history of *Magnus es tu*

Domine, from the time of its appropriation by Glarean and Ott through the nine-teenth-century German music historians to twentieth-century editors and theorists of the present day, an example drawing together the strands of this book in my growing awareness of the role of material determinants alongside intellectual para-digms in the history of music theory.

The perspective of my own analysis of *Magnus es tu Domine* acknowledges late twentieth-century musical and theoretical preferences and preoccupations in approaching a motet like *Magnus es tu Domine* or a treatise like the *Dodecachordon* while trying to understand them as their earlier readers did – an understanding that is created and sustained by a shifting dialogue of past and present. With some hesita-tion, I invoke "dialogue" here in the very specific sense in which it was used by Bakhtin in his early writings – hesitation, because the metaphorical use of the term is both so common and so easily misconstrued. The use of the term dialogue can easily place a false veneer of mutuality over the enterprise and suggest that a divider between two artificial worlds of past and present is easily or arbitrarily defined and somehow neutral. But what the concept offers is a point of mediation (of which our ownership is beyond dispute) that shifts as various historical and theoretical per-spectives are encountered and examined, highlighting the imaginative background against which dialogic meaning is configured.

It is just as impossible to re-create the past as it is to erase the present – the crucial element becomes the vantage point we adopt for negotiation. The disagreements among the accounts of near-contemporaneous theorists – whether they be Aron and Glarean or Salzer/Schachter and Berry – and their own occasional admissions of perplexity, should make it obvious that no music-culture is a homogeneous, self-consistent entity. The dialogic process offers the possibility of showing why earlier theorists offered certain insights and how they shape our own interpretation – of what it is that we share in our apprehension.

In ways many and varied, the conventions of exemplarity established by six-teenth-century theorists have shaped our own sense of how musical notation func-tions as a text within a text when embedded in a discursive format. Music examples provide material traces that beckon us to move outside the immediate context in which they are framed; they represent aural images that may be manipulated as visual representations that simultaneously manipulate and even disrupt the conven-tions of written texts; and they participate in a complicated intertextual rhetoric that constantly moves us between appropriations in strikingly different narrative contexts, between sounds and representations of sounds, between music and words *about* music. In reading other theorists, whether from the recent or more distant past, we also read ourselves.

BIBLIOGRAPHY

MUSIC MANUSCRIPTS

Sigla follow the *Census-Catalogue of Manuscript Sources of Polyphonic Music 1400–1550*, Renaissance Manuscript Studies 1 (Neuhausen-Stuttgart: Hänssler Verlag, 1979–88), 5 vols.

MunU 239 Munich, Universitätsbibliothek der Ludwig-Maximilians-Universität, MS 2° Art. 239.

MunU 322–25 Munich, Universitätsbibliothek der Ludwig-Maximilians-Universität, MS 8° 322–25.

MunU 374 Munich, Universitätsbibliothek der Ludwig-Maximilians-Universität, MS 4° Liturg. 374.

MunU 401 Munich, Universitätsbibliothek der Ludwig-Maximilians-Universität, MS 4° Art. 401.

RegB B211 Regensburg, Bischöfliche Zentralbibliothek, MS B.211–5

SGall 463 St. Gall, Stiftsbibliothek, MS 463 ("Tschudi Liederbuch").

SGall 464 St. Gall, Stiftsbibliothek, MS 464.

VienNB Mus. 15500 Vienna, Österreichische Nationalbibliothek, Musiksammlung MS Mus. 15500.

MUSIC PRINTS

Anthologies

Sigla follow RISM *Recueils imprimés, XVIe-XVIIe siècles*.

RISM 1501 *Harmonice musices odhecaton A*. Venice: Petrucci, 1501. Facsimile, Monuments of Music and Music Literature in Facsimile, 1, 10. New York: Broude Brothers, 1973. Facsimile, Milan: Bollettino bibliografico musicale, 1932. Ed. Helen Hewitt, *Harmonice musices odhecaton A*. Cambridge MA: The Mediaeval Academy of America, 1942.

RISM 1502[1] *Motetti A. numero trentatre. A*. Venice: Petrucci, 1502.

RISM 1505[2] *Canti B. numero cinquanta. B*. Venice: Petrucci, 1502. Facsimile, Monuments of Music and Music Literature in Facsimile, 1, 23. Ed. Helen Hewitt, *Ottaviano Petrucci Canti B numero cinquanta, Venice 1502*. Monuments of Renaissance Music 2. Chicago: University of Chicago Press, 1967.

RISM 1503[1] *Motetti De passione De cruce De sacramento De beata virgine et huius modi. B*. Venice: Petrucci, 1503.

RISM 1504[1] *Motetti C*. Venice: Petrucci, 1504.

RISM 1505[1]   *Fragmenta missarum.* Venice: Petrucci, 1505.

RISM 1505[2]   *Motetti libro quarto.* Venice: Petrucci, 1505.

RISM 1508[1]   *Motetti a cinque libro primo.* Venice: Petrucci, 1508.

RISM 1509[1]   *Missarum diversorum auctorum liber primus.* Venice: Petrucci, 1509.

RISM 1514[1]   *Motetti de la Corona. Libro primo.* Venice: Petrucci, 1514.

RISM 1516[1]   *Liber quindecim missarum electarum quae per excellentissimos musicos compositae fuerunt.* Rome: Antico, 1516.

RISM 1519[1]   *Motetti de la Corona. Libro secondo.* Venice: Petrucci, 1519.

RISM 1519[2]   *Motetti de la Corona. Libro tertio.* Venice: Petrucci, 1519.

RISM 1520[3]   *Motetti novi e chanzoni franciose a quatro sopra doi.* Venice: Antico, 1520.

RISM 1520[4]   *Liber selectarum cantionum quas vulgo Mutetas appellant sex quinque et quatuor vocum.* Augsburg: Grimm & Wyrsung, 1520.

RISM 1534[17]   *Hundert und ainundzewintzig newe Lieder von berümbtenn dieser Kunst gesetzt.* Nuremberg: Formschneider, 1534.

RISM 1537[1]   *Novum et insigne opus musicum, sex, quinque, et quatuor vocum.* Nuremberg: Formschneider, 1537.

RISM 1538[3]   *Secundus tomus novi operis musici, sex, quinque et quatuor vocum.* Nuremberg: Formschneider, 1538.

RISM 1538[7]   *Modulationes aliquot quatuor vocum selectissimae.* Nuremberg: Petreius, 1538.

RISM 1538[8]   *Symphoniae iucundae atque adeo breves quatuor vocum.* Wittenberg: Rhau, 1538.

RISM 1538[9]   *Trium vocum carmina a diversis musicis composita.* Nuremberg: Formschneider, 1538.

RISM 1539[1]   *Liber quindecim missarum.* Nuremberg: Petreius, 1539.

RISM 1539[2]   *Missae tredecim quatuor vocum.* Nuremberg: Formschneider, 1539.

RISM 1539[27]   *Ein Ausszug guter alter und newer teutscher Liedlein.* Nuremberg: Petreius, 1539.

RISM 1540[21]   *Der ander Theil, kurtzweiliger guter frischer teutscher Liedlein.* Nuremberg: Petreius, 1540.

RISM 1541[2]   *Trium vocum cantiones centum.* Nuremberg: Petreius, 1541.

RISM 1545[6]   *Bicinia gallica, latina, germanica.* Wittenberg: Rhau, 1545.

RISM 1548[9]   *Di Cipriano Rore et di altri eccellentisimi musici.* Venice: Scotto, 1548.

RISM 1549[3]   *Il primo libro de motetti a sei voce.* Venice: Scotto, 1549.

RISM 1549[7]   *Primo libro de motetti a cinque voci da diversi eccellentissimi musici composti.* Venice: Scotto, 1549.

RISM 1549[8]   *Il terzo libro di motetti a cinque voci di Cipriano de Rore, et de altri excellentissimi musici.* Venice: Gardano, 1549.

RISM 1550[1]   *Di Adriano et di Jachet. I salmi appertinenti alli vesperi per tute le feste dell'anno.* Venice: Gardano, 1550.

Single-composer prints

Agricola 1504   *Misse Alexandi Agricola.* Venice: Petrucci, 1504.

Gerle 1532   Gerle, Hans. *Musica teutsch auf die Instrument der grossen und kleinen Geygen auch Lautten.* Nuremberg: Formschneider, 1532.

Gerle 1533   *Tabulatur auff die Laudten.* Nuremberg: Formschneider, 1533. Ed. Hélène Charnassé, *Hans Gerle: Tablature pour les Luths (Nuremberg: Formschneider, 1533),*

Publications de la Société Française de Musicologie 5, 1 (Paris: Heugel, 1975–78). [Brown 1533/1; Gustavson F21]

Ghiselin 1503   *Misse Ghiselin*. Venice: Petrucci, 1503.

Isaac 1505   *Misse Izac*. Venice: Petrucci, 1505.

Josquin 1502   Josquin des Prez, *Misse Josquin*. Venice: Petrucci, 1502. 2nd ed., Fossombrone, 1514. 3rd ed., Fossombrone, 1516. Reprint, Rome: Dorico, 1526.

Josquin 1505   Josquin des Prez, *Missarum Josquin liber secundus*. Venice: Petrucci, 1505. 2nd ed., Fossombrone, 1515. Reprint, Rome: Dorico, 1526.

Josquin 1514   Josquin des Prez, *Missarum Josquin liber tertius*. Venice: Petrucci, 1514. Fossombrone, 1516. Rome: Dorico, 1526.

Obrecht   *Misse Obrecht*. Venice: Petrucci, 1503.

de Orto 1505   *Misse de Orto*. Venice: Petrucci, 1505.

Weerbecke 1507   *Misse Gaspar*. Venice: Petrucci, 1507.

Willaert 1559   *Musica nova di Adriano Willaert all'illustrissimo et eccellentissimo signor il signor Donno Alfonso D'Este prencipe di Ferrara*. Venice: Gardano, 1559. Edition in *Adriani Willaert: Opera Omnia*, Corpus mensurabilis musicae 3, Vol. 5: *Motets*, ed. Hermann Zenck and Walter Gerstenberg. Rome: American Institute of Musicology, 1957. Vol. 13: *Madrigals*, ed. Hermann Zenck and Walter Gerstenberg. N.p.: American Institute of Musicology, 1966.

Zarlino 1549   *Musici quinque vocum moduli, motetcta vulgo nuncupata opus nunquam alias typis excusum, ac nuper accuratissime in lucem aeditum. Liber primus*. Venice: Gardano, 1549.

Zarlino 1566   *Modulationes sex vocum, per Philippum Iusbertum musicum Venetum collectae*. Venice: Rampazetto, 1566.

THEORY TREATISES AND SIXTEENTH-CENTURY PRINTS

Aiguino, Illuminato. *La illuminata de tutti i tuoni di canto fermo, con alcuni bellissimi secreti, non d'altri più scritti*. Venice: Gardano, 1562.

Il tesoro illuminato di tutti i tuoni di canto figurato, con alcuni bellissimi secreti, non da altri più scritti. Venice: Giovanni Varisco, 1581.

anon. *Compendium musices*. Venice: Giovanni Battista Sessa, 1499. *Compendium musices: Venetiis, 1499–1597*, ed. David Crawford, Corpus scriptorum de musica 33. Stuttgart: American Institute of Musicology, 1985.

Aron, Pietro. *Compendiolo di molti dubii, segreti et sentenze intorno al canto fermo, et figurato*. Milan: Jo. Antonio da Castelliono, [c. 1550]. Facsimile, ed. Giuseppe Vecchi, Bibliotheca Musica Bononiensis II, 11. Bologna: Forni, 1970.

Libri tres de institutione harmonica editi a Petro Aaron Florentino interprete Jo. Antonio Flam. Foro Cornelite. Bologna: Benedictus Hectoris, 1516. Facsimile, ed. Giuseppe Vecchi, Bibliotheca Musica Bononiensis, II, 8. Bologna: Forni, 1970.

Lucidario in musica, di alcune oppenioni antiche, et moderne con le loro oppositioni, et resolutioni, con molti altri secreti appresso, et questioni da altrui anchora non dichiarati. Venice: Girolamo Scotto, 1545. Facsimile, Monuments of Music and Music Literature in Facsimile, II, 68. New York: Broude Brothers, 1978.

Thoscanello de la musica. Venice: Bernardino and Matheo de Vitali, 1523. Facsimile, Monuments of Music and Music Literature in Facsimile, II, 64. New York: Broude Brothers, 1969.

Toscanello in musica di Messer Piero Aron Fiorentino . . . nuovamente stampato con l'aggiunta da lui fatta et con diligentia corretto. Venice: Bernardino and Matheo de Vitali, 1529. Reprint Venice: Marchio Sessa, 19 March 1539. Reprint Venice: Domenico Nicolino, 1562. Facsimile of the 1539 edition, ed. G. Frey, Kassel, 1970. Trans. Peter Bergquist, Colorado College Music Press Translations 4. Colorado Springs: Colorado College Music Press, 1970.

Trattato della natura et cognitione di tutti gli tuoni di canto figurato non da altrui piu scritti. Venice: Bernardino de Vitali, 1525. Facsimile, ed. Willem Elders, Musica Revindicata. Utrecht: Joachimsthal, 1966. Chapters 1–7 translated in Oliver Strunk, *Source Readings in Music History.* New York: Norton, 1950, 205–18. Revised in Gary Tomlinson, ed. *Strunk's Source Readings in Music History*, volume 3: *The Renaissance.* New York: Norton, 1998, 137–50. A Supplement to the *Trattato* was published separately without title page or indication of the author. Venice: Bernardino de Vitali, 1531.

Bonaventura da Brescia. *Breviloquium musicale.* Brescia: Angelo Britannico, 1497.

Regula musicae planae. Brescia: Angelo Britannico, 1497, Reprint, Milan: Giovanni de Legnano, 1500. Facsimile, Milan: Bollettino Bibliografico Musicale, 1934.

Burzio, Nicolo. *Musices opusculum.* Bologna: Ugo Ruggerio for Benedetto Faelli, 1487. Facsimile, ed. Domenico Massera, Bibliotheca Musica Bononiensis II, 4. Bologna: Forni, 1969. Trans. Clement A. Miller, Musicological Studies and Documents 37. Neuhausen-Stuttgart: American Institute of Musicology, 1983.

Cochlaeus, Johannes. *De musica.* Cologne: Landon, 1507. Nuremberg: Weissenburger, 1511.

Tetrachordum musices. Nuremberg: Hans Stuchs, 1512. Reprint, Nuremberg: Peypus, 1514, 1516, 1520. Facsimile, Hildesheim: Georg Olms, 1971. Trans. Clement Miller, Musicological Studies and Documents 23. N.p.: American Institute of Musicology, 1970.

Coclico, Adrian Petit. *Compendiolum musices.* Nuremberg: Berg and Neuber, 1552.

Faber, Heinrich. *Ad musicam practicam introductio.* Nuremberg: Berg and Neuber, 1550.

Compendiolum musicae. Nuremberg: Berg and Neuber, 1564.

Frosch, Johann. *Rerum musicarum opusculum.* Strasbourg: Petras Schöffer and Mathias Apiarius, 1535.

Gaffurio, Franchino. *Angelicum ac divinum opus musice.* Milan: Gottardo da Ponte, 1508.

De harmonia musicorum instrumentorum opus. Milan: Gottardo da Ponte, 1518. Facsimile, Monuments of Music and Music Literature in Facsimile, II, 97. New York: Broude Brothers, 1979. Trans. Clement Miller, Musicological Studies and Documents 33. [Rome]: American Institute of Musicology, 1977.

Practica musicae. Milan: Guillaume Le Signerre for Giovanni Pietro da Lomazzo, 1496. Facsimile, Westmead: Gregg Press, 1967. Facsimile, Monuments of Music and Music Literature in Facsimile, II, 99. New York: Broude Brothers, 1979. Translation, Irwin Young. Madison: University of Wisconsin Press, 1969. Translation, Clement Miller, Musicological Studies and Documents 20. N.p.: American Institute of Musicology, 1968.

Practica musicae. Brescia: Angelo Britannico, 1497, 1508. Venice: Zani, 1512.

Theorica musicae. Naples: Francesco di Dino, 1480. Facsimile, ed. Cesarino Ruini, Musurgiana 15. Lucca: Libreria Musicale Italiana, 1996. Facsimile, Monuments of Music and Music Literature in Facsimile, II, 100. New York: Broude Brothers, 1967.

Theorica musicae. Milan: Filippo Mantegazza for Giovanni Pietro da Lomazzo, 1492. Facsimile, Bibliotheca Musica Bononiensis II, 5. Bologna: Forni, 1969. Translated Walter Kurt Kreiszig, *The Theory of Music*. New Haven: Yale University Press, 1993.

Glarean, Heinrich. ΔΩΔΕΚΑΧΟΡΔΟΝ [*Dodecachordon*]. Basel: Heinrich Petri, 1547. Facsimile, Monuments of Music and Music Literature in Facsimile, II, 65. New York: Broude Brothers, 1967. Facsimile, Hildesheim: Georg Olms, 1969. Translation, Clement Miller, Musicological Studies and Documents 6. [Rome]: American Institute of Musicology, 1965.

Isagoge in musicen. Basel: J. Froben, 1516. Translated with introduction by Frances Berry Turrell as "The *Isagoge in Musicen* of Henry Glarean." *Journal of Music Theory* 3 (1959), 97–139.

Musicae epitome ex Glareani Dodecachordon. Basel: Heinrich Petri, 1557. Basel: Hieronymus Curio, 1559.

Guerson, Guillaume. *Utillissime musicales regule*. Paris: Michel Thouloze, [*c.* 1495].

Heyden, Sebald. *Musicae stoicheiosis*. Nuremberg: Peypus, 1532.

Musicae, id est, artis canendi libri duo. Nuremberg: Petreius, 1537.

De arte canendi. Nuremberg: Petreius, 1540. Facsimile, Monuments of Music and Music Literature in Facsimile, II, 149. New York: Broude Brothers, 1969. Translation, Clement Miller, Musicological Studies and Documents 26. N.p.: American Institute of Musicology, 1972.

Listenius, Nicolaus. *Musica*. Wittenberg: Georg Rhau, 1537, 1539, 1542, 1544, 1548, 1549, 1554, 1555, 1557. Augsburg: Heinrich Steiner, 1538. Nuremberg: Petreius, 1539, 1541, 1544, 1547, 1548, 1549, 1550, 1551. Nuremberg: Gabriel Hain, 1557. Nuremberg: Dietrich Gerlach, 1569. Nuremberg: Katharina Gerlach, 1577, 1583. Leipzig: Blum, 1542, 1543, 1546, 1549, 1553.

Murmellius, Johannes. *Opusculum de discipulorum officiis: quod enchiridion scholasticorum inscribitur*. Cologne, 1505.

Niavis, Paulus. *Latinum idioma pro parvulis editum*. Nuremberg: Friedrich Creussner, 1494.

Ramis de Pareja, Bartolomé. *Musica utriusque cantus practica*. Bologna: [Baltasar di Hyrberia and Heinrich von Köln], 1482. Bologna: Baltasar di Hyrberia, 1482. Facsimile, ed. G. Vecchi, Bibliotheca Musica Bononiensis, II, 3. Bologna: Forni, 1969. Translation, Clement A Miller, Musicological Studies and Documents 44. Neuhausen-Stuttgart: Hänssler-Verlag, 1993.

Rhau, Georg. *Enchiridion utriusque musicae practicae*. Wittenberg: Georg Rhau, 1532.

Spangenberg, Johann. *Quaestiones musicae in usum scholoae Northusianae*. Nuremberg: Petreius, 1536. Wittenberg: Georg Rhau, 1536, 1542, 1548, 1551. Leipzig: Blum, 1542, 1544.

Spataro, Giovanni. *Errori de Franchino Gafurio*. Bologna: Benedetto Faelli, 1521.

Tractato di musica. Venice: Bernardino de Vitali, 1531. Facsimile, ed. Giuseppe Vecchi, Bibliotheca Musica Bononiensis, II, 14. Bologna: Forni, 1970.

Tinctoris, Johannes. *Opera theoretica*, ed. Albert Seay, Corpus scriptorum de musica 22. [Rome]: American Institute of Musicology, 1978.

Vanneus, Stefano. *Recanetum de musica aurea*. Rome: Dorico, 1533. Facsimile, ed. Suzanne Clercx, Documenta musicologica 28. Kassel: Bärenreiter, 1969. Partial translation, Albert Seay, Colorado College Music Press Texts and Translations 2. Colorado Springs: Colorado College Music Press, 1979.

Vicentino, Nicola. *L'antica musica ridotta alla moderna prattica*. Rome: Barre, 1555, 1557. Facsimile, ed. Edward E. Lowinsky. Documenta musicologica 17. Kassel: Bärenreiter, 1959. Translated by Maria Rika Maniates, *Ancient Music Adapted to Modern Practice*. New Haven: Yale University Press, 1996.

Wilphlingseder, Ambros. *Musica teutsch*. Nuremberg: Berg and Neuber, 1561. Nuremberg: Gerlach, 1569, 1570, 1574, 1585.

Erotemata musicae practicae. Nuremberg: Heussler, 1563.

Zarlino, Gioseffo. *Le istitutioni harmoniche*. Venice: [Pietro Da Fino], 1558. Facsimile, New York: Broude Brothers, 1965. Venice: Francesco Franceschi Senese, 1561, 1562. Enlarged, revised edition, Venice: Francesco Franceschi Senese, 1573. Facsimile, Ridgewood, NJ: Gregg Press, 1966. Revised edition as volume 1 of *De tutte l'opere del r.m. G. Zarlino*. Venice: Francesco Franceschi Senese, 1588. Facsimile and transcription in Gioseffo Zarlino, *Music Treatises*, ed. Frans Wiering, Thesaurus Musicarum Italicarum 1 [Utrecht: Universiteit Utrecht, 1997]. German translation and commentary on Parts I and II (1573 ed.) in Michael Fend, *Theorie des Tonsystems*. Europäische Hochschulschriften 36: 43. Frankfurt am Main: Peter Lang, 1989. English translation of Part III (1558 ed.) by Guy Marco, *The Art of Counterpoint*. New Haven: Yale University Press, 1968. English translation of Part IV (1558 ed.) by Vered Cohen, *On the Modes*. New Haven: Yale University Press, 1983.

Le dimostrationi harmoniche. Venice: Francesco Franceschi Senese, 1571. Facsimile, New York: Broude Brothers, 1965.

SECONDARY SOURCES

Ambros, August Wilhelm. *Geschichte der Musik*. Leipzig: F. E. C. Leuchart, 1887–1911.

Apel, Willi and Archibald Davison, eds. *Historical Anthology of Music*. Cambridge, MA: Harvard University Press, 1946.

Baldi, Bernardino. *Vite inedite di matematici italiani*, ed. Enrico Narducci. Rome: Tip. delle scienze matematiche e fisiche, 1887. Also published in *Bullettino di bibliografia e di storia delle scienze matematiche e fisiche* 19 (1886), 335–406; 437–89; 512–640.

Bellermann, Heinrich. *Die Mensuralnoten und Taktzeichen des XV und XVI Jahrhunderts*. Berlin: Walter de Gruyter, 1858.

Bent, Margaret. "Accidentals, Counterpoint, and Notation in Aaron's *Aggiunta* to the *Toscanello*." *Journal of Musicology* 12 (1994), 306–44.

"Diatonic ficta." *Early Music History* 4 (1984), 1–48.

Bergquist, Peter. "Mode and Polyphony around 1500." *Music Forum* 1 (1967), 99–161.

"The Theoretical Writings of Pietro Aaron." Ph.D. dissertation, Columbia University, 1964.

Bernstein, Jane. *Music Printing in Renaissance Venice: The Scotto Press (1539–1572)*. New York: Oxford University Press, 1998.

Bernstein, Lawrence. "Ockeghem the Mystic: A German Interpretation of the 1920s." In *Johannes Ockeghem: Actes du XLe colloque international d'études humanistes*, ed. Philippe Vendrix, 811–41. Tours: Klincksieck, 1998.

Berry, Wallace. *Structural Functions in Music*. New York: Dover, 1976.

Besseler, Heinrich, ed. Altniederländische Motetten von Johannes Ockeghem, Loyset Compère und Josquin des Prez. Kassel: Barenreiter, [1948].

Blackburn, Bonnie. J. "On Compositional Process in the Fifteenth-Century." *Journal of the American Musicological Society* 40 (1987), 210–84.

Blackburn, Bonnie J., Edward E. Lowinsky, and Clement A. Miller, eds. *A Correspondence of Renaissance Musicians.* Oxford: Clarendon Press, 1991.

Bolzoni, Lina. "L'Accademia Veneziana: splendore e decadenza di una utopia enciclopedica." In *Università, accademie e società scientifiche in Italia e in Germania dal cinquecento al Settecento*, ed. Laetitia Boehm and Ezio Raimondi, 117–67. Bologna: Il mulino, 1981.

Bonaccorsi, Alfredo. "Zarlino, Gioseffo," *Enciclopedia italiana di scienze, lettere ed arti.* Rome: Treccani, 1937.

Boorman, Stanley. "Early Music Printing: Working for a Specialized Market." In *Print and Culture in the Renaissance: Essays on the Advent of Printing in Europe*, ed. Gerald P. Tyson and Sylvia S. Wagonheim, 222–45. Newark DE: University of Delaware Press, 1986.

"The 'First' Edition of the *Odhecaton A.*" *Journal of the American Musicological Society* 30 (1977), 183–207.

"Limitations and Extensions of Filiation Technique." In *Music in Medieval and Early Modern Europe: Patronage, Sources and Texts*, ed. Iain Fenlon, 319–46. Cambridge: Cambridge University Press, 1981.

"Petrucci at Fossombrone: A Study of Early Music Printing, with Special Reference to the Motetti de la Corona (1514–19)." Ph.D. dissertation, King's College, University of London, 1976.

"Petrucci's Type-setters and the Process of Stemmatics." In *Formen und Probleme der Überlieferung mehrstimmiger Musik im Zeitalter Josquins Desprez*, ed. Ludwig Finscher, 245–80. Munich: Kraus International Publications, 1981.

"The Uses of Filiation in Early Music." *Text: Transactions of the Society for Textual Scholarship* 1 (1984), 167–84.

Bossuyt, Ignace. "*O socii durate*: A Musical Correspondence from the Time of Philip II." *Early Music* 26 (1998), 432–43.

Brandenburg, Sieghard. "The Historical Background to the 'Heiliger Dankgesang'." *Beethoven Studies* 3 (1982), 162–63.

Brothers, Thomas. "Vestiges of the Isorhythmic Tradition in Mass and Motet ca. 1450–1475." *Journal of the American Musicological Society* 44 (1991), 1–56.

Brown, Howard Meyer. "Hans Ott, Heinrich Finck and Stoltzer: Early Sixteenth-Century German Motets in Formschneider's Anthologies of 1537 and 1538." In *Von Isaac bis Bach: Studien zur älteren deutschen Musikgeschichte*, ed. Frank Heidlberger, 73–84. Kassel: Bärenreiter, 1991.

Butler, Bartlett. "Liturgical Music in Sixteenth-Century Nürnberg: A Socio-musical Study." Ph.D. dissertation, University of Illinois, 1970. 2 vols. UMI 71–14,690.

Buzás, Ladislaus. *Geschichte der Universitätsbibliothek München.* Wiesbaden: Otto Harrassowitz, 1972.

Cave, Terrence. *The Cornucopian Text: Problems of Writing in the French Renaissance.* Oxford: Clarendon Press, 1979.

Chartier, Roger. *The Order of Books: Readers, Authors, and Libraries in Europe between the Fourteenth and Eighteenth Centuries*, translated by Lydia Cochrane. Stanford: Stanford University Press, 1994.

"Texts, Printing, Readings." In *The New Cultural History*, ed. Lynn Hunt, 154–75. Berkeley: University of California Press, 1989.

Cicogna, Emmanuele. *Delle Inscrizioni Veneziane.* Venice: Picotti, 1830.

Cohen, Paul. *Die Nürnberger Musikdrucker im sechzehnten Jahrhundert.* Erlangen: Höfer & Limmert, 1927.

Corner, Flaminio. *Notizie storiche delle chiese e monasteri di Venezia e di Torcello.* Padua: Giovanni Manfrè, 1758. Facsimile, Bologna: Forni, 1990.

Ecclesiae Venetae antiquis monumentis nunc etiam primum editis illustratae ac in decadis distributae. Venice: Pasquali, 1749.

Crane, Mary Thomas. *Framing Authority: Sayings, Self, and Society in Sixteenth-Century England.* Princeton: Princeton University Press, 1993.

Crocker, Richard. "Perchè Zarlino diede una nuova numerazione ai modi?" *Rivista italiana di musicologia* 3 (1968), 49–58.

Dahlhaus, Carl, trans. Robert Gjerdigen. *Studies in the Origins of Harmonic Tonality.* Princeton: Princeton University Press, 1990.

Davidsson, Åke. *Bibliographie der Musiktheoretischen Drucke des 16. Jahrhunderts.* Baden-Baden: Verlag Heitz, 1962.

Drake, George Warren James. "The First Printed Books of Motets, Petrucci's *Motetti A numero Trentatre A* (Venice, 1502) and *Motetti de Passione, de Cruce, de Sacramento, de Beata Virgine et Huiusmode B* (Venice, 1503): A Critical Study and Complete Edition." Ph.D. dissertation, University of Illinois, 1972.

Duggen, Mary Kay. *Italian Music Incunabula: Printers and Type.* Berkeley: University of California Press, 1992.

Einstein, Alfred. *The Italian Madrigal*, trans. Alexander H. Krappe, Roger H. Sessions, and Oliver Strunk. Princeton: Princeton University Press, 1971.

Eisenstein, Elizabeth L. *The Printing Press as an Agent of Change.* Cambridge: Cambridge University Press, 1976.

Eitner, Robert. *Verzeichniss neuer Ausgaben alter Musikwerke aus der frühesten Zeit bis zum Jahre 1800.* Berlin: Trautwein, 1871. Supplement, 1877.

Erasmus, Desiderius. *De duplici copia verborum ac rerum commentarii duo.* Translated and annotated by Betty I. Knott as *Copia: Foundations of the Abundant Style.* Collected Works of Erasmus, Literary and Educational Writings 2. Toronto: University of Toronto Press, 1978.

Feldman, Martha. *City Culture and the Madrigal at Venice.* Berkeley: University of California Press, 1995.

Fellerer, Karl G. "Die Köllner Musiktheoretische Schule des 16. Jahrhunderts." In *Renaissance-muziek 1400–1600: donum natalicium Rene Bernard Lenaerts*, ed. Jozef Robijns, 121–30. Musicologica Lovaniensia 1. Leuven: Katholieke Universiteit Seminarie voor Muziekwetenschap, 1969.

Fenlon, Iain. "Heinrich Glarean's Books." In *Music in the German Renaissance*, ed. John Kmetz, 74–102. Cambridge: Cambridge University Press, 1994.

Flury, Roman. *Gioseffo Zarlino als Komponist.* Winterthur: Verlag P. G. Keller, 1962.

Fritzsche, Otto Fridolin. *Glarean, sein Leben und seine Schriften.* Frauenfeld: Verlag J. Huber, 1890.

Fromson, Michele. "Zarlino's Modal Analysis of Willaert's 'Avertatur Obsecro'." In *Secondo convegno europeo di analisi musicale: atti*, ed. Rossanna Dalmonte and Mario Baroni, 237–48. Trent: Dipartimento di storia della civiltà europea, Università degli studi di Trento, 1992.

Fuller, Sarah. "Defending the *Dodecachordon*: Ideological Currents in Glarean's Modal Theory." *Journal of the American Musicological Society* 49 (1996), 191–224.

Geering, Arnold. "Die Vokalmusik in der Schweiz zur Zeit der Reformation." *Schweizerisches Jahrbuch für Musikwissenschaft* 6 (1933), 36, 92.

Gehrenbeck, David. "*Motetti de la Corona*: A Study of Ottaviano Petrucci's Four Last-known Motet Prints." S.M.D. dissertation, Union Theological Seminary, 1970. UMI 7112440.

Gelley, Alexander, ed. *Unruly Examples: On the Rhetoric of Exemplarity*. Stanford: Stanford University Press, 1995.

Gottwald, Clytus. *Die Musikhandschriften der Universitätsbibliothek München*. Wiesbaden: Otto Harrassowitz, 1968.

Grafton, Anthony and Lisa Jardine. *From Humanism to the Humanities: Education and the Liberal Arts in Fifteenth- and Sixteenth-Century Europe*. Cambridge, MA: Harvard University Press, 1986.

Greenblatt, Stephen. *Renaissance Self-Fashioning: From More to Shakespeare*. Chicago: University of Chicago Press, 1980.

Gustavson, Royston. "Hans Ott, Hieronymus Formschneider, and the *Novum et insigne opus musicum* (Nuremberg 1537–38)." Ph.D. dissertation, University of Melbourne, 1998.

Haar, James. "The Frontispiece of Gafori's *Practica Musicae* (1496)." *Renaissance Quarterly* 27 (1974), 7–22.

"Orlande de Lassus: *Si bona suscepimus*." In *Music before 1600*, ed. Mark Everist, 154–74. Oxford: Blackwell, 1992.

Harrán, Don. "Burney and Ambros as Editors of Josquin's Music." In *Josquin des Prez*, ed. Edward Lowinsky, 148–77. New York: Oxford University Press, 1976.

In Search of Harmony: Hebrew and Humanist Elements in Sixteenth-Century Musical Thought. N.p.: American Institute of Musicology, 1988.

Hoffmann-Erbrecht, Lothar. *Henricus Finck – musicus excellentissimus (1445–1527)*. Cologne: Gitarre und Laute Verlagsgesellschaft, 1982.

Hyer, Brian. "Picturing Music." Paper read at the Society for Music Theory, Tallahassee, November 1994.

Jackson, Susan. "Berg and Neuber: Music Printers in Sixteenth-Century Nuremberg." Ph.D. dissertation, The City University of New York, 1998. 2 vols. UMI 9820545.

Jardine, Lisa. *Erasmus, Man of Letters*. Princeton: Princeton University Press, 1993.

Judd, Cristle Collins. "Aspects of Tonal Coherence in the Motets of Josquin." Ph.D. dissertation, King's College London, 1993. UMI 9501876.

"Musical Commonplace Books, Writing Theory, and 'Silent Listening': The Polyphonic Examples of the *Dodecachordon*." *The Musical Quarterly* 82 (1998), 482–516.

"A Newly-recovered Eight-Mode Motet Cycle: Zarlino's *Song of Songs* Motets." in *Theory and Analysis 1450–1650*, ed. Anne-Emmanuelle Ceulemans and Bonnie J. Blackburn. Louvain-la-Neuve, forthcoming.

"Reading Aron Reading Petrucci: The Music Examples of the *Trattato della natura et cognitione di tutti gli tuoni* (1525)." *Early Music History* 14 (1995), 121–52.

"Renaissance Modal Theory: Theoretical, Compositional, and Editorial Perspectives." In *The Cambridge History of Western Music Theory*, ed. Thomas Christensen. Cambridge: Cambridge University Press, forthcoming.

Judd, Cristle Collins and Christopher Amos. "Multi-layered Borrowing: Zarlino's *Si bona suscepimus* and a Complex of Motets." In *Early Musical Borrowing*, ed. Honey Meconi. New York: Garland, forthcoming.

Judd, Robert. "The Use of Notational Formats at the Keyboard: A Study of Printed Sources of Keyboard Music in Spain and Italy c. 1500–1700." D.Phil. thesis, University of Oxford, 1989.

Kelleher, John Emil. "Zarlino's 'Dimostrationi Harmoniche' and Demonstrative Methodologies in the Sixteenth Century." Ph.D. dissertation, Columbia University, 1993. UMI 9333801.

Kellman, Herbert and Charles Hamm. *Census-Catalogue of Manuscript Sources of Polyphonic Music 1400–1550*. Renaissance Manuscript Studies 1. Neuhausen-Stuttgart: Hänssler-Verlag, 1979–88. 5 vols.

Kemmler, Fritz. *"Exempla" in Context: A Historical and Critical Study of Robert Mannyng of Brunne's "Handlyng Synne."* Tübingen: Gunter Narr Verlag, 1984.

Kinsky, Georg, ed. *Versteigerung von Musiker-Autographen as dem Nachlaß des Herrn Kommerzienrates Wilhelm Heyer*. Cologne: Karl Ernst Henrici, 1926.

Kosel, Alfred. *Sebald Heyden (1499–1561): Ein Beitrag zur Geschichte der Nürnberger Schulmusik in der Reformationszeit*. Würzburg: Konrad Triltsch, 1940.

Krummel, Donald W. "Early German Partbook Typefaces." *Gutenburg Jahrbuch* 60 (1985), 80–98.

Krummel, Donald and Stanley Sadie, eds. *Music Printing and Publishing*. New York: Norton, 1990.

Leuchtmann, Horst. "Rochlitz, (Johann) Friedrich," *New Grove Dictionary of Music and Musicians*, ed. S. Sadie. London: Macmillan, 1980, XVI: 83–84.

Lewis, Mary. *Antonio Gardano, Venetian Music Printer, 1538–1569: A Descriptive Bibliography and Historical Study*. New York: Garland, 1988. 2 vols.

"Zarlino's Theories of Text Underlay as Illustrated in his Motet Book of 1549." *Music Library Association Notes* 42 (1985), 239–67.

Lincoln, Harry B. *The Latin Motet: Indexes to Printed Collections, 1500–1600*. Musicological Studies 59. Ottawa: The Institute of Medieval Music, 1993.

Lindberg, John E. "Origins and Development of the Sixteenth-Century Tricinium." Ph.D. dissertation, University of Cincinnati, 1988. UMI 9019795.

Loach, Donald. "Aegidius Tschudi's Songbook." Ph.D. dissertation, University of California, Berkeley, 1969.

Lodi, Pio. *Catalogo delle opere musicale della città di Modena R. Biblioteca Estense*. Parma: Fresching, 1923.

Lyons, John D. *Exemplum: The Rhetoric of Example in Early Modern France and Italy*. Princeton: Princeton University Press, 1989.

Macey, Patrick. "Josquin as Classic: *Qui habitat*, *Memor esto*, and Two Imitations Unmasked." *Journal of the Royal Musical Association* 118 (1993), 1–43.

Meier, Bernhard, trans. Ellen Beebe. *The Modes of Classical Vocal Polyphony*. New York: Broude Brothers, 1988.

"Heinrich Loriti Glareanus als Musiktheoretiker." In *Aufsätze zur Freiburger Wissenschafts- und Universitätsgeschichte*, ed. Clemens Bauer *et al.*, 65–112. Freiburg im Breisgau: Verlag Eberhard Albert Universitätsbuchhandlung, 1960.

Miller, Clement A. "Cochlaeus [Dobneck, Wendelstein], Johannes." *New Grove Dictionary of Music and Musicians*, ed. S. Sadie. London: Macmillan, 1980, IV: 512.

"The *Dodecachordon*: Its Origins and Influence on Renaissance Musical Thought." *Musica disciplina* 15 (1961), 155–66.

"Early Gaffuriana: New Answers to Old Questions." *Musical Quarterly* 56 (1970), 367–88.

"Gaffurius's *Practica Musicae*: Origin and Contents," *Musica disciplina* 22 (1968), 105–28.

"Sebald Heyden's *De arte canendi*: Background and Contents." *Musica disciplina* 24 (1970), 79–99.

Moss, Ann. *Printed Commonplace-Books and the Structuring of Renaissance Thought*. Oxford: Oxford University Press, 1996.

Müller, Peter O. "Sebald Heydens Nomenclatura." *Sprachwissenschaft* 18 (1993), 59–88.

Naegele, Philipp. "August Wilhelm Ambros: His Historical and Critical Thought." Ph.D. dissertation, Princeton University, 1954.

Newcomb, Anthony. "Editions of Willaert's *Musica nova*: New Evidence, New speculations." *Journal of the American Musicological Society* 26 (1973), 132–35.

Niemöller, Klaus Wolfgang. *Die Musica figurativa des Melchior Schanppecher*. Beiträge zur rheinischen Musikgeschichte 50. Cologne: Arno Volk Verlag, 1961.

Nicolaus Wollick und sein Musiktraktat. Beiträge zur rheinischen Musikgeschichte 13. Cologne: Arno Volk Verlag, 1956.

Untersuchungen zu Musikpflege und Musikunterricht an den deutschen Lateinschulen vom ausgehenden Mittelalter bis um 1600. Kölner Beiträge zur Musikforschung 54. Regensburg: Gustav Bosse, 1969.

"Zur Tonus-Lehre der italienischen Musiktheorie des ausgehenden Mittelalters." *Kirchenmusikalisches Jahrbuch* 40 (1956), 23–32.

Ongaro, Giulio M. "The Chapel of St. Mark's at the Time of Adrian Willaert (1527–1562): A Documentary Study." Ph.D. dissertation, University of North Carolina at Chapel Hill, 1986.

"The Library of a Sixteenth-Century Music Teacher." *Journal of Musicology* 12 (1994), 357–75.

Osthoff, Helmuth. *Josquin Desprez*. Tutzing: Hans Schneider, 1962–65. 2 vols.

Owens, Jessie Ann. *Composers at Work: The Craft of Musical Composition 1450–1600*. New York: Oxford University Press, 1997, 271–80.

"How Josquin Became Josquin." In *Music in Renaissance Cities and Courts: Studies in Honor of Lewis Lockwood*, ed. Jessie Ann Owens and Anthony M. Cummings, 271–80. Warren MI: Harmonie Park Press, 1997.

"An Illuminated Manuscript of Motets by Cipriano de Rore: München, Bayerische Staatsbibliothek, Mus. Ms. B." Ph.D. dissertation, Princeton University, 1979.

"Mode in the Madrigals of Cipriano de Rore." In *Altro Polo: Essays on Italian Music in the Cinquecento*, ed. Richard Charteris, 1–16. Sydney: Frederick May Foundation for Italian Studies, University of Sydney, 1990.

"Cipriano de Rore a Parma (1560–1565): nuovi documenti," *Rivista italiana di musicologia* 11 (1976), 5–26.

Owens, Jessie Ann and Richard Agee. "La Stampa della *Musica nova* di Willaert." *Rivista italiana di musicologia* 24 (1989), 213–305.

Palisca, Claude. *Humanism in Italian Renaissance Musical Thought*. New Haven: Yale University Press, 1985.

"Zarlino, Gioseffo," *New Grove Dictionary of Music and Musicians*, ed. S. Sadie. London: Macmillan, 1980, XX: 648.

Palumbo-Fossati, Isabella. "La casa veneziana di Gioseffo Zarlino nel testamento e nell' inventario dei beni del grande teorico musicale," *Nuova rivista musicale italiana* 20 (1986), 633–49.

Pellegrini, D. "Breve dissertazione previa al Sommario dell'Accademia Veneta della Fama." *Giornale dell'Italiana Letteratura* 22–23 (1808), 3–32, 113–28, 193–212; 49–68.

Perkins, Leeman. "Mode and Structure in the Masses of Josquin." *Journal of the American Musicological Society* 26 (1973), 189–239.

Powers, Harold. "Is Mode Real? Pietro Aron, the Octenary System, and Polyphony." *Basler Jahrbuch für historische Musikpraxis* 16 (1992), 9–52.

"Modal Representations in Polyphonic Offertories." *Early Music History* 2 (1982), 43–86.

"Mode." *New Grove Dictionary of Music and Musicians*, ed. S. Sadie. London: Macmillan, 1980, XII, 376–450.

"Monteverdi's Model for a Multi-modal Madrigal." In *In cantu et in sermone: For Nino Pirrotta on his 80th Birthday*, ed. Fabrizio della Seta and Franco Piperno, 185–219. Florence: Olschki, 1989.

"Music as Text and Text as Music." In *Musik als Text*, ed. Hermann Danuser and Tobias Plebuch. Kassel: Bärenreiter, 1998.

"Tonal Types and Modal Categories," *Journal of the American Musicological Society* 34 (1981), 428–70.

Quaranta, Elena. *Oltre San Marco: Organizzazione e prassi della musica nelle chiese di venezia nel rinascimento*. Florence: Olschki, 1998.

Rivera, Benito. "Finding the *Soggetto* in Willaert's Free Imitative Counterpoint: A Step in Modal Analysis." In *Music Theory and the Exploration of the Past*, ed. Christopher Hatch and David W. Bernstein. Chicago: University of Chicago Press, 1993. 75–80.

"Harmonic Theory in Musical Treatises of the Late Fifteenth and Early Sixteenth Centuries." *Music Theory Spectrum* 1 (1979), 80–95.

"Zarlino's Motets (1549): Keys to Interpreting His Teachings on Counterpoint and Mode." Unpublished paper read at the Conference on Medieval and Renaissance Music. London, August 1986.

Roberts, Kenneth Creighton. "The Music of Ludwig Senfl: A Critical Appraisal." Ph.D. dissertation, University of Michigan, 1965. UMI 66–6687.

Rochlitz, Friedrich. *Sammlung vorzüglichen Gesangstücke*, vol. I. Mainz, Paris, and Antwerp: Schott, 1835.

Rose, Paul. "The Accademia Venetiana: Science and Culture in Renaissance Venice." *Studi veneziani* 11 (1969), 191–242.

Salzer, Felix and Carl Schachter. *Counterpoint in Composition*. New York: Dover, 1969.

Saenger, Paul. "Silent Reading: Its Impact on Late Medieval Script and Society." *Viator* 13 (1982), 367–414.

Space Between Words: The Origins of Silent Reading. Stanford: Stanford University Press, 1997.

Sandberger, Adolf. *Bemerkungen zur Biographie Hans Leo Haßlers und seiner Brüder sowie zur Musikgeschichte der Städte Nürnberg und Augsburg im 16. und zu Anfang des 17. Jahrhunderts*. Denkmäler der Tonkunst in Bayern, Jg. V/I. Leipzig: Breitkopf and Härtel, 1904.

Sannemann, Friedrich. *Die Musik als Unterrichtsgegenstand in den Evangelischen Lateinschulen des 16. Jahrhunderts*. Musikwissenschaftlichen Studien 4. Berlin: E. Ebering, 1904.

Sansovino, Francesco. *Venetia, città nobilissima, et singolare, descritta in XIIII libri . . . Con aggiunta di tutte le cose notabili della stessa città, fatte, & occorse dall'anno 1580. Sino al presente 1663. das d. Giustiniano Martinioni.* Venice: S. Curti, 1663. Facsimile, Farnborough: Gregg International Publishers, 1968.

Scheller, Robert. *Exemplum: Model-Book Drawings and the Practice of Artistic Transmission in the Middle Ages.* Amsterdam: Amsterdam University Press, 1995.

Schering, Arnold. "Die Notenbeispiele in Glarean's Dodekachordon (1547)." *Sammelbände der Internationalen Musikgesellschaft* 13 (1912), 569–96.

Schiltz, Katelijne. "De 'Musica Nova' (1558–1559) van Adriaan Willaert: De muzikaal-historische context. Een analyse van de motetten." M.A. thesis, Katholieke Universtiteit Leuven, 1996.

Schlagel, Stephanie. "Josquin des Prez and His Motets: A Case Study in Sixteenth-century Reception History." Ph.D. dissertation, University of North Carolina-Chapel Hill, 1996. UMI 9715763.

Schubert, Peter. "The Fourteen-Mode System of Illuminato Aiguino," *Journal of Music Theory* 35 (1991), 175–210.

Sherr, Richard. "Illibata Dei virgo nutrix and Josquin's Roman Style," *Journal of the American Musicological Society* 41 (1988), 434–64.

Smith, Anne. "Willaert Motets and Mode." *Basler Jahrbuch für historische Musikpraxis* 16 (1992), 117–65.

Sorbelli, Albano. "Le due edizioni della *Musica Practica* di Bartolomé Ramis de Pareja." *Gutenberg-Jahrbuch* 5 (1930).

Spahn, Martin. *Johannes Cochlaeus: ein Lebensbild aus der Zeit der Kirchenspaltung.* Berlin: F. L. Dames, 1898.

Steude, Wofram. "Untersuchungen zu Herkunft, Verbreitung und spezifische Inhalt mittel-deutscher Musikhandschriften des 16. Jahrhunderts." Ph.D. dissertation, University of Rostock, 1972.

Strauss, Gerald. *Nuremberg in the Sixteenth Century: City Politics and Life Between Middle Ages and Modern Times.* Bloomington: Indiana University Press, 1976.

Subotnik, Rose Rosengard. "Toward a Deconstruction of Structural Listening: A Critique of Schoenberg, Adorno, and Stravinsky." In *Explorations in Music, the Arts, and Ideas*, ed. Eugene Narmour and Ruth Solie. Stuyvesant NY: Pendragon Press, 1988.

Teramoto, Mariko. *Die Psalmmotettendrucke des Johannes Petrejus in Nürnberg.* Frankfurter Beiträge zur Musikwissenschaft 10. Tutzing: Schneider, 1983.

Teramoto, Mariko and Armin Brinzing. *Katalog der Musikdrucke des Johannes Petreius in Nürnberg.* Catalogus Musicus 14. Kassel: Bärenreiter, 1993.

Tiozzo, Loris. *Gioseffo Zarlino: Teorico musicale.* Venice: Veneta Editrice, 1992.

Tirro, Frank. *Giovanni Spataro's Choirbooks.* Renaissance Musical Sources in the Archive of San Petronio in Bologna, vol. 1. Renaissance Manuscript Studies 4. N.p.: American Institute of Musicology, 1986.

Wienpahl, Robert. "Zarlino, the Senario, and Tonality," *Journal of the American Musicological Society* 12 (1959).

Wiering, Frans. "The Language of the Modes: Studies in the History of Polyphonic Modality." Ph.D. dissertation, University of Amsterdam, 1995.

Wüllner, Franz. *Chorübungen.* Munich, 1880. Revised ed., Eberhard Schwickerath. Munich: Theodor Ackermann, 1931. Revised and enlarged edition, Martin Stephani and Reinhart Stephani. Hamburg: Sikorski, 1959.

INDEX